# RELIGION AND THE CONTINENTAL CONGRESS
## 1774–1789

Recent titles in

RELIGION IN AMERICA SERIES
*Harry S. Stout, General Editor*

# RELIGION AND THE CONTINENTAL CONGRESS 1774–1789

## Contributions to Original Intent

Derek H. Davis

OXFORD

UNIVERSITY PRESS

2000

# OXFORD
UNIVERSITY PRESS

Oxford   New York

Athens   Auckland   Bangkok   Bogotá   Buenos Aires   Calcutta
Cape Town   Chennai   Dar es Salaam   Delhi   Florence   Hong Kong   Istanbul
Karachi   Kuala Lumpur   Madrid   Melbourne   Mexico City   Mumbai
Nairobi   Paris   São Paulo   Singapore   Taipei   Tokyo   Toronto   Warsaw

and associated companies in
Berlin   Ibadan

Copyright © 2000 by Derek H. Davis

Published by Oxford University Press, Inc.
198 Madison Avenue, New York, New York 10016

Oxford is a registered trademark of Oxford University Press

Library of Congress Cataloging-in-Publication Data

Davis, Derek, 1949–
Religion and the Continental Congress, 1774–1789 : contributions
to original intent / Derek H. Davis.
p.   cm.—(Religion in America series)
ISBN 0-19-513355-2
1. Freedom of religion—United States History.   2. Church and
state—United States History.   3. Constitutional history—United
States.   4. United States. Continental Congress.   I. Title.
II. Series: Religion in America series (Oxford University Press)
KF4783.D385   2000
322'.1'0973—dc21       99-26044

1 3 5 7 9 8 6 4 2

Printed in the United States of America
on acid-free paper

Dedicated to my parents,
Wanda Jean Martin Davis
and
David Keithley Davis

## ACKNOWLEDGMENTS

Any book is always much more than the work of its author. There are others who make inestimable contributions without which the project could never be completed.

I am indebted, first, to Tim Redman, Julie Reuben, Gerald Soliday, Victor Worsfold, and Ted Harpum for reading and critiquing the manuscript in its early stages. Whatever merit this book is deemed to have by its readers is in no small part attributable to their prudent suggestions. I also thank two graduate students in Church-State Studies at Baylor University, Mark Long and Susan Kelley-Claybrook, for their assistance in the preparation of the final two chapters.

I am grateful to Prometheus Books, Buffalo, New York, for the permission to include in chapter 1 of this book, in revised form, portions of the first two chapters of my *Original Intent: Chief Justice Rehnquist and the Course of American Church-State Relations* (1991); and I thank Mercer University Press for permission to include in chapter 11 of this book the major part of my essay, "Thoughts on a Civil Religion Solution to Religion Clause Jurisprudence," which appears in Jerry Vardaman, ed., *Chronos, Kairos, Christos II: Chronological, Nativity, and Religious Studies in Memory of Ray Summers* (Macon, Ga.: Mercer University Press, 1998).

The task of typing a lengthy manuscript should be wished upon no one. Beverly Toms and Wanda Gilbert were not only up to the task, but exercised their skills with considerable aplomb, speed, and spirit.

Finally, I would be remiss if I did not thank my wife, Kim, and children, Jeff and Melanie, who, for the period I was writing this manuscript, saw less of me than they—or I—would have preferred.

The Continental Congress was the body of delegates that represented the common interests of first the colonies and then the states from 1774 to 1789. The first and second of these congresses, which assembled in September 1774 and May 1775, respectively, were called to meet a pressing emergency—potential war with Great Britain—and served only in an advisory capacity to the colonies since they were extralegal bodies. Subsequent congresses, serving during and after the Revolutionary War, acted as the central government of the American union under the Articles of Confederation. The Continental Congress dissolved on 4 March 1789, when it was superseded by the new government established under the federal Constitution.

Historians have been prone to criticize the Continental Congress. Their evaluations are based largely on the inadequacies of the government of the states under the Articles of Confederation. In retrospect, however, the Congress had many notable achievements. It declared independence from Great Britain, then successfully prosecuted the war and negotiated the peace. It also managed to carry on the routine administration of matters that were of mutual concern to the states, while allowing the states to maintain their sovereignty. One of its greatest achievements was the passage of the Northwest Ordinance of 1787, legislation that enabled the western territories, once settled, to attain equal statehood with the existing states.

Most studies of the Continental Congress focus on various political events occurring in their secular context. Rarely is the Continental Congress examined from the perspective of the role that religion played in its proceedings and official acts. Because the Congress operated free of any formal notions of church-state separation, its work was in fact frequently imbued with a profound religious spirit. The present study examines the specific ways in which religion influenced the work of the Congress.

Such a study may be of interest to American religious historians seeking to know more about the character of American religion from 1774 to 1789, since the religious dimensions of the work of the Continental Congress were in many ways a reflection of a culture dominated by Protestantism but increasingly, at least among educated elites, influenced by Enlightenment rationalism. It is argued in chapter 6, for example, that the Declaration of Independence was drafted by three members of Congress of essentially rationalist persuasion, but who worded the document to appeal to a wider audience that included orthodox Protestants.

In preparing the manuscript for this book, my initial plan was to let the study rest merely as a historical investigation of the religious dimensions of the work of the Continental Congress. I was unable, however, to resist the urge to link the study to my own interest in modern American church-state relations. This linkage makes the study, I believe, more interesting and more relevant, although, admittedly, considerably more complex. Modern church-state relations, at least those aspects of it that are the most controversial and that most directly affect American citizens (e.g., prayer in public schools, government support of sectarian education, and religious symbols on public property) are mostly guided by U.S. Supreme Court interpretations of the First Amendment's religion clauses ("Congress shall make no law respecting an establishment of religion, or prohibiting the free exercise thereof"). It is generally held, and correctly so, that the American founding documents marked an important turn in human history—a shift from the interdependence of the institutions of religion and government to their mutual independence. But it remains unclear how the framers sought to implement this new framework of independence. Would any advancement of religion by the federal government be permitted? Would the federal government have any authority to deal with religious questions arising in the states? To what extent would religious exercises be allowed in government circles?

One might logically ask at this point how the work of the Continental Congress has anything to do with the subject of religion under the Constitution and the Bill of Rights. There is an important connection, which I contend has never been seriously pursued in the scholarly literature. The connection is to the "original intent" of the founding fathers who drafted the Constitution and Bill of Rights. It is submitted that an examination of the proceedings and official acts of the Continental Congress affecting religion will contribute to a narrowing of uncertainty about the framers' intent with respect to the role of religion in the United States.

The Constitution and Bill of Rights were not drafted in a vacuum, free from the influence of the nation's immediate history or of its leaders. They were drafted following a period in which the Continental Congress had served as the nation's first representative government. As a political body, the Continental Congress had confronted many difficult issues concerning religion: the religious grounding of human government in general, the propriety of employing religious means for political ends, the meaning of religious liberty for American citizens, and the expenditure of government monies for religious ends. Moreover, of the fifty-five delegates to the Constitutional Convention, forty-two had served as members of at least one of the Continental Congresses.[1] They brought with them certain practices and habits of thought that would inevitably influence their thinking in drafting the documents that would determine policy and practice for many years to come. It is my own view, then, that the present study of the Continental Congress's record on religion sheds valuable light on the framers' original intentions.

For more than 200 years a debate has raged between those who believe that jurists should follow the original intentions of the founding fathers and those who argue that the Constitution is a living, evolving document subject to interpretation by each succeeding generation.[2] While I believe there are definite limits to what original intent can tell us, I do not completely deprecate it as an important field of inquiry. The Supreme Court has historically considered the framers' intent to be important, if not decisive, when it is discoverable. The Constitution is the charter of the U.S. government. It is the binding framework for the law and public policy of the nation. Therefore, its original meanings, if ascertainable, necessarily guide its interpreters. So while the notion of a "living Constitution" is valid, the American constitution would someday lose much of its meaning if its primary guardians, the justices of the U.S. Supreme Court, were uncommitted to its original meanings.

At the same time, original intent is not always fully discoverable. In such cases, some measure of freedom must be given to constitutional interpreters. It has been the peculiar genius of the Constitution that while its provisions are sufficiently detailed to provide a necessary element of stability to government, it has nonetheless proved to be general and flexible enough to allow for growth to meet the altered requirements of an ever changing social order. Thus, original intent is a valid starting place in constitutional interpretation, but expansions on it must be permitted to meet changing requirements, especially when original intent, because of the inadequacy of available records, remains in many respects unclear.

The Continental Congress's proceedings and official acts affecting religion represent, somewhat ironically, the most neglected body of thought concerning church-state relations in the American founding era. As one might expect, studies investigating original intent tend to focus on the proceedings of the Constitutional Convention of 1787, the ratification debates that followed in the states, the proceedings of the First Congress that in 1789 adopted the Bill of Rights, and the subsequent state ratification debates. This ground has been plowed and re-plowed, although it remains soil in which all who investigate the issues must dirty their feet.[3] Other valuable studies examine the influence of church-state patterns in the colonies/states both before and after the Constitution and Bill of Rights were ratified.[4] Some studies highlight early America's most vigorous and pithy thinkers on church and state, hallowed names like Roger Williams, William Penn, Thomas Jefferson, and James Madison.[5] Still others trace judicial efforts to interpret the religion clauses, so that judges' interpretations of original intent become the focus.[6] All of these investigations are indeed relevant to the pursuit of the maddeningly elusive original intent of the framers, and they deserve the attention they have received and will continue to receive. But one looks in vain for a study of the period of the Continental Congress for what it might contribute to the debate.

Most scholars have correctly recognized religion as having a significant influence on the work of the Continental Congress and have, therefore, in searching for original intent, dismissed the period as an irrelevant phase preceding the revolutionary changes that were subsequently effected toward the separation of church and state in the ratification of the Constitution in 1789 and the Bill of Rights in 1791. Thus Edward Frank Humphrey's thirty-two-page chapter on the "Continental Congress and Religion," written in 1924, remains the most extensive account of the subject and characteristically concludes that "Congress rested heavily upon a religious authority and intended in every way possible to promote as a basis for a well-ordered government a dependence upon Protestant Christianity. There is no evidence that it for a moment contemplated a possible separation of the state and religion."[7] Neither Humphrey nor others, however, analyze in any detail the proceedings of the Continental Congress that legislated regularly on such subjects as sin, repentance, fasting, prayer, chaplaincies, and funerals, nor do they analyze adequately its official treaties, declarations, or resolutions that frequently invoked the name of God.

As the new nation's initial federal body, the Continental Congress was the first governing body required to measure its actions affecting religion because of possible conflicts with a federal arrangement that presupposed noninterference with the states' control over religious matters. Yet the Continental Congress, mostly because it was charged with the oversight of an epochal war, functioned with the belief that divine guidance and approval were essential to its success. Of course, a Congress merely acting religiously might not be violating the states' right of self-determination in matters of religion. But if the Congress's proceedings and official acts violated in various ways the religious liberty of American citizens or jeopardized in some manner the states' sovereignty over religion, then these are important factors that might have influenced the minimalist attention to religion that is obvious in the Constitution and the Bill of Rights. If concerns arose over these violations, and those concerns, expressed either by the delegates to the Congress or by other American citizens, were such that it became important to avoid them in later times, then that needs to be brought to light. Humphrey may be correct that Congress never "for a moment contemplated the separation of the state and religion," but if he is wrong, if there are in fact budding expressions of separationism in the proceedings and acts of the Continental Congress, then those need to be uncovered.

The aim of this study, then, is to discover those acts, proceedings, theories, ideas, and goals of the Continental Congress—in short, any-thing—that might shed light on the intended meaning of the Constitution and the First Amendment as they relate to the desired relationship between religion and government in the United States. It would be con-venient if the "original intent" of the framers was clear and unambigu-ous. But it is not. Therefore, the interpretation of the purposes and as-pirations of the framers regarding the relationship between religion and government in the new nation requires broader historical study. I con-tend that one legitimate place to locate the study—a place that heretofore has received little attention—is the experience of the Continental Con-gress.

This study has four claims. The first is that the U.S. Supreme Court should today consider "original intent" in deciding cases that deal with constitutional issues; this claim is considered in chapter 1. The second claim is that the record of the Continental Congress in regard to religion elucidates "original intent" in the realm of American church-state rela-tions; this claim is considered in chapters 2 through 10. The third claim is that "original intent" is important but not exclusive in constitutional adjudication: there were conflicting ideas and purposes among the foun-ders that make "original intent" difficult, if not impossible, to determine precisely; and there are important social and political developments since the founding era that must, in addition to the founders' original inten-tions, be considered by the Supreme Court in its interpretations of the

religion clauses. Finally, the study claims that the founding fathers'
"original intent" was to break with history and inaugurate a framework
of church-state "separation" in the new nation, although there are vital
reasons today to be sensitive to "accommodationist" claims and practices.
The concluding chapter 11 gives particular attention to these third and
fourth claims.

I should offer a word of explanation on the meaning of several terms
used repeatedly in this study. Terms such as "founding era," "founding
period," and "founding generation" refer generally to the period from
1774, when the Continental Congress convened, to 1791, when the ratification of the Constitution and its first set of ten amendments was completed. The terms "founding fathers" or "founders" therefore refer to
the members of the Continental Congress, Constitutional Convention, and
the First Congress who served during the same 1774–1791 period; they
are to be distinguished from "framers," which I use only in reference to
those who drafted the Constitution and the Bill of Rights.

*Waco, Texas*                                                   *D. H. D.*
*June 1999*

# CONTENTS

RELIGION AND THE CONTINENTAL CONGRESS
1774–1789

*One*


## ORIGINAL INTENT AS A BASIS
## FOR CONSTITUTIONAL INTERPRETATION


To more firmly establish the place of original intent in constitutional adjudication, it is necessary in this opening chapter to consider, first, a number of important historical and contemporary perspectives on the debate over original intent and, second, how original intent serves as a guideline to interpretation of the Constitution and First Amendment's provisions concerning religion. In this way, the relevance of examining the record of the Continental Congress on religion as an aid to recovering the framers' original intent will become more apparent.

### Original Intent as a Form of Inquiry

The term "original intent" stands for the idea that the judiciary should interpret the Constitution according to the understanding of its framers. The U.S. Supreme Court has professed an allegiance to original intent since the first years of its history. The Court has often stated that original intent is entitled to the utmost respect and consideration as an interpretive guide, at least when it is clearly discernible. The Court's commitment to original intent no doubt has much to do with Americans' feeling about their Constitution. As Leonard Levy has said, much that is part of original intent commands our loyalties, admiration, and affection: government by consent of the governed; a bill of rights that protects individual liberties; an elaborate system of checks and balances involving three complementary yet competing branches of government; and elections at fixed intervals.[1] So valued are these concepts to many Americans, the Constitution itself has achieved an almost sacred status. William Gladstone, the great British statesman and prime minister, once described the

American Constitution as "the most wonderful work ever struck off at a given time by the brain and purpose of man."[2] Americans cannot but be pleased by this tribute, and it is accepted by most as being literally true. Drafted by fifty-five delegates to the Constitutional Convention in 1787, the document survives today as the oldest written constitution in the world. Americans revere the framers as men of remarkable wisdom and foresight; maybe for this reason as much as any other, the purposes and intentions of the founding fathers have throughout the nation's history been considered relevant, to one degree or another, in construing and applying the Constitution's provisions.

## The Historical Debate

This commitment to original intent is somewhat strained, however, because the framers' intentions are not always as clear as we might hope. Moreover, it has never been clear to what extent the framers' intentions are relevant to the task of establishing constitutional norms. Even some of the founding fathers themselves disagreed on this point. James Madison, clearly one of the Constitution's primary draftsmen, felt strongly that future interpreters of the document should not look primarily to the intentions of the framers. Here was his position:

> I entirely concur in the propriety of resorting to the sense in which the Constitution was accepted and ratified by the nation. In that sense alone it is the legitimate Constitution. And if that be not the guide in expounding it, there can be no security for a consistent and stable, more than for a faithful, exercise of its powers.[3]

Madison's point here is that the intentions of the Philadelphia framers are not paramount; it is the intentions of the people of the various states who, through their representatives, ratified the Constitution that warrant primary consideration in construing the Constitution. Madison's view only makes constitutional interpretation more complex. If it is difficult to know the framers' intentions, it is even more difficult to know the intentions of all who were involved in the ratification process. Madison apparently was emphatic about this. He chose to delay publication of his notes of the Constitutional Convention until after his death, or, in his own words:

> at least, . . . till the Constitution should be well settled by practice, and till a knowledge of the controversial part of the proceedings of its framers could be turned to no improper account. . . . As a guide in expounding and applying the provisions of the Constitution, the debates and incidental decisions of the Convention can have no authoritative character.[4]

In an ironic twist, then, Madison's notes, not published until 1840, became the first authoritative source available for original intent analysis but were not considered by Madison himself to possess any authority for that purpose. In Madison's view, constitutional interpretation should rely on the intentions of the state ratifiers, not those who sat in Philadelphia. One scholar has expressed the opinion that Madison's view was prevalent in the late eighteenth and early nineteenth centuries; that is, in the nation's early years, the original intent relevant to constitutional discourse was not that of the Philadelphia framers, but rather that of the several parties to the constitutional compact—the states as political entities.[5]

Alexander Hamilton's view of constitutional interpretation likewise did not look principally to the framers, but neither did it look to the ratifiers. Instead, Hamilton looked to the Constitution itself. Hamilton was committed to giving to the Constitution, in the tradition of common law rules of construction, its face meaning: "Whatever may have been the intention of the framers of a Constitution, or of a law, that intention is to be sought for in the instrument itself, according to the usual and established rules of construction . . . [and] arguments drawn from extrinsic circumstances . . . must be rejected."[6]

This conclusion from the general principles of legal interpretation was confirmed, Hamilton added, by the language of the Constitution itself, in the necessary and proper clause:[7] "The whole turn of the clause . . . indicates, it was the intent of the convention, by that clause to give a liberal latitude to the exercise of the specified powers."[8] For Hamilton, then, the Constitution speaks for itself; there is no need to go behind it to ascertain the intent of the framers. However, in what it says, the Constitution is liberal in its granting of powers to the national government.

Thomas Jefferson advocated still another method of constitutional interpretation—the rule of strict constructionism. Jefferson strongly asserted that the Constitution was grounded on the principle embodied in the Tenth Amendment: that all undelegated powers are reserved "to the states respectively, or to the people."[9] For Jefferson, the principle of states' rights was supreme among the intentions of the framers and thus should be strictly adhered to.[10] Accordingly, Jefferson's view of constitutional interpretation was in one way similar to Hamilton's. Under both views, the intentions of the framers are apparent in the words of the Constitution. They differed, however, on the point of what the document said. Hamilton saw liberal powers granted to the new national government; Jefferson saw a very limited grant of power. In the first half of the nineteenth century, two conflicting approaches to constitutional interpretation emerged, roughly paralleling the differences expressed by Hamilton, on the one hand, and Jefferson, on the other. The nationalist school, championed by Daniel Webster and Supreme Court justice Joseph Story, explicitly rejected the Jeffersonian definition of the Constitution as a compact among sovereign states. The nationalists regarded the Supreme Court as the final and authoritative interpreter of the Constitution. John C. Calhoun headed the states' rights school, insisting that final interpretive authority rested with the states. Adherents of both camps, however, expressed their views as explications of the "original intent" of the framers, leaving behind earlier reluctances, such as those expressed by Madison, against the use of "extrinsic evidence" in constitutional interpretation.[11]

Immediately following the Civil War, a virtually uniform appeal to the framers' "original intent" was made by both schools of interpretation. States' rights advocates continued to appeal to the intentions of the framers in support of their views. Yet nationalists were equally vocal in their advocacy for a methodology of constitutional interpretation that stressed the intention of the framers. Senator Charles Sumner of Massachusetts, for example, reputedly one of the most radically nationalist members of the Union Congress, stated: "Every Constitution embodies the principles of its framers. It is a transcript of their minds. If its meaning in any place is open to doubt . . . we cannot err if we turn to the framers. . . ."[12]

The Union victory in the Civil War signaled its repudiation of the Confederacy's emphasis on states' rights; the Reconstruction witnessed an unprecedented era of statutory and constitutional lawmaking, greatly expanding the federal government's power to invade areas traditionally reserved to the states. Since that time, the struggle over the federal/state balance of power has been largely resolved in favor of virtually plenary federal power,[13] that is, until the Reagan and Bush administrations began to advocate a return of power to the states, relying upon the idea of "a written constitution with a fixed meaning . . . to limit the arbitrary exercise of governmental power."[14]

### The Contemporary Debate

The modern push for a jurisprudence of original intention became especially heated in 1985, when President Ronald Reagan's attorney general, Edwin Meese, castigated the Supreme Court in a speech before the American Bar Association for its refusal to give "deference to what the Constitution—its text and intention—may demand."[15] He went on to explain more clearly what he meant:

The intended role of the judiciary generally, and the Supreme Court in particular, was to serve as the "bulwark of a limited constitution." The Founders believed that judges would not fail to regard the Constitution as fundamental law and would regulate their decisions by it. As the "faithful guardians of the Constitution," the judges were expected to resist any political effort to depart from the literal provisions of the Constitution. The standard of interpretation applied by the judiciary must focus on the text and the drafters' original intent.[16]

For Meese, an adherence by the Supreme Court to the framers' original intentions would lead to more principled decisions and halt the Court's propensity to "roam at large in a veritable constitutional forest."[17] The federal courts, and especially the Supreme Court, Meese added, have lost sight of the central purpose of the Constitution, namely, to limit the power of the federal government.

Reaction to the Meese speech was swift and bitter. Abner Mikva, a judge of the U.S. Court of Appeals of the District of Columbia Circuit, termed Meese's remarks an attack on "settled and sensible law."[18] Irving R. Kaufman, presiding judge for the U.S. Court of Appeals, Second Circuit, remarked that as a federal judge, he often found it impossible to "ascertain the 'intent of the framers,' and even more problematic to try to dispose of a constitutional question by giving great weight to the intent argument."[19] Kaufman stated that "even if it were possible to decide hard cases on the basis of original intent or originalism, that methodology would conflict with a judge's duty to apply the Constitution's underlying principles to changing circumstances."[20]

Supreme Court justice William J. Brennan also took the opportunity to speak out publicly in response to Meese's remarks. In a speech to Georgetown University's Law Center, Brennan had harsh words for the advocates of "original intent":

> There are those who find legitimacy in fidelity to what they call "the original intentions of the Framers." In its most doctrinaire incarnation, this view demands that Justices discern exactly what the Framers thought about the question under consideration and simply follow that intention in resolving the case before them. It is a view that feigns self-effacing deference to the specific judgments of those who forged our original social compact. But in truth it is little more than arrogance cloaked in humility. It is arrogant to pretend that from our vantage we can gauge accurately the intent of the Framers on application of principle to specific, contemporary questions.[21]

For Brennan, who retired from the Court in 1990, a jurisprudence of original intention would "turn a blind eye to social progress and eschews adaptation of overarching principles to changes of social circumstance."[22]

The justice criticized one of federalism's principal claims: that "because ours is a government of the people's elected representatives, substantive value choices should by and large be left to them."[23] Brennan struck hard at such a claim:

> The view that all matters of substantive policy should be resolved through the majoritarian process . . . ultimately will not do. Unabashed enshrine- ment of majoritarianism would permit the imposition of a social caste system or wholesale confiscation of property so long as approved by a majority of the fairly elected, authorized legislative body. Our Constitution could not abide such a situation. It is the very purpose of our Constitu- tion—and particularly of the Bill of Rights—to declare certain values tran- scendent, beyond the reach of temporary political majorities.[24]

Given these points, Brennan, speaking on behalf of the federal judiciary, added that judges must "read the Constitution in the only way that we can: as 20th century Americans. We look to the history of the time of framing and to the intervening history of interpretation."[25]

In 1986 Robert H. Bork, then a judge of the U.S. Court of Appeals for the District of Columbia, became a chief spokesman for a jurispru- dence of original intention by arguing that judges who do not construe the Constitution in accordance with the original intent of the framers "will, in truth, be enforcing their own morality upon the rest of us and calling it the Constitution."[26] William H. Rehnquist, nominated by Pres- ident Reagan and confirmed as the nation's chief justice in 1986, has professed similar views.[27] The Bush administration subsequently was less vocal than the Reagan administration about reviving the "true inten- tions" of the framers, presumably because of the backlash of criticism directed at Edwin Meese and the outrage against Judge Bork's views that surfaced during Senate confirmation hearings on his nomination to the Supreme Court. Bork's "jurisprudence of original intention" was directly responsible for his failure to be confirmed as an associate justice. Still, the debate remains active today (even Bill Clinton occasionally appealed to the "original intent" of the founding fathers), but it is conducted more in scholarly circles than on the political front.

Thus, original intent remains important as a foundational doctrine in constitutional interpretation. The expectations of original intent, that is, its yield of specific designs or fundamental aspirations, of "original in- tentions" or principled visions, may vary from one interpreter to the next, but original intent remains an important inquiry for all.

This commitment to original intent is especially valid with respect to the religion clauses. An understanding of the original intent of the founding fathers with respect to the role of religion in America is a "necessary first step in reading the religion clauses of the Constitution."[28] The founding fathers were closer to the problem of religious despotism, having seen its effects in Europe and in the colonies. Their aspirations to provide guarantees for religious liberty in a constitutional government are instructive for a contemporary America that retains those aspirations. Thus, it is exceedingly important to consider the intentions of the framers who, so significantly, began the First Amendment with provisions concerning religion.

## Interpreting the Religion Clauses: The Quest for Original Intent

The first sixteen words of the First Amendment to the U.S. Constitution provide: "Congress shall make no law respecting an establishment of religion, or prohibiting the free exercise thereof." The first ten words are commonly called the Establishment Clause; the last six are often referred to as the Free Exercise Clause; together they are frequently referred to as the religion clauses.

The religion clauses are intimately interrelated in their purposes. It may be said that the framers' central purpose in both clauses was to protect religious liberty—to prohibit the coercion of religious practice or conscience, a goal that remains paramount today.[29] Justice Brennan's examination of the religion clauses in one case resulted in this conclusion:

> The two clauses, although distinct in their objectives and their applicability, emerged together from a common panorama of history. The inclusion of both restraints . . . shows unmistakably that the Framers of the First Amendment were not content to rest the protection of religious liberty exclusively upon either clause.[30]

The two clauses, on their face, express dual purposes: the prohibition of an establishment of religion and the guarantee of the free exercise of religion. The first clause prohibits; the second clause protects. In the words of one authority, the clauses express "a tradition of freedom *of* religious exercise and a tradition of freedom *from* religious exercise."[31] The clauses issue two separate mandates. The Establishment Clause was clearly intended to eliminate the possibility of an established church in the new nation; beyond that, full agreement as to the framers' intent ceases. There is less disagreement about the purpose of the Free Exercise Clause; it was intended to preserve the right of the citizen to believe,

following John Locke, "according to the dictates of his own conscience,"[32] free from civil coercion.

Because the meaning of the Establishment Clause is less clear than the
meaning of the Free Exercise Clause, most of the contemporary debate
over the framers' intent in the wording of the religion clauses focuses
on the Establishment Clause. Furthermore, the debate tends to revolve
around the Establishment Clause because the key issues focus on the
degree of permissible government sponsorship, promotion, advancement, or support of religious activities, and it is accepted by all that the
term "establishment" as contained in the Establishment Clause bears
most directly upon these issues. This is not to say, of course, that the
Free Exercise Clause is free from debate on its original meaning, but only
that it receives less attention than the controversy regarding the original meaning of the Establishment Clause. Nevertheless, the meaning of
the Free Exercise Clause can produce some very lively discussions. For
example, in the 1997 case of *Boerne v. Flores*,[33] Justices Sandra Day
O'Connor and Antonin Scalia used history to defend different interpretations of free exercise. O'Connor argued that the framers sought to exempt religious objectors from generally applicable laws, while Scalia was
convinced the very opposite was true.

Regarding the Establishment Clause, there are two basic interpretations of what the constitutional framers intended it to mean: the separationist and the accommodationist. One can argue that a twofold taxonomy is inadequate,[34] but even more nuanced positions on the meaning
of the religion clauses can be said to be mere deviations from these two
basic perspectives. The separationist interpretation was first advanced
by Justice Hugo Black for a five-to-four majority in the 1947 landmark
case of *Everson v. Board of Education*.[35] In what is certainly the most
frequently quoted portion of any Supreme Court opinion dealing with
church-state issues, Justice Black declared:

> The "establishment of religion" clause of the First Amendment means at
> least this: Neither a state nor the Federal Government can set up a church.
> Neither can pass laws which aid one religion, aid all religions, or prefer
> one religion over another. Neither can force nor influence a person to go
> to or to remain away from church against his will or force him to profess
> a belief or disbelief in any religion. No person can be punished for en-
> tertaining or professing religious beliefs or disbeliefs, for church atten-
> dance or non-attendance. No tax in any amount, large or small, can be
> levied to support any religious activities or institutions, whatever they
> may be called, or whatever form they may adopt to teach or practice
> religion. Neither a state nor the Federal Government can, openly or se-

cretly, participate in the affairs of any religious organizations or groups and vice versa. In the words of Jefferson, the clause against establishment of religion by laws was intended to erect "a wall of separation between church and State."[36]

Relying on the intent of the framers, the Court thus declared that the original purpose of the Establishment Clause was to create an absolute separation of the spheres of civil authority and religious activity by forbidding all forms of government assistance or support for religion. That is, the clause went far beyond merely intending to prohibit the governmental establishment of a single church or of preferring one religious sect over another. As Leonard Levy has stated, "The heart of this broad interpretation is that the First Amendment prohibits even government aid impartially and equitably administered to all religious groups."[37]

This "separationist" interpretation is also sometimes referred to as the "broad" or "no aid" view. Whatever its label, the idea is that there is to be a strict separation between civil authority and religion; no church or religious group should receive any form of governmental aid. This view is said to have grown out of the views of many of the leaders, notably Thomas Jefferson and James Madison, in the movement for religious liberty. For example, in Jefferson's "Bill for Establishing Religious Freedom" (1779) and Madison's "Memorial and Remonstrance" (1785), the idea is clearly expressed, in a number of ways, that religion should be totally independent of government interference. According to Leo Pfeffer, "In the minds of the fathers of our Constitution, independence of religion and government was the alpha and omega of democracy and freedom."[38]

In contrast to the separationist interpretation, the accommodationist view holds that the framers intended for the Establishment Clause to prevent governmental establishment of a single sect or denomination of religion over others.[39] According to this interpretation, J. M. O'Neill has said that the framers purposed to prohibit "a formal, legal union of a single church or religion with government, giving the one church or religion an exclusive position of power and favor over all other churches or denominations."[40] Sometimes called "non-preferentialists," proponents of this view would permit governmental aid to religious institutions as long as it preferred no particular group or sect. The framers, they contend, intended only to keep the government from abridging religious liberty by discriminatory practices generally or by favoring one denomination or sect over others. Accommodationists hold that the wall of separation between church and state "was not intended . . . to create a sharp division between government and religion or to enjoin government from fostering religion in general."[41] Accommodationists conclude that the founders intended only to remove religious requirements for public office, prevent the creation of a national church or religion, protect freedom of conscience in matters of religion against invasion by the national government, and leave the states to deal with the questions of religion as they saw fit.

As already noted, the separationist-accommodationist debate also embraces the Free Exercise Clause. The separationist position is that governmental bodies, having no inherent competence in matters of religion, should restrict the free exercise rights of individuals and religious bodies only to the extent that their religious exercise will endanger the health and welfare of themselves or others or if it violates public policy in some serious way. As a legal standard, this became the accepted view of the Supreme Court as early as 1878 in *Reynolds v. United States*.[42] More recently, however, due to the views of an increasingly accommodationist Supreme Court, state and local governments have been given considerable freedom to regulate religious activity, so long as it occurs pursuant to "neutral" laws not intended to discriminate specifically against religious activity.[43] In this sense, it is not religion being accommodated, as under the accommodationist interpretation of the Establishment Clause, but the majoritarian political process. This trend is troubling to separationists because it offers minority (and often unpopular) religions little protection or "separation" from legislative enactments that infringe upon their religious practices. Whether or not the framers believed that religious objectors should be exempt from valid "neutral" laws, such as conscientious objections to draft laws, remains a controversial topic.[44]

While the two opposing paradigms of separationism and accommodationism govern current interpretation of how the Constitution regulates the relationship of religion to the federal regime, neither was particularly well articulated, nor can either claim to have represented the clearly understood meaning of the religion clauses, in 1789. Still, each position claims to be historically validated and expressive of the "revolution" for religious liberty that became a national reality in the founding period.

Both positions have been worked out only in the last half of the twentieth century, since the Supreme Court determined that the religion clauses, through the application of the Fourteenth Amendment, were as binding on the states as on the national government.[45] Justice Felix Frankfurter sought to soften the delayed and indurate appearance of this "incorporation doctrine" by arguing that the religion clauses applied to the states, in spirit, for most of the nineteenth century, long before the adoption of the Fourteenth Amendment. In *McCollum v. Board of Education*, he stated:

> Long before the Fourteenth Amendment subjected the States to new limitations, the prohibition of furtherance by the state of religious instruction became the guiding principle, in law and feeling, of the American people. . . .
>
> Separation . . . was not imposed on unwilling States by force of superior law. In this respect the Fourteenth Amendment merely reflected a principle then dominant in our national life. To the extent that the Constitution thus made it binding on the States, the basis of the restriction is the whole experience of our people.[46]

Frankfurter's recognition is important for separationists, because it affirms the ongoing revolution in support of separation that was taking place in the late eighteenth and early nineteenth centuries and disaffirms the argument sometimes advanced by many that separationism is a twentieth-century creation.

The classic separationist position resolves the vexing question of how the two religion clauses relate to each other by positing a particular version of religious liberty. Religious liberty is understood as the absence of government constraint upon individuals in religious matters. This emphasis on individual freedom is the fulcrum upon which issues of church and state turn. Religious liberty entails unfettered *individual* action, which is then extrapolated to groups. It is the individual, devoid of participation in society, who engages in the most basic religious action without reference either to others or to an existing tradition. Further, liberty is conceived negatively—as absence of external or governmental restraint. This position arises out of an essentially Protestant view of faith focused through an Enlightenment emphasis upon the individual that deemphasizes the importance of communal dimensions of faith.[47]

The accommodationist position also conceives of liberty as a basic right that grew primarily out of the founding period. But accommodationists construe religion less in terms of individual action and give liberty a positive value—as something more than the absence of restraint. Thus they are more concerned with the communal aspects of religion than are separationists.[48]

The accommodationist position emphasizes that the religion clauses were never intended to deal harshly with religion. Accommodationists therefore interpret them to make religious liberty a positive right, the individual and communal exercise of which is to be encouraged, if not initiated, by government. This position is significantly different from that of the separationists and leads to markedly different contemporary policies and practices. With a very conservative Supreme Court makeup since the early 1990s, it is no surprise that the Court today is vocally accommodationist and inclined to "correct" the separationist decisions of the past several decades.[49] It is also interesting that accommodationists, including the Court's current chief justice, William Rehnquist, focus attention on the residual religious quality of the founding era. The same First Congress that adopted the First Amendment opened with prayer and later appointed its own chaplain. Indeed most of the early presidents, including a reluctant Madison, declared occasional days of thanksgiving. In the Northwest Ordinance, provision was arguably made for the support of religiously based education in the western territories.

In sum, accommodationists consider that the operative ideal of the early republic was a posture of support of religion by government on a nonpreferential basis. In turn, that posture seems to point toward a twentieth-century ideal of governmental accommodation to religion in ways that promote virtue among the citizens and generally secure the greater common civil good.[50]

Both positions have their strengths and weaknesses. Historical interpretation for each view does not yield tidy results. Each is more burdened by extrapolations than supported by hard, incontrovertible facts. The surviving data of the founding period, especially the debates of the founding fathers in formal session, as well as the records of the states' ratification proceedings, are regrettably inadequate in their treatment of the subject. Today, after more than 200 years of national experience and continuing debate on these issues, little has been resolved. This uncertainty regarding the framers' intent can be seen in a brief review of the proceedings that produced the Constitution's provisions on religion.

### The Constitutional Convention

The religion clauses contained in the First Amendment grew out of the concern of the states that the Constitution of 1787 gave little attention to the subject of religion. In contrast to the Declaration of Independence, the Constitution contained no references to God. Its only reference to religion was the prohibition against religious tests for federal officeholders contained in Article VI, clause 3: "No religious test shall ever be required as a qualification to any office or public trust under the United States." Only Roger Sherman of Connecticut disapproved of the provision, not because he disagreed with its purpose and effect, but because he thought including the provision in the Constitution was "unnecessary, the prevailing liberality being a sufficient security against such tests."[51]

One authority has noted that this provision "precluded the possibility of any church-state union or the establishment of a state church."[52] This is an important recognition. In the absence of the provision, Congress might have had the power to compel subscription to the tenets of a particular church, or to Protestantism, or to Christianity, or to any other religion, in order to hold office.[53] Instead, the provision rendered one's religion irrelevant to a capacity to serve the country in any official sense.

No further discussions on the subject of religion occurred at the Constitutional Convention. As will become more apparent in later chapters, the framers believed that the national government should have very little to do with religion; religious matters were best left to the states. Because of this reality, Congress was powerless, even in the absence of the First Amendment, to enact laws that aided religion.

The Convention delegates soundly rejected a proposal by George Mason of Virginia to include a bill of rights in the Constitution. The almost uniform belief of the delegates was that a bill of rights would be superfluous. The new federal government possessed only limited powers delegated to it by the states; no power had been granted to legislate on any of the subjects that might be included in a bill of rights. Because no such power existed, none could be exercised or abused, and, therefore, an enumeration of provisions against that possibility was unnecessary. In the words of Alexander Hamilton in *The Federalist*: "For why declare that things shall not be done which there is no power to do? Why, for instance, should it be said that the liberty of the press shall not be restrained, when no power is given by which restrictions may be imposed?"[54] It would be the states, though, fearful of a national government that would arrogate power unto itself, which would insist upon specific protections for individual freedoms, including religious liberty.

*Ratification Controversy*

From late 1787 until 1789 the proposed Constitution was considered by the various state ratifying conventions. A strong antifederalist element developed quickly; they opposed ratification, fearing that the new document's centralizing tendencies would crush the rights of states and individuals. For many of the states, the only solution to this problem was to mandate the inclusion of a bill of rights in the Constitution. Indeed, six of the thirteen states—Massachusetts, New Hampshire, North Carolina, New York, Rhode Island, and Virginia[55]—accompanied their instruments of ratification with a list of recommended amendments that would secure various personal liberties, such as "rights of conscience," "liberty of the press," and "rights of trial by jury."[56] However, the records of the debates of the state ratifying conventions are of little help in ascertaining the precise meanings that such liberties were to assume. Leonard Levy has suggested that the debate that took place over a bill of rights, both public and in the ratifying conventions themselves, "was conducted on a level of abstraction so vague as to convey the impression that Americans during 1787–88 had only the most nebulous conception of the meanings of the particular rights they sought to secure."[57]

Of the six states that recommended amendments to secure personal liberties, all but Massachusetts submitted proposals regarding religious freedom. Massachusetts, which maintained multiple establishments of religion at the time,[58] was the first state to ratify with amendments, but the only personal rights mentioned were those of the criminally accused. Massachusetts assemblymen obviously did not feel that the Massachusetts religious establishments were in any way threatened by the proposed Constitution; they believed that the new federal government was to be impotent in matters of religion.[59]

New Hampshire recommended the following amendment: "Congress shall make no laws touching Religion, or to infringe the rights of Conscience."[60] However, because there are no records of the debates in the New Hampshire assembly, little can be known about how the New Hampshire delegates understood the purpose and parameters of their proposal.

In Virginia, James Madison argued that no amendments to the Constitution were necessary. His efforts failed, however, and among the amendments recommended was one providing that "no particular religious sect or society ought to be favored or established, by law, in preference to others."[61]

In New York, not a single word of the week-long debates is recorded. Accordingly, the Convention members left no explanation of what they understood by their proposed amendment "that no Religious Sect or Society ought to be favored or established by Law in preference of others."[62] This wording was the same as that used in the state constitution of 1777, which abolished religious establishments in New York.

North Carolina, which had abolished its Anglican establishment in 1776, recommended an amendment virtually identical to those of Virginia and New York.[63] Rhode Island offered a similar proposal against establishment modeled after those of Virginia, New York, and North Carolina.[64]

It is clear from the amendments proposed by the various states that none favored the establishment of religion by Congress. But what was the meaning of an "establishment of religion" that was to be beyond the federal exercise of power? Did it mean that only a national church, sect, or denomination was not to be established? Or did it mean more—the prohibition of support of any church, sect, or denomination, or even religion in general? The evidence does not permit a conclusive generalization about what was meant by an establishment of religion. It is apparent that the states wanted to reserve jurisdiction over religion to themselves—indeed, many maintained establishments of religion—and that the federal government was not to meddle in religious matters. Whether or not the Congress was to be prohibited from offering any type of nondiscriminatory financial support to churches, however, or even from promoting religion in general, is unclear from an examination of the debates of the state ratifying conventions. Surely the First Congress, gathered to enact a bill of rights, would deal with these issues with considerably more precision.

## The First Congress and the Emergence of the Religion Clauses

James Madison had been among those who argued that a bill of rights was unnecessary. He insisted that the national government had no power to infringe upon individual rights. He soon came to appreciate the honest fears of the delegates to the state conventions, however, who insisted upon a clear prohibition of federal infringement upon the rights of conscience as well as other individual liberties. It was largely on the basis of his assurances that he would secure from the First Congress the kinds of amendments that the states wanted that most of the states were willing to ratify the Constitution.[65]

After the Constitution was ratified, Madison, feeling "bound in honor" to secure amendments,[66] was true to his word and offered a number of proposed amendments to the First Congress to allay the apprehension of many of the states. On 8 June 1789, at the opening of the First Congress, Representative Madison proposed, among others, the following amendment: "The civil rights of none shall be abridged on account of religious belief, nor shall any national religion be established, nor shall the full and equal rights of conscience in any manner or in any respect be infringed."[67]

Proponents of an accommodationist interpretation of the Establishment Clause claim that the word "national" is proof that Madison intended nothing more than a prohibition against the preference of one religion over another. Robert Cord, for example, argues that Madison's proposal supports his thesis that:

> the religion clauses ultimately adopted by Congress were meant to deny
> to Congress the constitutional authority to pass legislation providing for

the formal and legal union of any single church, religion, or sect with the Federal Government. . . . Consequently the separation of Church and the national State envisioned by the adopters of the First Amendment would leave the matter of religious establishments or disestablishment to the wisdom of the several States.[68]

On initial consideration, Cord's thesis seems persuasive. Yet a number of facts suggest that Madison might have opposed more than just the establishment of a national church.

Madison had led a fight in 1785 in the Virginia legislature against a bill calling for a general tax assessment for the support of not one but of all Christian religions. In his renowned "Memorial and Remonstrance," Madison repeatedly referred to the assessment bill as an "establishment of religion."[69] After his retirement from the presidency, Madison in 1817 expressed his disapproval of tax-supported chaplains for Congress and the armed services, as well as presidential proclamations of days of thanksgiving. Significantly, he described these as "establishments" and "the establishment of national religion."[70] All of this makes it difficult to know conclusively what Madison meant when he submitted his proposed amendment prohibiting the "establishment" of a "national religion." He may have been signifying not that the federal government had no business preferring one church or religion over others but that national action on behalf of any or all churches or religions was outside the purview of permissible government action.

Madison's proposed amendment was referred to a specially formed select committee, of which Madison was a member. The committee changed the wording of the amendment proposal several times but eventually settled on the following language: "No religion shall be established by law, nor shall the equal rights of conscience be infringed."[71]

Debate on the select committee's proposed amendment opened on 15 August 1789. Peter Sylvester, a fifty-year-old lawyer from New York, opened the debate and focused on the establishment question. He feared that the clause "might be thought to have a tendency to abolish religion altogether."[72] Michael Malbin has suggested that Sylvester had two premises in mind as he spoke:

1) He probably was concerned that the phrase "no religion should be established by law" could be read as a prohibition of all direct or indirect governmental assistance to religion, including land grants to church schools, such as those contained in the Northwest Ordinance, or religious tax exemptions. 2) Sylvester apparently thought some form of governmental assistance to religion was essential to religious survival. Unless these premises are assumed, it is difficult to see how Sylvester could have seen the establishment clause as a threat to religion.[73]

Malbin, then, finds in these two premises evidence that the House was concerned that the proposed amendment would prohibit nondiscriminatory governmental aid to various forms of religion. This gives support to his own view of the historical meaning of the Establishment Clause: Congress desired to encourage religion, which led it to accept nondiscriminatory aid to religion.[74] Yet there would seem to be at least one more plausible explanation of Sylvester's stated concern. Sylvester may have thought that the proposed amendment might be construed by the American people as a congressional outlawing of religion altogether. If that was the essence of Sylvester's thinking, which is altogether possible from a literal reading of the committee's proposal, he was not concerned with the issue of governmental aid to religion, as Malbin suggests, but with the much larger issue of the very survival of religion. In that case, he would merely be asking for a rephrasing of the amendment; his comment would say nothing about his views on establishment.

The debate continued. The only account of the debate, in the *Annals of Congress*, is given in paraphrased form. Levy's description of the debate is lugubrious:

> It [the debate] proves nothing conclusively. It was apathetic and unclear: ambiguity, brevity, and imprecision in thought and expression characterized the comments of the few members who spoke. That the House understood the debate, cared deeply about its outcome, or shared a common understanding of the finished amendment is doubtful.[75]

The House, acting as a committee of the whole, concluded the debate and, upon a motion by Samuel Livermore of New Hampshire, passed a revised amendment proposal: "Congress shall make no laws touching religion, or infringing the rights of conscience." Five days later, on 20 August, Fisher Ames of Massachusetts moved that the amendment read: "Congress shall make no law establishing religion, or to prevent the free exercise thereof, or to infringe the rights of conscience." Without debate, this proposal was adopted by the necessary two-thirds of the House. The amendment as submitted to the Senate, however, reflected a stylistic change that gave it the following reading: "Congress shall make no law establishing religion, or prohibiting the free exercise thereof, nor shall the rights of conscience be infringed." No record was left of proceedings that brought about this stylistic change.[76]

The Senate began deliberations on the House amendment on 3 September and continued through 9 September. The Ames amendment must have provoked controversy in the Senate, since several alternative versions were suggested in its place. In considering the House's draft, a Senate motion was made first to strike out "religion, or prohibiting the free exercise thereof" and to insert "one religious sect or society in pref-erence to others."[77] The motion was rejected, and then passed.[78] Thus, the first new Senate version read: "Congress shall make no law estab-lishing one religious sect or society in preference to others, nor shall the rights of conscience be infringed."[79]

After further debate, the Senate rejected two alternative wordings. First, it rejected language providing: "Congress shall not make any law, infringing the rights of conscience, or establishing any Religious Sect or Society."[80] Second, it rejected language providing: "Congress shall make no law establishing any particular denomination of religion in preference to another, or prohibiting free exercise thereof, nor shall the rights of conscience be infringed."[81]

Considerable disagreement exists among church-state scholars as to the meaning that should be given these Senate drafts. For example, Levy,[82] as well as Douglas Laycock, argue that all three of these drafts favored the "no preference" viewpoint, but all were rejected because the Senate clearly wanted a wording favoring the broad interpretation of the Establishment Clause. Laycock comments: "At the very least, these three drafts show that if the First Congress intended to forbid only preferential establishments, its failure to do so explicitly was not for want of ac-ceptable wording. The Senate had before it three very clear and felicitous ways of making the point."[83] Gerard Bradley, however, holding to the narrow interpretation, seems to suggest that the rejected versions all were aimed at prohibiting a national church, indicating, despite the fact that all three versions were rejected, the dominant idea among the senators—no national church.[84]

Later the same day, 3 September, the Senate adopted a draft that treated religion more generically: "Congress shall make no law establish-ing religion, or prohibiting the free exercise thereof."[85] Six days later the Senate again changed its mind and adopted, as its final form of the amendment: "Congress shall make no law establishing articles of faith or a mode of worship, or prohibiting the free exercise of religion."[86] Like the three defeated motions, however, this has the unmistakable meaning of prohibiting acts that prefer one church or sect over others—clearly a narrow intent.

The Senate version of the amendment was then sent to the House, which rejected it. Levy has suggested that this action indicates that the House was not satisfied with merely a ban on the preference of one church or sect over another—clearly, according to Levy, a broad intent.[87]

A House-Senate joint conference committee was then created to re-solve the disagreement over the religion amendment. A compromise amendment was eventually agreed upon on 25 September and passed by both branches: "Congress shall make no law respecting an establishment of religion, or prohibiting the free exercise thereof."[88] The joint committee left no records of its deliberations, but the congressional action was completed. The religion clauses, comprising a mere sixteen words, had been approved.

The First Amendment, with eleven other amendments, was submitted to the thirteen state legislations for ratification. Much to the disappointment of students of American constitutional law, there are no surviving records of the states' debates. By June 1790 the necessary nine states had approved ten amendments—the Constitution's Bill of Rights.[89]

## Concluding Remarks: The Search for Meaning

The foregoing sketch of the historic developmental phases that eventually produced the religion clauses of the First Amendment is not intended as an argument for either a separationist or accommodationist interpretation of the religion clauses; the point here is that during the entire developmental process, the framers left no record of any attempts to define terms so as to enable succeeding generations to determine with precision the intended meaning of the religion clauses. What is an "establishment"? What is a law "respecting" an establishment of religion? What is meant by "religion" or the "free exercise thereof"? Moreover, extrapolation on the meaning of such terms is frustrated by the paucity of records of the debates in Congress and the state ratifying conventions.

One writer has said that the "men who wrote the Constitution wrote under great duress and heightened pressure; they developed the document in a politically charged environment and were subject to compromise and negotiation."[90] Philip Kurland, in considering the enterprise of discovering the framers' original intent in fashioning the religion clauses, wrote: "At best, the past is never fully recapturable, and the parts that are recapturable may not be an accurate reflection of what actually happened. When the quarry is neither recorded words nor events, but rather the state of mind that gave rise to the words or events, and when the state of mind is not one person but of many persons, the pursuit of the past is almost hopeless."[91] Regarding the debates of the First Congress, Levy adds: "Not even Madison himself, dutifully carrying out his pledge to secure amendments, seems to have troubled to do more than was necessary to get something adopted in order to satisfy popular clamor and deflate anti-federalist charges."[92]

Despite the absence of perspicuous meanings in the religion clauses, seemingly every writer who embarks upon the arduous task of ascertaining the original intent of the framers in their crafting of the religion clauses concludes that his or her interpretation is the right one. The subject, particularly because of its implications in the formation of public policy (especially in education, both public and private), seems to transform into partisans all who approach it. The issue is, however, certainly more debatable than partisans on either side would have anyone believe. Close scrutiny of all of the available records simply does not produce irrefutable conclusions.[93]

University of Colorado law professor Steven Smith has argued recently that the search for substantive principles in the religion clauses is futile because they are not there. He suggests that the founders assigned the substantive problem to the states; they disagreed on the substantive principles, so to produce a Constitution and Bill of Rights that could be ratified, "they simply made it explicit that religion was within the jurisdiction of the states, not the national government."[94] Thus, there was no national principle delivered by the founders prescribing the desired relationship between religion and government. Moreover, Smith says, the Supreme Court's decision in the 1940s to "incorporate" the religion clauses represented, in effect, a reversal of this entire approach:

> By undertaking to review and regulate church-state relations at both the national and state levels, the federal judiciary necessarily committed itself to developing a substantive constitutional law for the subject. It would therefore be more accurate to say that this decision, far from "incorporating" the religion clauses, effectively repudiated—and hence repealed—those clauses.[95]

There is much to commend in Smith's thesis. What he says is basically true. But the place of "original intent" in our constitutional schema is more complex. Yes, the framers *did* choose to confer on the states jurisdiction over religion. But where does this leave us? While the framers collectively may not have sought formally to advance a substantive rational principle of religious liberty, we still need one today. The "incorporation" doctrine, no matter what one thinks of its merits, is nevertheless a constitutional reality, thus making the religion clauses binding today on governments at every level. It is therefore essential to formulate sound policy regarding the relationship between religion and government. Smith recognizes this, of course, and thus contends that we are free to debate and work toward a workable framework. His point is that "as long as we keep trying to find in those clauses what isn't there, we will continue to get divisive and contradictory answers to some of the most fundamental and important questions that can be asked by a people who cherish their religious freedoms."[96]

But does this render irrelevant the issues of "original intent?" Hardly. In formulating a sensible and workable policy on the relationship between religion and government, among the bodies of material we *must* consult are the framers' views. That the Constitution initially deflected jurisdiction over many questions pertaining to religion to the states in no way suggests that the founders did not have principled ideas about religious liberty. Their ideas, theories, and practices are perhaps the *most* important source of material we can consult. Because the founders declined, collectively, in crafting the Constitution and Bill of Rights, to formally announce a comprehensive, national principle of religious liberty in no way lessens the fact that many founders thought and wrote profoundly on the subject. They may have disagreed on principles, but that is no reason to ignore their contributions to the debate. Being attentive to "founding" issues and the overall framework of government contemplated for the new nation, the founders' ideas on the public role of religion, to be applied in the states *or* at the federal level, remain vital data for us to examine. Moreover, *after* passage of the religion clauses, a number of key issues arose at the federal level that called for interpretations of the meaning of those clauses—issues such as national prayer proclamations, the appointment by Congress of legislative and military chaplains, and the applicability of the religion clauses to activities in the western territories. These were matters that could not be assigned to the states, thus requiring deliberation at the federal level and the formulation of "original intent."

While Smith is right in suggesting that the formulation of substantive principles on religious freedom is largely the renewed task of each generation, it is suggested here that the ideas of the founders, what we can still refer to loosely as "original intent," are permanently relevant to the ongoing debate. Toward this end, scholars should continue to investigate the relationship between religion and government in the colonies, then the states; the debates at the Constitutional Convention and the First Congress; the state ratification debates on the Constitution, then later, the Bill of Rights; eighteenth-, nineteenth-, and twentieth-century practices, court decisions, and theory; and any other body of relevant material. This book simply seeks to investigate another body of material not heretofore systematically examined: the role of religion in the Continental Congress. As will be shown, this is a reservoir of material that can add much to the discussion about the place of religion in American public life.

With these parameters in mind, it is necessary in the next chapter, prior to commencing a direct examination of the work of the Continental Congress, to consider the church-state frameworks that existed in the colonies when the Continental Congress convened in 1774, a familiarity with which is essential to an understanding of various acts and policies relating to religion adopted by the Continental Congress.

*Two*

## THE POLITICAL STATUS OF RELIGION
## IN THE FOUNDING ERA

In 1902 historian Sanford Cobb called religious liberty the "great gift of America to civilization and the world."[1] The religious liberty he referred to was built upon the unique principle of the disestablishment of religion by civil authority, adopted first in America as a political principle in the 1630s in Rhode Island, a tiny colony founded by the able and imaginative Roger Williams. In Rhode Island, no churches received financial support from government; they were all maintained only by voluntary, private contributions. Citizens could attend churches of their own choice, without fear of governmental reprisal. These practices were in stark contrast to the traditional European pattern adopted in nearby Massachusetts Bay, where all citizens not only were obligated to attend the established Puritan churches but were taxed for their support as well. The disestablishment principle was subsequently adopted in the colonies of Pennsylvania and Delaware and by 1833 had been embraced by all of the states.

The disestablishment movement, in turn, contributed to the progress of other aspects of religious liberty. As tax-supported churches were recognized to be unessential to the stability of political society, religious tests for civil office gradually began to disappear. Also, because minority religious groups were accorded an essentially "equal" status before the law, civil penalties for "unorthodox" religious worship likewise receded. The drive for religious liberty in early America, embodied primarily in the disestablishment movement, was a revolution of monumental proportions that eventually resulted in a clean break from the European tradition that understood a common religion to be essential to the stability of the political and social order.

When the Continental Congress convened in Philadelphia on 5 September 1774, this revolution was ideologically still in its early stages across the American colonies. Most of the colonies still had tax-supported, "established" churches. On a national level, the difficulty of breaking with traditional ideas on government, society, and religion was an imbroglio so recondite that it was to receive special consideration only some years later—during the pressurized Constitution-making period of 1787 to 1791. It was during this period that a remarkable new framework for the relationship between religion and government, aided by the passage of the First Amendment's proscription on religious establishments and its guarantee of the free exercise of religion, formally became part of America's national identity. This arrangement, binding on the federal government, left in place the states' jurisdiction over religion. Rabidly protective of their autonomy, the states would have it no other way; thus many states continued their traditional "establishments." Subsequently, however, those states that had not already done so adopted, on the model of the federal Constitution's First Amendment religion clauses, similar provisions that formally broke all remaining ties with the churches (Massachusetts was the last to do so in 1833), setting all churches free to be self-supporting and independent of governmental fiscal support. In this regard, Steven Smith's argument that the framers of the Constitution offered no substantive principle of religious liberty, leaving to the states complete authority over religion,[2] begins to break down. There *were* substantive principles enunciated in the religion clauses, disestablishment being the primary one, and so compelling was its merits that the states eventually, without exception, adopted it. This was a development for which the states, not the Supreme Court through the "incorporation" doctrine, voluntarily were responsible. Thus the *meaning* of nonestablishment, a national principle, indeed a product of "original intent," must, among other related principles, be analyzed.

The meaning of the religion clauses will be taken up in more detail in later chapters. The point to be made here is that it was not a primary task of the Continental Congress to forge national principles respecting the desirable relationship between government and religion. That would be undertaken, at least to some degree, by the new federal government some fifteen or so years later. The tasks of the Continental Congress were more patently political, more directly related to dealing with the growing schism between the colonies and Great Britain. The exclusive jurisdiction over religion claimed by the colonies was not challenged by the Continental Congress. This jurisdictional claim assumed by the states after independence was solidly affirmed in the Articles of Confederation, adopted by Congress on 15 November 1777. The convening of the Congress thus involved no mission to alter the state or character of religion in any of the colonies or to compel the rearrangement of existing church-state frameworks. The colonies all jealously guarded their autonomy on virtually all political, economic, military, and religious matters. That the Continental Congress, the first national political body in America, was formed at all was only because of the exigencies of the times, the growing troubles and faltering relationship with the mother country, which forced the colonists to form a coalition to deal effectively with their common problems.

An earlier effort to federate the colonies had failed. In 1754 delegates from seven colonies had met in Albany, New York, to consider ways to deal with the perennial Indian danger and the threat of war with France. Benjamin Franklin in particular was interested in the overall problem of colonial unity and defense, and with the aid of other delegates he devised a plan (the Albany Plan) for intercolonial government. The plan was not approved for the sole reason that none of the colonies wished to give up any of their own powers. Thus it took the experience of the French and Indian War and, later, the keen resentment of British measures against the colonies to bring the colonial assemblies to the realization that union was essential.[3] As already mentioned, among the powers that the colonies did not wish to relinquish to a federated body was the right to set and direct the course of religion within their own boundaries. The character of religion and the relationships between religion and political authority varied greatly from colony to colony. Some colonies regulated religious activity to a considerable degree, some barely at all. Some financially supported several denominations, some only one, some none at all. Self-determination in religious matters was inviolable territory for the colonies. Thus, in a work such as the present one that seeks to describe, analyze, and interpret the proceedings and official acts of the Continental Congress related to religion, it is necessary to first examine briefly the political status of religion in the colonies at the time the Continental Congress convened in 1774.

## Colonial Patterns of Establishment

Those coming to the New World in the seventeenth century brought with them the ideals, traditions, and customs with which they had grown up. As one writer has noted, "There is a deeply rooted idea in American historical lore that the colonists came to America in search of religious liberty."[4] In fact, most of the colonists had no intention of tolerating any religion other than their own. They had ventured to America not to experiment, but to practice and preserve already fully developed systems of belief.[5] Consequently, most of the colonies established their own churches and persecuted, to one degree or another, those outside the approved form of worship. Notable exceptions to this pattern were Rhode Island, Pennsylvania, and Delaware, which never had formally established churches.

### Chesapeake and New England Colonies

In 1774 a majority of the people of British North America still lived in the Chesapeake (Virginia and Maryland) or New England colonies under an Anglican or Congregational establishment. Since the passage of the English Act of Toleration in 1689, these colonies' toleration of dissenting sects had increased, but only grudgingly so. Quakers, Presbyterians, and Baptists always had a presence in the Chesapeake and New England colonies,[6] but the Act of Toleration only granted to them the right to hold their own religious services, provided they properly registered their ministers and places of worship. It did not extend to them, however, the right to hold public office, and Catholics and Unitarians were excluded from all the benefits provided by the Act.[7] It was not until after the Great Awakening that a notable increase in the number of dissenting sects—especially Baptists, Presbyterians, and Congregational Separatists— began to be apparent. The Virginia population of Baptists in particular swelled after 1765. Asserting their right to religious liberty, large numbers of Baptist ministers either refused to apply for licenses to preach or failed to confine their preaching to authorized locations. In 1774 Virginia authorities responded by imprisoning some fifty Baptist ministers, an event that led such Virginia statesmen as James Madison, Thomas Jefferson, and Patrick Henry to side with the cause of replacing the principle of toleration in Virginia with one of full religious liberty. The effort led to the complete disestablishment of the Church of England in Virginia, accomplished progressively between 1776 and 1786.[8]

Throughout the New England colonies of Massachusetts, Connecticut, and New Hampshire, the Congregationalists were the overwhelming majority in nearly every town. Typically, non-Congregationalists were taxed for the support of Congregational ministers and buildings. In Connecticut and New Hampshire this establishment was maintained by force of law, in Massachusetts, by sheer force of numbers. In 1692 the Massachusetts General Court provided for an establishment of religion on a town basis by simply requiring every town to maintain an "able, learned and orthodox" minister, to be chosen by the voters of the town and supported by a tax levied on all taxpayers.[9] This made it theoretically possible for several different denominations to install a non-Congregational minister in their own town.

In a limited number of Massachusetts towns, Baptists settled in sufficient numbers to enable them to elect their own minister. In Swansea, for example, settled and dominated by Baptists long before the 1692 statute, two Baptist churches began to receive support from mandatory public taxation. This turning of the tables was too much for local Congregationalists. In 1708 they sued in the county court, claiming that the Swansea church failed to maintain the required "learned and orthodox" minister. The court ruled that religious taxes in Swansea must be divided equally between the two denominations, a victory for the Congregationalists. Thus Swansea possessed a dual establishment, at least until 1717. In that year the Congregationalists, who continued to complain of religious persecution by the Baptists, received additional relief from an act of the General Court incorporating the Congregational section of Swansea into the adjoining town of Barrington, where the standing order prevailed. Swansea reverted to its exclusive Baptist establishment, which lasted until 1727, when the General Court enacted a statute exempting Baptists from religious taxes.[10]

Thereafter, Massachusetts, New Hampshire, and Connecticut all experimented with granting tax exemptions to Baptists, Quakers, and even Anglicans in towns in which they held a majority of the population. This was unsatisfactory, however, to the same groups living in towns where they did not constitute a majority, who argued that they also should be exempted from taxes collected to support Congregational ministers. The 1760s and 1770s witnessed an increasing pattern of refusal by Baptists and Quakers to pay religious taxes on grounds of conscience. These recalcitrant taxpayers were frequently jailed and some even lost personally owned real estate levied upon for payment of the required taxes. These developments led Isaac Backus, a Baptist minister converted from Congregationalism, to become politically active throughout New England and in Virginia in the cause of convincing the reigning orders that government had no lawful authority over religion and that religious taxes should be eliminated altogether, leaving all churches to be supported voluntarily. Backus enjoyed little success in New England.[11]

In 1774, when the patriots were shouting "No taxation without representation," Backus protested in vain to the Boston patriots against the inconsistency and injustice of sectarian taxation. The more realistic John Adams contemptuously replied that it would be easier to effect a change in the solar system than to alter the church-state structure in Massachusetts.[12] However, Backus's efforts were instrumental in the overthrow of

the Anglican establishment in Virginia in the years immediately following independence.


### Middle Atlantic Colonies

The overwhelming tendency in the New England and Chesapeake
regions to cling tightly to traditional patterns was not being emulated
elsewhere in 1774. The political status of religion in the Middle Atlantic
colonies (New York and New Jersey) marked a most striking departure
from the European norm of an established church. In New Netherland,
the Dutch Reformed Church was actively supported by government, and
the church's first and foremost clergyman, Peter Stuyvesant, grimly persecuted Quakers and other dissenters. The English conquest of 1664,
however, ended the Dutch Reformed establishment, and it was replaced
by the Church of England.[13] Only gradually, though, did the Dutch in
fact see its culture fade, first as a result of the Anglican presence, which
did not establish a formal parish anywhere in the colony before the
1670s, and then from a strong evangelical influence in the first half of
the eighteenth century.[14] The Anglican establishment was never very
strong. The legislature provided for formal support of the Church of
England only in four southern counties of the New York province in the
1690s. By 1700 toleration vanquished establishment if only because even
those who favored establishment were divided over which church to
support. By 1774 a remarkable diversity of Anglicans, Baptists, Methodists, Presbyterians, Catholics, Quakers, Jews, and German Pietists pop-
ulated New York and neighboring New Jersey, with none holding a preeminence that could command an establishment.[15]

In the Pennsylvania and Delaware region non-establishment was from
the beginning the preferred choice of its settlers. Some Lutheran, German
Reformed, and Presbyterian clergymen, accustomed to the more traditional practice of governmental financial support of churches, lamented
the "disorder" they detected all around them,[16] but in the late seventeenth century, for those who sought habitated regions in which to settle,
removed from Puritan or Anglican dominance and privilege, the Delaware Valley was a good option. After various experiences under the
Swedes, the Dutch, and the English, Delaware was transferred to William
Penn in 1682. The "three lower counties," as the portion making up
modern Delaware was then called, received autonomy in 1701.[17]

Beginning in the 1680s, Quakers became dominant in the region, but
the open-door policy of William Penn encouraged citizens of a diversity
of faiths to settle there as well. Although the "Great Law" of 1682 required Sunday observance and penalized profanity, the first fundamental

of Penn's government was freedom of faith and worship to all those who acknowledged one God.[18] At no point thereafter did an established church even seem remotely possible in either Pennsylvania or Delaware. Churches became voluntary societies that people of faith joined only if they so desired and then supported through private contributions. They had to compete with one another for members and received no governmental privileges.[19] In its tiny space in southern New England, Rhode Island, under the direction of the Massachusetts Bay outcast Roger Williams, had already moved in this direction beginning in the 1630s.

Thus it may be said that Pennsylvania, Delaware, and Rhode Island were all founded on principles of religious freedom. They cherished with great pride their liberality in matters of religion, and this attitude was still maintained with steady vigor when the Continental Congress commenced its business in the fall of 1774.

### Southern Colonies

Somewhat less obviously, the two Carolinas and Georgia stumbled in the same direction within the colonial South. The Church of England was established in all three colonies in the early 1700s, but most settlers seldom saw an Anglican clergyman.[20] Freedom of worship was therefore taken for granted. Formal disestablishments in North Carolina and Georgia occurred uneventfully during and after the Revolution—North Carolina in 1776 and Georgia in 1798. South Carolina's Anglican establishment created little disturbance until 1777, when the Reverend William Tennent, a Presbyterian acting as spokesman for various non-Anglican denominations, appeared before the state legislature to disestablish the Anglican church, which was by then calling itself the Protestant Episcopal church. The existence of an established church, Tennent argued, abridged the "free and equal liberty in religious matters" to which all good Christian (Protestant) subjects were entitled. He declared his objection to "all religious establishments" because they infringed religious liberty, but he did not favor the complete separation of religion and government. Few Christians in the revolutionary era did. Like Tennent, they believed that the state should "give countenance to religion" by protecting all denominations and "do anything for the support of religion, without partiality to particular societies" and without abridging "the rights of private judgment" by exacting taxes to promote religion.[21]

Tennent emphasized that the establishment in South Carolina made invidious distinctions among people of different religious beliefs, merely tolerating dissenters as if they stood "on the same footing with the Jews," unmolested but unequal.[22] It also taxed all for the support of one religion. Discriminatory distinctions and tax support constituted its chief characteristics. "The law," he declared:

> knows and acknowledges the society of the one as a Christian church; the law knows not the other churches. The law knows the clergy of the one as ministers of the gospel; the law knows not the clergy of the other churches, nor will it give them a license to marry their own people. . . . The law makes provision for the support of one church; it makes no provision for the others. The law builds superb churches for the one; it leaves the others to build their own churches. The law, by incorporating the one church, enables it to hold estates and to sue for rights; the law does not enable the others to hold any religious property not even the pittances which are bestowed by the hand of charity for their support. No dissenting church can hold or sue for their property at common law.[23]

Although Tennent railed against "all religious establishments," he in fact favored a "general establishment" that supported and nurtured all Protestants without preferring one denomination over others. He therefore proposed to the South Carolina legislature the establishment of "Protestant Christianity."[24] In 1778 the new constitution of South Carolina created the establishment of religion endorsed by Tennent.[25] By 1790, however, South Carolina had discontinued the "Protestant Christianity" establishment, opting to place all churches on voluntary support.

### Statehood and the Question of Religious Establishment

Thus, it can be seen that the political status of religion in 1774 varied greatly from colony to colony. Broadly speaking, the disestablishment movement was gaining a momentum that would accelerate dramatically in the tumultuous Revolutionary War years. Between 1776 and 1784 eleven of the thirteen original colonies adopted new state constitutions,[26] and in the process each was forced to deal once again with the question of formal ties with religion that it might begin, retain, or terminate as it entered statehood. For states like North Carolina and New York, the decision to end all ties to religious establishments was easy.[27] For states like Massachusetts and Connecticut, the decision to retain their establishments or, as with Rhode Island, Pennsylvania, and Delaware, to continue without establishments was equally easy. For some states, however, like Virginia and South Carolina, the question of what to do about maintaining its formal links to religion was cause for acrimonious debate, and the solutions did not come easily.

In Virginia, the move to sever all ties with the Church of England, which had been established since 1619, was quickly accomplished after independence in 1776. But a ten-year struggle ensued over the question of whether religion ought to be placed on a private, voluntary basis or be supported on a nonpreferential basis by a new "general" assessment. The general assessment proposal, introduced by Patrick Henry, was similar to the one proposed by William Tennent in South Carolina in that it sought to make Christianity "the established religion," whereby each taxpayer would have the right to designate the church of his preference, and that church alone would receive his taxes; money collected from a taxpayer failing to designate a church was to be divided proportionately among all churches of his county.[28]

Religious minorities, especially Baptists, Presbyterians, and Methodists, aggressively fought against the general assessment proposal and were supported by the less religiously orthodox Thomas Jefferson and James Madison. Their efforts proved successful. Madison won popular support for Jefferson's "Statute for Religious Freedom" by the dissemination of his own "Memorial and Remonstrance against Religious Assessments," and the Virginia legislature eventually passed Jefferson's bill in January 1786. Since that time, no churches in Virginia have received financial support from the state.[29] Jefferson was later to describe the struggle for disestablishment in Virginia as the most difficult of his entire career.[30]

By the time of the convening of the Constitutional Convention in 1787, seven states, including Virginia, had altogether abandoned governmental support of religion.[31] In all of those states, government support of any church or churches was considered contrary to the basic principles of religious liberty. The remaining six of the original thirteen states were to eventually be likewise convinced on this point, but it took forty-six more years before Massachusetts, the last holdout, was to join the disestablishment movement.[32]

The disappearance of church establishments in the United States in the early nineteenth century was the culmination of a movement for disestablishment that had been active from the very time of the settlement of Rhode Island in the 1630s. While the meaning of the First Amendment's prohibition against Congress's passing laws "establishing" religion was open to some debate, clearly the growing conviction in the late eighteenth and early nineteenth centuries was that it meant at least that churches were to receive no financial support from the federal government. It was the appeal and the success of this model that led all of the states to enact similar provisions against the financial support of churches. While the meaning of religious liberty has always had many dimensions, the revolution for religious liberty that occurred in America from the 1630s to the 1830s had as its chief component the proscription of financial support of churches by civil authority. This was a revolution "in process" in 1787, the fullest expression of which was in Virginia, the final results of which were only to be realized in years to come in all of the states. But, to again affirm the principal contention of this chapter, it was a revolution that had barely begun in 1774 when the Continental Congress convened. The delegates to the Congress understood at that time, to be sure, that a diversity of tightly guarded establishments still existed in the colonies and that the legal status of those establishments lay outside of their authority.

### Religious Tests for Civil Office

Following Old World practices, all of the thirteen original colonies required an attestation of religious belief or affiliation as a prerequisite for holding public office. These oaths were viewed as instruments of social control, given the traditional view that citizens were only trustworthy as civil servants if they were willing to affirm their allegiance to basic religious tenets. All of the colonial oaths went beyond requiring only a belief in God, often mandating a belief in the Trinity, the Scriptures, or, in some cases, a commitment to Protestantism.

As already noted, in the eight-year period following Independence, eleven of the thirteen original states adopted new constitutions. As we have seen, many of the states ended their religious establishments, but most continued to require religious oaths for civil officeholders. Only Connecticut and Rhode Island failed to adopt new constitutions, but the constitutions of both states required officeholders to be Protestants.[33]

Among the states adopting new constitutions, most simply reaffirmed the religious tests that had been in force during the colonial era. The states that limited state officeholders to Protestants were Georgia (1777), Massachusetts (1780), New Hampshire (1784), New Jersey (1776), North Carolina (1776), South Carolina (1778), and Vermont (1777). One only had to be a Christian in Delaware (1776), Maryland (1776), and Pennsylvania (1776), although Delaware required a belief in the Trinity, and Pennsylvania and Vermont required a belief in the Scriptures (both Old and New Testaments).[34]

Of the new state constitutions adopted prior to the Philadelphia Convention of 1787, only the Virginia and New York constitutions declined to require religious oaths for civil servants.[35] In the case of New York, in absence of a constitutional provision addressing the matter of test oaths, state legislation continued until the turn of the century to require a test oath that prevented Catholics from holding office. In Virginia, Thomas Jefferson's "Statute for Establishing Religious Freedom," enacted

1 January 1786, proscribed religious test oaths. For Jefferson, one's religious opinions were irrelevant to one's ability to hold public office.[36]

Neither the Articles of Confederation (adopted by the Continental Congress in 1777, but not ratified by the states until 1781) nor the Constitution of 1787 required religious test oaths of federal officeholders. The Articles were silent on the matter; the Constitution, of course, prohibited religious tests for federal officials in Article VI, clause 3. In crafting these documents, members of the Continental Congress and the Constitutional Convention did not displace existing religious tests in the states, just as they did not displace religious establishments. Neither body sought to interfere in any way with the states' exclusive jurisdiction over religion, nor would any attempted interference have been tolerated. As Daniel Dreisbach notes, in reference to the ratification of the Constitution, "Many delegates to the state [ratifying] conventions were unwilling to grant the new national regime authority to implement a practice [i.e., religious tests] that was common at the state level precisely because they wanted to retain the state tests and they feared a federal test might displace existing state tests."[37]

Nevertheless, the "no religious test" clause of the federal Constitution became a model that many of the states themselves chose to adopt. Before the turn of the century, the states of Georgia (1789), South Carolina (1790), Delaware (1792), Vermont (1793), and Tennessee (1796) either prohibited or removed their constitutions' religious tests. Moreover, as a newly admitted state, Kentucky, in its 1792 constitution, opted not to require a religious test for civil officeholders.[38] Other states retained their religious tests, however, well into the nineteenth and even the twentieth centuries.[39]

The U.S. Supreme Court did not rule on religious tests until 1961 in *Torcaso v. Watkins*,[40] when it ruled that the Maryland constitution's requirement that every state official declare a "belief in the existence of God" was a violation of the First Amendment's Free Exercise Clause. The case effectively ruled out the possibility that government at any level can impose constitutionally valid religious tests for public office.

For purposes of this study, what do we learn from the fact that the founders (delegates to the Continental Congress and the Constitutional Convention) did not permit religious tests for federal officeholders? Specifically, do we learn anything about "original intent?" Significantly, we learn that both federal bodies, by not imposing religious tests on federal officials, sought not to interfere with the states' autonomy over religion. This mirrored the strategy adopted with respect to state religious establishments. But while this strategy was the driving force behind the absence of federal religious tests, there were other important theoretical reasons for doing so, at least as pertains to the religious test ban in Article VI of the Constitution. Oliver Ellsworth, a respected delegate to the Constitutional Convention from Connecticut, wrote that the sole purpose of the ban on religious tests was "to secure . . . the important right of religious liberty."[41] Federalist James Iredell of North Carolina, Baptist leader Isaac Backus of Massachusetts, and New Hampshire's Reverend Samuel Langdon likewise made the point that the ban advanced freedom of conscience and religious liberty.[42]

Some colonial leaders considered religious tests to be a form of tyranny. A letter from new England Presbyterians to George Washington called religion tests "that grand engine of persecution in every tyrant's hand."[43] Isaac Backus echoed these sentiments: "Let the history of all nations be searched from that day (Constantine's) to this, and it will appear that the imposing of religious tests hath been the greatest engine of tyranny in the world."[44] Ellsworth added that religious tests emanated from "tyrannical kings, popes and prelates."[45] Indeed, the notion that religious tests were a tool of tyranny and religious persecution was prominent in the founding era.

Others argued that religious tests were unjust and unnecessary. One North Carolina delegate argued that test oaths "exclude from office conscientious and truly religious people, though equally capable as others."[46] Oliver Ellsworth thought that religious tests unfairly discriminated against "honest men, men of principle."[47] The Reverend Daniel Shute labeled them "unnecessary" because Americans "will choose for their rulers men of known abilities, of known probity, of good moral characters" in the absence of such tests.[48]

Finally, religious tests were thought to violate democratic principles of equality. Along these lines, James Madison, in *Federalist* No. 51, argued that the surest protection for religious liberty was a multiplicity of tests equal before the law. Religious majorities (including those who could meet religious tests for office) were the greatest threat to religious liberty for all and thus should be checked at every opportunity. Concerning Article VI, clause 3, James Iredell of North Carolina added: "This article is calculated to secure universal religious liberty, by putting all tests on a level—the only way to prevent persecution."[49]

Of course, there were also arguments against the federal ban on religious tests for officeholders,[50] but the many arguments in favor of the ban not only contributed toward the inclusion of the "no religious test" clause in the Constitution but, perhaps more significantly, also contributed to the subsequent movement in the states to ban their own religious tests. The federal test ban, therefore, contributed to a growing and widespread "public perception that religious test oaths had no place in republican governments."[51] The various sentiments just highlighted decrying religious tests are a part of "original intent." The arguments opposing religious tests do not necessarily lead to the conclusion that the framers, by constitutionally banning religious tests for holding federal office, intended to create a thoroughly secular state. Some have suggested this,[52] but the inclusion of the "no religious test" clause in Article VI had less to do with political theory—whether America was to be a religious state or a secular state—than it had to do with the expedient resolve that matters of religion were to be left to the states. But neither is it enough to say, as Stephen Smith does, that religion was left to the states by the framers, and so no significant "original intent" on substantive issues regarding the desired relationship between religion and government can be located.[53] The founders had much to say about the drawbacks of religious oaths, and if the states subsequently chose to eliminate their own religious tests, based on the federal model, then we learn something about the meaning of religious liberty in the founding era, which in turn is valuable for us today in formulating policy regarding the appropriate role of religion in public life. And again, in examining the position of the earliest federal governments in America (the Continental Congress under the Articles of Confederation and the First Congress under the Constitution) on the matter of religious tests for federal officeholders, we see that another significant aspect (religious tests) of what we previously referred to as a 200-year movement for religious liberty in America (1630s to 1830s) was in process, still undeveloped, still incomplete in the years where we typically look for original intent (1774–1791). We must always look beyond the founding era for the latent *effects* and *outcomes* of an inchoate "original intent." It is there that we find in the case of religious test bans, as with state disestablishments, the more mature notion of religious liberty, indeed the more fully developed manifestations of the founding fathers' "original intent."

## Concluding Remarks

Had the Continental Congress aspired to obtain the authority to alter the character of the colonies' control over religion, by modification, unification, or elimination, the colonies probably would never have permitted the Continental Congress to convene. John Adams was to write a few years later that the Continental Congress should stay out of religious matters altogether, except to pray, fast, and give thanksgiving annually.[54] To the chagrin of Adams and other delegates, as will be seen, the Congress's involvement with religion far exceeded Adams's suggested parameters.

The Continental Congress's considerable reliance upon religion was in great measure a product of the trying times in which it served. This point can hardly be overstated. Committing Americans to a full-scale, seven-year war against a powerful enemy naturally fostered a reliance on divine assistance. Moreover, the Continental Congress, as well as most colonials, interpreted the American Revolution in religious terms. As it is essential to understand the Congress's record on religion in these important contexts, we turn now to an examination of the religious aspects of the American Revolution.

*Three*


RELIGION AND THE AMERICAN REVOLUTION


Prelude to War

The Continental Congress was formed for the single purpose of giving leadership to the American colonies in the growing disputes with Great Britain that were increasingly pointing to a full-scale war for independence. For the most part, the colonists had been loyal to Britain prior to 1763. They enjoyed access to British markets and the protection of the British military and naval forces. But beginning in 1763, the policies of the British government increasingly antagonized the colonists, who began to look more at the disadvantages of British connections than the benefits. Britain imposed a series of measures—the Intolerable Acts (the Stamp Act, the Townshend Acts, the Tea Acts, and others)—that were designed to increase British revenues. From the British standpoint, these measures had a very logical and pragmatic justification, which historian Charles Akers has aptly described:

> In English eyes the revenue question was simple. The British debt was staggering; the American debt insignificant. Englishmen paid high taxes; Americans low taxes. Much of the British debt had been acquired defending the colonies from the French, and now the territory to guard and administer had been enlarged by the recent [French and Indian] war. Therefore, tax revenues from the colonies must be increased.[1]

The colonists, however, interpreted the British measures in a dramatically different way. They protested the measures as the unlawful taking of property, in short, as "taxation without representation." This basic response soon expanded to claims that the British acts were threats against the colonists' natural rights and fundamental liberties, without which the enjoyment of their very human existence stood in jeopardy.

The arguments against Great Britain did not remain merely on the level of the deprivation of natural rights and fundamental liberties. Inextricably woven into the colonial rhetoric were transcendent values, religious arguments, and appeals to the God of the universe as the witness to these violations of liberties of which he was the author.[2] So powerful were the religious influences on the independence movement that it becomes possible to say that those in the Continental Congress who made the political decision to separate from Great Britain did so only because they fully believed with the majority of the American people that such a monumental act was their religious duty. In order to understand the religious dimensions of the work of the Continental Congress, it thus becomes necessary to examine some of the ways in which the American public, and indeed the members of Congress themselves, understood a revolution to be countenanced, if not demanded, by religious sentiment. This chapter will examine the religious influences on the Revolution under two categories: pietistic influences and rationalistic influences. In many ways pietism and rationalism in the eighteenth century were but opposite sides of a single movement that gathered enough power and momentum to support the idea of independence from Great Britain. Yet as categories of religious thought, they were clearly distinguishable. Sidney Mead has identified pietism and rationalism as the two live movements in American religion in the eighteenth century.[3] While this taxonomy might legitimately be criticized as overly simplistic,[4] it does provide a useful way to discuss revolutionary religion, because eighteenth-century pietism and rationalism both can be defined broadly. In the case of pietism, it can be understood as comprising overlapping elements of Protestantism: New England Puritanism, revivalist evangelicalism produced by the Great Awakening, and the pietism of European immigrants who stressed the inner workings of the Holy Spirit in the believer's life. Denominationally, pietists could be found among Congregationalists, Baptists, Methodists, Presbyterians, Quakers, Hugenots, and a host of pietistic German and Dutch sects. An equally broad definition can be assigned to eighteenth-century rationalism. Influenced by the Enlightenment, rationalists assigned to reason a primacy over revelation in apprehending religious truth. They could be found scattered throughout the Protestant denominations, although they were most heavily concentrated within the Anglican and what later became the Unitarian churches.

While pietism and rationalism differed in their fundamental theological presuppositions, Mead has argued that pietism discovered its incompatibility with rationalism only *after* the War for Independence, leading it to "divorce itself and remarry traditional orthodoxy."[5] But during the revolutionary epoch itself, he says, pietism and rationalism joined hands to achieve common goals. Mead focuses mainly on the achievement of religious freedom and the separation of church and state as shared ideas that found their way into the American system, but he also mentions that these two faces, pietism and rationalism, were allies in their support of the independence movement.

Rationalists and pietists were alike in that both, in their own way, managed to shrug off the theological questions that had divided their forebears, and both developed and practiced their own way of unity. The rationalist, as befitted the learned, found that "the essentials of every religion" could be reduced to a set of intellectual propositions about God, the life of virtue, and immortality of the soul. And, as the much revered Benjamin Franklin put it, these propositions being "found in all the religions we had in our country, I respected them all."[6] The pietist clergyman might be as learned as any rationalist, but his concern was for the hungry sheep in his church who could never be nourished either on formal creeds and theologies or on intellectual propositions. For the pietist, the "walk with Christ" was paramount and the basis for unity. These basic tenets the pietists proclaimed, spreading "scriptural religion throughout the land, among people of every denomination; leaving every one to hold his own opinions, and to follow his own mode of worship."[7]

Thus, rationalists appealed to the head and concluded that the manifold differences over which Christian sects fought were matters of nonessential opinion, while pietists appealed to the heart and concluded that the differences over which Christians had battled and bled since the apostolic era were immaterial to those of "like heart."[8] One important result was that when it came to discussing independence and other important political issues of the day, rationalists and pietists had little difficulty in overlooking their respective religious differences. They continued to go their own ways in their personal religious lives, of course, but they did not permit theological differences to prevent them from finding bonds of unity in commitments to liberty and republican government.

The injection of religious concerns into the revolutionary discussion, even if not all of it favored independence, was widespread. As there was much argument concerning the wisdom of the revolutionary course, so was there a variety of ways in which religious perspectives were infused into the revolutionary debate. Eighteenth-century America was, to a much greater degree than in England, suffused with an intensely religious spirit. Even among those who had left behind the dogmas of orthodox Protestantism, the values and attitudes of that belief system continued to exert considerable influence. For the many colonials who practiced one of the many varieties of traditional Christianity, religious

perceptions became an unmistakable part of the revolutionary arguments.[9] Together, then, pietistic as well as rationalistic religious perspectives contributed to the revolutionary debate, and as those perspectives
overwhelmingly tended to favor independence, it is little wonder that
most American historians have attributed importance, to one degree or
another, to religious sentiment on the momentum of the independence
movement. This assessment stops short of asserting that religious grievances or religious ideology in fact *caused* the Revolutionary War. The
war, it seems, was principally a problem of political power. But religion,
as a powerful force that motivated political behavior, can be discovered
within the atmosphere of the times.

The literature on the connections between religion and the American
Revolution is extensive, and because any comprehensive exploration of
the subject is beyond the scope of the present study, the discussion that
follows seeks only to highlight some of the major links between the
Revolution and, first, pietism, and second, rationalism.

### Pietistic Influences on the Revolution

Patrick Henry's famous speech of 23 March 1775, which ended in the
cry for liberty or death, was typical of the revolutionary appeals to
heavenly authority for a vindication of the colonists' rights. He urged
the colonials to "make a proper use of those means which the God of
nature hath placed in our power." He affirmed that "we shall not fight
our battles alone. There is a just God who presides over the destinies of
nations, and who will raise up friends to fight our battles for us." And
to his own question, "Is life so dear, or peace so sweet, as to be purchased
at the price of chains and slavery?" the answer came, "Forbid it Almighty God!"[10]

Clergymen across the colonies preached to their congregations the
justness of the colonists' cause. Samuel Langdon from Massachusetts, for
example, preached on 31 May 1775:

> If God be for us, who can be against us? The enemy has reproached us
> for calling on his name, . . . They have made a mock of our solemn fasts,
> and every appearance of serious Christianity in the land. . . . And may we
> not be confident that the Most High, who regards these things, will vin-
> dicate his owner, and plead our righteous cause against such enemies to
> his government, as well as our liberties?[11]

Other patriotic preachers joined in a chorus of dissent against the
British attack on American liberties, leading John Adams to say, in the

months just before the signing of the Declaration of Independence, "They [the clergy] engage with a fervor that will produce wonderful effects. Those . . . of every denomination . . . thunder and lighten every Sabbath."[12]

The close connection in the minds of the colonists between political and religious rights explains the nature of the clerical protest. The ministers thus viewed the Stamp Act as the first stage of a subversive plot against the spiritual as well as the civil liberties of the colonists. Not surprisingly, in the years after 1765 the dissenting ministers also feared that the Church of England would soon appoint a bishop for the colonies, and they lashed out defensively against such proposals. The passage of the Intolerable Acts along with the Quebec Act in 1774 confirmed the clergy's belief in a conspiracy against the American churches. By permitting the worship of the Roman Catholic religion in the former French province the English government was thought to be laying the groundwork for the ultimate destruction of American Protestantism. Gradually, especially after Lexington and Concord, independence indeed seemed the only logical course.[13]

Modern scholars have identified a number of links between religion and the American Revolution. Gordon Wood has made the connection between religion and the Revolution by defining religion in such a broad way as to describe the Revolution itself as a quasi-religious movement. He describes revolutionary ideology as a combination of Enlightenment ideas of progress and religious ideas of destiny, both subsumed under a predominantly political framework of "republicanism."[14] Republicanism was then, and remains, a loosely defined circle of ideas stressing democratic ideals, religious destiny, separation of powers in government, a system of checks and balances to minimize the potential for corruption in political leaders, and moral virtue among the citizenry. Wood sees the Revolution as a necessary means to achieve these ideals in the new nation.

Other historians have made more direct connections between religion and the Revolution.[15] Alan Heimert, for example, holds that the roots of the Revolution as a political movement are so deeply imbedded in the soil of the First Great Awakening (roughly 1735–1755) that it can be truly said that the Revolution was the natural outgrowth of that profound and widespread religious movement.[16] He suggests that as a result of the thousands of conversions that took place during the Awakening's revivals, colonials gradually began to sense a new importance of the individual vis à vis the authorities in society. This new outlook resulted in the belief that God was using ordinary people, not elites, to transform and redeem society. The Revolution, then, was a major step in over-throwing the old social order, its leaders and its ideals, and installing a new one based on God's power working through the individual person.[17]

This description actually squares quite well with the interpretation of the Awakening offered by its most important theologian, Jonathan Edwards (1703–1758). Edwards saw America becoming the center of God's kingdom on earth. The conversions of the Awakening were proof that world history was culminating in a new Age of the Spirit. The creation of new men, converted men, especially political leaders, would make possible the realization of God's promised kingdom. Change, thought Edwards, was good for man and good for society.[18] The new evangelicalism, then, provided one of the most powerful forces that helped to focus American discontent and offered a new vision that allowed for a breaking with the past.[19]

William G. McLoughlin likewise emphasizes the role of the Great Awakening as a preparation for the independence movement. The Awakening, he says, seen as an evangelical religious reaction either to Arminian or Enlightenment forces in the colonies, was really the beginning of America's identity as a nation—the starting point of the Revolution.[20] He adds:

> The forces set in motion during the Awakening broke the undisputed power of religious establishments from Georgia to . . . Maine, but more than that, the Awakening constituted a watershed in the self-image and conceptualization of what it meant to be an American. The old assumptions about social order and authority that underlay Colonial political economy and produced cultural cohesion dissolved. The corporate and hierarchical society began to yield to an individualistic and equalitarian one. While the medieval concept of a Christian commonwealth lingered, its social foundations crumbled.[21]

McLoughlin concludes that, after 1735, a new evangelical spirit caused the colonists to redefine their social principles into a cohesive structure sufficiently radical to necessitate a political break with Great Britain.[22]

But while the evangelical fervor of the Great Awakening may have had a direct bearing on colonials' perception that their political ties to Britain were an impediment to the growth and development of America, the independence movement could never have been sustained on the strength of evangelical ideas alone. Puritanism, still a powerful force in the colonies, especially in New England, would have to support the cause as well. Edmund S. Morgan has said that the independence movement "in all its phases, from the resistance against Parliamentary taxation in the 1760s to the establishment of a national government and national policies in the 1790s was affected, not to say guided, by a set of values inherited from the age of puritanism."[23] Moreover, the majority of American citizens during the Revolution were in many ways identified with Puritanism. Bernard Bailyn has asserted that New England Puritanism was "channeled into the main stream of eighteenth-century political and social thinking . . . by almost the entire spectrum of American Protestantism."[24] More specifically, Mark Noll has estimated that 75 percent of the colonists in 1776 were identified with denominations that had arisen from the Reformed, Puritan wing of European Protestantism: Congregationalism, Presbyterianism, Baptists, and German and Dutch Reformed.[25] Another writer has estimated that Congregationalists, Presbyterians, and Baptists alone made up at least 54 percent of the American population during the Revolution.[26] Thus, both in terms of its ideology as well as in the sheer numbers of its adherents, Puritanism was indeed pervasive throughout the colonies, and any sustained independence movement would require the active support of those of Puritan heritage.[27]

How is the Puritan strain in the nation's early history best described? It defies simple definition, but certain generic qualities can be identified. First of all, the Puritan perspective saw life as a whole. It made few distinctions among social, political, and theological concerns. Since the battle between good and evil, God and Satan, was carried into every aspect of life, decisions in the communal life of the wider society had a moral significance equal to those enacted within the narrow confines of the church. Puritanism refused to compartmentalize life or separate religious affairs from the body politic.[28]

For the Puritan, the Bible was God's authoritative revelation to mankind, and its pages contained necessary and sufficient guidelines for the proper ordering of all dimensions of human life on earth. All aspects of life, whether political, social, cultural, economic, ecclesiastical, or personal, needed to be brought into subjection to God. In the Reformed tradition, Puritans believed that all men were under sin and only God's grace could bring salvation. Without God's supernatural call, effected most often through the message of the gifted, educated, authoritative Puritan preacher, the ordering of one's life to the glory of God was impossible.[29] But among all the Puritan doctrines, the ones that were the most influential in allowing a patriotic response to the independence movement were those of "covenant" and "consent."

The covenant symbol was one of the most basic and pervasive in Puritan life. Covenant was a model of association, appearing at several points in the Bible. It was best illustrated in the manner in which God called Israel into being by the means of a covenant with Abraham. God was the instigator, moving in history to bind himself in covenant with his chosen people.

Jerald Brauer mentions three items essential for the Puritan understanding of covenant. First, all initiation in creating and sustaining the covenant is in God's hands. Second, the covenant is conditional; that is, God lays down the covenant and its terms, but man can break the covenant by disobedience to those terms. Third, covenant is not just between God and the individual, but is communal—between God and his elect people, the church.[30]

Just as covenant was between God and the spiritual community, so also covenant was between God and human government—at least it should be if God was properly acknowledged. The Mayflower Compact was such a covenant in which the Pilgrims as a body politic covenanted with God to commit their ways to Him. The compact was "looked upon as a special act of Providence sealing the covenant made [by God] with His people."[31] The settlements that spread throughout the New England colonies were founded upon similar compacts.

Puritan society also emphasized the theme of consent. This notion held that man's consent is required at all key points of human existence. While salvation was the result of God's election, consent by man was required to seal it. Members of a congregation must consent to their own minister. In government, magistrates and rulers cannot rule without the consent of their subjects. Rulers retained their right to rule, says Brauer, "only insofar as they embodied the main values of the people and made necessary adjustments in order to retain consent."[32]

The political implications of the covenant and consent symbols became especially important when colonial discussions reached the point of serious consideration of severing all ties with Great Britain. The essential link between politics and religion was forged when the ideas of covenant plus consent were extended to encompass the British empire and its American colonies.[33] According to Kenneth Wald, "If the relationship between colonist and king was a contract sealed by the authority of God—in other words, a covenant—then the terms of that contract bore divine authority."[34] The king and his citizens owed mutual respect to one another. However, the king was entitled to the respect of his citizens only as long as he held to the terms of the contract. If he breached the contract, the citizens could withdraw their consent and establish a new government.

It is clear from this type of reasoning that the Puritans understood the relationship between a government and its citizens as one of mutual obligation. Clearly, the force of such beliefs superseded and overruled the biblical texts suggesting unlimited obedience to ordained rulers. The Puritan understanding was further supported by the social compact and natural right theories of such philosophical divines as Milton, Sydney, Hoadly, and especially John Locke. It is traditionally held that the Puritans were influenced by Locke in arriving at their views on human government, but Perry Miller suggests that the reverse is true—that Locke was influenced by the covenant motif developed in the sixteenth and seventeenth centuries by the Puritans.[35] But regardless of the original source of the covenant and social compact theories, the essential point is that such theories were a bedrock of Puritan theological thought, reinforced by eighteenth-century philosophical thought.

It is fundamentally important also to understand that the eighteenth-century Christian patriot, insofar as he carried with him the influence of the Puritan traditions, never considered himself to be subordinating theology to philosophy or even adopting an admixture of theology and philosophy. The Bible still reigned supreme. He may have accepted, preserved, extended, and popularized various doctrines of political philosophy, but only because they in no way contravened biblical theology. To the extent that his ideas about government and the rights of man were derived, whether consciously or not, from secular sources, they were strengthened and sanctioned by Holy Writ. What he believed and taught about government was required to have the authority of the divine. This divine sanction may not have been essential for Enlightened patriots outside of the Puritan mainstream in the development of philosophical underpinnings for the Revolution, but no matter, the final outcome for all patriots, Christian or not, was the same—a revolution was countenanced.

The final outcome of the application of these doctrines in the revolutionary era is well summarized by Wald:

> The colonists repeatedly invoked the covenant tradition to justify the breaking of their bonds with Great Britain. Almost a year to the day before the Declaration of Independence was made public, the Continental Congress called upon Americans to observe a day of national confession, marked by "publick humiliation, fasting, and prayer." After promising this confession and pledging repentance, the colonists asked God for help in persuading the British to respect the terms of the compact that bound the colonies to the mother country. When the British proved resistant to these prayers, the colonists once again stressed the breaking of the covenant as justification for revolt. The Declaration of Independence begins with the assertion that the colonists deserved independence under "the Laws of Nature and Nature's God." Consistent with covenant theory, the colonists asserted that the bond between rulers and ruled was dependent

on the rulers' respect for those rights that God granted to men. Once the terms of the compact had been violated by a despotic King George (as the colonists attempted to demonstrate in great detail), the people of America could claim a divine mandate to dissolve their ties. The Declaration concludes with the submission of the purity of the rebel's claims to "the Supreme Judge of the World."[36]

Thus, the views of the Congregationalists and Presbyterians—not to mention other colonial groups that had their origins in separations from the Puritan line—produced an ideology that merged with other patriots' parallel and similar values of freedom, liberty, and consent of the governed and helped shape the resistance of the colonies against George III and Parliament.

In some ways the emphases of the Great Awakening were a reaffirmation of Puritanism; in other ways they were a departure. Like Puritan theology, the Awakening emphasized the need for personal salvation and the importance of the sanctified life. In the Puritan world, however, revivals were not common; salvation occurred when God efficaciously moved to bring one's mind and heart into agreement with the Word of God's call for repentance. Revivalism was the mark of the Great Awakening, and God's moving through the power of the Holy Spirit was a given; one only had to "receive Christ" to gain salvation.

With the Great Awakening, individualism, egalitarianism, and optimism became the dominant attitudes, transforming in the process the static, corporate, stratified view of class structure within Puritanism. As a result of the Awakening, churches lost power to individuals; divine sanction in institutions—in particular the theocratic structuring of society within Puritanism—was diluted and authority was invested in inward experience. As a colony-wide movement, the Awakening united the colonials as never before and spurred a new emphasis in political activity in which state control of religion was the main issue. Many traditional Puritans left the ranks of the staid Congregational, Presbyterian, and Anglican churches to join the new Baptist and Separatist Congregational churches that were formed during the Awakening. These new adherents were usually called "New Lights" (within Congregationalism) or "New Sides" (within Presbyterianism). But many "Old Lights" and "Old Sides," unimpressed by the emotion and "enthusiasm" of the Great Awakening, were no less supportive of the independence movement. For them the political implications of covenant and consent, the desire for political change, the belief that change was possible, and the widespread opinion that English control of American political, economic, social, and religious life was the main obstacle to change united them with New

Lights, New Sides, and many other Americans in the view that a separation from Great Britain was imperative.[37]

The New England Puritans' perennial image of themselves as God's "New Israel" also influenced revolutionary thinking. From the time of the earliest Puritan settlements in Massachusetts in the 1620s, the Puritans understood themselves as a "chosen people" of God, just as Old Testament Israel was a "chosen nation." As God had brought Israel from out of bondage in Egypt to Canaan, so he had brought the Puritans out from the bondage of the Old World into a "new Canaan." Moreover, just as God had many times in the Old Testament entered into covenants with Israel, he had covenanted with the New Israel whereby it would be the focus of his plan to usher in a millennial age of righteousness on earth.

Harry Stout has impressively demonstrated that in the 1760s and early 1770s, New England still looked to biblical Israel as the model of its relationship to God. He also documents how the unity of the American people in the independence movement led the New England Puritans to expand the circle of earthly participants in God's covenant with them to the nation as a whole.[38] In this way, Puritans and their various denominational descendants became intellectually supportive of independence, believing that America was the central focus of God's purpose to usher in a reign of righteousness upon the earth.

Preachers and patriots across the colonies adopted the New Israel theme. In a sermon preached in 1770, Charles Chauncy of Boston preached to his parishioners that, just as the Jews had been delivered from Egypt and, later, from the destruction threatened by King Ahasuerus, so had the colonies been delivered from the Stamp Act. Chauncy assured Americans that "there are no people, now dwelling on the face of the earth, who may, with greater pertinency, adopt the language of King David, and say, 'our fathers trusted in thee; they trusted, and thou didst deliver them.' "[39]

In 1777 George Duffield, a Presbyterian from Philadelphia, preached a sermon in which Britain was likened to Babylon and to Egypt while America was described as Judah. If the war could be seen as a struggle between God and this people against the hosts of darkness, just as depicted so often in the Old Testament, the colonists' confidence in the ultimate outcome would sustain them throughout their great time of trial.[40] Ministers frequently observed, both before their congregations and on election, fast, and thanksgiving days, that "what was said of Canaan" in the Old Testament "will apply to these states."[41]

One anonymous layman sounded the same likeness of America (as the offspring of England) to Israel:

That the English nation, as such having universally received the Christian religion . . . and having formed all their laws and regulations of civil society, agreeable to its holy precepts, have a right to look upon themselves as much in visible covenant with God as ever the Jews had.[42]

Another abiding line of thinking in eighteenth-century America that helped to support the Revolution was biblical millennialism. As already indicated, Puritans held the belief that a major element of God's covenant with them was that they would be God's principal instrument in establishing a millennial reign of righteousness on earth. But millennialism, under a diversity of interpretations, was a part of the faith of many American Christians. Sometimes postmillennial, sometimes premillennial, sometimes a muddled combination of both, such themes were prominent among American Protestants. It was widely believed that the millennial age of peace and righteousness foretold in Scripture could be dawning in America. With the prospect of political liberty and the unique opportunity for virtuous citizens to create their own institutions, it seemed increasingly likely that the millennial age would arise from the struggle for liberty and Christianity in which the colonists were engaged. In the frantic days preceding Congress's Declaration of Independence, Ebenezer Baldwin of Connecticut was only one of many contemplating the possibility that America might become "the principal seat of that glorious kingdom, which Christ shall erect upon Earth in the latter days."[43]

In the years leading up to the Revolutionary War, millennial themes were spurred by earthly events that were interpreted as divinely ordained signs of the imminent millennial age. Earthquakes in Boston in 1727 and in New Hampshire, Peru, Spain, and Portugal in 1755 raised millennial expectations.[44] Colonials were also encouraged by what they interpreted as a clarification on the identity of the Antichrist. The anti-Catholic crusade of the French and Indian War had frequently seen the pope as the Antichrist, whose presence must be purged before the millennium would begin. In Boston and elsewhere, traditional anti-Catholic Pope Day celebrations became occasions for dramatizing the cause of Protestants. Once the Catholic threat lessened after the French and Indian War, however, and was replaced by the increasing British threat, the identity of the Antichrist was easily transferred from the pope to George III. This raised the colonial consciousness of the need to go to war with the mother country and expel the British king's presence from America forever so that God might more expeditiously usher in his new reign of righteousness on earth.[45]

It is not possible in the space here to address the number of ways in which religious pietism influenced the independence movement. It should be pointed out, however, that the American patriots, who according to one estimate were two-thirds of the population,[46] were comprised of a large number claiming pietistic commitments. For the great many of them, their biblically orthodox theology, once tested by the turbulent issues of the day, allowed for a commitment to the revolutionary cause. Without this religious sanction, the American colonies probably would never have gone to war with Britain.

### Rationalistic Influences on the Revolution

While religious pietism had a profound influence on the independence movement, the rationalism associated with the eighteenth-century Enlightenment also played an important role. Rationalists were fewer in number than pietists but nevertheless were dominant among the educated and intellectual classes. Broadly speaking, rationalism holds that reason is the chief source and test of knowledge. Its religious manifestations appeared prominently during the Enlightenment in the form of deism. Deists accepted the existence of God but spurned supernatural revelation. Deism and its ecclesiastical offspring, eventually to be called Unitarianism, had been slowly but steadily gaining influence in the colonies since the early 1700s and by 1776 could claim a wide following among the intellectual classes in the colonies. They helped lead an intellectual, but nevertheless religiously grounded, movement calling for separation from Great Britain, and with such political leaders as Benjamin Franklin, Thomas Jefferson, Richard Henry Lee, and, arguably, John Adams and George Washington in their corner, it does not seem an exaggeration to say that deists maintained a dominant presence in the Continental Congress. This is not to suggest, of course, that there was not a strong presence of more pietistically oriented men in the Congress, but only that many of the most prominent and influential members were deists.

The impact of Enlightenment religious rationalism on American revolutionary thought is more difficult to assess than purely Christian religious ideas. This is because Enlightenment ideas draw so eclectically from religion, philosophy, and science, whereas Christian pietism is so thoroughly grounded in a single source—the Bible. Nevertheless, the Enlightenment influences in America during the revolutionary era were pervasive, and they clearly played an important role in supporting revolutionary ideals. The achievements of Sir Isaac Newton and other seventeenth-century astronomers and mathematicians gave to humankind a new confidence in the power of human reason, without the assistance of divine revelation, to grasp God's government of the universe. The Enlightenment, as the new movement came to be called, promised to reveal the mysteries of God's created handiwork simply through the application of human intelligence.[47] As Sidney Ahlstrom stated in assessing the impact of the Enlightenment on the revolutionary era, "More and more thinkers came to accept its primary assertion that reason and scientific knowledge could supply all the necessary elements of religion and ethics, though many might concede that revelation was still needed by the masses."[48] The American Revolution, from the perspective of Enlightenment ideals, was a natural occurrence in a larger revolution involving the progress of the human race.[49] Looking back on the Revolution in 1790, Ceasar Rodney, a Delaware lawyer and wartime governor, wrote to Thomas Jefferson with such a perspective:

> The Revolution of America, by recognizing those rights which every Man is entitled to by the laws of God and Nature, Seems to have broken off all those devious Tramels of Ignorance, prejudice, and Superstition which have long depressed the Human Mind. Every door is now Open to the Sons of genius and Science to enquire after Truth. Hence we may expect the darkening clouds of error will vanish fast before the light of reason; and that the period is fast arriving when the Truth will enlighten the whole world.[50]

Most American clergymen at first perceived no threat to religion from the Enlightenment. Although they thought poorly of human reason, they were themselves assiduous in making the most of it. They had certainly applied it in biblical interpretation, but they now welcomed every new piece of scientific knowledge in the assurance that it would help to fill out the data derived from the Bible. With the success of Newton to motivate them, they began to pay more attention to the physical world by becoming students of plants and animals, of planets, comets, and stars.[51]

Puritan preachers in particular had no quarrel initially with the Enlightenment, insofar as it lifted the burden of mankind with its scientific discoveries and inventions. For Levi Hart, the Enlightenment was "a thing to be rejoiced in,"[52] and for Samuel Finley, "if duly applied, an excellent handmaid to divinity," because learning of all sorts, properly used, was serviceable in the cause of Christ and humanity.[53] The Puritan divines' real quarrel was rather with unabashed reason, which they believed denied the authority of the Bible and ultimately led to "the sapless morality" of heathens.[54]

It became evident only gradually—first in Europe in the sixteenth and seventeenth centuries, then in America in the eighteenth century— that reason, instead of assisting revelation, might replace it. Though Newton himself retained a firm belief in the Scriptures and spent his later years attempting to sort out biblical prophecies, many of his admirers became deists.[55] Institutionally, this meant that many began turning away from the more conservative denominations, such as the Congregationalists, Presbyterians, and Baptists, to the more liberal ones, such as the Episcopalians and Unitarians.

Emerging from the Enlightenment during the revolutionary era was a secular utopian vision. It saw the Revolution as promising an imminent and radical transformation of the world and the universal establishment of peace, freedom, and morality. This utopian vision saw the need for America to rid itself of all foreign restraints on the realization of its destiny. As the colonists moved toward the conclusive indictments of the British king and Parliament, a process completed with the Declaration of Independence, the vision of a new order gained intensity.

The relationship between this Enlightenment utopianism and biblical millennialism, as with the relationship between Enlightenment and biblically orthodox clergymen in general, was at first not antagonistic but complementary. The sense of their incompatibility did not become clear until the very end of the eighteenth century.[56] In contrast to biblical millennialism, secular utopianism's key terms were not those of Scripture but more exclusively those of secular political ideals: liberty, reason, and the rights of man. Elements of both visions, however, were often blended together into what could be called a "millennial utopianism." Newspaper columns upheld visions of a future era of liberty and peace that suggested the fulfillment of biblical prophecy even though they were not explicitly millennial. Articles in the *Boston Gazette* described America rising to that "happy period" when "virtue and liberty [shall] reign here without a Foe, until rolling years shall measure time no more."[57] And the *New York Journal* urged perseverance in the revolutionary cause until "true freedom and liberty shall reign triumphant over the whole globe."[58]

Political leaders also voiced the same millennial aspirations. Thomas Paine's *Common Sense* must be read against this background of millennial utopianism: "The birthday of a new world is at hand."[59] Even the Continental Congress, in its early years, alluded to biblical prophecy in their visions of "the golden period, when liberty, with all the gentle arts of peace and humanity, shall establish her mild dominion," and "that latest period, when the streams of time shall be absorbed in the abyss of eternity."[60]

Religious rationalism, especially in its emphasis on themes of progress and the perfection of humanity, contributed significantly to the colonial aspirations for independence. In effect, the American Enlightenment represented something of a translation into secular terms of the millennial goals, and even the spirit, of more biblically oriented Christians. Perhaps the best way to understand the ideological background of the American Revolution is as a combination of disparate, competing traditions of Christian pietism and Enlightenment rationalism that came together to produce the image of a new Golden Age. As Patricia Bonomi has so eloquently put it, these two traditions "did not carve separate channels but flowed as one stream toward the crisis of 1776."[61]

## Concluding Remarks

In summarizing the religious impulses that contributed to the independence movement, it is possible to conclude that, to a great degree, orthodox Protestant convictions lay at the root of the revolutionary movement. In particular, it can be argued that the Puritan concepts of covenant and consent—involving belief in divine sovereignty over the relationships between God and humankind—provided a perspective on life and society without which revolutionary thought could not have developed as it did. Because of the prevailing presumption of God's special guidance and protection over the colonies, one can readily view colonial resistance to Great Britain as a product of a particularly religious way of looking at the world. Indeed, the prevailing thought that existed during the prerevolutionary days emphasized a covenantal relationship between human governments and men that demanded moral integrity on the part of both parties to the covenant. Patriotic libertarians acquired such notions from Enlightenment religious rationalism and political philosophy; pietistic Christians disposed to the patriotic cause named Scripture as their source of the same views. Though both groups may have apprehended their views from different sources, the final outcomes were essentially the same and formed a common bond that would support the revolutionary cause.

The religious history of the United States will never be adequately understood apart from the knowledge of religious thought and behavior at the time of the Revolution. During this period, those with religious commitments were called upon to examine and update the elements of their religious heritages, and determine whether they could support a revolution. For most Americans, the Revolution united religious beliefs and political principles into convictions about the proper nature of life as earthly and heavenly citizens. For a lesser number, the Revolution called forth demanding sacrifices when personal convictions went against the grain of the patriot majority. What is clear, however, is that for virtually all Americans, convictions about the rightness or wrongness of the Revolution were fundamentally grounded in religious perspectives.

As the First Continental Congress convened in Philadelphia in 1774, its delegates, being political men responsible to represent the interests of their constituencies, were not unaware of the strong religious outlooks that framed Americans' perspectives on the issue of independence. Indeed, many, if not all, of the delegates themselves had similar religious perspectives. The convergence of the citizens' religious outlooks with those of their political representatives was a combination that proved to make religious impulse one of the driving forces of the Continental Congress as it led the country through what has come to be known as the central event in American history, the American Revolution.

*Four*

# A SUMMARY VIEW OF POLITICS AND
# RELIGION IN THE CONTINENTAL CONGRESS

## Religious Differences and Political Consensus

On 20 January 1775, in the British House of Lords, the illustrious Lord
Chatham (William Pitt) delivered a very remarkable speech. Formerly
prime minister, he was an outspoken defender of the struggling colonists
of America in their protracted controversy with the British king and
parliament. He vindicated, in the fullest and clearest manner, the right
of the colonists to refuse to be taxed without their consent. "The spirit,"
he said, "which now resists your taxation in America, is the same which
formerly opposed loans, benevolences and ship money in England; the
same spirit which called all England on its feet, and by its bill of rights
vindicated the English Constitution, the same spirit which established
the great, fundamental, essential maxim of your liberties, that *no subject
of England shall be taxed but by his own consent.*" On this great principle,
and in this cause, the American colonists, he added, "are immovably
allied; it is the alliance of God and nature, immutable, eternal, fixed as
the firmament of Heaven."[1]

At that same time, the Continental Congress, a rather impressive collection of colonial leaders, was in session in Philadelphia and had barely
initiated those plans and purposes that only months later found expression in the great charter of the colonists' rights and liberties, the Declaration of Independence. Of this body of patriotic men, William Pitt, in
the speech just quoted from, made this memorable declaration:

When your Lordships look at the papers transmitted to us from America;
when you consider their decency, firmness, and wisdom, you can not but
respect their cause, and wish to make it your own. For myself I must
declare and avow, that in all my reading and observation—and it has

been my favorite study, I have read Thucydides, and have studied and admired the master States of the world—that for solidity of reasoning, force of sagacity and wisdom of conclusion, under such a complication of difficult circumstances, no nation or body of men can stand in preference to the General Congress assembled at Philadelphia.[2]

This was high eulogy, and, from the lips of one so familiar with the great men of history, it was exalted praise. Naturally, Pitt's assessment of the men of the Continental Congress would not have seemed to most Americans an exaggerated estimate. Suddenly brought together to meet a pressing emergency, Congress's membership was made from the most thoughtful and talented men in the country. And the importance of the hour was recognized by these men who, as members of America's first national assembly, would set the course for the historic events centered around the formation and shaping of a new nation.

Perhaps it was John Adams who was most sensitive to the magnitude of the situation. "It has been the will of Heaven," he wrote in January 1776, "that we should be thrown into existence at a period when the greatest philosophers and lawgivers of antiquity would have wished to live. A period when [we have] an opportunity of beginning government anew from the foundation. . . . How few of the human race have ever had any opportunity of choosing a system of government for themselves and their children."[3] Only weeks before independence, as Congress drew closer and closer to making a formal declaration, Adams wrote: "Objects of the most stupendous magnitude, and measures in which the lives and liberties of millions yet unborn are intimately interested, are now before us. We are in the very midst of a revolution, the most complete, unexpected, and remarkable, of any in the history of nations. . . . When these things are once completed, I shall think that I have answered the end of my creation."[4]

Given the Congress's talented composition, as so keenly sensed by William Pitt, and the magnitude of the hour in which Congress was called to serve, as so eloquently expressed by John Adams, one might easily conclude that the potential for self aggrandizement, contention, and impasse in congressional deliberations was considerable. This potential was not realized, however, for while congressional debates often were passionate and heated, the men of the Continental Congress were for the most part remarkably able to set aside their political, geographical, and ideological differences in charting the course for America's political destiny.

Fundamental differences among the congressional delegates could also be observed in their personal religious views. The delegates, however, fully aware that religious dissension had so often in history been the downfall of great nations, were determined to set aside these differences as well. Both the official records of the Continental Congress and the delegates' personal correspondence are remarkably free of signs that the delegates permitted sectarian religious differences to interfere with congressional deliberations and actions. Consequently, we know less about the specific religious beliefs of the 337 men who served for one or more terms as delegates to the Continental Congress than we do about the ways in which the delegates allowed their religious beliefs to support shared political commitments. It is appropriate, then, to identify these shared commitments and consider the ways in which they were supported by the diversity of religious views represented in the Continental Congress.

If we continue to permit pietism and rationalism to describe the basic categories of religious commitment that were represented in revolutionary America, we can readily observe that pietists and rationalists in the Continental Congress—both were well represented—joined not only in their support of the independence movement but also in believing that religion and revolutionary politics were connected in a variety of ways. Pietists and rationalists in the Congress seemed specifically to share three separate but interrelated commitments.

### The Interdependence of Nature and Liberty

First, rationalists and pietists both believed that the American independence movement was in keeping with eternal principles of nature, liberty, good government, and justice. All human affairs, they believed, are imbedded in the natural order conceived on the pattern of creation and Creator. Thus, Thomas Jefferson could say, "The God who gave us life gave us liberty at the same time."[5] The same belief led the chaplain of the Continental Congress, Jacob Duché, to share with his congregation in 1775 his opinion that "liberty, traced to her true source, is of heavenly extraction, that divine virtue is her illustrious parent, that from eternity to eternity they have been and must be inseparable companions, and that the hearts of all intelligent beings are the living temples in which they ought to be jointly worshipped."[6]

The Continental Congress communicated this same conviction in 1774 when it told the American people in a circular letter that only the Creator could give to government a solid foundation and that it was every citizen's "duty to God, the creator of all," to consider whether English rule was not in keeping with the natural order.[7] A decade earlier, in 1764, James Otis had clearly adumbrated the Congress's perspective:

I think it [government] has an everlasting foundation in the *unchangeable will* of GOD, the author of nature, whose laws never vary. The same omniscient, omnipotent, infinitely good and gracious Creator of the universe who has been pleased to make it necessary that . . . celestial bodies . . . perform their various revolutions . . . has made it *equally necessary* that . . . different sexes should sweetly *attract* each another, form societies of *single* families, of which *larger* bodies and communities are as naturally, mechanically, and necessarily combined as the dew of heaven and the soft distilling rain is collected by the all enlivening heat of the sun.[8]

The connection between religion and liberty as understood by most Americans was perhaps most succinctly stated by patriot minister William Smith. "Religion and liberty," he said, "must flourish or fall together in America."[9] To be sure, Congress shared with most Americans the belief that the eternal principles that regulated the affairs of men supported their desire for independence.

### A Just Cause, Providentially Ordered

Second, both pietists and rationalists in the Continental Congress believed that God controlled history and that the Americans' cause against the British held God's favor. Oliver Wolcott, a pietistic Congregationalist from Connecticut, held firmly to his belief that God would not "consign this Country to Destruction; Light in due Time will arise and the happy Days of Peace; Fair, equitable and just Peace will Return."[10] For him, the "God who takes care of and Protects Nations, will take care of this People."[11] Maryland's Samuel Chase, son of an Anglican clergyman, was "grateful to our God for . . . his favour and protection;[12] without it, "our Country is undone."[13] John Adams was convinced that "we have nothing to depend upon for our Preservation from Destruction, but the kind Assistance of Heaven."[14] Speaking from the steps of the Continental State House at Philadelphia in 1776, Samuel Adams from Massachusetts told a large crowd that "the hand of heaven appears to have led us on to be, perhaps, humble instruments and means in the great providential dispensation which is completing."[15] Elbridge Gerry, Adams's fellow delegate from Massachusetts, apparently agreed. In a letter to Samuel Adams, he wrote that "history could hardly produce such a series of events as has taken place in favor of American opposition. The hand of Heaven seems to have directed every occurrence."[16]

Meanwhile, Dr. John Witherspoon, the Presbyterian delegate and clergyman from New Jersey, thought it would be "a criminal inattention not to observe the singular interposition of Providence hitherto, in behalf of

the American colonies."[17] Only delegate William Williams, writing to
Oliver Wolcott, seemed willing to express any doubt about the eventual
outcome of the war:

> What will be the event of Things God only knows. If we were to view
> only the rage and Strength of our Enemies, our Divisions and the Wick-
> edness of the People, we might well despair but They [the British] are
> wicked also. Their cause is certainly most unjust. The Judge of all the
> Earth will do right, He has done great things for Us. He will not forsake
> us I believe, tho most of Us have forsaken him, I trust many, many,
> thousands have not bowed the knee to Baal. . . . Let our Trust and Hope
> be in the Lord Jehovah and with Him is everlasting Strength.[18]

Even Congress itself, in a circular letter to Americans in 1779, was
certain that the British had behaved in ways that were tantamount to
"courting the vengeance of heaven and revolting from the protection of
Providence,"[19] under which, it was assumed, the colonies assuredly
rested. If confidence counted for anything among the members of Congress, indeed victory against England was virtually assured.

### Republican Government

A third bond between rationalists and pietists was the belief in republican government. Mark Noll has suggested that two crises dominated
the founding era—the crisis with Britain resolved by the American Revolution and the crisis of government resolved by the adoption of the
Constitution—and that both represented an effort by Americans to preserve the virtues of republican government.[20]

How did eighteenth-century American political leaders understand
"republican" government? Republicanism was more an idea than a
sharply defined system. In simplified terms, republicanism was the conviction that power defined the political process and that unchecked
power led to corruption even as corruption fostered unchecked power.
Holding that unchecked power must by its very nature result in the
demise of liberty, law, and natural rights, republicanism favored separation of power in government. Adherents of republicanism usually held
that a good government must mix elements of executive authority (monarchy), aristocratic competence and learning (aristocracy), and popular
influence (democracy). Although most republicans doubted the wisdom
of complete democracy, or total rule by the people, they believed deeply
that humankind possessed a store of rights grounded in nature (John
Locke defined these as "life, liberty, and property)." Finally, republican

theory drew a close connection between the morals of a people and the safety of its government—virtue in public men made it more likely that government would succeed, vice more likely that it would verge toward tyranny.[21]

In late eighteenth-century America, political leaders were convinced that England had ventured away from republican principles and sought to stifle republican ideals in the colonies. American leaders knew that "whig" political thought, as republicanism was then often styled, had played a large role in England's Glorious Revolution of 1688, when Parliament removed King James II in favor of William and Mary of the Netherlands. In that crisis, as the leaders of 1688 saw it, the tyrannical aims of James II had imperiled the liberties of Englishmen. Leaders of the Glorious Revolution replaced James II not only because he acted capriciously as a monarch, but also because he was a Catholic and threatened Protestant liberties won by the English Reformation. Besides replacing their king in 1688, following the theories of Locke, leading "whigs" went further to compose a bill of rights that spelled out the irreducible liberties of English citizens and the concrete limits beyond which royal power could not go.[22]

Republicanism, or "whig" ideas, gradually receded in England over the course of the eighteenth century. Prime ministers such as Horace Walpole and their Parliaments became consumed by struggles for power at court and expanding economic problems and paid less and less attention to efforts to define and describe republican liberties. This lack of concern for liberty and related republican ideals became a primary basis for resistance to Great Britain and the construction of a new national government.[23]

Americans contributed a great deal to the formation of republicanism, though that process involved numerous individuals and groups over a long period of time. Republican thought had its roots in classical philosophy, especially with Plato and Aristotle, and was recovered and developed as a set of political ideas by Machiavelli in the early sixteenth century. Republican values were also given biblical links by the Puritans who supported Oliver Cromwell and the Scottish Calvinists agitating for independence. Many American political leaders felt that republicanism represented a political recognition of Scripture's realistic teaching about human sinfulness. This specifically biblical emphasis contributed to the theory of the separation of powers, which limits abuse and provides for checks on political power, that was eventually written into the Constitution. Perhaps James Madison best expressed this emphasis in *Federalist* No. 51:

But what is government itself, but the greatest of all reflections on human nature? If men were angels, no government would be necessary. If angels were to govern men, neither external nor internal controls on government would be necessary. In framing a government which is to be administered by men over men, the great difficulty lies in this: you must first enable the government to control the governed; and in the next place oblige it to control itself. A dependence on the people is, no doubt, the primary control on the government; but experience has taught mankind the necessity of auxiliary precautions.

The constitutional framers knew that other societies had sought to curb self-interest and ambition in political leaders through rigorous education in the virtues, constant surveillance, and severe punishment for wrongdoing. But they also knew that these measures more often than not failed to prevent tyranny and the loss of freedom by the people. Their plan was not to attempt to eliminate self-interest and ambition but to encourage it, and then when power was acquired, to counteract it in a system in which the holder of power was forced to compete with others also holding power. In this way, it was believed that natural tendencies toward self-advancement would be turned to the benefit of the people. As Publius explained it in *Federalist* No. 51, "ambition must be made to counteract ambition."

Other influences on the development of republicanism, however, were less biblical and more deistic or agnostic. Some of Britain's eighteenth-century whigs had given up traditional Christianity for a religion of nature with no place for miracles, the Incarnation, or special revelation. Others, following Isaac Newton, wanted to see the political order display the same harmony as the laws of nature. Thus, the heritage of republicanism was mixed, but as a basic framework for government in revolutionary America it enjoyed wide support in the Continental Congress.[24]

In his careful study of the development of American political ideals from 1776 to the time of the Constitutional Convention in 1787, Gordon Wood notes that republicanism became not merely "a matter of suitability" but "a matter of urgency."[25] Thomas Paine exclaimed in 1776 that it was only common sense for Americans to become republicans.[26] In the Continental Congress, rationalists and pietists alike frequently spoke of their commitment to republican ideals. Thomas Jefferson, for example, was pleased that by 1777 Americans "seem to have deposited the monarchical and taken up the republican government with as much ease as would have attended their throwing off an old and putting on a new suit of clothes."[27] Jefferson's fellow rationalist, John Adams, was of the view in 1776 that republicanism is "better calculated to promote the general happiness than any other form [of government]."[28] Moreover, Adams had not altered his opinion of republican government more than four decades later. In 1819 he wrote that "there is no good government but what is republican."[29] Adams's more pietistically oriented friend from Pennsylvania, Benjamin Rush, for whom American independence proclaimed "glory to God in the highest—on earth peace—good will to man,"[30] lauded the communal benefits of republicanism. "Every man in a republic," he stated, "is public property. His time and talents—his youth—his manhood—his old age—nay more, life, all belong to his country."[31] Indeed, the spirit of republicanism pervaded the Continental Congress and was to become the guiding ideology behind the Articles of Confederation adopted in 1777 (ratified in 1781) as well as the new Constitution (Article IV guarantees to each state a republican form of government) adopted in 1787.

### Religion and the Continental Congress—An Overview

Western political theory since the advent of the Christian era has been dominated by the belief that religion is central to a rightly-ordered polity. Religion has usually been understood to have an ontological status that demands its formal recognition by the civil order. The inevitable result has been the struggle between "church" and "state" in which each has sought to dominate the other. The American constitutional system was a unique experiment in which this struggle was sought to be eliminated by making church and state essentially independent of one another. This experiment, as discussed in later chapters, was attempted for reasons having to do with a mixture of expedience and principle, but the outcome was nevertheless unique in the history of Western civilization.

The Continental Congress, whose experience predated the experiment sanctioned by the Constitutional Convention, functioned essentially under traditional Western political theory, that is, on the belief that religion is central to a well-ordered polity. Yet in many ways the period of the administration of the Continental Congress was a transitional phase between the old traditional theory, under which religion served as the glue of the social and political order, and the newer theory, under which it was thought that both religion and government might function best if constitutionally separated from one another. So while the Continental Congress operated essentially with religion as an important support to its overall function, separationist elements can be detected as well. For example, as discussed in chapter 7, the Continental Congress painstakingly attempted to respect the desire of the colonies and then the states to support or regulate religion within their own jurisdictions. This deference to the sovereignty of its members on religious matters was indeed a form of separation, but, as will be demonstrated in the remainder of this chapter, the Congress in no way understood this policy to mean that religion would not provide an important framework for it to address publicly and internally the political and social problems of the day. It is the purpose of the remainder of this chapter, then, to demonstrate, in overview fashion, the manner in which the Continental Congress frequently engaged in religious acts and legislated with respect to religious matters. Subsequent chapters will examine more specifically the variety of ways in which the Congress operated with a religious dimension, and how that dimension may have influenced the original intent of the constitutional framers in regard to the role of religion in American public life.

### Politicians or Priests?

Not only did the Continental Congress frequently engage in prayer and hear sermons as an assembled body, but it also legislated on a wide range of religious themes, such as sin, repentance, humiliation, divine service, morality, fasting, prayer, mourning, public worship, funerals, chaplains, and "true" religion. Sabbath recognition, moreover, was important enough that Congress declined to meet on Sundays except for rare special sessions.

The proclamations and official state papers of the Congress are, as Edward F. Humphrey remarked, "so filled with Biblical phrases as to resemble Old Testament ecclesiastical documents."[32] The documents frequently invoke, as a sanction for their acts, the name of "God," "Nature's God," "Lord of Hosts," "His Goodness," "Providence," "Creator of All," "Great Governor of the World," "Supreme Judge of the Universe," "Supreme Disposer of All Events," "Jesus Christ," "Holy Ghost," and "Free Protestant Colonies." One document alone, Congress's Declaration of Rights of 6 July 1775, written to justify the use of arms against Great Britain (see appendix A), contained references to "the divine Author of our existence," "reverence for our great Creator," the "Divine favour towards us," and "those powers, which our beneficent Creator hath graciously bestowed on us," before closing with an expression of "humble confidence in the mercies of the supreme and impartial Judge and Ruler of the Universe."[33] Even the Declaration of Independence, as discussed in detail in chapter 6, called upon God as a witness to Parliament's callous indifference to the colonists' rights. Indeed, from the opening to the final session of the Continental Congress, its assemblies were sometimes imbued with a profoundly religious spirit.

Catherine Albanese has likened the members of the Congress to a group of priests laboring on behalf of a new national church, "performing the functions appropriate to authority in an ecclesiastical situation: teaching and preaching, governing and celebrating."[34] As a collection of men who looked upon their congressional role as fundamentally political, the delegates probably would have had little appreciation for Albanese's depiction of them as "priests." Nevertheless, there can be no doubt that the Continental Congress frequently undertook its work in ways that made politics and religion close allies. The religious dimension of Congress's work can be accounted for on at least three bases.

First, although the Enlightenment in America by the 1770s had begun to make inroads into the traditional understanding of Christianity, the nation was still overwhelmingly biblically orthodox in its worldview, and, as already suggested, the religious dimensions of civil government were in that day still generally taken for granted. These perspectives combined to produce within Congress a steady stream of Christian rhetoric that the Congress felt was appropriately related to its political function. Second, Congress's insistence on religious sanction was in part due to the fact that it had no specific legislative authority. Variously elected by colonial assemblies or by extralegal meetings, delegates to the Congress were aware of the absence of any clear legislative authority for the Congress and thus may have sought to remedy this deficiency by reliance upon a higher authority.[35] Third, and most important, the Congress was convened under the extraordinary circumstances surrounding the foreboding turn of events in the colonies' relationship with Great Britain. Independence and war were growing possibilities in 1774, when the First Continental Congress convened. The seriousness of the times, especially after war broke out, demanded, in the eyes of the congressional delegates, a reliance upon a higher authority for guidance and assistance. The presence of each of these factors can be seen in a brief review of the various forms of religiosity demonstrated by the Congress in many of its acts and proceedings.

### Prayer, Worship, and Other Religious Acts

Only one day after convening on 5 September 1774, Congress appointed a chaplain to lead prayer at its sessions. The proposal to appoint a chaplain, the controversy it generated, and the functions of Congress's chaplain are discussed in chapter 5. Congress also appointed army chaplains and encouraged them to promote before the Continental Army the regular observance of Congress's designated days of colony-wide fast and thanksgiving. Each time one of its members died, Congress issued its standard resolution that its members "in a body, attend the funeral [at various Christian churches] . . . with a crape around the arm, and . . . continue in mourning for the space of one month."[36] When the war led to a scarcity of Bibles, a congressional committee recommended that Bibles be imported from European nations other than the customary Britain because "the use of the Bible is so universal, and its importance so great."[37] Similarly, as discussed in chapter 8, the Congress passed a resolution in 1782 praising the "pious and laudable" work of Robert Aitken, who had published an American edition of the Bible at a time when it was impossible to import any copies.

The Continental Congress not only engaged in public religious rituals but also sometimes encouraged all Americans in the pursuit of moral perfection as well. Soon after convening in 1774, believing God's favor in resolving the colonies' growing tensions with the mother country depended upon the morality of the people, Congress resolved to:

> encourage frugality, economy, and industry, and promote agriculture, arts and the manufactures of this country, especially that of wool; and . . . discountenance and discourage every species of extravagance and dissipation, especially all horse-racing, and all kinds of gaming, cockfighting, exhibitions of shews, plays, and other expensive diversions and entertainments; and on the death of any relation or friend, none of us, or any of our families, will go into any further mourning-dress than a black crape or ribbon on the arm or hat, for gentlemen, and a black ribbon and necklace for ladies, and we will discontinue the giving of gloves and scarves at funerals.[38]

As inappropriate as this type of legislation might seem to the student of twentieth-century politics, it was actually somewhat common in the eighteenth century. The moralizing contained in the legislation can be appreciated if it is seen as an earnest effort by Congress to implement "republican" ideals. Moreover, there is little doubt that the congressional delegates took the legislation seriously, for a year later, in 1775, when the Marquis de Lafayette invited the president of Congress to a play, Henry Laurens of South Carolina politely declined. Pressed by the Marquis for an explanation, Laurens replied that since "Congress . . . passed a resolution, recommending to the several States to enact laws for the suppression of theatrical amusements, he could not possibly do himself the honor of waiting upon him to the play."[39]

There is evidence too that the American people took Congress's pronouncements with equal seriousness. The day that Congress had designated in July 1775 for its first fast day was observed in Philadelphia "with a decorum and solemnity never before seen on a Sabbath."[40] The

Presbyterian Synod of New York and Philadelphia, which had appointed its own fast day in June 1775, had made provision that if there should be a congressional fast it should "be observed in preference to the day appointed by themselves."[41] Almost a year later, on the eve of independence, a Philadelphia resident described his neighborhood on the 17 May fast day as "extremely quiet, observant and composed, in compliance with the resolve of the Honorable Congress."[42] Even three years later, on 6 May 1779, the same Philadelphian described his city as "very quiet" on a congressionally designated fast day.[43] Those who failed to observe the fasts were frowned upon by the faithful and often suspected of being disloyal to American interests.

Congress reserved Independence Hall for most of its official business but made collective worship in various churches a regular practice. It frequented Episcopalian, Lutheran, Presbyterian, and Congregational services during the war and occasionally attended Catholic mass as a body.[44] After the victory over Cornwallis, Congress paraded in solemn procession to a Dutch Lutheran church to give thanks to God for America's great victory.[45]

In diplomatic correspondence, members of the Congress regularly employed religious language. In 1779, for example, the president of Congress, John Jay, concluded a letter to the king of France, Louis XVI, with a petition "That the Supreme Ruler of the universe may bestow all happiness on your Majesty is the prayer of your faithful and affectionate friends and allies."[46] John Hanson, president of Congress in 1782, opened his letter to the same king: "Among the many instances that Divine Providence has given us of his favor, we number the blessings he has bestowed on your Majesty's family and kingdom." And Hanson closed with: "We pray God, great, faithful, and beloved friend and ally, always to keep you in his holy protection."[47] In a letter written by John Adams to President Hanson, while the former was in England, he asked Congress to be mindful of "the utmost cause of gratitude to Heaven for ordering events in the course of his Providence so decidedly in their favor."[48] Indeed, in formal written correspondence, even in communications between nations, religious language was nearly as routine as affixing a date or a signature.

### The Clergy as Civil Servants

In spite of the prevalence of religious acts and religious language in Congress's work, however, it should be pointed out that those looked to by Americans as religious leaders, the clergy, were not unanimously thought to have a place of service as members of the Continental Congress. One might think that their religious training and outlook would be looked upon favorably by a Congress that employed religious language and engaged in religious acts so frequently. But many of the delegates perceived clergymen as having inherent limitations that made them unfit for civil service. John Adams, for example, writing to his wife on 17 September 1775 concerning the newly arrived delegates from Georgia, described the minister Dr. John Zubly in the following way:

> [H]e is the first Gentleman of the Cloth who has appeared in Congress, I can not but wish he may be the last. Mixing the sacred Character, with that of the Statesman, as it is quite unnecessary at this time of day, in these Colonies, is not attended with any good Effects. The Clergy are universally too little acquainted with the World, and the Modes of Business, to engage in civil affairs with any Advantage. Besides those of them, who are really Men of Learning, have conversed with Books so much more than Men, as to be too much loaded with Vanity, to be good Politicians.[49]

Actually, Adams's view that ministers were unqualified for public service was quite common in the founding era. Many of the colonies and, following independence, seven of the original states,[50] disqualified ministers from public office. The colonial practice was kindled by Old World influences. In England the practice had a history dating to the early sixteenth century. As the U.S. Supreme Court observed in 1978, the exclusion was thought to prevent a minister from failing to give himself totally to his "sacred calling and to prevent ministers, who after 1533 were subject to the Crown's powers over the benefices of the clergy, from using membership in Commons to diminish its independence by increasing the influence of the King and the nobility."[51] The later practice of several of the states in providing for disqualification was for a fundamentally different reason: to assure the success of a new political experiment, the separation of church and state.[52] In 1783 Thomas Jefferson advocated such a position in a draft of a constitution for Virginia. In a letter to Jeremiah Moore in 1800, he explained his rationale: "The clergy, by getting themselves established by law, and ingrafted into the machine of government, have been a very formidable machine against the civil and religious rights of man."[53] Although Jefferson later reversed his position, his view at this stage in his career was that civil government was better served if clergymen, having many pretensions of power and privilege, were disqualified from holding civil office.

Others, who thought the practice to be opposed to liberty, were against the exclusion. Benjamin Rush, a delegate from Pennsylvania, saw no reason to distinguish ministers from any other citizens; "they had children, wives, and were community citizens like anyone else."[54] John Witherspoon, a Presbyterian from New Jersey and the only clergyman to sign the Declaration of Independence, was likewise opposed on the grounds that no good reason existed for limiting a minister's citizenship status. Later, James Madison argued that the disqualification violated "a fundamental principle of liberty by punishing a religious profession with the privation of a civil right."[55]

Thus the practice of disqualifying clergymen from public office was a matter of some disagreement among the best thinkers of the founding period. These disagreements, however, did not prevent clergymen from serving in the Continental Congress, at least not those who happened to be from states where clergy were not disqualified from holding public office. The significance of the debate is that it reveals that many members of the Continental Congress, who generally held to traditional political theory upholding religion as essential to good government, made theoretical distinctions affirming that political service was essentially a civil rather than a religious function.

### Preserving Religious Liberty

Notwithstanding concerns such as these, the Continental Congress from the beginning seems to have understood one of its main goals to be the preservation of colonial religious liberties in the face of English measures perceived as challenges to such liberties. This emphasis can perhaps be traced to 17 June 1774, when the Massachusetts legislature, on motion of Samuel Adams, issued an appeal for the convening of the First Continental Congress. Among the stated purposes was that the representatives of the colonies should devise measures "for the recovery and establishment of their just rights and liberties, civil and religious."[56] Then on 17 September, only twelve days after convening, the Congress was presented with the Suffolk County Resolves, which Suffolk County, Massachusetts, officials had written and presented only eight days earlier to the royal governor of Massachusetts, Thomas Gage.[57] The "Resolves" were a list of denunciations of the British government in protest of four parliamentary acts (the Intolerable Acts) imposed upon Massachusetts as a result of the "Boston Tea Party" and other Massachusetts protests against British taxes. The four acts constituted a policy of coercion, to be applied not against all of the colonies but only against one, the chief center of resistance, Massachusetts. After a sharp debate on the Resolves, the Continental Congress gave them its full endorsement. "This was one of the happiest days of my life," wrote John Adams, because "this day convinced me that America will support Massachusetts or perish with her."[58] The Resolves included these resolutions:

2. That it is an indispensable duty which we owe to God, our Country, ourselves, and posterity, by all lawful ways and means in our power to maintain, defend and preserve those civil and religious rights and liberties, for which many of our fathers fought, bled and died, and to hand them down entire to future generations.

17. That this country, confiding in the wisdom and integrity of the Continental Congress, now sitting in Philadelphia, pay all due respect and submission to such measures as may be recommended by them to the colonies for the restoration and establishment of our just rights, civil and religious.[59]

These Resolves were not specific about how the Intolerable Acts were a threat to the religious liberties of the colonists. In colonial revolutionary rhetoric, the term "civil and religious," as appears in paragraph seventeen of the Resolves, became a generic, coined phrase to describe the various rights and liberties that the colonists believed were threatened by British measures. So completely were civil and religious liberties believed to be interdependent that Massachusetts divine Charles Turner, in typical fashion, preached that "religious liberty is so blended with civil, that if one falls it is not expected that the other will continue."[60] The colonials' fear of the loss of "religious" liberties referred generally to no more than the dislike of what many colonials considered to be an excessive Anglican presence in the colonies and, more specifically, the widespread but probably unrealistic (see chapter 9) fear that the Church of England would soon impose a colony-wide "establishment" and even appoint an American bishop to oversee the new establishment. Nevertheless, as chapter 9 demonstrates, the right to worship according to one's conscience was cherished by the colonists and became, whether justified or not, an emotionally charged issue in anti-British revolutionary rhetoric. This perhaps explains why John Adams, in describing to his wife the Congress's unanimous support for the Suffolk Resolves, and specifically its commitment to the protection of the colonists' religious liberties, wrote, "These votes were passed in full Congress with perfect unanimity . . . the fixed determination . . . was enough to melt a heart of stone."[61]

## Concluding Remarks

The creation of the Continental Congress and the performance of its tasks must be evaluated in the context of the Revolutionary War. The potential for war with Great Britain resulted in the formation of the Congress; the prosecution of the war occupied more of Congress's time than all other matters combined. The war between the American colonies and Great Britain was a watershed event in human history. While the British perhaps never saw it in those terms, the Americans did and were energized by the magnitude and significance of the war for themselves as well as for their young and developing nation. One essayist in 1778 adumbrated that at stake was the freedom of an "empire yet in embryo," extending from "the bay of the Hudson to the gulf of California"; on this basis he believed the continental fast days promulgated by Congress to be merited.[62]

Moreover, at stake for the Americans from their own perspective was not just their own civil and religious liberties, but also the freedom to order human government in such a way that might best protect those liberties, to the end that American liberties might never again be diminished and that the American way might become the standard for the rest of the world. Thomas Paine's *Common Sense* perhaps said it most succinctly: "The cause of America is in great measure the cause of all mankind. . . . We have it in our power to begin the world over again. A situation similar to the present has not happened since the days of Noah until now."[63] And as with *Common Sense*, these goals were generally seen in religious terms, as being ordered by Providence, which of course meant that God was on the side of the Americans and the war was something like a "rite of passage," a proving ground for Americans in which their readiness for what lay beyond the war was being tested.

When the Revolutionary War is understood in these terms, it is hardly surprising that the delegates to the Continental Congress, despite being men of considerably diverse faith commitments, were able for the most part to achieve consensus on their political goals. Most of the delegates, it would appear, understood those goals to some degree in religious terms and thus were not reluctant to combine religious zeal with political responsibility.

## Five

## CHAPLAINCIES AND DAYS OF RELIGIOUS
## OBSERVANCE UNDER THE CONTINENTAL CONGRESS

The religious outlook of the Congress can most readily be observed in a closer examination of two specific areas of activity briefly alluded to in the previous chapter: the role of legislative and military chaplains and the declaration of national days of fast and thanksgiving. These practices, which to some degree have become national traditions, originated under legislation passed by the Continental Congress. They are practices that accommodationists today point to as proof that the First Congress (which permitted the continuance of all but the fast day observances) could not have understood the Establishment Clause to prohibit the federal government from advancing religion. Nevertheless, they can be explained on contextual and pragmatic grounds, thus weakening the accommodationist assertion.

### Legislative Chaplaincies

The First Continental Congress assembled 5 September 1774. The next day Thomas Cushing of Massachusetts moved that the daily sessions be opened with prayer. Abraham Clark, a delegate from New Jersey, claims to have been responsible for this motion, although the official record credits Cushing. In a letter to James Caldwell dated 2 August 1776, Clark referred to his motion as well as the cold reception it apparently received from many of the delegates. He wrote: "At my coming to Congress, I moved for a Chaplain to attend prayers every morning which was carried—and some of my Starch brethren will scarcely forgive me for naming Mr. [Jacob] Duché. This I did knowing without such a one many would not attend."[1] Irrespective of who made the motion, formal objections were lodged by John Jay, the orthodox Congregationalist from New

York, and by John Rutledge of South Carolina, on the ground that, "proper as the act would be," it was rendered impractical by the "diversity of religious sentiments represented in Congress."[2] Samuel Adams, also a Congregationalist, rose to speak in favor of the motion: "I am no bigot. I can hear a prayer from a man of piety and virtue, who is at the same time a friend of his country. I am a stranger in Philadelphia, but I have heard that Mr. Duché deserves that character; and therefore, I move that Mr. Duché, an Episcopalian clergyman, be desired to rend prayers to the Congress tomorrow morning."[3]

Adams's motion carried without further discussion. The position of Jay and Rutledge should not go unappreciated, however. Their view represents the classic concern that governmental religious exercise, when there is no officially approved form of faith, will inevitably offend some and therefore should be avoided as an aspect of religious liberty. Adams's response in essence represents the classic rebuttal: governments should acknowledge God's sovereignty over all human affairs through prayer and other religious acts, regardless of who might be offended. The propriety of legislative prayers remains a lively issue today, as indicated by the fact that many federal and state legislators excuse themselves from chaplain-led prayers, not in protest of prayer per se, but of government-promulgated prayer.[4]

Upon final vote, the Continental Congress agreed that Jacob Duché should be asked to lead the Congress in prayers the following morning. Duché agreed to do so and thus returned the following morning with his clerk and in full pontificals. He read from Scripture and then prayed extemporaneously for about ten minutes.[5] Here is the account of John Adams written to his wife, Abigail:

> [He] read several prayers in the established form; and then read the Collect for the seventh day of September, which was the thirty-fifth Psalm. You must remember this was the next morning after we heard the horrible rumor of the cannonade of Boston. I never saw a greater effect upon an audience. It seemed as if Heaven had ordained that Psalm to be read on that morning.
>
> After this, Mr. Duché, unexpected to everybody, struck out into an extemporary prayer, which filled the bosom of every man present. I must confess I never heard a better prayer, or one so well pronounced, Episcopalian as he is. Dr. Cooper himself[6] never prayed with such fervor, such earnestness and pathos, and in language so elegant and sublime—for America, for Congress, for the Province of Massachusetts Bay, and especially the town of Boston. It has had an excellent effect upon everybody here.

Mr. Duché is one of the most ingenious men, and best characters, and greatest orators in the Episcopal order, upon this continent. Yet a zealous friend of Liberty and his country. I long to see my dear family. God bless, preserve, and prosper it. Adieu.[7]

The minutes of Congress for that day contain this official approbation of Duché's service: "Voted, that the thanks of the Congress be given to Mr. Duché, by Mr. Cushing and Mr. Ward, for performing divine Service, and for the excellent prayer, which he composed and delivered on the occasion."[8]

Jacob Duché's prayer and psalm-reading were an inspiration to many of the delegates. The source of that inspiration was apparently the way in which the Thirty-fifth Psalm was used to imply God's sympathy with the revolutionary spirit in the colonies. The psalm begins, "Plead thou my cause, O Lord, with them that strive with me, and fight thou against them that fight against me." Joseph Need, a patriot sitting in on the congressional proceedings, called the prayer and reading a "masterly stroke of policy."[9] Delegate Samuel Ward, a former Governor of Rhode Island, remarked that it was "one of the most sublime, catholic, well-adapted prayers I ever heard."[10]

Jacob Duché had won the hearts of the men of Congress. At Congress's request, he continued his service to Congress as its chaplain, offering regular prayers and an occasional sermon. His appointment was renewed when the Congress declared its independence from Great Britain. President John Hancock stated that his reappointment was due to his "piety" and "uniform and zealous attachment to the rights of America."[11] Duché's prayer upon the occasion of his reappointment was a strong plea for America. It included these words:

Look down in mercy, we beseech Thee, on these our American States, who have fled to thee from the rod of the oppressor, and thrown themselves on thy gracious protection, desiring to be henceforth dependent only on Thee. To Thee do they now look up for that countenance and support which Thou alone canst give. Take them, therefore, Heavenly Father, under thy nurturing care. Give them wisdom in council, and valor in the field; defeat the malicious designs of our cruel adversaries; convince them of the unrighteousness of their cause; and if they still persist in their sanguinary purposes, Oh! let the voice of Thine own unerring justice, sounding in their hearts, constrain them to drop the weapons of war from their unnerved hands in the day of battle.[12]

Although this prayer clearly indicates Duché's identification with the patriot cause, he apparently changed his mind about the merits of the colonial separation from Britain very soon after independence was declared. He resigned his chaplaincy and wrote a fourteen-page letter to George Washington, the commander-in-chief of the American Army, exhorting him to rescind the Declaration of Independence. Washington referred the letter to Congress. Duché was ruined; one influential member of Congress, in a bold and bitter satire, called him a "fop," a "turncoat," a "hypocrite," a "blasphemer," a "vain conceited Creature," a "liar," and an "ass," among other epithets.[13] Duché endured the war as a loyalist, then returned to England after the defeat of the British army. He did return to his native America in 1792, however, old, paralytic, and, due to his stained reputation, virtually unnoticed.[14]

On 21 December 1776 Congress appointed two chaplains to replace Jacob Duché. William White (1748–1838) was an Episcopalian pastor in Philadelphia and a leader in the formation of the Protestant Episcopal church in the United States. George Duffield (1732–1790) was pastor of a Presbyterian church in Philadelphia and had served briefly as a chaplain during the war. When the British troops brought the war to the Philadelphia region in late 1776 and early 1777, the Congress departed that city and resumed its daily sessions at York, Pennsylvania. For both White and Duffield, the chaplain's role in the Congress was important enough to cause them to temporarily move their residences to York, where they resided with local pastors for several months until Congress was able to return to Philadelphia.[15] They served until 1784, offering prayer at each session, preparing and delivering sermons for days of fast, humiliation, and thanksgiving, assisting in patriotic celebrations, supervising the preparation and publication of an American Bible, and generally acting as the officially constituted (sometimes spiritual) leaders of the nation's first national representative body.[16]

In 1784 the Reverend Daniel Jones was elected chaplain of Congress,[17] and it was determined that appointments should be made to fill the office annually.[18] Jones, like his predecessors and most of his successors, served without compensation. In 1788, however, it was resolved that the chaplain was to receive an annual salary "not to exceed three hundred dollars." The last chaplain, the Reverend Dr. John Rodgers, received only one year's salary, since the Congress dissolved in 1789 when the Constitution was ratified.[19]

Although prayers were not offered during the Constitutional Convention in 1787, the First Congress, as one of its early items of business, adopted the policy begun in the Continental Congress of selecting a chaplain to open each session with prayer. With no officially recorded reasons, Congress decided on 15 April 1789 that each branch of Congress would appoint its own chaplain and that they would be of different denominations.[20] The Senate elected its first chaplain, Samuel Provost, an Episcopalian, on 25 April;[21] the House, on 1 May, elected Congregationalist William Linn.[22] The official record of the proceedings of Congress, the *Annals of Congress*, do not record the vote in either chamber or how many members voted. We do know, however, that James Madison, a member of the House of Representatives, disapproved at the time of Congress's action. In a letter of 1822 to Edward Livingston, he stated:

> I observe with particular pleasure the view you have taken of the immunity of religion from civil jurisdiction. . . . This has always been a favorite principle with me; and it was not with my approbation, that the deviation of it took place in Congress when they appointed Chaplains, to be paid from the National Treasury.[23]

Several months after appointing chaplains, Congress, on 22 September 1789, agreed on the wording of the First Amendment, whose proscription on "establishments" of religion was apparently not thought by a majority of the delegates to be inconsistent with Congress's practice of hiring chaplains.

Largely on the strength of this historical record, the Supreme Court in 1983 held in a 6 to 3 vote that the Nebraska legislature's practice of opening each legislative day with a prayer by a chaplain paid by the state did not violate the Establishment Clause.[24] The Court reasoned: "Clearly the men who wrote the First Amendment Religion Clause did not view paid legislative chaplains and opening prayers as a violation of that Amendment, for the practice of opening sessions with prayer has continued without interruption ever since that early session of Congress."[25] Justice William Brennan dissented on the grounds that the "unique history" of officially sponsored legislative prayer does not raise the practice to a level requiring constitutional protection. Such prayers, he argued, infringe on individual legislators' rights to conscience, violate required government neutrality toward religion by involving government directly in religious activity, and trivialize and degrade religion by too close of an attachment to the organs of government.[26]

Despite the Court's holding, it should not be assumed that congressional chaplaincies were uniformly sanctioned in the founding period. The objections of John Jay and John Rutledge to opening sessions of the Continental Congress with prayer have already been noted. James Madison later explained his opposition to congressional chaplaincies:

> The Constitution of the U.S. forbids everything like an establishment of religion. The law appointing Chaplains establishes a religious worship for

the national representatives, to be performed by ministers of religion . . .
and these are to be paid out of the national taxes. Does this not involve
the principle of a national establishment . . . ?[27]

Chaplaincies for Madison not only were religious establishments, but
they were inconsistent with the pure principle of religious freedom:

> The establishment of the chaplainship to Congress is a palpable violation
> of equal rights, as well as of Constitutional principles. The tenets of the
> chaplains elected [by the majority] shut the door of worship against the
> member whose creeds and consciences forbid a participation in that of
> the majority. To say nothing of other sects, this is the case with that of
> Roman Catholics and Quakers who have always had members in one or
> both of the Legislative branches. Could a Catholic clergyman ever hope
> to be appointed a Chaplain? To say that his religious principles are ob-
> noxious or that his sect is small, is to lift the evil at once and exhibit in
> its naked deformity the doctrine that religious truth is to be tested by
> numbers, or that the major sects have a right to govern the minor.[28]

Religion, after all, Madison believed, must be a voluntary act, and, he
queried, if congressmen believe they must have the benefit of clergy,
then why not let them do as other citizens do: voluntarily contribute to
the support of their chaplains.[29]

It might also be pointed out that congressional chaplaincies, although
held generally by worthy and capable men, do not seem to have been
uniformly successful in the early years of the nation. For instance, the
Reverend Ashbel Green, pastor of the Second Presbyterian Church of
Philadelphia and a congressional chaplain for eight years from 1792 on,
complained of thin attendance of congressmen at prayers. He attributed
the usual absence of two-thirds or so (who would dismiss themselves
during prayer and then return) to the prevalence of "freethinking."[30]
After watching Congress for thirty years continue the practice of hiring
chaplains, Madison commented that few bothered to attend the services
of these "legal Ecclesiastics," and the whole exercise, he thought, had
become "a tiresome formality."[31]

Chaplaincies, it would seem, are one of the categories of governmental
involvement in religion that, on its face, violates a policy of strict neutrality toward religion. They have always been somewhat controversial,
even as far back as the opening session of the Continental Congress. Yet
they have been upheld by the American judiciary because they are longstanding practices and are less coercive than other kinds of government-
promulgated religious exercises, such as state-approved prayers in public
schools. Legislative prayer and public school prayer are similar in that
they both represent a kind of government imprimatur on prayer. But as

the Supreme Court has held, the situations are distinguishable because impressionable young children are more likely to feel pressured to participate in school prayer exercises than are mature, adult legislators in legislative prayer exercises.[32]

What of the practice of the Continental Congress and its influence on the appointment of chaplains by the House and Senate in the First Congress? In its *Marsh* decision, although making made passing reference to the fact that the Continental Congress, beginning from its inception in 1774, regularly appointed paid chaplains, the Supreme Court gave no emphasis to how this practice contributed to the First Congress's decision to appoint chaplains. This, it is submitted, is an oversight, as there seems to have been no other reason (at least none that was publicly discussed by congressional members) for the continuation of chaplaincies in the First Congress. The Court seemed to rely mostly on the fact that the wording of the First Amendment came only *after* the House and Senate had each agreed to appoint and pay chaplains, as if this were strong proof that the framers did not consider chaplaincies to be inconsistent with the religion clauses. In fact, the evidence seems to suggest that most congressmen in the First Congress gave little thought to the issue of the possible inconsistency of chaplaincies with the First Amendment and therefore somewhat casually allowed tradition (the established practice of chaplaincies) to rule over principle (the possibility of "establishment" problems). On this interpretation, the decision of the First Congress to appoint chaplains seems to have been done as a matter of course, based primarily on the fact that the appointment of chaplains had been a long-standing practice in the Continental Congress.

This interpretation is, of course, at odds with that of most accommodationists. Justice Antonin Scalia, for example, a leading accommodationist on the Supreme Court, argued in a dissenting opinion in *Lee v. Weisman* that minister-led prayers at high school commencement exercises should be permitted, in part because the First Congress's decision to appoint chaplains is strong evidence that the framers did not intend to eliminate all religious exercises from public life.[33] Robert Cord also cites the appointment of chaplains by the First Congress as certain proof that the framers never intended for the federal government to be neutral toward religion but instead advocated nondiscriminatory aid toward religion. His most reliable proof is that "James Madison was a member of the Congressional Committee that recommended the Chaplain system."[34] The implication here, of course, is that if so strong a separationist as Madison would vote in favor of congressional chaplains, then obviously no one at the time could have countenanced a separationist position on the religion clauses. It is true that Madison served on the committee that recommended the appointment of chaplains,[35] but there is absolutely no proof that he supported the committee's recommendation. As stated earlier, there is no record of Madison's or of any of the other congressmen's votes on the issue. What we do have in Madison's case, however, is his 1822 letter to Edward Livingston, discussed above, that indicates Madison's disapproval of the chaplaincy system not only in 1822, but in 1789 as well. It may be that there were many congressmen in the First Congress who, unlike Madison, were in support of a chaplaincy system for the principled reason that they believed the new government should officially engage in religious acts. But there is no written record of this, leading one to conclude that it was tradition, not principle, that generated the resumption of the chaplaincy system in the First Congress.

### Military Chaplaincies

Just as chaplains have traditionally served in Congress since 1774, so also have government-paid military chaplains served the nation since the days of the Revolutionary War. Before the war, chaplains generally had served the colonial militias under a volunteer and rotation system. But as the Continental Army grew and took shape under General George Washington, this system increasingly proved to be inadequate. Responding to this development, the Continental Congress on 29 July 1775 created the Chaplain Corps in the Continental Army and provided that the pay of a chaplain ($20 per month) be that for a captain.[36]

On the eve of the war, General Washington increased efforts to appoint qualified chaplains. Emphatic in his belief that religion and public worship were essential to morale among soldiers, he issued this order on 9 July 1776:

> The honorable Continental Congress having been pleased to allow a chaplain to each regiment, the colonels or commanding officers of each regiment are directed to procure chaplains accordingly, persons of good characters and exemplary lives, and to see that all inferior officers and soldiers pay them a suitable respect. The blessing and protection of Heaven are at all times necessary, but especially so in times of public distress and danger. The General hopes and trusts, that every officer and man will endeavor to live and act as becomes a Christian soldier, defending the dearest rights and liberties of his country.[37]

Both the original and revised Articles of War adopted by the Continental Congress recommended that all officers and men attend divine worship and that if any behaved indecently or irreverently they were to be brought before a court martial to be reprimanded and fined or possibly confined. For swearing or blaspheming God's name, a soldier was compelled to wear a wooden collar for as long as his commander deemed proper. As early as the French and Indian War (1755–1763), General Washington had expressed the view that there should be found in a chaplain a "gentleman of sober, serious and religious deportment, who would improve morale and discourage gambling, swearing, and drunkenness."[38] But even qualified chaplains in the Revolutionary War were apparently unable to check the profanity over which Washington continued to be concerned, resulting in this order issued by Washington on 3 August 1776:

> The General is sorry to be informed that the foolish and wicked practice of profane cursing and swearing (a vice hitherto little known in the American Army) is growing into fashion; he hopes the officers will, by example as influence endeavor to check it and that both they and the men will reflect that we can have but little hopes of the blessing of heaven on our Arms, if we insult it by our impiety and folly added to this it is a vice so mean and low, without any temptation, that every man of sense and character, detests and despises it.[39]

A year after independence, Washington showed his deep interest in selecting chaplains who would as far as possible hold religious views sympathetic to those of the men he served. With this in mind, and to avoid religion disputes, he protested a proposal to substitute brigade for regimental chaplaincies. He preferred the latter on grounds that it "gives every Regiment an Opportunity of having a chaplain of their own religious sentiments, it is founded on a plan of a more generous toleration . . . a Brigade . . . composed of four or five, perhaps in some instances six Regiments, there might be so many different modes of worship."[40]

On 2 May 1778 an order regarding chaplain-led worship services was issued by General Washington from his headquarters at Valley Forge:

> The Commander-in-Chief directs that Divine service be performed every Sunday at 11 o'clock, in each Brigade which has a Chaplain. Those Brigades which have none will attend the place of worship nearest to them. It is expected that Officers of all Ranks will, by their attendance, set an example to their men. While we are duly performing the duty of good soldiers, we certainly ought not to be inattentive to the higher duties of religion. To the distinguished character of a Patriot, it should be our highest glory to add the more distinguished character of a Christian.
>
> The signal instances of Providential goodness which we have experienced, and which have almost crowned our arms with complete success, demand from us, in a peculiar manner, the warmest returns of gratitude and piety to the Supreme Author of all Good.[41]

It is clear from these orders that General Washington maintained a commitment to advancing the interests of religion and that his commitment played an important part in the early development of the military chaplaincy in the United States.

The First Congress, by a law enacted 3 March 1791, authorized President Washington, "by and with the advice and consent of the Senate," to appoint a chaplain for the "Military Establishment of the United States."[42] The compensation for the chaplain was to be "fifty dollars per month, including pay, rations and forage."[43] This action indicates that the First Congress—as a body—probably did not embrace a broad concept of the separation of religion and government. But again, as with legislative chaplaincies, the practice was already longstanding, dating from the era of Continental Congress (and the exigencies of the Revolutionary War), and thus the desire to continue a strong tradition may have been the chief factor (with little regard for possible First Amendment conflicts) in Congress's decision to provide for the appointment of a military chaplain. Moreover, the possible conflict with the First Amendment was probably not in full view since, while the Bill of Rights had been adopted by Congress, it was not ratified by the necessary number of states until 15 December 1791, six months after the enactment into law of the authorization for the president to appoint a chaplain.

Despite the action of the First Congress in providing for the appointment of a military chaplain, not all of its delegates favored such an appointment. James Madison, for example, after playing such a determinative role in the drafting of the Constitution, formed views concerning military chaplaincies that differed markedly from Washington's. For him, mixing religion with political and military authority was establishing religion. "The object of this establishment," he remarked, "is seducing; the motive to it is laudable." But he was quick to emphasize that we have a Constitution. "Is it not safer to adhere to a right principle, and trust to its consequences, than confide in the reasoning however [alluring] in favor of a wrong one?" Madison conceded that arguments against his position could be especially strong when troops were far away or isolated from ordinary means of religious counsel. Nevertheless, Madison could not divorce himself from the general truth "that it is safer to trust the consequences of a right principle than reasonings in support of a bad one." He went so far as to call military chaplaincies an "establishment of a national religion," which he believed was proscribed by the Constitution.[44]

Despite the U.S. Supreme Court's determination in the twentieth century that the Establishment Clause prohibits "all legislative power respecting religious belief or the expression thereof,"[45] the Court has not

banned military chaplaincies. The clearest rationale for the constitutionality of military chaplaincies was offered by Justice Brennan in the 1963
case of *Abington School District v. Schempp*:

> There are certain practices, conceivably violative of the Establishment
> Clause, the striking down of which might seriously interfere with certain
> religious liberties also protected by the First Amendment. Provisions for
> churches and chaplains at military establishments for those in the armed
> services may afford one such example. . . . Since government has deprived
> such persons of the opportunity to practice their faith at places of their
> choice . . . government may, in order to avoid infringing the free exercise
> guaranteed, provide substitutes where it requires such persons to be.[46]

Brennan went on to say that "hostility, not neutrality, would char-
acterize the refusal to provide chaplains and places of worship for soldiers cut off from all civilian opportunities for public communion."[47]
Thus the Court has upheld, in the interest of the free exercise rights of
those serving in the armed forces, the long-practiced program of military
chaplaincies that finds its national aspects rooted in the actions of the
Continental Congress. Under this rationale, military chaplaincies have
less to do with possible violations of the Establishment Clause than with
violations of the Free Exercise Clause.

One nineteenth-century scholar argued that the early chaplains were
not understood by most people to be ministering to the government at
all. Instead, they were thought to be supplying personal pastoral assistance to individuals.[48] This is consistent with the Supreme Court's rationale in the *Schempp* case that military chaplaincies are justifiable constitutionally because they protect the free exercise rights of soldiers.
Viewed from this perspective, military chaplaincies should not be a major
issue in the contemporary debate over the original intent of the framers
in drafting the religion clauses. If military chaplaincies protect free exercise rights, the question of whether they are unlawful advancements
of religion in violation of the Establishment Clause remains far in the
background, if not altogether out of view. Moreover, the issue of whether
military chaplaincies were unconstitutional, either on free exercise or
establishment grounds, was not significantly under review by members
of Congress for the primary reason that the continuance of the Continental Congress's practice of appointing military chaplains was the simple
and expedient rationale for approving the practice.

## Days of Humiliation, Fasting, and Thanksgiving

Special fast days each spring and days of thanksgiving each fall were
traditions of the New England colonies dating back to the seventeenth

century. As colonial relations with the mother country increasingly de-
teriorated in the late 1760s and early 1770s, local communities as well
as some of the southern colonies began to appoint special days of prayer
and thanksgiving. In 1768, in the Massachusetts towns of Boston, Braintree, Charleston, and Lexington, for example, a day in September was
observed as a special day of fasting and prayer in protest of the coming
of the troops, "The Town," as Braintree declared, "having under consideration the Distressing and Alarming circumstances they are now subjected to as also those impending."[49]

The idea of colonial fasts was introduced into the southern colonies
in 1774. Thomas Jefferson recorded that he and several other members
of the Virginia House of Burgesses, especially Patrick Henry and Richard
Henry Lee, "were under conviction of the necessity of arousing our
people from the lethargy into which they had fallen as to passing events;
and thought that the appointment of a day of general fasting and prayer
would be most likely to call up and alarm their attention."[50] The House
of Burgesses appointed 1 June of that year as a day of fasting and prayer,
and every member sent a copy of the resolution to the clergymen of his
county. Jefferson described the observance as a "shock of electricity"
that had a very positive effect on the people.[51] Other colonies followed
suit. The provincial congress of South Carolina set aside 17 February
1775 as a day of fasting and prayer, Maryland appointed 11 May, and
Georgia followed later with a day in July 1775.[52]

It was the Continental Congress, however, that really unified the
prayers of the people. It set 20 July 1775 as a day of humiliation and
prayer for the restoration of the just civil and religious privileges of
America, which was observed throughout the colonies. Thereafter, the
Congress appointed a day in the spring for fasting, humiliation, and
prayer, and a day in the autumn for thanksgiving. These were proclaimed by the governors of the states and were observed throughout
the country. Delegate William Livingston was convinced of their value.
He wrote Henry Laurens in 1778: "I cannot but think that such a measure
is our indispensable Duty, and I dare affirm that it would be very agreeable to all pious people, who are all friends to America; for I never met
with a religious Tory in my life."[53] George Mason was similarly convinced of their merit. As he said to Richard Henry Lee, "I have no
objection to the Fast they have recommended; these solemnities, if properly observed, and not too often repeated, have a good effect upon the
minds of the people."[54]

Of the several fast days, perhaps the most significant was the first,
issued 12 June 1775, calling for a day of fasting to be observed on 20

July in all of the colonies. The proclamation, authored by John Witherspoon and signed by John Hancock as president of the Congress, is rather lengthy but is quoted here in full to give the sense and spirit of the fast day prayers that were subsequently to be offered twice each year until the war was concluded:

> As the great Governor of the world, by his supreme and universal providence, not only conducts the course of nature with unerring wisdom and rectitude, but frequently influences the minds of men to serve the wise and gracious purposes of his providential government; and it being, at all times, our indispensable duty devoutly to acknowledge his superintending providence, especially in times of impending danger and publick calamity, to reverence and adore his immutable Justice as well as to implore his merciful interposition for our deliverance: This Congress, therefore, considering the present critical, alarming, and calamitous state of these Colonies, do earnestly recommend that, Thursday, the twentieth day of July next, be observed by the inhabitants of all the English Colonies on this Continent, as a day of publick humiliation, fasting and prayer; that we may, with united hearts and voices, unfeignedly confess and deplore our many sins, and offer up our joint supplications to the allwise, omnipotent, and merciful Disposer of all events; humbly beseeching him to forgive our iniquities, to remove our present calamities, to avert those desolating judgments with which we are threatened, and to bless our rightful Sovereign, King George the Third, and inspire him with wisdom to discern and pursue the true interest of all his subjects, that a speedy end may be put to the civil discord between Great Britain and the American Colonies, without further effusion of blood; and that the British Nation may be influenced to regard the things that belong to her peace, before they are hid from her eyes; that these Colonies may be ever under the care and protection of a kind Providence, and be prospered in all their interests; Representatives of the people in the several Assemblies and Conventions, that they may be directed to wise and effectual measures for preserving the union, and securing the just rights and privileges of the Colonies; that virtue and true religion may revive and flourish throughout our land; and that America may soon behold a gracious inter position of her invaded rights, a reconciliation with the Parent state on terms constitutional and honourable to both; and that her civil and religious privileges may be secured to the latest posterity. And it is recommended to Christians of all denominations, to assemble for publick worship, and to abstain from servile labour and recreation on said day.[55]

Referring to this fast day, John Adams, writing to his wife from Philadelphia, commented: "We have appointed a Continental fast. Millions will be upon their knees at once before their great Creator, imploring his forgiveness and blessing, his smiles on American Councils and arms."[56] Indeed, the fast day was widely supported. It was printed in newspapers and handbills in all of the states, and regular activities, save the delivery of appropriate sermons in churches everywhere, essentially came to a halt.[57] On the day of the fast, Congress attended *en masse* Reverend Jacob Duché's Episcopalian church in the morning and Dr. Francis Alison's First Presbyterian Church in the afternoon. After the fast day was concluded, Adams remarked that the day was "kept more strictly and devoutly than any Sunday was ever observed" in Philadelphia.[58]

The Continental Congress's first thanksgiving proclamation was issued 1 November 1777, to be observed 18 December 1777. Authored by Richard Henry Lee of Virginia, it declared not a day of fast, but of special praise and thanksgiving, and sought God's blessing on the war effort. It too is quoted in full here as representative of the wartime proclamations that were to follow:

> Forasmuch as it is the indispensable duty of all men to adore the superintending providence of almighty God; to acknowledge with gratitude their obligation to him for benefits received, and to implore such farther blessings as they stand in need of: And it having pleased him in his abundant mercy, not only to continue to us the innumerable bounties of his common providence; but also to smile upon us in the prosecution of a just and necessary war, for the defence and establishment of our unalienable rights and liberties; particularly in that he hath been pleased, in so great a measure, to prosper the means used for the support of our troops, and to crown our arms with most signal success:
>
> It is therefore recommended to the legislative or executive powers of these United States, to set apart Thursday, the eighteenth day of December next, for solemn thanksgiving and praise: that at one time and with one voice, the good people may express the grateful feelings of their hearts, and consecrate themselves to the service of their divine benefactor; and that, together with their sincere acknowledgements and offerings, they may join the penitent confession of their manifold sins, whereby they had forfeited every favour; and their humble and earnest supplication that it may please God through merits of Jesus Christ, mercifully to forgive and blot them out of remembrance: that it may please him graciously to afford his blessing on the governments of these States respectively, and prosper the public Council of the whole: to inspire our commanders, both by land and sea, and all under them, with that wisdom and fortitude which may render them fit instruments, under the providence of almighty God, to secure for these United States, the greatest of all human blessings, independence and peace: that it may please him, to prosper the trade and manufactures of the people, and the labour of the husbandman, that our

land may yield its increase: to take schools and seminaries of education, so necessary for cultivating the principles of true liberty, virtue and piety, under his nurturing hand; and to prosper the means of religion, for the promotion and enlargement of that Kingdom, which consisteth "in righteousness, peace and joy in the Holy Ghost."

And it is further recommended, that servile labour, and such recreation, as, though at other times innocent, may be unbecoming the purpose of this appointment, be omitted on so solemn an occasion.[59]

President Henry Laurens mailed a copy of this proclamation to each of the governors in the thirteen states, encouraging them "to take the necessary measures for carrying this resolve into effect in the state in which you reside."[60] The day of thanksgiving, much like the fast days, was widely observed throughout the states.

The thanksgiving proclamation quoted above contains only a passing reference to the old harvest home custom of colonial days. This observance did not become nationally prominent until President Abraham Lincoln set aside 26 November 1863, during the turmoil of the Civil War, as a day of thanksgiving to God as "the Beneficent Creator and Ruler of the Universe."[61] It was in that year that Thanksgiving officially became a holiday in the United States, to be observed the fourth Thursday of each November. Nevertheless, the 1777 enactment may be considered the first national thanksgiving day proclamation. Its distinctly Christian elements are readily noticeable; later state and federal proclamations almost uniformly omitted Christological references, most likely so that they might be acceptable to Christians, Jews, as well as other theists.[62]

General George Washington, whose army was then at Valley Forge, referred to the Congress's proclamation in his orderly book:

Tomorrow being the day set apart by the honorable Congress for Public Thanksgiving and praise, and duty calling us devoutly to express our grateful acknowledgements to God for the manifold blessings he has granted us, the general directs that the army remain in its present quarters, and that the chaplains perform divine service with their several corps and brigades, and earnestly exhorts all officers and soldiers whose absence is not indispensably necessary to attend with reverence the solemnities of the day.[63]

Undoubtedly, Congress's regular proclamation of days of fast and thanksgiving served to reinforce the belief of Americans that God was acting for them. Each victory in the war fostered the conviction reported in the *Constitutional Gazette*, that "the Lord hath done this, and it is marvelous in our eyes."[64] Members of Congress echoed the same sentiments. Early in the war, in 1775, Jonathan Trumbull wrote to

George Washington, encouraging him to be "strong and courageous."
He added, "May the God of the armies of Israel shower down the
blessings of his Divine Providence on you, give you wisdom and fortitude, cover your head in the day of battle and danger, add success,
convince our enemies of their mistaken measures, and that all their
attempts to deprive these Colonies of their inestimable constitutional
rights and liberties are injurious and in vain."[65] Later that year Elbridge
Gerry wrote to Samuel Adams that history could "hardly produce such
a series of events as has taken place in favor of American opposition.
The hand of Heaven seems to have directed every occurrence."[66] Adams
agreed. Speaking to a large gathering at the statehouse at Philadelphia,
Adams confidently asserted that "the hand of Heaven appears to have
led us on to be, perhaps, humble instruments and means in the great
providential dispensation which is completing."[67] Benjamin Rush wrote
to a friend in England in 1774 that "the God of armies cannot be an
indifferent spectator of these things. Victory must at last declare herself
in favor of justice. Our cause is a righteous one. It is the cause of
Heaven."[68]

Congress itself was equally convinced that God was fighting its battles. In an open letter addressed to all U.S. citizens in 1778, Congress
assured them that "at length that God of battles, in whom was our trust,
has conducted us thro' the paths of danger and distress to the thresholds
of security."[69] A year later Congress reminded them how "America, without arms, ammunition, discipline, revenue, government or ally, with a
'staff and a sling' only, dared, 'in the name of the Lord of Hosts,' to
engage a gigantic adversary, prepared at all points, boasting of his
strength, and of whom even mighty warriors 'were greatly afraid.' "[70]
Congress may have been relying on a higher authority for victory in
battle, but it was not itself prone to relax, working, in the words of
Delaware delegate Thomas McKean, "double tides [overtime]," even "on
the Fast Day."[71]

Once the Revolutionary War was concluded, in special thanksgiving
to the "God of Battles" who had given victory to the American colonies,
the Continental Congress issued two additional thanksgiving proclamations. The first, issued 11 October 1782, called for a day of gratitude to
"Almighty God, the giver of all good."[72] After the Treaty of Paris was
signed on 3 September 1783, formally ending the war, Congress set aside
11 December 1783 as a special day of thanksgiving.[73] It was to be the
Continental Congress's final thanksgiving proclamation.

Although fast days and government proclamations of thanksgiving
and prayer began during the early period of the Continental Congress,

none was forthcoming from 1784 until 1789. Following the establishment of the new Constitution, fast days were never reinstated, but thanksgiving days were. While one scholar has interpreted the end of thanksgiving and fast days as a sure sign that the Continental Congress's reliance upon God receded in its enjoyment of war success,[74] it is possible to see the end of the observance days only as the natural result of peace. The thanksgiving and fast days promulgated by the Continental Congress had been instituted as wartime events, so why should they not have been discontinued once the war was concluded? After the war, the Continental Congress never discontinued the practice of having its chaplain begin each daily session with prayer, and this would seem to be a better measure of whether the Continental Congress entered a period of spiritual declension after the war was concluded.

One might also attempt to argue that the fast days were not resumed after 1789 because the new Constitution carried the notion of religion being beyond the purview of the federal government, but if that is true, why were thanksgiving days reinstated? The best explanation, again, seems to be that the fast days were essentially related to the war effort; when the war ended, so did the fast days. Days of national thanksgiving, however, which have continued off and on since the First Congress, are best explained as holdovers from the colonial period and as practices deemed substantially harmless by most governmental leaders under the new Constitution who sought to acknowledge God's authority over all things in heaven and earth.[75]

It would be erroneous, however, to assume that the constitutionality of thanksgiving days has always been accepted without question. When, in the First Congress after the adoption of the Constitution, a resolution was offered in the House to request the president to "recommend to the people of the United States a day of public thanksgiving and prayer, to be observed by acknowledging with grateful hearts the many signal favours of Almighty God,"[76] objection was raised by at least two members of Congress. Thomas Burke of North Carolina, for example, thought that such an observance would be a "mimicking of European customs, where they made a mere mockery of thanksgivings."[77] Thomas Tucker of South Carolina suggested that "it is a business with which the Congress have nothing to do; it is a religious matter, and as such is proscribed to us. If a day of thanksgiving must take place, let it be done by the authorization of the several states."[78] Tucker's comment is of special interest because it occurred on the same day, 25 September, that the wording of the First Amendment was approved by Congress after more than a month of debate in House and Senate committees. His view that a thanksgiving proclamation, as a "religious matter," was "proscribed" to Congress, strongly suggests that he understood the Establishment Clause, its meaning fresh on his mind, to prohibit Congress from engaging in religious acts.

To the objections of Burke and Tucker, however, Roger Sherman of Connecticut argued that not only was the practice of public thanksgiving a "laudable one," but one justified by scriptural precedents: "for instance the solemn thanksgivings and rejoicings that took place in the time of Solomon, after the building of the temple."[79] Elias Boudinot cited a more recent precedent: the thanksgiving days observed by "the late [Continental] Congress."[80] Sherman and Boudinot carried the resolution over the objections of Burke and Tucker, and on 3 October 1789, President Washington proclaimed a national day of thanksgiving, which he followed with several others during his administration.

While Washington made every effort to frame his proclamations in language acceptable to all faiths, his successor, John Adams, called for Christian worship. Jefferson refused to issue any religious proclamations, believing that "the Constitution has precluded them."[81] James Madison, who sought a "perfect separation"[82] between religion and government, stated that "Religious proclamations by the Executive recommending thanksgivings and fasts are shoots from the same root with the legislative acts [the chaplaincies]."[83] He regarded such proclamations as violating the Establishment Clause: "They seem," he wrote, "to imply and certainly nourish a *national* religion."[84] As president, however, Madison gave in to demands to proclaim days of thanksgiving, finding extenuating circumstances in the fact that he was president during the time a war was fought on American soil. Still, he used prayers that were generic and nondiscriminatory as far as possible.[85]

With one exception, Madison's successors followed his example and issued prayer and thanksgiving proclamations in nonsectarian language. The one exception was Andrew Jackson, who shared Jefferson's views and steadfastly refused to issue any thanksgiving proclamations because he thought he "might disturb the security which religion now enjoys in the country, in its complete separation from the political concerns of the General Government."[86] All of the presidents since Jackson have issued prayer proclamations, either annually or in connection with important or critical events, such as American entries into war. Moreover, in 1952 the Congress passed a law providing for a National Day of Prayer, observed annually since, and which from 1988 has been observed on the first Thursday in May.

## Concluding Remarks

The appointment of legislative and military chaplains and the proclamation of national days of fasting, humiliation, and thanksgiving by the Continental Congress, while revealing the theistic, if not essentially Christian, worldview of the nation's earliest leaders, must be understood in an even broader historical context. These practices were not new; they had been commonplace in the colonies from the earliest days of American settlement.[87] They were so much a part of the fabric of American social life that hardly anyone noticed when the Continental Congress adopted the same practices. Furthermore, the adoption of these practices was in large measure precipitated by the special circumstances and demands of the Revolutionary War; in the case of the days of fast and thanksgiving, their demise was coterminous with the war's end. Legislative chaplains, however, continued to serve in the Continental Congress until that body ceased to function upon ratification of the Constitution.

The First Congress chose not to resume the observance of national days of fasting and humiliation. It did, however, continue to appoint its own legislative chaplains, and it made provision for the appointment of military chaplains and special presidential proclamations of days of thanksgiving. There is little evidence that the appointment of chaplains, both legislative and military, were occasioned by much controversy, although at least James Madison voiced strong objections based on conflicts with the First Amendment. Presidential proclamations of prayer and thanksgiving came under some scrutiny (as indicated by the objections of Thomas Tucker and Thomas Burke in the First Congress) after the First Amendment brought into issue the propriety of governmental entanglements with religion.

All of these historical practices are far more controversial today than they were in the early years of the nation, only because in every modern discussion of church-state relations, those advocating an accommodationist interpretation of the religion clauses invoke the early post-Constitution chaplain appointments and thanksgiving prayers as evidence that the founding fathers intended no clear separation of religion from the federal government. The evidence, however, does not immediately allow for this conclusion. For example, on the issue of thanksgiving day proclamations, some of the framers, like Roger Sherman, favored the practice and saw no inconsistency with the Establishment Clause; others, like James Madison, believed vehemently that it was a practice inconsistent with the First Amendment; most, it seems, gave the whole matter little thought and were swayed more by the tradition of thanksgiving prayers in the Continental Congress than possible conflicts the practice might have with the Establishment Clause. Elias Boudinot, for example, as one of only two congressmen who stated recorded objections to thanksgiving proclamations, cited only the practice of the Continental Congress as a justification for thanksgiving proclamations. There is likewise little evidence that reasons other than the continuation of longstanding traditions of the Continental Congress were behind the First Congress's action calling for the appointment of legislative and military chaplains.

In the contemporary debate concerning the extent to which early post-Constitution chaplaincies and prayer proclamations inform the framers' original intent, it thus becomes vitally important to evaluate such practices in the context of traditions that reach at least as far back as the administration of the Continental Congress. These were inherited practices that the First Congress more or less assumed, as a matter of course, to be consistent with the First Amendment. Discerning the framers' "original intent" as to how such practices influenced the wording of the First Amendment assumes that the framers were attentive to (considered, analyzed, debated) the consequences of their actions. In fact, very little attention seems to have been given to the relationship of these practices to the First Amendment. Thus, one must be careful not to read too much into the framers' purposes by an overemphasis on the early chaplaincy and prayer practices of Congress. Accommodationists in particular have usually assigned too much significance to these early governmental traditions. Such traditions simply do not say as much about "original intent" as accommodationists like to claim. Accommodationists typically assume that the members of the First Congress approved of such practices because they believed, as members of the Continental Congress for the most part believed, that religion is vital to the maintenance of sound republican government. It may of course be true that the majority of the First Congress's membership held this belief, but the written record they bequeathed to us does not offer overwhelming proof for this conclusion.

In support of the argument here advanced that emphasizes tradition over principle, annual thanksgiving prayers by presidents in particular must be seen in the context of the longstanding colonial practice (by the states and by the Continental Congress). The practice had such a long tradition that it would have indeed been difficult for members of the First Congress to object to the adoption of the practice, even had they sensed that it might be in conflict with First Amendment strictures. Furthermore, the proposal for reinstatement of the practice in 1789 (after a five-year absence) occurred in the midst of great excitement over the ratification of the new Constitution and the considerable hopes and expectations surrounding the new "republican" form of government that the document embraced. Add to this the realization that Congress's proposal was for the nation's first president, George Washington, already a national hero of mythical proportions, to offer the special prayer of thanks to God for bestowing his blessings on the new nation, and one has the prescription for an event that could hardly have been voted down, no matter what the First Amendment said.

*Six*

## RELIGIOUS DIMENSIONS OF THE
## DECLARATION OF INDEPENDENCE

The Declaration of Independence is arguably the most widely known and influential political document in the history of the world. When the Continental Congress at Philadelphia on 4 July 1776 adopted the Declaration of Independence, it marked an abrupt end to America's acceptance of British authority over the American colonies. This dramatic step was not taken hastily or unadvisedly. It came as the culmination of a long series of events that convinced Americans that their freedom and happiness could never be attained under British rule.

It is important to realize that a majority of the American people would never have endorsed a colonial separation from the mother country unless they believed that it had God's sanction. Thus it is necessary to examine the ways in which the Continental Congress's formal act of separation, the Declaration of Independence, was theologically grounded and therefore deserving, from the colonists' perspective, of the widespread support it enjoyed. This chapter argues that the "laws of nature" provided the needed theological and philosophical underpinnings of the Declaration. Also examined is the relationship of religious liberty in the colonies to the Declaration as well as the Declaration's relevance in ascertaining the constitutional framers' original intent regarding the relation of religion and government in the new nation.

### Drafting the Declaration

When the Continental Congress met on 7 June 1776, Richard Henry Lee from Virginia offered a resolution calling for the independence of the several colonies from Great Britain. The resolution read, in part, that

"these United Colonies are, and of right ought to be, free and independent States, that they are absolved from all allegiance to the British
Crown, and that all political connection between them, and the State of
Great Britain is, and ought to be, totally dissolved."[1] The resolution was
seconded by John Adams of Massachusetts. After two days of debate,
consideration was postponed for several weeks in order that public support for independence, especially in the more conservative colonies,
might mature. Meanwhile, so that no time would be lost, a committee
was appointed to draw up a declaration to accompany the resolution of
independence in the event of its adoption. This committee, selected on
11 June 1776, was composed of Thomas Jefferson, John Adams, Benjamin
Franklin, Roger Sherman, and Robert R. Livingston.

Before we consider the Declaration and its underlying ideology, in
particular its religious dimensions, it might be useful to examine briefly
the religious views of the five members of the Declaration committee.
While Jefferson was the principal draftsman of the document, the Declaration draft that was submitted to the Continental Congress for approval must be considered the work of the entire committee and accordingly influenced by their collective religious views.

These five men, like many of the nation's earliest leaders, are difficult
to describe because while they were all genuinely religious, they were
not all specifically Christian. Thomas Jefferson's views are perhaps best
known. While generally regarded by orthodox Christians of his day as
an "infidel," he was by birth and baptism affiliated with the Church of
England and in his early days served as a vestryman. He was a regular
attendant at church services and maintained an active interest in religion
all of his life.

Late in life Jefferson summarized the basic religious convictions he
had held for most of his eighty-four years by affirming that Jesus' doctrines "tend all to the happiness of man . . . that there is only one God
. . . that there is a future state of rewards and punishments, that to love
God with all thy heart and thy neighbor as thyself, is the sum of religion." For the remaining Christian fundamentals—Christ's deity and resurrection, the Trinity, the divine authorship of Scripture, the earthly
return of Christ—these were for Jefferson the "deliria of crazy imagi-
nations."[2] Also late in life, he wrote James Smith expressing confidence
that "the present generation will see Unitarianism become the general
religion of the United States."[3] In a letter to Benjamin Waterhouse that
same year, he wrote: "I trust that there is not a young man now living
in the United States who will not die a Unitarian."[4] And regarding the
Bible, he wrote to Peter Carr that it was just another history book, to
be read "as you would read Livy or Tacitus."[5] Jefferson, then, was no

atheist, but neither was he an orthodox Christian. He is perhaps best described as an enlightened deist.

John Adams was more complex than Jefferson in his religious sentiments. To be called a Puritan, orthodox Christian, deist, and humanist in one lifetime was no small achievement, but Adams was easily equal to it and certainly untroubled by it. Though he criticized ritual he insisted on the importance of attending church; he reconciled the two because he got out of church exactly what he felt it should give, nothing more or less. He identified himself with and became one of the leading Unitarians in America. David Hawke writes of Adams: "He verged on deism in religion and found it no easier than Jefferson to admit his waywardness publicly. He respected the findings of natural philosophy and was inclined to extend those findings into the political and social world. He believed that natural law resembled the axioms of mathematics—'Self evident principles, that every man must assent to as soon as proposed.' "[6]

In their final years, Adams and Jefferson renewed their friendship of earlier years, and their letters reveal that they were almost totally agreed on religion. After surveying their letters, Cushing Strout offered this conclusion: "Whatever their political differences, Jefferson and Adams were virtually at one in their religion." He suggested that their common creed was Unitarianism.[7]

Benjamin Franklin was less outspoken than either Jefferson or Adams against traditional Christian beliefs, but he too saw Christ as primarily a moral teacher and true religion as an expression of perfectible human virtues. In spite of exertions by his more orthodox friends, Franklin never went farther in his Christian faith than acknowledging Christ as the greatest model of the virtue of humility. A few weeks before he died, Franklin wrote to Ezra Stiles, president of Yale University: "Here is my creed. I believe in one God, Creator of the Universe. That He governs it by His providence. That He ought to be worshipped. That the most acceptable service we render Him is doing good to His other children. That the soul of man is immortal, and will be treated with justice in another life respecting its conduct in this. These I take to be the principles of sound religion."[8]

Franklin prized his membership in the Masonic movement. In 1779 he became the Grand Master of the most influential lodge in France, the "Nine Sisters," to which Voltaire had also belonged before his death in 1778.[9] Masonic membership was generally looked upon more favorably by the public in the eighteenth and nineteenth centuries than in the twentieth. While Freemasonry as a social movement has always been difficult to define, describe, or trace, it at least did not undergo in the

eighteenth century the kind of organized movement against it that
emerged in the nineteenth century and continues in some quarters even
today. Its eighteenth-century strength was related to the new faith in the
future of humanity and the ideal of progress that characterized the thinking of the day. This new outlook became a social force and a concrete
fact through the agency of Freemasonry, which at once accepted it and
advocated it. Thus it was not unusual for revolutionaries seeking political
change to discover in the Masonic movement ideas that corresponded to
their own.[10]

Both Robert Livingston and Roger Sherman supposedly were also Ma-
sons, although this is disputed in the case of Sherman.[11] More traditionally known as a conservative Connecticut Calvinist Congregationalist,
Sherman made a lifelong effort to base his life on biblical teaching. He
was a dedicated and pious churchman, and this was well known to his
fellow congressional delegates. Once when Congress was backed up with
business, it resolved to meet on Sunday. Sherman objected—out of "a
regard of the commands of his Maker." To his face delegates addressed
the stern and serious Sherman as "Judge Sherman" but behind his back
often called him "Father Sherman." One delegate described his speaking
abilities as "grotesque and laughable," but he was praised by his colleagues for being thorough and intelligent and for possessing a pure
heart and a clear head. Thomas Jefferson described him as "a man who
never said a foolish thing in his life." He was so well respected by his
colleagues that he served on virtually every important committee created
by the Continental Congress. He was, therefore, a natural choice to the
committee appointed to write the Declaration.[12] But while he met several
times with the committee, there is no evidence of what, if anything, he
contributed to its final wording.[13]

Robert R. Livingston from New York was the most unlikely member
of the drafting committee. In every debate in congressional assemblies,
his had been the firmest voice in opposition to independence. He was
most likely placed on the committee to assure those for postponement
that, while separation might be inevitable, the document that would
declare it to the world would contain nothing to offend the more conservative members of Congress.[14] "Every good man wishes that America
remain free," he said, "in this I join heartily; at the same time I do not
desire she should be wholly independent of the mother country. How to
reconcile these jarring principles, I profess I am altogether at a loss."[15]

Livingston was not known as a strongly religious man. As already
mentioned, he was an active Mason, suggesting a latitudinarian approach
to religion.[16] His religious views are of little consequence in the present
context, however. He neither voted for independence nor signed the

Declaration. His participation on the committee was formal only; like Sherman, he contributed virtually nothing to the process of planning and drafting the Declaration.

According to Jefferson, the committee pressed on him alone to prepare a draft of a declaration.[17] After submitting his draft to Adams and Franklin, who made a few minor revisions, the 33-year-old Jefferson reported it to the full committee, which made no further revisions. The committee's report was made to Congress on 28 June 1776. Richard Henry Lee's resolution for independence, which had been debated in several sessions in the month of June, was considered on 1 July in nine hours of uninterrupted debate. It was finally put to vote and approved the following day. Congress then undertook consideration of the Declaration submitted by the committee. It was debated 2–4 July, during which passages condemning the British people and the slave trade were stricken. Other stylistic changes were made, and in approved form the Declaration was adopted by the Continental Congress on 4 July to supplement Lee's resolution for independence, which had been adopted two days earlier.[18]

The Declaration of Independence has been much lauded for its eloquence. Its greatest strength, however, lies in the succinct way in which it states religious and philosophical ideas that were commonly accepted in 1776. As he later wrote to Richard Henry Lee in 1825, Jefferson's goal in 1776 was:

> Not to find out new principles, or new arguments, never before thought of, not merely to say things which had never been said before; but to place before mankind the common sense of the subject, in terms so plain and firm as to command their assent. . . . Neither aiming at originality of principles or sentiments, nor yet copied from any particular and previous writing, it was intended to be an expression of the American mind. . . . All its authority rests then on the harmonizing sentiments of the day, whether expressed in conversation, in letters, printed essays, or the elementary books of public right, as Aristotle, Cicero, Locke, Sidney, etc.[19]

Jefferson's remarks express his belief that the Declaration's philosophy reflected "the American mind." Whether or not its essence was as widely adhered to as Jefferson would have us believe, the philosophy of the Declaration was certainly nothing new to the members of Congress. Much of the content of the Declaration, including most of the enumerated grievances against Great Britain, had been debated in the First Continental Congress in 1774 and 1775 in contemplation of a "Declaration of Rights" to be adopted and presented to the mother country (see appendix A). Preliminary drafts of this document had been prepared by Thomas Jefferson and John Dickinson.[20] These drafts and Congress's debate on them represented the belief of most Americans that Great Britain would in the end break down if the colonies only remained united and made it clear that they would not stand for their rights being trampled on.

Congress's "Declaration of Rights" was finally agreed upon and passed on 6 July 1775.[21] That the Declaration of Independence was framed on ideas and themes thoroughly set forth in the Declaration of Rights was confirmed in an 1822 letter from John Adams to Timothy Pickering: "There is not an idea in it but what had been hackneyed in Congress for two years before. The substance of it is contained in the declaration of rights and the violation of those rights, in the Journals of Congress, in 1774."[22] And Jefferson himself late in life attested to the familiarity of all the Declaration's contents: "I turned to neither book nor pamphlet while writing it. I did not consider it as any part of my charge to invent new ideas altogether, and to offer no sentiment which had ever been expressed before."[23] If, then, the Declaration contained only familiar ideas and themes that Jefferson said represented "the American mind" and that Adams asserted were thoroughly known to Congress, it becomes necessary to examine the basic philosophy of the Declaration.

### The Philosophy of the Declaration

The basic philosophy behind the Declaration is that all people are endowed by God with natural rights that are unalienable, and when a government acts to destroy such rights its subjects are entitled to revolt and establish a new government. This basic philosophy appears in the first part of the second paragraph of the Declaration:

> We hold these truths to be self-evident. That all men are created equal, that they are endowed by their Creator with certain unalienable rights; that among these are life, liberty, and the pursuit of happiness; that to secure these rights governments are instituted among men, deriving their just powers from the consent of the governed; that whenever any form of government becomes destructive of these ends, it is the right of the people to alter or to abolish it, and to institute new government, laying its foundation on such principles and organizing its powers in such form, as to them shall seem most likely to effect their safety and happiness.

Not all Americans, to be sure, would have accepted the philosophy of the Declaration as, to use Jefferson's phrase, "the common sense of the subject." Yet the premises of the natural rights philosophy stated in the Declaration were widely held in eighteenth-century America: that there is a "natural order" of things in the universe, expertly designed by God for the guidance of mankind; that the "laws" of this natural order may be discovered by human reason; that these laws so discovered furnish a reliable and immutable standard for testing the ideas, the conduct, and the institutions of men.[24] An important part of this natural order as it was commonly understood was the notion of a social compact between peoples and governments. Under the theory of the social compact, so thoroughly elaborated by John Locke in his *Second Treatise on Human Government*, governments are formed when people come together and by agreement transfer certain of their "natural rights" to rulers to ensure their safety, protection, and welfare. Some of these natural rights, such as life and liberty, are unalienable and cannot be transferred because they are fundamental to the enjoyment of one's life. When the compact is violated by the ruler, the compact is dissolved, and the people are thereby free to establish a new government.[25]

The idea that secular political authority rests upon compact did not originate with Locke. Late medieval theorists, beginning with Marsilius of Padua in the early fourteenth century, had conceived of the authority of princes as resting upon a compact with their subjects, a compact on their part to rule righteously, failing which their subjects were absolved from allegiance. But most political theorists of the fourteenth century argued that this absolution became operative only through the intervention of the pope, who, as God's earthly representative, possessed by divine right authority over princes as well as over all subjects.[26] This was the position, for example, of fourteenth-century theorists Hervaeus Natalis, professor of theology at the University of Paris, and William of Ockham. Marsilius, however, viewed papal authority in civil matters as myth and held that all legitimate government, whether secular or sacred, rests entirely on the consent of the governed. By the seventeenth century, Protestant theorists held that kings' right to rule came directly from God, conveniently eliminating the agency of the pope.[27]

But the social compact theory in Locke, Thomas Hobbes, and Jean-Jacques Rousseau, among others in the early modern period, rejected the notion of the divine right of kings to rule and posited that social compacts between rulers and subjects were "approved" by God as transactions of "nature." Governments were human institutions, the details of which were worked out by men. God was still involved, but as an approving observer, not as a participating party. In this way, a compact broken by a ruler was automatically dissolved; there was no need to be concerned with violating the will of God by ending an arrangement that God himself had not established in the first place.

It was fundamentally important to Jefferson and the Continental Congress that the colonies' right to independence be grounded in a philosophy that had a theistic framework. Although they did not articulate this position specifically, the delegates undoubtedly knew that without divine sanction, a declaration of independence would never be countenanced by the American people. Thus it is not surprising that there are several references to God in the Declaration. While four such references appear in the final text—"Nature's God," the "Creator," the "Supreme Judge of the world," and "Divine Providence"—only the first one, "Nature's God," appears in Jefferson's original draft. The reference to the "Creator" resulted from Franklin's recommendation that Jefferson's wording "that from that equal creation they derive rights inherent and inalienable" be altered to read "that they are endowed by their Creator with rights some of which are certain inherent and unalienable."[28] Congress then further changed this to "they are endowed by their Creator with certain unalienable rights."[29] The last two references to the deity were added by Congress, seemingly to buttress the argument that God was on the side of American independence.

This perspective is not intended to suggest, of course, that the references to the deity, either Jefferson's or those added by Congress, were included for expedience only. There is every reason to believe that Jefferson strongly held to natural law theory as the essence of the universal order established by God and that most of the delegates also saw it that way. How was it, then, that Congress and particularly Jefferson, as the Declaration's chief author, understood the relation between natural law and the deity?

Carl Becker, who has written perhaps the best volume on the philosophy of the Declaration of Independence, offers an important insight into the way Jefferson understood the Declaration. Jefferson and other Enlightenment rationalists, he says, had lost that sense of intimate intercourse and familiar conversation with God that religious men of earlier ages had enjoyed. Since the later seventeenth century, says Becker, God was not conceived by enlightened thinkers as having contact with human beings and therefore had become no more than the Final Cause or Prime Mover of the universe. As such (and here is where Jefferson would most have differed with orthodox Christians), God was conceived as exerting his power and revealing his will indirectly through his creation rather than directly by miraculous manifestation or through inspired revelation. In the eighteenth century as never before, "nature" had stepped in between God and man so that there was no longer any way to know God's will except by discovering the "laws" of nature, which of course would be the laws of "Nature's God" (the Declaration's wording). Why look any further than the natural order to discover the true nature of God? Was there any other valid revelation? The eighteenth-century rationalists, says Becker, seeking a modified version of the orig-inal compact, had to find truth in nature or forever abandon the hope of finding it.[30]

The concept of nature was not new, of course, even in the eighteenth century. Philosophers in the early Greek city-states reflected on the na-ture of the order that governed the relations of humankind. In the fifth and fourth centuries B.C.E., the Sophists appealed to a law of nature, which was thought to govern the evolution of all natural phenomena, including human relations. Later, Socrates, Plato, and Aristotle asserted the discoverability of immutable standards with reference to which pos-itive law (formulated human law) might be evaluated.[31]

Aristotle went farther than those before him in holding that there is a natural law or justice that everywhere possesses the same authority and is readily identifiable. As the natural law was discoverable by reason, Aristotle restricted the apprehension of it to the elite—those especially favored by education, talent, wealth, and the cultivation of virtues.[32]

In the third century B.C.E., the Stoics became the first to develop natural law into a formal philosophical system. Unlike Aristotle, how-ever, they asserted that all persons, not just elites, could by the exercise of reason comprehend the natural law. The state of nature, they said, was one of harmony, regulated by reason. This, they thought, had been perverted by selfishness, and the task confronting humankind was to fashion its laws in such a way as to recover the ancient ideal. To live according to nature was to live naturally. The laws of nature and of morality were considered identical. Reason, moreover, was common to people everywhere, and natural law was therefore all pervading.[33]

In the Roman era, a significant development was the evolution of the *jus gentium*, or law of nations, applicable to all non-Roman citizens. As a body of law common to all people, its underlying basis was the natural law as developed by the Stoics. Another important development in the Roman era was the work of Augustine of Hippo, who in the fifth century became the first to contrast natural law and revelation. The natural law, he held, allowed men to live freely before the fall but thereafter enslaved all humankind who in sin sought to live apart from its demands. It was not until the thirteenth century that a comprehensive system seeking a harmonization of natural laws, God's law, and human law was attempted, by the brilliant Dominican, Thomas Aquinas.[34]

Aquinas defined natural law as that part of law discoverable by right reason. According to Aquinas, the highest of all laws, comprehending all others, was the eternal law, which was nothing less than the all-encompassing knowledge possessed by God. Part, but not all, of the eternal law could be known by man: part of it was revealed in Scripture (divine law); part of it could be discovered by reason (natural law). Natural law was in fact not the laws of nature, but a natural method of learning about the law of God.[35]

The concept of nature in the eighteenth century as developed by rationalist thinkers of the Enlightenment was somewhat different from Aquinas's account. Enlightenment thought did not abandon the effort to share in the mind of God; it only had the increased confidence to think that *all* of the mind of God could be known. This confidence arose through the progress of scientific investigation, which had been creating, since the time of Copernicus, a strong presumption that the mind of God could be discovered with greater precision by studying the mechanism of his created universe than by meditating on his revealed word. Most of the laws of this curious mechanism had already been formulated by Johann Kepler, Galileo Galilei, and especially Isaac Newton. Their discoveries led many rationalists to believe that all of the "laws" of God's universe could be discovered through the exercise of human reason. If this were really possible, would not the infinite mind of God be fully revealed, and the natural law be identical with the eternal law? In the final analysis, eighteenth-century rationalists answered, yes. Having thus deified nature, many eighteenth-century Enlightenment thinkers would conveniently dismiss Holy Writ and drop the concept of eternal law altogether. Natural law could explain everything.[36]

No modern scholarship disputes that natural law philosophy is what undergirds the Declaration. Becker's classic work, *The Declaration of Independence: A Study in the History of Political Ideas*, written in 1922, was the first work that investigated in depth the natural law foundation of the Declaration, and it enshrined the view that Jefferson relied most heavily on John Locke for his understanding of natural law. Becker's work remains for most scholars the beginning and end of investigation into the ideas of the Declaration. Two more recent works, however, have added much to the scholarly discussion about not only the ideas underpinning the Declaration but also colonial revolutionary thought in general.

Garry Wills's *Inventing America: Jefferson's Declaration of Independence*, published in 1978, is a penetrating book that seeks to discover the intellectual influences on Jefferson as the Declaration's chief author. He affirms Becker in acknowledging natural law as the core of Declaration philosophy but claims that Locke has been overrated as Jefferson's primary source. Rather, he argues that Jefferson was a disciple of the French and Scottish Enlightenment who wrote into the Declaration definable portions of the moral philosophy of Jean Jacques Burlamaqui, Francis Hutcheson, Thomas Reid, Henry Kames, David Hume, and Adam

Smith. Though he never lets polemics get in the way of faithful exposition, Wills's motive is to rescue the early nation from the individualist
tradition associated with Locke and replace it with more communitarian,
fraternal doctrines. For Wills, Locke is the evil genius of the harsh and
calculating liberalism of nineteenth- and twentieth-century America:
minimize Locke at the founding and one has the essential formula for
remaking modern America.

Another revisionist text also published in 1978 was Morton White's
*The Philosophy of the American Revolution.*[37] Because the book focuses,
like Wills's, on the paramount importance of Thomas Jefferson and natural law theory in the drafting of the Declaration of Independence, it
probably does not deserve such a comprehensive title. Nevertheless, it
is an important work that seeks to discover the "real" Jefferson. White,
too, wants to go beyond Locke to understand the sources of the revolutionary political mind, to Burlamaqui, Kames, and especially Hutcheson. But he is far less ready than Wills to dismiss Locke as a primary
influence.

The heart of White's investigation is the search for the meaning of
"self-evident" truths[38] (the Declaration contained many), which were believed by most seventeenth- and eighteenth-century thinkers to be an
outcome or result of natural law. White shows that Lockean epistemology
held that self-evidence did not mean evident to all but immediately
knowable, as when the eye is turned toward something clearly illuminated. Thus the term carries the unfortunate implication of being apparent only to elites, which in turn means that the colonists did not
expect the truth of their argument for revolution to be universally recognized. White believes that Jefferson and the Continental Congress
never embraced such a view—in fact, he claims, they wanted all the
world to understand the philosophical logic of the nation's act of independence. Thus White considers the possibility that Jefferson's use of
the term self-evident was rooted in a later non-Lockean tradition, namely,
the Scottish Enlightenment. Might the term have been meant to suggest
that the rights upon which the colonists depended were evident to the
moral sense, as Frances Hutcheson taught? White concludes that it probably was not so intended and that, even if it were, still only elitists
might apprehend the self-evident truths claimed by the Declaration. He
shows that Jefferson was heavily influenced by the Swiss jurist Burlamaqui, who stood, on this point, closer to Locke than to Hutcheson.
Burlamaqui thought that the "stupid wretches"[39] among the people were
unable to perceive self-evident truths. White's point is not that the Revolution was essentially elitist but that it was more ambiguous on this
point than is often realized.

No attempt is made here, on the models of Wills and White, to trace the various antecedents of Jefferson's beliefs about epistemology, philosophy, political theology, and metaphysics, all of which can be speculated about in studying the Declaration. It is sufficient in the present context to say that in many indirect ways, the antecedents are endless and can be traced beyond Locke, Hobbes, Burlamaqui, or other early modern thinkers, even to Plato and Aristotle, if not to preclassical sources. The present study is of the religious dimension of the work of the Continental Congress, not of the multiple sources of the Declaration of Independence. The purpose of the foregoing discussion in relation to the overall study has been merely to show the complexity of natural law theory as embraced by Jefferson and Congress in writing the Declaration of Independence and to demonstrate how that theory was never far removed from theology, or at least political theology, and as such, natural law indeed was a notable religious influence on the work of the Continental Congress.

Morton White's concern for the "self-evidenced" nature of the Declaration's argument for independence raises a related question. To what extent did the colonists themselves understand Congress's Declaration? In particular, to what extent did the non-elites among the colonists understand the niceties of natural law theory upon which the document was built? When Jefferson said that the Declaration merely represented "the American mind," was he not implying that more than the elite educated classes, indeed that most Americans, understood and believed in natural law theory and the other basic ideas of the document? While it may never be possible for scholars to answer this question with certainty, there is evidence that the channels through which the philosophy of natural law made its way in the colonies in the eighteenth century were several. Many Americans had been educated at British universities, where the doctrines of Newton and Locke were gospel, while those who were educated at American universities were well acquainted with these works as well.[40]

For the general reader, the so-called non-elite, the political philosophy of the eighteenth century was available not only through newspapers, pamphlets, and tracts, but was also expounded from the church pulpits far more than is often realized. Both in England and America clergymen laid firm hold of the Newtonian conception of the universe as an effective weapon against infidelity. Dr. Richard Bentley studied Newton in order to preach a "Confusion of Atheism," deriving a proof of divine providence from Newton's physical construction of the universe.[41] The so-called "argument from design" was a powerful polemic for the truth of the existence and goodness of God, and the sermons of the century were filled with it.

In 1750 there was published at Boston a book of twenty sermons, delivered in the Parish Church at Charleston, South Carolina, by the Reverend Samuel Quincy. In one of these sermons the natural law philosophy is fully elaborated:

> For a right knowledge of God by the Light of Nature, displays his several amiable Perfections; acquaints us with the Relation he stands in to us, and the Obligations we owe to him. . . . It teaches us that our greatest Interest and Happiness consists in loving and fearing God, and in doing his Will; that to imitate his moral Perfections in our whole Behaviour, is acting up to the Dignity of our Natures, and that he has endowed us with Reason and Understanding (Faculties which the Brutes have not) on purpose to contemplate his Beauty and Glory, and to keep our inferior Appetites in due Subjection to his Laws, written in our Hearts.[42]

In his election sermon of 1754, Jonathan Mayhew, a prominent Congregationalist minister, expounded the same philosophy for deriving the authority of government. Government, he said, arising out of the natural order of things, "is both the ordinance of God, and the ordinance of man: of God, in respect to his original plan, and universal Providence; of man, as it is more immediately the result of human prudence, wisdom and concert."[43] In Massachusetts election sermons from 1768 to 1773, the natural law philosophy is evident in addresses by Daniel Schute, Jason Haven, Samuel Cooke, Frederick Tucker, and Moses Parsons. In each sermon, the Enlightenment trinity of God, Nature, and Reason are made the foundation of human government.[44]

Earlier in 1719, John Wise, another Congregationalist minister from New England, had argued that the "laws of nature" supported the American colonial governments' desire to improve their condition. For Wise, while no particular form of government is ordained by God, God has established the "law of nature as the general rule of government," so that all who wish to do so may, by the use of their reason, comprehend those basic principles of "sociableness" on which every sound government is based.[45] It was this conviction, that God's laws, the laws of nature, could be discerned only by human reason, that gave many Americans the courage to launch themselves on the perilous task of establishing a new government.

And so there became established in the minds of many Americans, elites as well as non-elites, the conception of natural law to confirm their faith in the majesty of God while destroying their faith in the majesty of kings. In other words, by 1776 a great many Americans understood human government to be an outgrowth of God's natural law, and that tyrannical kings were an aberration of such laws and could be resisted with God's approval.

While the basic notion of natural law and its political implications were widely accepted in eighteenth-century America, not all of its details, at least among orthodox Christians, were so readily believed. To the extent that the natural law philosophy was perceived by them as rejecting such vital doctrines as the infallibility of the Scriptures, original sin and total depravity, the virgin birth and deity of Christ, and the atonement and resurrection, it was untenable. To be sure, the natural law philosophy was compatible with, and to some degree constructed by, deists like Thomas Jefferson, Benjamin Franklin, Richard Henry Lee, Thomas Paine, and Ethan Allen. Following David Hume, they banished the possibility of miracles in a world ruled by natural law, rejecting the Scriptures as the final source and guarantee of truth. They were willing to grant to the Scriptures a relative authority to the extent that they agreed with the laws of nature and conformed to the dictates of right reason, but they reserved the right to judge Scripture in the light of human reason.[46] Samuel West, for example, a Massachusetts Arminian clergyman, was deliberate in subordinating Scripture to natural law: "A revelation," he preached, "pretending to be from God, that contradicts any part of natural laws, ought immediately to be rejected as an imposture; for the Deity cannot make a law contrary to the law of nature without acting contrary to himself."[47]

It was not the intention of the deists to banish Christianity from the American scene; they actually held its ethical principles in very high regard, but it was their vision to break the monopolistic hold of the historic Christian theology on the political and social life of the American people. Jefferson, according to his *Notes on the State of Virginia*, was convinced that only a liberal religion could offer the most favorable atmosphere for the realization of the democratic millennium.[48]

But most of the natural law doctrines could be viewed in tandem with traditional Christianity. It was on the basis of natural law that Samuel Adams in 1772 wrote to Elbridge Gerry that the colonists should vindicate against the British their "Rights *as Christians* as well as Men and Subjects."[49] Christian writers were accustomed to thinking of "the laws of God and nature" as identical.[50] Certainly the basic idea of natural rights, the social compact theory, and the right of revolution were not viewed as incompatible with biblical faith; knowing this, it was these features of the natural law philosophy that Jefferson highlighted in the

Declaration of Independence. Moreover, the numerous references to God were enough to place the Declaration in an overall theistic framework so as to satisfy virtually anyone who held a theistic worldview. Thus in drafting the Declaration of Independence, Thomas Jefferson and his congressional colleagues seized upon, and indeed helped to further shape, a bond between Enlightenment latitudinarianism and Christian orthodoxy that made it possible to formally dissolve all bonds with Great Britain and at the same time confidently assert "the protection of Divine Providence."

A number of conservative Christian scholars today acknowledge this mixture of Christian and Enlightenment influences on the Declaration. Reconstructionist theologian Gary North, for example, calls it a "Deistic document."[51] He is disappointed that the deity of the Declaration is only "the undefined god of nature" and not the God of Scripture,[52] but he nevertheless finds the Declaration more Christian than the Articles of Confederation, which refers to God once, and the Constitution, which contains no references to God. For North, the Declaration acts as the "incorporating" document for the nation, and the Constitution as its set of bylaws. The Constitution, however, trumps the Declaration and in identifying a new deity, "We the people," becomes nothing more than "an atheistic, humanist covenant."[53]

Gregg Singer, an evangelical scholar, also calls Jefferson's document a "Deist Declaration" but finds the Constitution somewhat more conservative, if not more Christian. The United States, he holds, is a Christian nation whose founding fathers affirmed the relevance of biblical law but left open its application by making no specific references to it in the Constitution.[54]

The status of the Declaration as a Christian or deist document has been much debated. In this author's view, the document is actually neither. The Declaration of Independence was primarily a foreign policy document aimed at England, France, and Europe, although it was also designed to unify those at home. It is written in a theistic framework primarily because Jefferson, his committee, and indeed the Continental Congress at-large understood the colonists' authority to sever their relationship with Britain as resting upon a theistic, natural rights philosophy. Yet this theistic framework also was adopted because it was broad and general enough to capture the theistic framework in which most colonists understood all earthly events to take place. Thus it was neither specifically deistic (scientific worldview) nor Christian (biblical worldview), as either position would have excluded those adherents of the other; as a theistic document, it appealed to both.

## Religious Liberty and the Declaration

In the Declaration's inventory of twenty-eight specific grievances against the king of Great Britain, there is no reference made to religion. Given the pervasiveness of American opposition in the eighteenth century to the possible appointment by the king of an American bishop, why was no complaint concerning British infringements on religious liberty in the colonies registered in the Declaration? The controversy regarding an American bishop was a lively one in the 1760s and early 1770s, and even most American Anglicans did not want a resident bishop. Indeed, the controversy probably consumed as much paper as the Stamp Act dispute and perhaps exceeded it over the long run, since the question of "episcopacy" was debated from about 1700 onward.[55] John Adams would later claim that "the apprehension of Episcopacy" contributed as much as any other cause to the American Revolution, capturing the attention "not only of the inquiring mind, but of the common people. . . . The objection was not merely to the office of a bishop, though even that was dreaded, but to the authority of parliament, on which it must be founded."[56] The real fear in all of this, of course, was a combined church and state in the colonies—the formal establishment of the Church of England throughout colonial America. The possibility was repugnant to almost all Americans.

Then why the omission of a grievance against British threats to religious liberty in the Declaration of Independence? The answer may well be that Congress did not believe that the religious liberty of the nation was seriously endangered. The threat of a nationwide establishment was minimal, given that colonial America had for almost 200 years been a rather diverse band of independent colonies. Great Britain, especially before 1750, dealt with each colony as an independent entity, transacting business, formulating policy, and otherwise generally overseeing each colony without regard to the others. Each colony maintained its own policy on church establishments; in the early seventeenth century, England had been mostly glad to be ridded of Anglican dissenters and therefore gave to each colony considerable leeway in forming its own religious establishments. The only significant period in which England had become active in imposing religious policy was after the passage of the Act of Toleration in 1689, when it sought to enforce greater standards of religious toleration in the colonies, especially in New England, where Congregationalism was so well entrenched. Even then, changes in colonial policy occurred mostly because they were desired locally, not because of British pressure. Generally speaking, then, each colony had the religious affiliation and practices that the majority of its citizens wished.

Therefore, from the standpoint of religious liberty, there was little cause for public grievance against George III.

Most colonial grievances on grounds of religious liberty were in fact lodged against fellow colonists. Baptists and Anglicans in the North and Baptists and Presbyterians in the South, as examples, sought a degree of religious toleration that the established *colonial* governments would not give them. New Light Baptist and Presbyterian itinerants in Virginia defied laws to preach or build church buildings and won increasing sympathy after 1776 from nominal but alienated Anglicans. New Light Baptists and Separates in New England refused to pay taxes or even to turn in the certificates that would have entitled them to tax exemption.[57]

Furthermore, so dominant were the Protestant establishments that Catholics and Jews were legally disenfranchised in most of the colonies. In this respect, English authorities would have had little reason to pressure for change, since persecution of Catholics and Jews had been a longstanding practice in England. Only in Rhode Island, Pennsylvania, and Delaware was there anything approaching full religious liberty.[58] Not embittered by this status, Charles Carroll of Maryland, the only Catholic among fifty-six signers of the Declaration, declared in his later years that he had signed the document to bring about the toleration of all Christians. His sentiments appear in this excerpt from a letter dated 9 October 1827, addressed to John Stanford, a New York Baptist minister:

> I was yesterday favored with your friendly letter of the 10th past, and the discourses on the opening of the House of Refuge and on the death of Jefferson and Adams. The former I have not yet read. With the latter I am highly pleased and I sincerely thank you for your pious wishes for my happiness in the life to come. Your sentiments on religious liberty coincide entirely with mine. To obtain religious, as well as civil liberty, I entered zealously into the Revolution, and observing the Christian religion divided into many sects, I founded the hope that no one would be so predominant as to become the religion of the State. That hope was thus early entertained, because all of them joined in the same cause, with few exceptions of individuals. God grant that this religious liberty may be preserved in these States, to the end of times, and that all believers in the religion of Christ may practice the leading principle of charity, the basis of every virtue.[59]

These factors, then, all pointing to the greater concern over threats to religious liberty arising from within the colonies than from without, make a strong case that the Continental Congress was not sufficiently concerned about British interference with religious liberty in the colonies to warrant its mention in the Declaration.

There remains the possibility that Jefferson and the Congress at-large, by unintentional omission only, neglected to include language in the Declaration specifically complaining of imperial infringement of the colonists' religious liberty. This is not likely, however, since colonial concerns over an Anglican establishment were widespread and familiar to members of the Continental Congress. It may be that while the concerns over an Anglican bishop and its repercussions for America were genuine, Jefferson and Congress believed that since the king had not formally appointed a bishop, any specific complaint of interference with the colonies' right to govern themselves regarding religion was premature. There may also have been real concerns about imperial efforts to enforce the British Act of Toleration in the colonies, but it would hardly have made sense to complain in the Declaration of British violations of religious liberty that were in fact only efforts to enhance religious liberty by forcing colonial establishments to further their tolerance of dissenting sects. Thus, to sum up, it is probably best to understand the omission in the Declaration as intentional, based on the lack of any realized British threat to religious liberty in the colonies. On this interpretation, Congress was sophisticated enough in its analysis of the problem to set aside as overstated the popular perception that Britain intended to stamp out religious liberty in the colonies.

### Concluding Remarks: The Declaration in Modern Context

What place does the Declaration of Independence have in modern political discourse? Is it a basis for the formulation of law and public policy? Are its principles still binding? Are its themes preserved in the Constitution? Does it aid in interpreting the religion clauses? What does it contribute to the debate over original intent?

The first thing that can clearly be stated about the Declaration is that it is not law. That is, none of its provisions can be law unless enacted into law. The Declaration is inspiring, but its most inspirational parts today remain in the realm of politics, not law. It mostly represents a ringing statement of political philosophy from a past age. The Declaration did not purport to create a new government or to enact any new laws. The bulk of it is exactly what it claimed to be: an announcement to the world of American reasons for renouncing its ties to Great Britain. New governments and new laws were created later—in state constitutions and the Articles of Confederation.

The present Constitution depends on the Declaration's theory that the people are empowered to alter their form of government. The Constitution was not ratified under the procedures for amending the Articles of Confederation but instead by a new and independent act of the American people. The people today could again abandon their Constitution and adopt an entirely new one. They need not use the Constitution's amendment procedures unless they wish to leave the present Constitution in effect.[60]

Constitutional interpretation is aided little by the Declaration. The thirteen years between the adoption of the Declaration and the ratification of the Constitution was a period of intense political change. The Declaration's loose, free-wheeling philosophy of the people's "rights," preserved to a large degree in the Articles of Confederation, gradually gave way to the Constitution's more structured framework that was necessary to support a strong national government. If today we find tensions between the Declaration and the Constitution, it is mostly because new views had come to prevail. Throughout the debates of the Convention, there was virtually no discussion of Nature's God, natural rights, or consent of the governed. As Roger Sherman understood it, the question was "not what rights naturally belong to man, but how they may be most equally and effectually guarded in society."[61] The Declaration cannot change the meaning of the Constitution; at most it can make proposed interpretations seem more or less plausible.[62]

The Declaration might be helpful in construing the Ninth Amendment, which provides, "The enumeration in the Constitution, of certain rights, shall not be construed to deny or disparage others retained by the people." Though it is largely ignored in modern constitutional adjudication, this clause writes the Declaration's philosophy of unalienable natural law rights into positive law. The Declaration is too broadly written, however, to be of much help in defining the content of these unenumerated rights.

What should be made of the Declaration's repeated references to God? Does the Declaration found the American political system on the belief that rights come from God? Does it mean that our governments are also theistic and free to act on their belief in God by erecting religious symbols on public property or requiring prayer in public schools? Probably not, on all of the aforementioned counts, for reasons having to do more with the Constitution than the Declaration. It is important to remember that the Declaration only severed the colonies from Britain; it did not establish a new government. The Articles of Confederation did, but that charter, which contained one reference to God, was replaced by the Constitution, which contained none. It is probably best to read the religion clauses as leaving religion wholly to the states and to the people. The Constitution expresses a disassociation from any competence concerning religion, leaving it to the people and, to the extent they wished to exercise some jurisdiction over religion, to the states.

There is, of course, contrary evidence. The references to God in the Declaration and the Articles of Confederation, as well as the religiosity associated with much of the work of the Continental Congress, are part of this contrary evidence, much like post-Constitution presidential thanksgiving proclamations and congressional chaplains. But these evidences do not necessarily override other arguments about the meaning of the religion clauses. The original intentions of those who drafted the Constitution—the ascertainment of which is the primary goal of this study—should not be grounded primarily in this contrary evidence. Once again, the transitional character of the founding era must be considered. Traditional Western political theory, in which religion was thought to be central to a well-ordered polity, was on the decline and essentially rejected by the Constitution. This accounts for the Constitution's lack of any reference to God. This omission, as further explained in chapter 11, in no way suggests that the framers' were irreligious; in fact, they were, perhaps to the man, profoundly religious. Nor does it suggest that the framers did not acknowledge God's sovereignty over all human affairs, including political ordering; it posits only that they saw God's oversight in the realm of a somewhat distant Providence in which the details of a well-ordered polity are the work of man, not God.

Also, the disestablishment movement was well under way, from 1774 to 1789, marked by the view that human government should, as much as possible, leave religion to the individual. Post-Constitution acts like presidential thanksgiving proclamations and legislative chaplaincies, however, reflect the practical impossibility of achieving this end entirely.

Finally, as already noted, the Declaration was not a document written to specifically address issues such as government neutrality toward, or accommodation of, religion. However, as Douglas Laycock has noted, it is not clear that the Declaration taken as a whole is at odds with government neutrality toward religion. "We hold these truths to be self-evident" is the secular argument for natural rights law; that individuals are "endowed by their Creator with certain unalienable rights" is the religious argument. The Declaration involves "the Laws of Nature" as well as the laws of "Nature's God." Just as the religion clauses call for people of all religious faiths or of none to live compatibly in civil society, so the argument of the Declaration appeals to both religious and secular audiences, as Jefferson intended. The Declaration prefigures both the religious neutrality of the religion clauses and the political reality that most Americans are religious.[63]

To conclude this chapter, a final note concerning the context of the Declaration should be offered. The Declaration is by no means primarily a religious document, or even a philosophical one. It was mainly intended as an appeal to public opinion—an attempt to draw favorable attention to the revolutionary cause—among the French, among colonial sympathizers in Britain, and even among waverers in the colonies. Treason is at best an ominous business, and the Continental Congress was determined that Great Britain and not the revolting colonies should stand condemned before the bar of world public opinion.[64]

But the Declaration is a masterpiece of political literature for the primary reason that it succinctly expresses political ideas widely accepted in 1776. These political ideas embodied an eighteenth-century philosophy of natural rights arising out of a philosophy of natural law that reached back to antiquity. Moreover, this philosophy was stated in a compelling theological framework, assuring those who would fight and even die for the cause of independence that their efforts were looked upon with favor from heaven.

*Seven*

# RELIGION AND FEDERALISM DURING
# THE CONFEDERATION PERIOD

Issues of federalism, that is, matters related to the distribution of powers between the federal government and the states, did not originate with the Constitution. The Continental Congress, the first representative body of the American colonies, frequently found itself enmeshed in considerations of the degree of its own sovereignty in relation to that of the colonies and later the states. Congress's authority on matters such as interstate trade and commerce, settlement of boundary disputes between states, and foreign affairs was not easily wrested from the states. Federalism affected virtually every area of government. The subject of this chapter is how federalism influenced the formation of the Continental Congress's policies regarding religion. The focus will be upon identifying those policies adopted for distinguishing a federal matter from a state matter, and how those policies affected the provisions concerning religion that were written into the Constitution.

Claude Van Tyne, in an important article published early this century, listed a formidable array of commentators who have considered that in the relationship between the Continental Congress and the states, the Continental Congress was sovereign.[1] Modern scholars have tended to go the other way, arguing that the states, not the Continental Congress, were sovereign.[2] The older school has lost favor, because it tended too much to adhere to, and to apply retroactively to the entire confederation period, Federalist arguments of the mid-1780s that a new Constitution was needed to broaden the authority possessed by the Continental Congress under the Articles of Confederation. The older school therefore erroneously read the entire confederation period as a time of rule by a strong Continental Congress that needed to be stronger. The commission of this error minimizes the independent and sovereign status of the states before the adoption of the Constitution, a status that indeed was the principal reason for the convening of a Constitutional Convention. It is now widely accepted that the Federalists pictured the confederation period as one of chaos, born solely of the existing form of government. Through the *Federalist Papers* and other advocacy efforts, the Federalists were able to persuade the American people of the wisdom of the new Constitution, which expanded considerably on the powers given to the central government. But the need for greater national sovereignty only became evident by the mid-1780s. To impress upon the period of 1774 to 1787 the notion that the sovereignty of the Continental Congress was superior to that of the colonies/states, as some have sought to do, is indeed a misreading if not a revisionism of the worst kind.

The sovereign status of the several colonies/states from 1774 to 1787 vis-à-vis the Continental Congress can readily be established by reference to a number of factors. To begin with, as Raoul Berger has pointed out, the term "congress" arose only in the seventeenth century and referred generally to a conference for the discussion or settlement of some question. The Continental Congress, says Berger, as a meeting of the representatives of sovereign states, was properly a "congress" in this sense.[3] Van Tyne observed that Congress "was never forgetful that the member was there in the capacity of a diplomat from a foreign state."[4] Justifiably, Merrill Jensen concludes that "the delegates to the first Continental Congress came as ambassadors of twelve [Georgia sent no representative until later] distinct nations."[5]

That the states considered their sovereignty superior to that of the Continental Congress is further validated by the ways in which they were separated by vast distances; the mere geographical distances between many of the colonies and Philadelphia, the seat of Congress, made it impractical for such colonies to give over to Congress a comprehensive governmental sovereignty. As Berger appropriately reminds us, "The taming of the continent's vast distances by modern technology makes it difficult today to appreciate how the primeval wilderness appeared to the colonists."[6] Of Georgia and Carolina, it has been said that "a delegate to the Congress . . . obliged to travel 700 or 800 miles . . . could scarcely have entered upon the duties of his appointment, before the year would be past."[7] When William Houston was sent from Georgia to the Continental Congress in 1785, he "thought of himself as leaving his 'country' to go to 'a strange land amongst strangers.' "[8] In South Carolina, James Lincoln declaimed that adoption of the Constitution meant the surrender of self-government "into the hands of a set of men who live one thousand miles distant from you."[9]

Moreover, while the Declaration of Independence was titled "The Unanimous Declaration of the Thirteen United States of America," implying the collectivity and union of the states, the Declaration's final paragraph asserts "that these united colonies are . . . free and independent states" and then declares the new powers derived—"power to levy war, conclude peace, contract alliances, establish commerce" and the like—to be claimed not for the union, but for the "independent states." This squares with the view of the Declaration of Justice Samuel Chase, formerly a member of the Continental Congress, as he expressed it in 1796:

> I consider this a declaration, not that the united colonies jointly, in a collective capacity, were independent states, &c. but that each of them was a sovereign and independent state, that is, that each of them had a right to govern itself by its own authority and its own laws, without any control from any other power on earth.[10]

The resolution proffered to Congress on 7 June 1776 by Richard Henry Lee regarding a plan of confederation also supports the view that the states were sovereign. Lee moved "that these United Colonies are . . . free and independent states. That a plan of confederation be prepared and transmitted to the respective colonies for their consideration and approbation."[11] Note that the "United Colonies" were not declared to be a "United States," but rather "independent states," a result that Merrill Jensen ascribes to the instructions delegates had received from their states.[12]

When the Continental Congress agreed on 15 November 1777 to recommend the Articles of Confederation to the states, it made the independent sovereignty of the states emphatically plain. As "delegates of the States affixed to our Names," the members provided in Article II that "each state retains its sovereignty, freedom and independence, and every Power . . . which is not by this confederation expressly delegated . . . to the United States, in Congress assembled." In logical sequence, Article III provided that "the said states hereby severally enter into a firm league of friendship with each other for their common defence." The drafters then recited that they acted "in the name and in behalf of our respective constituents," not the aggregate people of the United States, and proceeded to sign "on the part and behalf of the State of New Hampshire," and in like fashion for each of the remaining twelve states.

In view of these facts, it is difficult to disagree with the assessment of John Jay, secretary of foreign affairs to the Continental Congress in

1786, that "the thirteen independent sovereign states . . . [had], by express delegation of power, formed and vested in Congress a perfect
though limited sovereignty for the general and national purposes specified in the Confederation."[13] Whatever new limitations on state sovereignty were legalized upon ratification of the Constitution, the unmistakable conclusion is that the states under the Articles of Confederation
had a superior sovereignty to that of the Continental Congress.[14]

In matters of religion, it was therefore natural for the Continental
Congress to assume a limitation upon Congress's sovereignty and to acknowledge the authority of the states. From the time of its first convening the Continental Congress adopted a policy of noninterference with
the states in matters of religion. Most of the delegates had specific instructions from their own state assemblies to prohibit Congress's interference in state matters, including matters of religion. Rhode Island's
instructions to its delegates in 1776 were typical: "You are to take the
greatest care to secure to the Colony in the strongest and most perfect
manner its present form and all of the powers of government so far as
relates to the internal police and government of our own affairs, civil
and religious."[15] This policy of deference applied, however, to only those
matters in which congressional involvement would clearly invade the
states' liberty. Thus, for example, Congress forbade itself from giving
edicts or even advice to the states on questions concerning the taxation
of individuals for the support of established churches. Such matters were
uniformly thought to be off limits; the states would have it no other
way.

Under some circumstances, no infringements of state liberty were at
issue. In these instances, Congress felt free to act. For instance, Congress's
appointment of its own chaplain was in no way interpreted by the states
as an intrusion on their own jurisdictional privileges; after all, a chaplain
only aided the work of Congress. Likewise, Congress's collective attendance at Catholic mass or its issuance of proclamations for national days
of fasting and thanksgiving were never interpreted as encroachments on
the states' reserved jurisdiction over religion. As noted earlier, utterances
by a small segment of congressional delegates expressing dissatisfaction
with Congress's religious approach to its work occurred occasionally, but
these objections were only mild complaints about mixing religion and
politics and had nothing to do with questions concerning state versus
federal jurisdiction.

This chapter highlights a number of religious questions over which
the Continental Congress, as opposed to the states, exercised jurisdiction.
In some cases, its jurisdictional authority was evident, but in other cases
it was far from clear. One domain considered by Congress to be under

the inviolable jurisdiction of the colonies/states was religious taxes. Thus, it will be seen that when the prominent Baptist Isaac Backus arrived in Philadelphia in October 1774 to plead before Congress the cause of New England Baptists imprisoned for failure to pay religious taxes for conscience sake, he was unable to get a hearing, since Congress had no authority to deal with the question.

One obvious area of federal jurisdiction was foreign relations. The Continental Congress, even before it officially commenced operating under the authority of the Articles of Confederation, assumed the responsibility of acting for the united colonies/states on religious questions that arose in connection with its dealings with foreign nations. It will be shown in a later chapter that Congress assumed the right to address issues of religious liberty in entering into treaties with other countries. On at least one occasion, however, Congress decided that a foreign policy matter should be dealt with by the states. Thus, as discussed later in this chapter, when a French papal representative sought permission from the Continental Congress to appoint a papal representative for American Catholics, Congress replied that it was required to defer to the states regarding such matters.

The war also gave rise to situations in which Congress and the states, because of the inherent difficulty of the religious questions at issue, each sought to defer to one another. This was particularly the case, as this chapter will show, when it came to resolving the problem of what to do with a group of American pacifists who were mistakenly thought to be aiding the British war effort.

All of these situations were complicated and were made even more complex by the presence of an emerging system of federalism yet ill-defined in its particulars. The discussion that follows will demonstrate that the uncertainties of an emerging federalism at times caused unfortunate delays of needed action as well as unwarranted injustices against religious minorities. In the end, however, these complications proved fortuitous since they sharply raised the level of consciousness in the young nation about the meaning of religious liberty.

## The Resolutions of Congress Regarding the Appointment of an American Catholic Bishop

No sooner was peace with Great Britain established in 1783 than the Continental Congress was forced to take a stand on religious questions affecting foreign relations. A crisis in American-papal relations arose on 28 July 1783, when the papal nuncio in Paris delivered a note of inquiry to Benjamin Franklin, the U.S. minister to France. The note explained

the pope's desire to appoint a French official to oversee American Catholicism and requested Congress's approval. The note, in part, read:

> Note . . . as it is necessary that the Catholic Christians of the United States
> should have an ecclesiastic to govern them in matters pertaining to reli-
> gion, the *Congregation de Propaganda Fide*, existing at Rome, for the es-
> tablishment and preservation of missions, have come to the determination
> to propose to Congress to establish, in one of the cities of the United States
> of North America, one of their Catholic brethren, with the authority and
> power of Vicar-Apostolic and dignity of Bishop, or simply with the rank
> of Apostolic Prefect. The institution of a Bishop-Apostolic appears the
> most suitable, inasmuch as the Catholics of the United States may have
> within their reach the reception of Confirmation and Orders in their own
> country. And as it may sometimes happen that among the members of the
> Catholic body in the United States, no one may be found qualified to
> undertake the charge of the spiritual government, either as Bishop or
> Prefect-Apostolic, it may be necessary under the circumstances, that Con-
> gress should consent to have one selected from some foreign nation on
> close terms of friendship with the United States.[16]

According to this note, the Congress was being asked to sanction the
manner of governance of Roman Catholicism in the United States. At first
blush, the plan proposed by the papal legate seems rather innocuous.
After all, it only involved replacing the vicar-apostolic in London, who
had previously represented American Catholics in Rome, with a new
representative from France. Eventually, the note explained, an American
ecclesiastic with a more elevated rank of bishop or apostolic prefect
would be appointed to represent American interests, but that likely
seemed to Franklin a rather natural progression.

Dr. Franklin seems to have been willing initially to lend his support
to the plan, but without the involvement of the Continental Congress.
Here are Franklin's own observations on the matter as transmitted to the
French papal nuncio:

> Mr. Franklin, after reading the note of M. the Nuncio and reflecting upon
> it maturely, believes that it would be absolutely useless to send it to the
> congress, which, according to its powers and its constitutions, can not,
> and should not, in any case, intervene in the ecclesiastical affairs of any
> sect or of any religion established in America. Each particular State has
> reserved to itself by its own constitutions the right to protect its members,
> to tolerate their religious opinions, and not to interfere with the matter,
> as long as they do not disturb civil order.
>
> Mr. Franklin is therefore of opinion that the Court of Rome may take,
> of its own initiative, all the measures that may be useful to the Catholics
> of America, without disregard to the constitutions, and that Congress will

not fail to give its tacit approval to the choice that the Court of Rome, in concert with the minister of the United States, may make of a French ecclesiastic, who, residing in France, may regulate the spiritual affairs of the Catholics who live, or who may come to establish themselves, in those States, through a suffragan residing in America.

Besides many political reasons that may make that arrangement desirable, M. the Apostolic Nuncio must find in it many others that may be favorable to the intentions of the Court of Rome.[17]

Franklin thus from the beginning did not consider that the papal nuncio needed to seek the approval of Congress; he understood such a power to be vested exclusively in the several states. To further impress this point of state autonomy on the nuncio, he sent to the nuncio an additional note in which he pointed out that "in the greater number of the colonies, there is no endowment, no fixed revenue, for the support of a clergy of whatever denomination; legislation, viewing this subject from the standpoint of a more general freedom, has been unwilling to make a public charge of a tax that should be only voluntary and private."[18]

On 13 September Franklin decided that it might after all be prudent to communicate the nuncio's request to the Continental Congress. The leading Catholic in the United States, John Carroll, heard rumors of the plan for a French bishop-apostolic to represent American interests in Rome, and on 26 September he wrote to an English friend, Charles Plowden, that "a foreign temporal jurisdiction will never be tolerated here; and even the spiritual supremacy of the Pope is the only reason why in some of the United States the full participation of all civil rights is not granted to the Roman Catholics. They may therefore send their agents when they please; they will certainly return empty-handed."[19]

The first official indication of the attitude of Congress appeared in a communication from the French papal nuncio, Chevalier de la Luzerne, to the French prime minister, the Count Charles de Vergennes, dated 31 January 1784:

Monseigneur the Apostolic Nuncio has made some propositions in the name of His Holiness to Doctor Franklin in regard to the sending of a bishop, or vicar-apostolic, whom the Holy Father desires to place over the Roman Catholic churches of this continent. The Congress has respectfully welcomed that overture; it has been unable, however, to take action in this matter, which is not of the competency of Congress. It is a matter that concerns the Catholics alone; and the delegates who have spoken to me on the subject have assured me that a Catholic bishop would be very well received in the state of Pennsylvania, and much more so in Maryland, where there are many Catholics, providing the prelate carefully avoided to assume any temporal jurisdiction or authority. The congress, in general, would be pleased at the residence of a prelate, who by conferring the sacrament of Holy Orders on the priests of these parts, would relieve them of the necessity of receiving it in London or in Quebec, as has been done in the past. Some of the delegates even believed that a Catholic bishop would not refuse to confer Holy Orders on the Anglican ministers of America, who, until now, have been obliged to procure their ordination at London; but this practice does not seem to me to be compatible with the profession that those who receive Holy Orders must make, or with the examination that they must undergo. The state Legislatures and Congress refrain from entangling themselves with religious matters.[20]

The last sentence of the nuncio's statement appears to represent, based on his understanding of the opinion of the Continental Congress, his view that the appointment of a Catholic bishop in America was strictly a religious matter, and that neither Congress nor any of the states, as temporal bodies, could therefore interfere or in any way assume jurisdiction over the issue. This seems to contradict Franklin's view set forth in his previous letter to the papal nuncio that the states, but not Congress, could lawfully pass upon the issue (see note 17), but Congress held solidly to the view that this was a matter of state jurisdiction, as appears from the following resolution of Congress in May 1784:

> Resolved, That Doctor Franklin be desired to notify to the Apostolic Nuncio at Versaille, that Congress will always be pleased to testify their respect to his sovereign and state; but that the subject of his application to Doctor Franklin, being purely spiritual, it is without the jurisdiction and powers of Congress, who have no authority to permit or refuse it, these powers being reserved to the several states individually.[21]

In this resolution, then, the Continental Congress expanded its policy of noninterference with the states on official matters of religion to include matters of foreign as well as domestic relations. That it happened to be an issue of foreign policy was likely insignificant; the position of Congress turned on the fact that the issue was preeminently a religious one, and if any temporal body was to assume jurisdiction, it must be one of the states. It should, of course, be mentioned that Congress's attitude had nothing to do with any bias against the Catholic faith; it represented only a resolute determination to keep church and state separate at the federal level.

Although Congress recommended that Catholic officials consult the states on the matter, in fact they declined to consult any of the states. Pope Pius VI proceeded to appoint a prefect apostolic for the United States in 1784—not a Frenchman as originally planned, but an American,

Father John Carroll.[22] In 1790 Carroll was consecrated as the first American bishop, and in that same year, to advance the cause of American Catholicism and to respond to anti-Catholic attacks, he published a notable work, *An Address to the Catholics of the United States*.[23] In the *Address*, Carroll strongly supported the American principle of religious liberty, praising the way in which it enabled American Catholics to freely exercise their faith without fear of governmental repression.

## Baptist Pleas to Congress for Religious Liberty

Barely before members of the First Continental Congress had the opportunity to become mutually acquainted, a delegation sent by New England Baptists arrived in Philadelphia in October 1774 to appeal to the Congress for assistance in securing relief from religious taxes. This delegation was officially commissioned by the Warren Baptist Association of Massachusetts and was headed by Isaac Backus, a Baptist minister from Middleborough, Massachusetts. A brief description of the background to the delegation's visit to Philadelphia is essential to an understanding of the purpose and outcome of the Baptists' mission.

During and after the Great Awakening in Massachusetts, New Hampshire, and Connecticut, so many Congregationalists became Baptists that George Whitefield is reported to have said upon a return trip to the American colonies: "Behold all my chickens have become ducks."[24] Many of these converts, including Backus, objected to being required to pay taxes to support the established Congregational church. Massachusetts had an exemption law designed to exempt Baptists from the tax, but the law was so complex that compliance was virtually impossible. Even when Baptists succeeded in securing the required exemption certificates, local authorities often refused to recognize their validity and proceeded to seize land belonging to individuals, and on several occasions many were jailed. Certificates of exemption, moreover, required the payment of fourpence in paper currency, so the Baptists complained that they were not really exempt. They also objected that only a few specified denominations, including Baptists, were exempt and that this was unfair to the nonexempted denominations.[25]

In view of this state of affairs, Backus became an active writer on religious liberty and a frequent lobbyist before the Massachusetts legislature. As the most profound American thinker of his day in regard to church-state relations and religious liberty, Backus drew upon Roger Williams and John Locke and wrote several voluminous works, the most important being *A History of New England with Particular Reference to the Denomination of Christians Called Baptists*, which was published in three volumes (1777, 1784, 1796). The thrust of his argument was that the exemption laws were against the law of God, since the government had assumed the right to determine those whom it would tolerate and at what price and those who were entitled to exemptions.[26]

The efforts of Backus and others, however, brought about little change in the Massachusetts laws. Thus in 1774 the Warren Association (consisting of twenty-one Baptist churches) decided that it would appeal to the newly created Continental Congress for possible redress. Backus accepted the Association's request that he be their spokesman at Philadelphia. Backus later offered an explanation for the decision to petition Congress: "[Since] it appeared likely that in the future they [Congress] would be our highest resort as to civil power, many judged that it was expedient for us to endeavor to procure some influence from them in our favor. For it was most evident that our former sufferings would have been much greater than they were, if the ruling party here had not been restrained by a higher power."[27] In short, because they were no longer able in 1774 to appeal to the British "higher power," the King's Council, the Baptists turned to the new "higher power" as a check on their suppressors. As McLoughlin notes, in this respect the Baptists were not advocates of "states' rights" in 1774. They were eager to transfer to the Congress the same authority over the colonies that the British had possessed for the securing of basic rights. This kind of thinking was not unusual.[28] As Peter Onuf has reminded us, the "American people were accustomed to monarchy, and it was easy to imagine Congress as successor to George III."[29] If the Congress had defended the minority rights of the Baptists in 1774, it might have set a useful precedent and stemmed the tide of antifederalism in later years. By 1787 the Baptists were strongly antifederalist.[30]

Upon arriving in Philadelphia on 8 October 1774, the Baptist delegation was approached by three leading Philadelphia Quakers—Israel Pemberton, James Pemberton, and Joseph Fox—who sought to be helpful in the Baptists' cause. The Quakers advised Backus and his delegation "not to address the Congress as a body at present, but to seek for a conference with the Massachusetts delegates, together with some others who were known to be friends to religious liberty."[31] This suggestion was adopted and perhaps it was a good one, for possibly it would have embarrassed the Massachusetts delegates to be upbraided for intolerance in front of all the other delegates. But as it turned out, they might have had nothing to lose by addressing the whole Congress and might have even gained from the pressure it would have put on the Massachusetts delegates and from the increased publicity of their grievances.

A meeting was arranged for Friday night, 14 October, in Carpenter's Hall, the meeting place of the Continental Congress. Attending were the four members of the Baptist delegation, the four Massachusetts delegates (John Adams, Samuel Adams, Robert Treat Paine, and Thomas Cushing), five other members of Congress, and about fifteen other Baptists and Quakers. A memorial prepared by Backus was read to open the discussion. It summarized the tax exemption acts and described some of the oppressions committed under them. It included excerpts from "the great Mr. Locke" intended to prove that the magistrates' power did not extend to spiritual affairs, thus supporting the argument that the Baptists were in effect being taxed without representation by being forced to support a religious system that was established by civil authority and that they could not for conscience sake adhere to.[32]

According to Backus's diary, the response was that "John Adams made a long speech, and Samuel Adams another, both of whom said, 'There is indeed an ecclesiastical establishment in our province; but a very slender one, hardly to be called an establishment.' And they exerted all their art for near an hour in trying to represent that we had no cause to complain of encroachments upon our religious liberties at all. As soon as they would permit we brought up facts to the contrary which they tried to take off the edge of, but could not."[33]

The meeting lasted several hours and, as Backus noted, ended with "their promising to do what they could for our relief."[34] No relief was forthcoming, however. John Adams and Robert Paine looked upon the whole affair as only an attempt to disrupt colonial unity and to break up the Continental Congress by introducing extraneous and contentious issues.[35] When Backus returned to Middleborough in November, he found that Paine had already spread the view that the Baptists and Quakers had been employed in Philadelphia by enemies of the American cause to divide the country in its time of danger.[36]

The petitions of the Baptists were never considered by the Continental Congress acting as a body. Had Congress considered the matter, it likely would have recommended to Backus that he resume his struggles at the local level on account of a lack of authority of Congress to deal with religious disputes. This is in fact what occurred: Backus and other Baptists continued to pursue their cause before the Massachusetts legislature. It was not until 1833, however, twenty-seven years after Backus's death, that taxation in Massachusetts for the support of Congregational churches was discontinued. Moreover, Backus's trip to Philadelphia, his first trip out of New England, helped to expose the plight of Massachusetts Baptists to other areas of America. Eventually the Baptists in the

South were able to find champions of their cause among members of the ruling elite (like Jefferson, Madison, and Mason) who would help them. The Baptists in Massachusetts, and most of the New England region for that matter, never had such assistance from any of the ruling elite of New England.[37]

### Congress and Wartime Dissidents

Religious pacifists were unpopular with most Americans during the Revolutionary War. Quakers, Moravians, and others not only were mistreated for their unwillingness to bear arms, but also were frequently falsely accused of being informants and traitors against the American cause. In 1777 a group of Pennsylvania Quakers were made to undergo an especially rancorous episode of religious persecution perpetrated against them by not only the State of Pennsylvania, but the Continental Congress as well. While the episode clearly qualifies, in the words of one of the Quakers involved, as a poor example of "the principles of justice and liberty then advocated for the nation,"[38] it is cited here in a different context—as an example of conflicts over religious matters that arose between states and the national government that, however unfortunate, were probably inevitable in a yet new, undeveloped federal system.

According to eighteenth-century Quaker Thomas Gilpin's autobiographical account, in 1777 repeated accusations against a number of Pennsylvania Quakers, later to be proven false, developed into a national scandal. Pennsylvania law authorized law enforcement officials to "disarm and secure" all persons "notoriously disaffected" to the "common cause" (the Revolutionary War) and to search such persons' homes for "firearms, swords, bayonets, etc."[39] Several sworn documents surfaced in which certain Quakers were accused of being "disaffected to the American cause" and acting to "communicate intelligence to the enemy, and, in various other ways, injured the counsels and arms of America."[40] At about the same time, General John Sullivan discovered and presented to the Continental Congress a letter supposedly written by certain Pennsylvania Quakers to General Howe of the British Army, wherein the general was given valuable wartime information about various plans of the Continental Army.

When the sworn documents and the letter from General Sullivan were presented to Congress as proof of the threat these Quakers posed to the American war effort, Congress, on the recommendation of a committee consisting of John Adams, Richard Henry Lee, and John Drew, resolved that the Pennsylvania Supreme Executive Council (thirteen key members of the Pennsylvania legislative) should carry out the required punishment, which Congress recommended should be, pursuant to Pennsylvania law, imprisonment of the accused Quakers and seizure of all personal papers that might relate to their guilt.[41]

The Pennsylvania Executive Council, acting on this suggestion from Congress, promptly apprehended forty alleged informants for incarceration. Believing that American interests would be better served if the prisoners were secured in Virginia, further removed from British troops, Pennsylvania officials wrote Congress asking for its suggestion of a suitable location in Virginia. Congress in turn, on 3 September 1777, recommended Staunton, Virginia, as an ideal place for confinement.[42]

The affected Quakers filed a written protest with the Continental Congress, which was taken into consideration on 6 September 1777. Congress must have already been aware that it had acted precipitously, for it passed on that day this resolution: "That it be recommended to the Supreme Executive Council of the State of Pennsylvania, to hear what the said remonstrants can allege, to remove the suspicion of their being disaffected or dangerous to the United States, and act therein as the said Council judge most conducive to the public safety."[43] Although the arrest of the Quakers by Pennsylvania officials had been encouraged by Congress, the Congress now sought to shift responsibility for further investigation of the original charges to the State of Pennsylvania. Two days later Congress decided to take firmer action to transfer the matter to Pennsylvania:

> Resolved, That it would be improper for Congress to entertain any hearing of the remonstrants or the other prisoners in the Lodge, they being inhabitants of Pennsylvania; and, therefore, as the Council declines giving them a hearing, for the reasons assigned in their letter to Congress, that it be recommended to the said Council to order the immediate departure of such of the said prisoners as yet refuse to swear or affirm allegiance to the State of Pennsylvania, to Staunton in Virginia.[44]

While Congress might appropriately have assumed jurisdiction over the case as a war matter, it decided instead to steer clear of direct involvement as far as possible. Still, urgent and numerous appeals and protests were filed by the Quakers with the Continental Congress in the hope that it might use its influence on the Pennsylvania Council to absolve the Quakers, but to no avail. Without trial, and under conditions of considerable harshness, a large number of Quakers were imprisoned by Pennsylvania officials. One protest, signed by 113 Friends, addressed "To the President and Council of Pennsylvania," dated 9 September 1777,

characterized the proceedings against the Quakers as "an alarming violation of the civil and religious rights of the community" and set forth
the following additional charges:

> The remonstrance and protest of the subscribers, herewith; That your
> resolve of this day was this afternoon delivered to us; which is the more
> unexpected, as last evening your secretary informed us, you had referred
> our business to Congress, to whom we are about to apply.
>
> In this resolve, contrary to the inherent rights of mankind, you con-
> demn us to banishment unheard.
>
> You determine matters concerning us, which we could have disproved,
> had our rights to a hearing been granted.
>
> The charge against us, of refusing "to promise to refrain from corre-
> sponding with the enemy," insinuates that we have already held such
> correspondence, which we utterly and solemnly deny.
>
> The tests you proposed, we were by no law bound to subscribe, and
> notwithstanding our refusing them, we are still justly and lawfully enti-
> tled to all the rights of citizenship of which you are attempting to deprive
> us.
>
> We have never been suffered to come before you to evince our inno-
> cence, and to remove suspicions, which you have labored to instill into
> the minds of others; and at the same time knew to be groundless; although
> Congress recommended you to give us a hearing,[45] and your president
> assured two of our friends this morning we should have it.
>
> Upon the whole, your proceedings have been so arbitrary, that words
> are wanting to express our sense of them. We do therefore, as the last
> office we expect you will now suffer us to perform for the benefit of our
> country, in behalf of ourselves and those freemen of Pennsylvania who
> have any regard for liberty, solemnly remonstrate and protest against your
> whole conduct in this unreasonable excess of power exercised by you.
>
> That the evil and destructive spirit of pride, ambition, and arbitrary
> power with which you have been actuated, may cease and be no more;
> and "that peace on earth and good will to men," may happily take the
> place thereof, in your and all men's minds, is the sincere desire of your
> oppressed and injured fellow citizens.[46]

The prisoners, on 11 September, were sent to Staunton, Virginia. After
receiving still more written protests, Congress was growing less and less
proud of its role in the proceedings and soon acted to cover its part in
the matter. On 29 January 1778 Congress passed a resolution for the
discharge of the prisoners on their taking an oath of allegiance to the
State of Pennsylvania as a free and independent state.[47] Being opposed
to oaths on religious grounds, this the imprisoned Quakers declined to
do, even though many of their number were badly suffering from sick-

ness caused by winter exposure. Congress then resolved on 16 March 1778 to place the prisoners at the disposal of the Council of Pennsylvania.[48] The Council decided to set them free, provided "that the whole expense of arresting and confining the prisoners sent to Virginia, the expenses of the journey, and all other incidental charges, be paid by the said prisoners."[49] The prisoners agreed to these conditions and at last were brought back to Pennsylvania and discharged. Two of the prisoners, however, including one of Pennsylvania's leading Quakers, Israel Pemberton, had died while in confinement.

Several years later the Quakers were able to prove that the documents and letter to General Howe upon which the original accusations against them had been made were indeed forgeries. Thus they not only cleared their names but vindicated their principles as well.[50] The episode helped to impress upon Americans the loyalty of the Quakers to the nation, but more important it helped define the meaning of religious liberty in a country where liberty supposedly meant everything. Specifically, the meaning of religious liberty was expanded to embrace the right to wartime exemption from military service (without the requirement for substitute service) for those who might conscientiously object on religious grounds; rarely in the future would disloyalty to the nation be presumed against religious minorities.

The episode also helped expose a weakness in the newly emerging federal system of government—the tendency of one party in the system to deflect difficult problems to another. The State of Pennsylvania saw the problem as a "war" matter and therefore sought to shift responsibility to Congress as the party overseeing the war effort. Congress, however, saw the problem as a "religious" matter involving the violation of state law and therefore wanted Pennsylvania to assume responsibility. The whole matter was of course exacerbated by wartime hysteria, but had jurisdictional lines been more clearly marked, either Congress or the State of Pennsylvania, whichever party upon which responsibility devolved, would perhaps have undertaken with greater seriousness its duty to resolve the problem with greater attention to fairness and justice.

This is not to suggest, of course, that a jurisdictional controversy such as the one here described is ever easily resolvable—even today. Federalism remains a governmental arrangement allowing for dual sovereignty between the states and the federal government. The Quaker controversy, if duplicated today, would likely produce many of the same disputes about location of responsibility that it produced more than two centuries ago. The differences today would be the constitutional questions raised under both federal and state constitutions and the opportunities for immediate redress for the aggrieved Quakers in a system of multiple legal forums at least arguably sensitized to violations of religious liberty by more than 200 years of experience.

## Concluding Remarks

What concluding observations can be made from the data discussed in this chapter? To begin with, it is apparent that problems associated with federalism in the confederation period produced some interesting results in matters of religion. On the one hand, Congress from the beginning established a policy of deferring to the states on religious matters that had traditionally been handled by the states. Thus the rights of states to tax for the support of specific churches, to require religious tests for holding public office, or to legislate Christian morals were not interfered with. On the other hand, Congress did not hesitate to engage itself in a religious matter if it was one in which the states had not traditionally assumed jurisdiction. Thus, for example, because Congress was responsible for prosecuting the war effort, it did not hesitate to proclaim colonial fast days and encourage American citizens toward right living—all to commend the nation to God's favor during a difficult war with an uncertain outcome. Between these two settled realms of jurisdiction, however, lay a region of shared, if not disputed, jurisdiction created by the nation's emerging system of dual sovereignty. The episode in which Congress and the State of Pennsylvania each sought to defer to the other in the punishment of Quaker war dissidents fits squarely within this region.

In what ways did these policies influence the treatment of the relation of religion and government under the Constitution and Bill of Rights? In other words, what does this information contribute to our knowledge of the framers' original intent? Two things stand out. First, Congress's policy of deferring to the states in matters of religion was preserved under the new Constitution. The reason for this requires a few extended remarks.

What must be fundamentally understood is that the framers' primary object in writing a constitution was to secure an adequate federal government for the new nation. We experience some difficulty in our own day in appreciating the pride with which each of the states in the founding era looked upon itself as a sovereign jurisdiction. For a state to relinquish any measure of that sovereignty was to forfeit part of its own identity. But each of the states in 1787 sent delegates to the Constitutional Convention prepared to assign sufficient power to the central government to make the new nation credible. The particulars of creating a governmental framework of dual sovereigns was an especially challenging one for the framers. The Constitution that they presented to the American people for ratification was not well received in all quarters. The Antifederalists, as we have seen, mounted a formidable campaign against ratification of the new document, arguing, principally, that the Constitution robbed too much power from the states and assigned it to the new central government.

In expectation of this assault, the framers were especially careful to leave in place state sovereignty wherever it could. On considering the question of how to treat religion in the new regime, the framers well understood that it was potentially one of the most, if not the most, divisive issues facing them. This becomes one subject in which an understanding of how the Continental Congress handled questions of religion is quite helpful to an understanding of how the constitutional framers proposed to treat religion. The Continental Congress essentially deferred to the states on all issues of establishment, aid to religion, freedom of belief, and sundry other religious matters. This policy was adopted because these were matters concerning which the states rigorously guarded their right to determine their own destiny. The framers chose not to alter this policy of deference; they knew that any alteration would cause certain defeat of the Constitution in the ratification process.

This interpretation is adequately confirmed in Madison's *Federalist* No. 10, in which he suggested strategic grounds, beyond the practical ones, for making the federal government independent of churches. He was convinced that religious disagreements held the potential to undermine the ability of the new federal government to function. In his view, the states' differences in religious preferences, much like their geographical, economic, and political differences, should not be eliminated but instead allowed to flourish to the end that they might counterbalance one another. All of these differences, then, would be neutralized and rendered less capable of destroying the new regime.[51]

In like fashion, the proposed Constitution could not include religious tests for office if it were to survive the ratification process, even though most of the states had them in their own constitutions. How could the framers, even had they wanted to, draft a religious test that would be satisfactory to the plurality of sects and denominations across the states? The goal of achieving an adequate federal government could only be frustrated if the issue of religion's relationship to the new regime was allowed to encourage divisiveness among the citizens of the union.

The delegates' solution—and the idea seems to have originated with South Carolina's Charles Pinckney—was to prohibit *any* kind of religious test for holding federal office. Thus, Article 6, clause 3, provided: "No religious Test shall ever be required as a Qualification to any Office or public Trust under the United States." The secularity of this provision was bothersome to many, but most Americans came to agree with Connecticut delegate Oliver Ellsworth's logic: "A test in favor of any one denomination of Christians would be to the last degree absurd in the United States. If it were in favor of either Congregationalists, Presbyterians, Episcopalians, Baptists, or Quakers, it would incapacitate more than three-fourths of the American citizens for any public office."[52] The provision did nothing to improve the status of any sect or denomination before the federal government; rather it served to enhance religious liberty among the peoples of the various states, an aim of government to which Americans had become accustomed during the confederation period.

We have already noted the preratification appeals by the Antifederalists for a bill of rights. Federalists agreed to one, not because they believed that one was necessary, but to ensure a ratified Constitution. Moreover, a specific provision guaranteeing religious liberty, thought the Federalists, would only spell out a right that the people already owned as a nondelegated, and therefore reserved, right. The only remaining question was how the guarantee should be worded. At the First Congress, the House first considered four alternative wordings.[53] Not satisfied with the House's product, the Senate considered four additional wordings. Finally, a joint House-Senate committee agreed on the amendment's present language: "Congress shall make no law respecting an establishment of religion or prohibiting the free exercise thereof." As noted earlier, this provision remained virtually uninterpreted until the mid-twentieth century, having since judicially passed through a roughly forty-year separationist phase of interpretation and then, beginning in the mid-1980s and continuing through the present time, an accommodationist phase.

What specifically, then, was the central objective of the framers respecting church and state? What must be realized is that the framers were not prone to think in separationist-accommodationist terms. The church-state question was for them subordinate to the central objective of securing an adequate government for the union. As John Wilson has said, the framers were neither pro- nor anti-religion in the abstract; they wanted only to neutralize religion as a factor that might jeopardize the achievement of a newly constructed federal government.[54] Thus, they fashioned the new central government to be incompetent and without authority to supervise or to depend upon religious institutions. Seeing the framers' perception of the church-state question in these terms, interpreting their objectives as the product of political necessities rather than as a deduction from theological and philosophical doctrines, makes it more comprehensible than formulating it strictly according to either the separationist or accommodationist paradigm.

Thus, the founding fathers' vision for the relationship between government and religion in the new nation was based more on expedience—securing an adequate government—than the highly principled separationist and accommodationist readings of history that have developed in the twentieth century. By designing a government that at the federal level would be conducted without regard to religion, the states were left free to conduct their own governmental affairs with as much or as little attention to religion as they desired. This freedom was altered in the twentieth century by the incorporation doctrine, but the U.S. Supreme Court's implementation of that doctrine had little to do with interpreting the framers' intent but, rather, that of the Congress that passed the Civil War amendments to the Constitution.[55] This does not imply that we should abandon the search for original intent. But it does tell us that we are not always likely to find the data we seek toward ascertaining original intent. In terms of the development of the desirable relationship between religion and state, the founding era (1774–1791) was a period of transition, and thus "original intent," in terms of its implementation, is sometimes better located in the post-founding era.

A second observation about how the policies of the Continental Congress influenced the framing of the Constitution and Bill of Rights is actually the reverse of the first. If it can be determined from Congress's general policy of deferring to the states in matters of religion that it held to no strong precepts of church-state separation, this can be affirmed in the observation that Congress in fact exercised jurisdiction over religious matters in which the states chose not to assume jurisdictional authority. The unmistakable conclusion here is that the Continental Congress did not see itself as a temporal body that should generally remain neutral toward religion. Notions of the institutional separation of church and state were "in the air"—as previously seen, states like Virginia and South Carolina were moving in that direction—but those principled ideas were not a part of the mindset of the Continental Congress. Thus it is not surprising that many of the religious practices of the Continental Congress—chaplaincies, regular prayer, and observation of days of thanksgiving, as examples—were resumed once the Congress began acting under the new Constitution. Many members of Congress in the early post-Constitution period simply considered these to be realms of religious involvement that were neither reserved to the states nor proscribed to Congress under the Constitution's provisions on religion.

## Eight

## A NATIONAL SEAL AND A
## (NATIONAL?) BIBLE

The first of two sections in this chapter considers the religious overtones of the Continental Congress's creation and adoption of the nation's official seal. The design of the seal indicates again Congress's irreluctance to assign religious meaning to the events surrounding the formation of the new nation. The second section examines Congress's consideration of a proposal to pay for the publication of 20,000 copies of an American edition of the Bible needed to meet a severe shortage of Bibles in the colonies during the Revolutionary War.

### Congress and the Great Seal

After adopting the Declaration of Independence on 4 July 1776, none of the members of the Continental Congress departed Independence Hall, since there were other pressing business matters for Congress to deal with. Among those items was a decision on what it should do about adopting an official seal for the newly formed United States of America. After discussing the matter at some length, Congress made the decision to appoint a small but distinguished committee to look further into the matter; accordingly, it was, "Resolved, that Dr. Franklin, Mr. J. Adams and Mr. Jefferson, be a committee, to bring in a devise for a seal for the United States of America."[1] Thus three of the five men who had drafted the Declaration of Independence, indeed three of the finest minds serving in the Congress, were brought together to design a permanent insignia signifying the beliefs and values of the new nation.

The Congress believed that an emblem and national coat of arms were needed to give visible evidence of a sovereign nation and a free people with high aspirations and grand hopes for the future. The task proved

far more difficult than anticipated; it took six years, two more committees, and the combined efforts of fourteen men before the Great Seal of
the United States became a reality on 20 June 1782.[2]

Throughout its history the American Seal has been known by two
names, both equally correct: "the seal of the United States" and "the
Great Seal" (or, "the Great Seal of the United States"). The two names
were employed indiscriminately by the Continental Congress, although
the secretary of Congress, Charles Thomson, seems to have preferred "the
Great Seal." The device or design of the Great Seal is the coat of arms
of the United States. Used for numerous official purposes, the coat of
arms is the symbol and badge of the U.S. government. The Great Seal
has undergone a number of changes over the course of its history, which
now exceeds 200 years, but the changes have not been significant, and
the Great Seal of today, as well as its reverse side, both appearing on the
reverse side of U.S. one dollar notes, remain substantially in the form
originally adopted by the Continental Congress.

### The First Committee

The committee of Franklin, Adams, and Jefferson was as distinguished
a group of men as ever served the U.S. government. There was little in
their backgrounds, however, to qualify them specially for the task of
choosing or creating a design for the national seal.[3] The challenge facing
the committee was to translate intangible ideals and principles into
graphic symbols. Each of the committee members experimented with
biblical and classical themes. Franklin proposed as the device the following:

> Moses standing on the Shore, and extending his Hand over the Sea,
> thereby causing the same to overwhelm Pharaoh who is sitting in an open
> Chariot, a Crown on his Head and a Sword in his Hand. Rays from the
> Pillar of Fire in the Clouds reaching to Moses, to express that he acts by
> Command of the Deity. Motto, Rebellion to Tyrants is Obedience to God.[4]

It is interesting to note that although Franklin's motto, "Rebellion to
Tyrants is Obedience to God," was never adopted by Congress, Jefferson
was so impressed with the phrase that he later suggested it as an alternative motto for the Great Seal of Virginia, and he later added it to his
personal seal.[5]

Thomas Jefferson's first proposal was the only one of the committee
that contemplated a pendant seal with designs on the two sides. For the
obverse he proposed the Children of Israel in the wilderness, led by a
cloud by day and a pillar of fire by night. For the reverse he suggested

the two brothers, Hengist and Horsa, legendary leaders of the first Anglo-Saxon settlers in Britain. Jefferson withdrew this proposal, however, upon discovering that he preferred Franklin's "Israel" theme.[6]

John Adams proposed the allegorical picture known as "The Judgment of Hercules" as engraved by Simon Gribelin. This picture, with which he was familiar as an illustration in a book in his library, had impressed him deeply. According to the editors of the Adams Family Correspondence, the picture depicted:

> a succession of appeals to the young Hercules, by female impersonations of Virtue and Vice or Sensuality. . . . Vice speaks first and points out the flowery path of self-indulgence; Virtue follows and adjures Hercules to ascend the rugged, uphill way of duty to others and honor to himself. . . . Gribelin's engraving, executed according to these principles, had a profound effect on Adams' attitude toward the fine arts, which to him typified luxury and therefore the threat of moral and social decadence.[7]

Unable to agree upon a suitable design, the committee sought the help of a talented Philadelphia "drawer" and portrait artist, Pierre Eugene du Simitiere. To the post of consultant, Du Simitiere brought a familiarity with heraldry (the art of describing coats of arms), and he had experience in designing seals. He had designed great seals for Jamaica and Barbados, as well as for the American Philosophical Society, and was highly regarded.[8]

Du Simitiere's proposal for a coat of arms included a shield, crest, supporters, and motto. His design included no reverse side and is shown in illustration 1. Within the main shield is a smaller shield, and this inner shield is divided into six parts, arranged in two columns of three each. Each of the six small divisions bears a device symbolizing a country of Europe whose settlers came to America: England, Scotland, Ireland, France, Germany, and the Netherlands. In the space between the outer and the second shield are thirteen smaller shields, symmetrically arranged and each bearing an initial letter or letters of one of the thirteen states. The thirteen small shields are linked together in a band by a chain. The crest is the eye of Providence in a radiant triangle, its glory extending over the shield and beyond the supporters. The supporters are an American soldier in buckskin garb, who holds the left side of the shield, and the Goddess Liberty, who leans against its right side. The motto is E Pluribus Unum (Out of many, one).[9]

On 20 August 1776 the committee submitted its report, apparently written by Jefferson, to Congress. That report, which contemplated a pendant seal, drew on Du Simitiere's design for the obverse and on Franklin's proposal for the reverse. There were several changes, however,

such as the American soldier being replaced on the obverse by the Goddess Justice bearing a sword in her right hand and a balance in her left,
and a legend round the whole achievement, "Seal of the United States
of America MDCCLXXVI."[10]

On the same day, immediately following the report to Congress, the
*Journals of the Continental Congress* record the proposal's unfortunate
fate: "Ordered, To lie on the table."[11] This action had the effect of killing
the proposal. Although no other record of the reaction of Congress has
been located, that the Congress-at-large was dissatisfied with the device
is obvious. So ended the work of the first committee.

Of significance for this study is the religious symbolism of the various
proposals, especially as seen in the proposals of Franklin and Jefferson.
Both Adams and Jefferson, acting independently of one another, landed
upon the idea of using ancient Israel as the theme for the nation's seal.
It is well known that the colonial Puritans considered themselves less a
New *England* than a New *Israel*; as Harry Stout has observed, "Geneal-
ogy tied them to the Old World, but providence linked them to ancient
Israel so thoroughly and explicitly that words in the Old Testament could
be taken as if literally intended for New England."[12] So pervasive was
this theme in New England that by the time of the revolutionary era, its
imprint on the whole of American culture can hardly be overstated. That
two non-Puritan intellectual statesmen such as Franklin and Jefferson
would so readily adopt the analogy to permanently symbolize the nation's birth and destiny is proof enough of its influence on the American
mind. Furthermore, the "Eye of Providence" appearing on the obverse,
which was ultimately preserved in the final design approved in 1782,
alludes to the many signal interpositions of providence that the colonists
believed God had performed on behalf of the American cause.

### The Second Committee

So consumed was the Continental Congress by the demands of war that
it did not again turn its attention to the matter of a device for a Great
Seal until it appointed a second committee on 25 March 1780. The members named to this committee were James Lovell of Massachusetts, Chairman; John Morin Scott of New York; and William Churchill Houston of
New Jersey. They asked Francis Hopkinson, a former member of the
Continental Congress and a gifted Philadelphian who had designed the
American flag and the great seal of the State of New Jersey, to serve as
their consultant.[13]

So far as the records show, Hopkinson did the work of this committee,
except for clerical assistance and occasional suggestions from Houston.

Hopkinson produced two sets of drawings, each consisting of an obverse and a reverse, with the second set superseding the first. The obverses have a shield between two supporters, and both have above the shield a constellation of thirteen six-pointed stars. Both reverses use a female figure representing Liberty as the basic device.[14]

The committee submitted Hopkinson's drawings along with their report to Congress on 10 May 1780.[15] One week later, on 17 May, Congress considered the report, debated it, and referred it back to the committee.[16] The committee apparently made no further serious effort to produce an acceptable seal design. On 4 May 1782 a new (the third) committee would be appointed to undertake the task.

### The Third Committee

On 4 May 1782 Congress appointed two newly elected members of the Congress from South Carolina, Arthur Middleton and John Rutledge, as well as Elias Boudinot from New Jersey, as a committee on a "Device for the Seal of the U.S."[17] Like its predecessor committee, the members of this committee did little or no serious work themselves, relying instead on the services of William Barton, a talented Philadelphia lawyer who was also an accomplished historian, economist, and artist. Barton worked quickly and within days produced drawings that contained features and concepts that eventually would appear in the Great Seal as finally adopted.[18]

Barton's chief contribution at this stage was the eagle, not the American bald eagle, but a small crested white eagle "displayed" (with its wings spread). He combined it with a small American flag and two Latin inscriptions on the obverse: *In vindiciam libertatis* (In defense of liberty) and *Virtus sola Invicta* (Only virtue is unconquered). The design for the reverse contained a thirteen-step "unfinished" pyramid and the first committee's Eye of Providence. The reverse also bore two Latin inscriptions: *Deo Favente* (With God's favor) and *Deo Favente Perennis* (With God's everlasting favor).[19] See illustration 2 for a representation of Barton's sketches.

On 9 May, only five days after it was appointed, the committee submitted to Congress its report, which included Barton's drawings. Still not satisfied, Congress did nothing until 13 June 1782, when it placed the whole matter of a device for the Great Seal in the hands of Congress's secretary, Charles Thomson. Thomson, a businessman, teacher, and politician, had been serving as secretary of the Continental Congress for eight years. Thomson had no experience in heraldry, but he was a man of industry, common sense, and love of his country. Congress turned over to Thomson all of the collected work and recommendations of the three committees, believing that he was the man to get the job done.[20]

Thomson selected what he believed to be the best features of all the previous designs and gave them fresh and novel arrangement and a pleasing simplicity. Thomson decided to assign prominence to the eagle, but, feeling that the new nation's symbol should be strictly American, he replaced Barton's crested imperial eagle with the native American bald eagle, wings extending downward as though in flight. He placed in the left talon a bundle of arrows and in the right an olive branch.[21]

Thomson's modified crest (a device placed above the shield) was a constellation of thirteen stars surrounded by clouds. The shield, borne on the eagle's breast, was a chevron design with alternating red and white stripes. Adopting the motto *E Pluribus Unum* (Out of many, one) from the first committee's report, Thomson included it on a scroll clenched on the eagle's beak. His was the first proposal in which the final design of the obverse can be seen.[22]

In his design of the seal's reverse, Thomson retained the pyramid with the Eye of Providence in a triangle at the zenith and, as the products of his Latin proficiency, introduced the mottos *Annuit Coeptis* (God has favored our undertakings) over the eye and *Novus Ordo Seclorum* (A new order of the ages) beneath the pyramid. He gave his sketches and reports to Barton, depending on him to polish the designs. Thomson's design, without Barton's modifications, is shown in illustration 3.

Barton portrayed the eagle with its wings displayed, but with wing tips upward, and simplified Thomson's chevron arrangement of stripes on the shield. He arranged thirteen vertical stripes, alternately red and white, beneath the upper part of the shield. And he specified that the arrows in the eagle's left talon should number thirteen.[23] See illustration 4.

On 20 June 1782 Charles Thomson submitted to Congress his report recommending a design, the one on which he and William Barton had collaborated, for the Great Seal. Congress adopted the device the same day and adopted for its explanation the following "Remarks" submitted by Thomson:

> The Escutcheon is composed of the chief [upper part of shield] and pale [perpendicular band], the two most honorable ordinaries [figures of heraldry]. The Pieces, paly [alternating pales], represent the several states all joined in one solid compact entire, supporting a Chief, which unites the whole & represents Congress. The Motto alludes to this union. The pales in the arms are kept closely united by the chief and the Chief depends on that union & the strength resulting from it for its support, to

Portrait artist Du Simitiere's design for Franklin. Adams and Jefferson suggested the shield, the Eye of Providence in radiant triangle, and motto, *E Pluribus Unum*, all used in the final design. Drawn from original in Thomas Jefferson Papers.

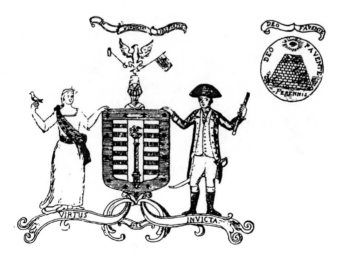

Lawyer William Barton's design for third committee combined white eagle, flag, and reverse side with a 13-step pyramid and the first committee's Eye of Providence. Drawn from original in National Archives.

Secretary of Congress Charles Thomson united earlier suggestions and gave them a fresh and novel arrangement, pleasing in its simplicity and lack of clutter. His design was the first to foreshadow the one Congress adopted. Drawn from original in National Archives.

Charles Thomson's design with William Barton's modifications. Drawn from original in National Archives.

denote the Confederacy of the United States of America & the preservation of their union through Congress.

The colours of the pales are those used in the flag of the United States of America; White signifies purity and innocence, Red, hardiness & valour, and Blue, the colour of the Chief signifies vigilance, perseverance & justice. The Olive branch and arrows denote the power of peace and war which is exclusively vested in Congress. The Constellation denotes a new State taking its place and rank among other sovereign powers. The Escutcheon is born on the breast of an American Eagle without any other supporters [figures represented as holding up the shield] to denote that the United States of America ought to rely on their own Virtue. Reverse. The pyramid signifies Strength and Duration: The Eye over it & the Motto allude to the many signal interpositions of providence in favour of the American cause. The date underneath is that of the Declaration of Independence and the words under it signify the beginning of the new American Era, which commences from that date.[24]

The first die for the Great Seal was cut from brass later in 1782. The first document impressed with the seal was an authorization from the Continental Congress for George Washington to negotiate and sign with the British an agreement for the exchange, subsistence, and better treatment of prisoners of war. The document was signed by the president of the Congress, John Hanson, and, as fate would have it, countersigned by the Seal's primary creator, Charles Thomson, as secretary.[25]

No die was cut for the reverse. The reverse was intended to be impressed on the back surfaces of wax pendant seals. The United States used pendant seals for treaties from 1815 to 1871, but the backs were never impressed. Enthusiasm for cutting a die for the reverse thereafter diminished, and to this day one has not been cut. The current official design of the reverse follows fairly closely the design submitted by Thomson in 1782, and it appears on the back side of one dollar bills opposite the design for the Great Seal, which itself has undergone five changes in detail since 1782.[26]

### The Meaning of the Great Seal

Symbolically, the seal reflects the beliefs and values the founding fathers attached to the new nation. The obverse has less spiritual meaning than the reverse. As Charles Thomson reported in his "Remarks" to Congress, the red and white stripes of the shield "represent the several states . . . supporting a [blue] Chief which unites the whole and represents Congress." The colors are adopted from the American flag—white signifies purity; red, valor; and blue, perseverance and justice. The shield signifies the virtue of the American people.

The number thirteen, denoting the thirteen original states, is represented in the bundle of arrows, the stripes of the shield, and the stars
of the constellation. The olive branch and the arrows "denote the power
of peace and war." The constellation of stars symbolizes a new nation
taking its place among other sovereign nations. The motto *E Pluribus
Unum*, emblazoned across the scroll and clenched in the eagle's beak,
expresses the union of the thirteen states. Recent scholarship has identified the probable source of this motto.[27] *Gentleman's Magazine*, published in London from 1732 to 1922, was widely read by the educated
in the colonies. Its title page carried that same motto, and it is quite
possible that it influenced the creators of the seal.

The reverse has more obvious religious implications. The pyramid,
with the year 1776 in Roman numerals on the base, has thirteen steps
but is unfinished, which contemplates the increase of the number of
states comprising the union. Along the lower circumference of the design
appear the words *Novus Ordo Seclorum*, heralding the beginning of the
new American era in 1776. At the summit of this entire display is the
Eye of Providence in a triangle surrounded by a Glory (rays of light),
and above it appears the motto *Annuit Coeptis* (God has favored our
undertakings). The plain implication is that God providentially super-
intended the birth of the new nation, giving favor to the colonists' cooperation and courage. The image probably had greater appeal to congressional members than the more obviously biblical allusions to Israel
suggested by Franklin and Jefferson, for the reason that its symbolism
was generic and therefore more acceptable to a broader spectrum of
Americans. What is unmistakable, however, is the theistic framework in
which the Continental Congress sought to have the world understand
the creation of the American republic.

### Endorsement of an American Bible

A critical lack of Bibles in the states led to the involvement of the Continental Congress in 1777 to solve the problem. No edition of the Bible
in the English language had been published in the colonies before Independence. As a result of the war, ministers experienced a lack of Bibles
for their services, causing Dr. Patrick Allison, pastor of the First Presbyterian Church in Baltimore, and a large number of ministers from diverse faiths to petition Congress to do something to remedy the shortage.
The petition prayed that, "unless timely care be used to prevent it, we
shall not have Bibles for our Schools, and families, and for the publick
Worship of God in our Churches. We therefore think it our Duty to our
Country and to the Churches of Christ to lay this design before this

honourable house, humbly requesting that under your care, and by your encouragement, a copy of the holy Bible may be printed, so as to be sold nearly as cheap as the Common Bibles, formerly imported from Britain and Ireland, were sold."[28]

On 11 September 1777 Congress appointed a committee of John Adams, Daniel Roberdeau, and Jonathan Bayard Smith to look into the matter. That same day the committee returned this report:

> The committee to whom the memorial of Dr. Allison and others was referred, report, "That they have conferred fully with the printers, &c., in this city, and are of opinion, that the proper types for printing the Bible are not to be had in this country, and that the paper cannot be procured, but with such difficulties and subject to such casualties, as render any dependence on it altogether improper: that to import types for the purpose of setting up an entire edition of the bible, and to strike off 30,000 copies, with paper, binding &c. will cost £10,272 10, which must be advanced by Congress, to be reimbursed by the sale of the books: that, in the opinion of the committee, considerable difficulties will attend the procuring the types and paper; that afterwards, the risque of importing them will considerably enhance the cost, and that the calculations are subject to such uncertainty in the present state of affairs, that Congress cannot much rely on them: that the use of the Bible is so universal, and its importance so great, that your committee refer the above to the consideration of Congress, and if Congress shall not think it expedient to order the importation of types and paper, the committee recommend that Congress will order the committee of commerce to import 20,000 Bibles from Holland, Scotland, or elsewhere, into the different ports of the states of the Union."[29]

In voting on this report, New Hampshire, Massachusetts, Connecticut, Rhode Island, New Jersey, Pennsylvania, and Georgia were in favor of acting on the recommendation to import, at Congress's expense, 20,000 Bibles; New York, Delaware, North Carolina, South Carolina, Virginia, and Maryland opposed such action. Despite the affirmative vote, the margin of one vote led Congress to table the matter, and no final action was taken.[30]

The reason for the reluctance of six states to approve the measure cannot be determined from available records. There are no available records of Congress's debate on this question, and this writer's own search for other records on this issue has been fruitless. It can only be determined that Congress was thoroughly divided on this very difficult issue. The reason for this division, however, remains undetermined. The only writers who have considered the congressional action on this point in any depth make no attempt to analyze Congress's rationale for voting against the committee's recommendation.[31] It could have been nothing more than Congress's belief that it could not afford the project.

Because of the exigencies of war,[32] the matter did not again arise until 1780. Concerned that the demand for Bibles still had not been met, Congress adopted the following resolution on 26 October 1780:

> That it be recommended to such of the States who may think it convenient for them that they take proper measures to procure one or more new and correct editions of the Old and New Testament to be printed and that such states regulate their printers by law so as to secure effectually the said books from being misprinted.[33]

In the meantime, Robert Aitken (1734–1802), a patriotic Philadelphia printer and a Presbyterian elder, had proceeded on his own initiative and published an American edition of the Bible. In January 1781 he petitioned Congress for an endorsement of his project and for financial support. He received the former but not the latter.[34] Congress's endorsement of the Bible without allocating funds for the project is indeed a strong evidence that Congress was deeply committed to the importance of religion for the new republic, but equally unwilling, for whatever reason, to become financially involved.

Although Congress gave no financial aid to the project, the Pennsylvania legislature advanced $700 to Aitken to complete the work.[35] The Aitken Bible is now a rare Americanum and greatly sought after. Only about seventy-five copies are known to exist.[36] On the two pages that follow the title page appear the four endorsements received from the Continental Congress. Each of them is here reproduced to show Congress's subservience to, in the language of the 10 September 1782 endorsement, the "interest of religion":

> By the United States in Congress Assembled:
> September 12th, 1782
> The Committee to whom was referred a Memorial of Robert Aitken, Printer, dated 21st January, 1781, respecting an edition of the Holy Scriptures, report, "That Mr. Aitken has, at a great expense, now finished an American edition of the Holy Scriptures in English; that the Committee have from time to time attended to his progress in the work; that they also recommended it to the two Chaplains of Congress to examine and give their opinion of the execution, who have accordingly reported thereon; the recommendation and report being as follows:
> "Philadelphia, 1st September 1782.
> "Reverend Gentlemen
> "Our knowledge of your piety and public spirit leads us without apology to recommend to your particular attention the edition of the Holy Scriptures publishing by Mr. Aitken. He undertook this expensive work

at a time when, from the circumstances of the war, an English edition of the Bible could not be imported, nor any opinion formed how long the obstruction might continue. On this account particularly he deserves applause and encouragement. We therefore wish you, Reverend Gentlemen, to examine the execution of the work, and if approved, to give it the sanction of your judgment, and the weight of your recommendation.

We are, with very great respect,

Your most obedient humble servants.

(Sign'd)        JAMES DUANE, Chairman in behalf of a Committee of Congress on Mr. Aitken's Memorial.

Reverend Doct. White and Revd. M. Duffield,

Chaplains of the United States in Congress assembled.

Report.

Gentlemen:

AGREEABLY to your desire we have paid attention to Mr. Robert Aitken's impression of the Holy Scriptures of the Old and New Testament. Having selected and examined a variety of passages throughout the work, we are of opinion that it is executed with great accuracy as to the sense, and with as few grammatical and typographical errors as could be expected in an undertaking of such magnitude. Being ourselves witnesses of the demand for this invaluable book, we rejoice in the present prospect of a supply; hoping that it will prove as advantageous as it is honorable to the Gentleman, who has exerted himself to furnish it, at the evident risque of private fortune. We are, Gentlemen,

Your very respectful and humble servants,

(Sign'd)                                    WILLIAM WHITE

                                            GEORGE DUFFIELD.

Philadelphia, September 10th, 1782.

Honble James Duane, Esq. Chairman, and the other

Honble Gentlemen of the Committee of Congress on

Mr. Aitken's Memorial.

Whereupon,

RESOLVED,

THAT the United States in Congress assembled highly approve the pious and laudable undertakings of Mr. Aitken, as subservient to the interest of religion, as well as an instance of the progress of arts in this country, and being satisfied from the above report of his care and accuracy in the execution of the work, they recommend this edition of the Bible to the inhabitants of the United States, and hereby authorize him to publish this Recommendation in the manner he shall think proper.

CHA. THOMSON, Sec'ry.[37]

Some have referred to the 1782 Congress as "the Bible Congress," because it endorsed Aitken's Bible, making it the only Bible ever officially authorized in America.[38] Yet one scholar has provided an interesting explanation for Congress's endorsement. Edwin Rumball-Petre, writing in 1940 after a thorough investigation of the history of the Aitken Bible, suggested that Congress was less interested in importing or publishing Bibles than it was in being kind to Robert Aitken. Aitken was the congressional printer who printed the *Journals of Congress*[39] and, according to Rumball-Petre, undertook the publication of an American edition of the Bible at some financial risk. When peace was proclaimed shortly after he published an unknown number of copies of his edition, the importation of cheaper Bibles was again made possible, and congressmen were among the first to realize that Aitken's investment would be a loss. The Congress therefore recommended "this edition of the Bible to the inhabitants of the United States, and hereby authorize him to publish this recommendation in the manner he shall think proper." Aitken acted on this authorization and printed the recommendation among the preliminary pages of his Bible, which no doubt helped him to dispose of his published copies.[40]

Whether this account is true or false (Rumball-Petre himself admitted that it had never before been expressed in print) is not of paramount importance in the present context. What is important is that Congress was unwilling, possibly even for its good friend and servant, Robert Aitken, to expend congressional monies on a project that many of the states found objectionable. Whether this objection centered on the recognition that the Bible could not possibly satisfy all readers across the states, the more principled rationale that congressional financing would violate the states' jurisdiction over religion, the lack of funds to finance the project, or some other reason is uncertain. Laboring without the restraints on its involvement in religion that would follow the passage of the Constitution's First Amendment, Congress probably did not perceive the project as an improper advancement of religion. It did, however, seem to view as one of its primary responsibilities the preservation of the liberty of the various states in things pertaining to religion. Therefore, it is more likely that Congress believed that because of the likelihood that the Aitken Bible would not appeal to all citizens of the various states, it would be an infringement upon the states' liberty for Congress, which represented all of the states, to expend the monies required to publish the needed Bibles.

## Concluding Remarks

This chapter has examined two specific areas of congressional action that had religious implications: the creation and adoption of the U.S. Seal and the endorsement of the Aitken Bible. As the foregoing discussion has shown, Congress's involvement in settling on a national seal with obvious religious symbolism and its endorsement of the Aitken Bible point to a Congress that understood its function to some degree in religious terms. There is no evidence that any of the congressional delegates objected to Congress's role in these activities on the grounds that it violated some nascent notion of the separation of church and state. While this may have been Congress's reason for declining to subsidize the printing of the Aitken Bible, it is more likely that Congress thought this was a "states' matter" or even that the project was too expensive for Congress's limited bank account. All of this only supports the conclusion that formal discussions of the separation of church and state—at the national level— arose later with the passage of the First Amendment.

*Nine*

## THE CONTINENTAL CONGRESS
## AND RELIGIOUS LIBERTY

Many of the colonial leaders who led the independence movement had in mind from the beginning both political and religious
freedom. Two late colonial actions reflect this emphasis. First was
the Massachusetts legislature's call on 17 June 1774 for the convening
of the First Continental Congress. Among the purposes stated in this
appeal, as noted in chapter 4, was that the colonial representatives should
devise measures "for the recovery and establishment of their just rights
and liberties, civil and religious."[1] The second action occurred the following year, when the New York Provincial Congress resolved that "neither the Parliament of Great Britain, nor any other earthly legislature or
tribunal, ought or can of right interfere or interpose in anywise how-
soever in the religious and ecclesiastical concerns of the colonies."[2] These
two actions reveal the early commitment of the colonial leaders to religious liberty, at least leaving to each colony its own independence from
the king and Parliament in matters of religion.

Independence from Great Britain was a major factor in allowing religious freedom to progress in the colonies. No longer were any of the
Protestant churches required to look to Europe for authority; many colonial religious establishments were maintained, but in time all American
churches were separated from government support and controls. Independence not only changed corporate religious liberty but individual
religious liberty as well. The Declaration of Independence laid emphasis
not only on the worth of the individual but on the individual's right to
determine his or her own religious beliefs and to act upon those beliefs.
Indeed, the individual gained a religious freedom that had never before
been known on such a large scale at any time or place in history.

The new conception of religious liberty was in great measure made possible by evolving changes in the way government viewed its responsibility to the individual. The long-held view that it was the duty of government to propagate religious truth, achieved by compulsion if necessary, slowly began to give way to the view that mankind and God were better served by giving the individual freedom, absent any coercion, to determine truth regarding matters of faith and conscience. Individual liberties thus became a limitation on government; they increased the dignity of the individual person and simultaneously reduced the sphere of influence of government.

In America from 1774 to 1789 these extraordinary notions of religious liberty were taking firm root. During this remarkable period, most of the states enacted new and sweeping provisions to remove civil disabilities imposed because of religious views and to protect the rights of citizens to worship freely. The disestablishment movement was also making progress. In 1774 only four colonies made no provision for the support of religion. By 1789 the states of Virginia, New York, and New Jersey had also discontinued the practice, and by 1833 none of the original thirteen states gave any financial support to churches. This gradual shift in the formal church-state framework in the states reflects the growing idea in the early life of the nation that religion would survive and even thrive if set free from the support of and linkage to government. The prediction of prominent Connecticut Congregationalist Elihu Hall in 1749 that without state support religion would collapse and "there would not be . . . one regular visible church left subsisting in this land fifty years hence"[3] never materialized. By 1800, Hall's predicted year of doom, the number of churches in America had doubled from about 2,000 at the time of Hall's prediction to approximately 4,000,[4] and establishments were on the decline.

The delegates to the Continental Congress, as political leaders who above all else sought to see the growth of liberty in the young nation, regularly legislated in favor of religious liberty—for the states, for American citizens, and for foreigners on American soil. Their efforts to foster and protect religious liberty, imperfect as they were at times, are the subject of this chapter.

## The Enlistment of Quebec

One of the earliest acts of the Continental Congress was to enlist the province of Quebec in resistance against England. The great majority of the people of that province were Roman Catholic, but Congress wanted to invite Quebec to join the revolting colonies in securing a redress of their grievances. This was a difficult task, however, in view of Parliament's passage of the Quebec Act earlier in 1774.

The Quebec Act reversed Parliament's earlier plan to anglicize Quebec and allowed the French Canadians to retain their old semi-feudal system and civil law even as it introduced English criminal law. It also included within the boundaries of Quebec the old northwest region (ceded to the United States at the Treaty of Paris in 1783 and from which the states of Ohio, Indiana, Illinois, Michigan, and Wisconsin were later carved). The Act's provisions admitted Roman Catholics to citizenship and to eligibility for public office. In effect, parts of the system of New France were restored under British sovereignty, with controls actually lighter than under the French Crown.[5]

In the colonies, the Quebec Act was widely interpreted as an "establishment" of the Roman Catholic religion in Canada. Indeed, the Roman Catholic religion was given such favorable treatment in the Act as to cause great resentment among Protestants in the thirteen colonies, who feared its effects on their own traditions.[6] Alexander Hamilton's reaction was typical: "This act makes effectual provision not only for the protection, but for the permanent support of Popery."[7]

It is difficult to overestimate the degree to which, on the eve of the Revolution, Catholics in America were still widely discriminated against. Several members of the Continental Congress, including Congregationalist Roger Sherman, were opposed to hiring Catholics to fight in the Continental Army.[8] Only three colonies allowed Catholics to vote. They were banned from holding public office in all New England colonies save Rhode Island. New Hampshire law called for the imprisonment of all persons who refused to repudiate the pope, the mass, and transubstantiation. New York held the death penalty over priests who entered the colony; Virginia boasted that it would only arrest them. Georgia did not permit Catholics to reside within its boundaries; the Carolinas merely barred them from office. Only Pennsylvania permitted Catholic schools. Elsewhere forbidden to have schools of their own, Catholics could enter Protestant schools only at the price of Protestant instruction or even of denying their Catholic belief.[9]

In an American environment thoroughly hostile to Roman Catholicism, the Quebec Act was anathema. American Protestants (except some Anglicans) were already alarmed by rumors that the Church of England schemed to appoint a bishop in the colonies with the intention of enforcing Anglican authority upon all of the various denominations. To these Protestants the line between the Church of England and the Church of Rome always had seemed dangerously thin. When Catholics ceased to be actively persecuted in the mother country, alarmists in the colonies began to fear that Catholicism and Anglicanism were about to merge, and at the passage of the Quebec Act they became convinced that a plot was afoot in London for subjecting Americans to the tyranny of the pope. No such plot existed, says Carl Bridenbaugh, who has concluded that English authorities were far more interested in increasing Anglican than Catholic influence in the colonies.[10] The only plot in the situation, according to one English observer, was the one perpetrated by the colonial leaders to make the colonists "verily believe" that "the Romish is going to be established in America by an act of Parliament."[11]

In considering the implications of the Quebec Act, the Continental Congress was far less interested in masterminding plots to increase American sentiment for independence than it was in making serious efforts to win the support of the citizens of Quebec in the colonies' dispute with Great Britain. This would not be easy in view of the popularity of the Quebec Act among Canadians; after all, did the Act not guarantee to Canadian Catholics the right to freely exercise their faith without civil penalties of any kind? The strategy that Congress settled on was to convince the Canadians that the religious freedom granted them in the Act was already theirs—granted by God—and that their submission to British grants of pre-existing rights would strengthen the power of Parliament to arbitrarily remove such rights in the future. Congress hoped the Canadians would recognize that America, not England, was the true advocate of religious liberty and that Protestant America and Catholic Quebec could be good neighbors and allies. The Congress carefully placed these arguments in a letter addressed to the citizens of Quebec[12] (see appendix B), dated 26 October 1774. The letter was of little effect, however; the Canadians remained neutral in the British-American dispute, believing that Canadians were better off under the British than they would be under the Americans, mostly because they were put off by the considerable American hostility to Catholicism.[13]

Congress's liberal attitude toward the Canadian Catholics was not, however, free from concerns arising from the Quebec Act. On the same day that it wrote the letter to the inhabitants of Quebec, Congress petitioned the king, complaining of his policy of allowing Catholicism to become firmly established as the religion of the Quebec province:

> In the last session of parliament an act was passed . . . for extending the limits of Quebec, abolishing the English and restoring the French law, whereby great numbers of the British freemen are subjected to the latter, and establishing an absolute government and the Roman Catholic religion throughout those vast regions.[14]

Congress undoubtedly acted somewhat duplicitously here—on the one hand, suggesting to the Canadians that fundamental principles of religious liberty entitled them to believe and worship as they desired, apart from any grant of such liberty by Parliament, and on the other hand, pleading to the king to deny to the Canadians the right to determine their own course in religious matters. There is no evidence that this duplicity gave offense to the only Catholic member of Congress, Charles Carroll, but Congress obviously wanted a double benefit: to enlist the support of Catholic Quebec, but simultaneously to raise colonial ire against England for giving too much consideration to a Roman Catholic population.

Congress continued to court Quebec in its cause against England. On 29 May 1775 Congress issued a statement that had as its thematic affirmation, "We perceived the fate of the Protestant and Catholic colonies to be strongly linked together."[15] A thousand copies of this statement were sent to Canada to be dispersed among the inhabitants of Quebec. Congress attempted to assure the Canadians that their religious preferences were no obstacle to good relations with the American colonies. On 14 September 1775 Benedict Arnold, who was preparing to depart for Canada with his troops, was given a letter by General George Washington regarding his proper attitude in meeting the sensibilities of the Roman Catholic population of the province of Quebec. The letter included these instructions:

And as the contempt of the religion of a country, by ridiculing any of its ceremonies, or affronting its ministers or votaries, has ever been deeply resented, you are to be particularly careful to restrain every officer and soldier from such imprudence and folly, and to punish every instance of it. On the other hand, as far as it lies in your power, you are to protect and support the free exercise of the religion of the country, and the undisturbed enjoyment of the rights of conscience in religious matters with your utmost influence and authority.[16]

Still, Washington, like most Americans of his day, viewed the Catholic faith with contempt. In the same letter, he added these words:

I also give it in charge to you to avoid all disrespect of the religion of the country, and its ceremonies. Prudence, policy, and a true Christian spirit, will lead us to look with compassion upon their errors without insulting them. While we are contending for our own liberty, we should be very cautious not to violate the rights of conscience in others, ever considering that God alone is the judge of the hearts of men, and to him only in the case they are answerable.[17]

These instructions to Arnold formed the basis of more detailed and important instructions given by the Continental Congress to several of its members sent on a diplomatic mission to Canada in February 1776. The members first chosen for this mission were Benjamin Franklin, Samuel Chase, and Charles Carroll, but Congress desired that "Mr. Carroll be requested to prevail on Mr. John Carroll to accompany the committee to Canada, to assist them in such matters as they shall think useful."[18] John Carroll, Charles Carroll's cousin and who was later to become the first Catholic bishop in the United States in 1790, accepted the commission, and the committee proceeded to Canada, under the injunctions of Congress, dated 20 March 1776, which in part read as follows:

> You are further to declare that we hold the sacred rights of conscience any may promise to the whole people, solemnly in our name, the free and undisturbed exercise of their religion; and, to the clergy, the full, perfect and peaceable possession and enjoyment of all their estates. That the government of everything relating to their religion and clergy, shall be left entirely in the hands of the good people of that province and such legislature as they shall constitute: provided, however, that all other denominations of Christians be equally entitled to hold offices and enjoy civil privileges and the free exercise of their religion and be totally exempt from the payment of any tithes or taxes for the support of any religion.[19]

While the commission's efforts to win Canadian support for the American cause were unsuccessful, Congress's instructions to the diplomatic commission are indicative of its committed efforts to accord the utmost respect to the Canadians' Catholic religion.

The repeated overtures of friendship and cooperation toward Canada must be understood in the light of political developments that had occurred there in the years leading up to the American revolutionary movement. During the French and Indian War (1756–1763) a strong anti-Canadian bias existed in the colonies because Canada was under French rule and the colonists believed that a French victory in the war would mean a stronger Catholic presence in North America. It was not uncommon for colonists to believe that the pope was the Antichrist and that America, surely the location of Christ's coming millennial reign, needed a purging of Catholic influences that were undoubtedly responsible for delaying the onset of the millennium. The New England Congregationalist James Dana, for example, preached in 1770 that the decline of the papal Antichrist since the Reformation was nearly complete and that in a very short time, "The millennium will come and true Christianity will prevail."[20] When the French were defeated in the war and Canada was ceded to Britain pursuant to the terms of the Treaty of Paris, colonial fears of a widening Catholic presence in America greatly subsided. By 1776, after scarcely more than a decade under British rule, Canada did not have particularly strong allegiances to Great Britain. In fact, many political leaders in the colonies hoped that Canada would join the colonies as a member of the new confederation to be formed. Indeed, in the Articles of Confederation, as finally adopted in 1778, specific provision was made for this possibility. In effect, a place was reserved for Canada without the approval of nine states that was required for the admission of any other states. If this goal was to be achieved, it was essential both to assure the Catholic inhabitants of Canada that their religion would be respected and to assure the increasing English Protestant population that it need not fear losing its religious freedom.

Although the American religious makeup was overwhelmingly Protestant in the revolutionary era,[21] that the American leadership was so respectful of Canadian Catholics and apparently intent on preserving their religious liberty suggest that the increasingly pluralistic character of religion in America more and more demanded political recognition through guarantees of religious freedom for all. While Congress was obviously concerned about an increased Catholic presence, it settled on a policy of religious freedom even for Catholics. To achieve consistency, Congress could not have decided on any other policy. Because Congress broadly acknowledged the right of self-determination in religious matters for each colony, it was compelled to attempt, within limits, to treat Quebec, potentially a colony, much the same, despite its overwhelmingly Catholic population.[22]

## Religious Liberty under the Articles of Confederation

Formal separation from Great Britain made necessary the reorganization of government in the colonies, which had proclaimed themselves free and independent states. Under the encouragement of the Continental Congress, most of the colonies drafted new constitutions. Most of these constitutions provided for governments similar to those of pre-Independence years, except that central authority, which previously had rested with the royal governors, was now vested in legislative assemblies. Many of the constitutions restrained governmental authority by bills of rights that echoed the popular opposition to arbitrary power and reasserted the doctrine that government existed only with the consent of the governed.

Until the establishment of the state governments, the Continental Congress was the principal organization providing leadership in the struggle for independence. Once established, the state governments began to ac-

quire prestige above that of Congress. They possessed affirmative powers, while the Continental Congress was largely advisory, lacking the
power of compulsion over either the states or the people. Congress could
organize the war effort and make requests for money, men, and equip-
ment, but it was without the power to demand them if the requests went
unheeded. Some central authority was needed for the efficient conduct
of the war, and a permanent framework of union had to be devised.[23]

The Continental Congress began serious consideration of a plan of
confederation on 7 June 1776. It was on that day that Richard Henry
Lee had introduced his resolution proposing that a Declaration of Independence be drawn up; what is frequently overlooked is that on the
same day he also proposed that "a plan of confederation be prepared
and transmitted to the respective colonies for their consideration and
approbation."[24] Acting on this proposal, Congress appointed a committee
composed of one representative from each colony, which began work
immediately on a proposal.[25] Only five weeks later, on 12 July 1776, the
committee submitted to Congress a proposal for "Articles of Confederation."

The quick work of the committee was possible because it was able to
draw from three earlier drafts of a confederation plan prepared by Benjamin Franklin, Silas Deane, and John Dickinson, respectively. Franklin's
plan was presented to Congress on 21 July 1775[26] but never formally
considered—the First Congress adjourned only twelve days later. Deane's
draft, probably composed in November 1775, was never seriously considered by Congress. Both the Franklin and Deane texts suffered from
hasty draftsmanship and reflected a striking lack of concern with the
task of dividing power between Congress and the colonies.

Neither of these drafts had any major impact on the proposed set of
articles that John Dickinson, one of the thirteen members of the congressional committee appointed on 7 June 1776, prepared in late June
and early July 1776; their importance rests instead on what they reveal
of the delegates' earliest conceptions of confederation. The Franklin and
Deane texts were saddled with the paradox of having to preserve colonial
unity in a comprehensive federal system while somehow preserving the
lingering hope of securing a reconciliation that would leave the colonies
within the British empire.[27]

This formidable difficulty no longer applied in June 1776, when Dickinson and the other members of the confederation committee set to work
on a new plan of confederation. Independence was imminent, and by
the time the committee had submitted its proposal to Congress on 12
July,[28] the thirteen British colonies had become thirteen sovereign states
in critical need of some formal union. Historians have usually labeled

the text that the committee presented to Congress as the "Dickinson Plan."[29]

Many difficulties stood in the way of approval of the proposed plan. The overall difficulty was the fact that the colonists had not yet developed awareness of important common interests, except for the immediate interest of waging war against a common enemy. Every state was leery of the delegation of authority to a government that it would be unable to dominate. The particular difficulties included inability to agree upon bases for representation for voting, for the allocation of taxes among the states, for military selective service, and for the proper division of various other rights and responsibilities. Because of the many grounds of disagreement, the inevitable tendency was to allot to the union the absolute minimum of authority necessary for performance of functions that could not be performed adequately by the state governments.[30]

It is impossible to overstate the degree to which the colonies treasured their autonomy and the resulting reluctance they had toward assigning federal authority. It involved retreating from the experience of a century and a half of self-governance, interrupted only occasionally by a parent nation located a vast ocean away. Of all the problems in political theory that engaged the colonies in the revolutionary era, none ultimately proved more challenging than the framing of a federal union. To reduce the evolution of the colonial leaders' ideas on this subject to manageable proportions is not an easy task. The sources for understanding the Articles of Confederation are far less imposing than the comparable sources for the Constitution, but the assortment of ideas on federalism, democracy, power, representation, human nature, and other topics that contributed to the creation of the former are almost as impressive as those for the latter. Of these multiple themes, however, it is the role that religion played in the framing of the Articles of Confederation that is the subject of the present discussion.

The passage by Congress of the Articles of Confederation on 15 November 1777 and their ratification by the states was an important achievement for the colonies. Once agreed upon, the Articles served as the framework of national government until superseded by the Constitution upon its ratification by the states in 1789. But agreement on the Articles as drafted by Dickinson and his committee did not come easily. And one of the obstacles to agreement was the way in which the authority of the states in matters of religion was dealt with in Dickinson's plan.

Dickinson's draft reflected his view that the problem of confederation involved more than alleviating potential sources of jealousy among the states. Implicit in his conception of confederation was the premise that the states were incapable of entirely regulating their activities in the best interest of the union and that any plan of confederation would therefore have to impose restraints on their sphere of authority—and not merely in areas where authority clearly rested with Congress. Dickinson rejected the idea that exclusive spheres of authority should be blocked off both for Congress and the states. He envisioned a confederation whose authority would have clear precedence over the rights of the states.[31]

The early portion of Dickinson's draft revealed his belief that the authority of the states should be restrained. He accepted the formula of the Franklin plan to reserve to each state "as much as it may think fit of its own present Laws, Customs, Rights, Privileges, and peculiar Jurisdictions," but to it he added the proviso, "in all Matters that shall not interfere with the Articles of this Confederation."[32] In Dickinson's view this confirmation of existing laws and practices did not confer upon the states an absolute control over the future regulation of their internal affairs. For in the very next article, what Jack Rakove has called "the most innovative of the entire draft,"[33] Dickinson gave attention to a topic that was closely connected with government and politics in virtually all of the states: the rights of religious minorities. Here Dickinson sought to freeze the pattern of church-state relations existing in each of the states by prohibiting the new governments from enacting any additional laws requiring dissenters to support established churches, imposing religious tests as a qualification for holding civil office or exercising any other civil liberty, and compelling persons to take oaths who objected to the practice on religious grounds. Dickinson's Article IV read as follows:

Art.[4]. No person in any Colony living peaceably under the Civil Government, shall be molested or prejudiced in his or her person or Estate for his or her religious persuasion, Profession or practice, nor be compelled to frequent or maintain or contribute to maintain any religious Worship, Place of Worship, or Ministry, contrary to his or her Mind, by any Law or ordinance hereafter to be made in any Colony different from the usual Laws & Customs subsisting at the Commencement of this War—provided, that such person frequents regularly some Place of religious Worship on the Sabbath; & no religious Persuasion or practise for the Profession or Exercise of which, persons are not disqualified by the present Laws of the said Colonies respectively, from holding any offices Civil or military, shall by any Law or Ordinance hereafter to be made in any Colony, be rendered a Disqualification of any persons profession or exercising the same from holding any such offices, as fully as they might have done heretofore: Nor shall any further Tests or Qualifications concerning religious persuasion, Profession or Practise, than such as have been usually administered in the said Colonies respectively, be imposed by any Law or Ordinance hereafter to be made in any Colony; and whenever on Election or Appointment to

any Offices, or on any other occasions, the Affirmation of persons conscientiously scrupulous of taking an Oath, hath been admitted in any
Colony or Colonies, no Oath shall in any such Cases be hereafter imposed
by any Law or Ordinance in any such Colony or Colonies, it being the
full Intent of these united Colonies that all the Inhabitants thereof respectively of every Sect, Society or religious Denomination shall enjoy
under this Confederation, all the Liberties and Priviledges which they
have heretofore enjoyed without the least abridgement of their civil Rights
for or on Account of their religious Persuasion, profession or practise.[34]

Although this provision might have been interpreted as a challenge
to existing church establishments in many of the states, Dickinson was
not calling for an eventual end to existing establishments. His immediate
concerns were more narrowly political and thus provide a key for understanding his approach toward confederation. Recognizing the extent
to which sectarian rivalries generated domestic political strife—most dramatically in the middle colonies, where the mix of religious sects was
more evident—Dickinson hoped to use the confederation to prevent religious hostilities from being injected into the struggles for power that
would accompany the formation of new state governments. By allaying
fears that dominant sects—especially the Congregationalists in the
North—might use their political power to harry their opponents, adoption of this article might eliminate a dangerous source of internal conflict.[35]

Congress rejected Dickinson's entire article dealing with religious liberty, not because Congress opposed religious liberty, but because it did
not agree with the radical nature of Dickinson's efforts to vest substantial
authority in Congress and impose explicit limitations upon the states.
Since most of the delegates believed that the rights of individuals, especially rights of belief and conscience, were a local matter unrelated to
the problem of constructing a confederation among independent states,
it is not surprising that the article was rejected out of hand.

Dickinson's plan of confederation, without its language dealing with
religious liberty, and otherwise greatly revised, was finally adopted by
Congress on 15 November 1777.[36] Congress immediately began operating
under the charter, although "The Articles of Confederation," the plan's
official title, was not ratified by all of the required thirteen states until
March 1781.

In its final form, the Articles guaranteed states' rights—a matter of
great importance to those states who wished to retain their religious
establishments. Article II stated: "Each state retains its sovereignty, freedom, and independence, and every Power, Jurisdiction and right, which
is not by this confederation expressly delegated to the United States, in

Congress assembled." This doctrine of delegated powers, so often associated with the Constitution, was actually only a carryover from the Articles of Confederation. So firmly impressed upon the minds of the American people was this doctrine that many demanded its inclusion (in what became the Tenth Amendment)[37] as a prerequisite to ratification of the Constitution.

If the states' rights guarantee in Article II was not enough to secure the exclusive jurisdiction of each state over religion, Article III served as a strong reinforcement:

> The states hereby severally enter into a firm league of friendship with each other; for their common defense, the security of their liberties, and their mutual and general welfare, binding themselves to assist each other against all force offered to, as attacks made upon them, or any of them, on account of religion, sovereignty, trade, or any other pretense whatever.

This was a straightforward acknowledgement by the states of respect for one another's official treatment of religion, even pledging to mutually protect the integrity of each state's religion or of its religious freedom. It guaranteed, for instance, the probable continued dominance of Congregationalism in Connecticut, Episcopalianism in Georgia, and religious liberty in Rhode Island. This policy of deference to the states in matters of religion was to be retained in the Constitution; it was assumed and implied in the document written in 1787 and more affirmatively stated in the First Amendment, which placed absolute limitations on the federal government's ability to legislate establishments or restrict free exercise rights. The lack of any such specific restraints on the Continental Congress under the Articles of Confederation may in one sense, from the perspective of Congress, have been an advantage. The prohibitions erected against the federal government in the First Amendment religion clauses inevitably led to controversies, persisting to this day, over the meaning and scope of the enumerated prohibitions. For the Continental Congress, this issue never arose, enabling it to operate with a theistic, if not manifestly Christian, worldview, seldom reluctant to advance Christian causes unless its acts would clearly interfere with the liberty and sovereignty of the states.

This point is perhaps best made by pointing out that the members of the Continental Congress were confident enough of the merits of this arrangement (and of its acceptance among a citizenry equally committed to a theistic perspective) to include in the final article this affirmation: "And Whereas it hath pleased the Great Governor of the World to incline the hearts of the legislatures we respectively represent in congress, to

approve of, and to authorize us to ratify the said articles of confederation
and perpetual union."

### Religious Liberty and Foreign Mercenaries

Once the war broke out, the Continental Congress pursued a policy of
actively dissuading foreign mercenaries from fighting for Great Britain.
It wanted to persuade them to desert from the redcoat army and encourage them to become American citizens. They were almost exclusively
Germans, of whom there were nearly 30,000 troops—about one-third of
the land forces fighting for Great Britain in the American colonies.
Slightly more than half of these came from Hesse-Cassel (hence they were
called Hessians); the rest came from Brunswick and other German prin-
cipalities. They included Calvinists, Lutherans, Unitarians, Roman Catholics, and men of other faith backgrounds.[38]

The strategy adopted by Congress was to encourage desertion by these
soldiers by promising them citizenship, fifty acres of land, and full religious freedom. On 14 August 1776, on the recommendation of a committee that had been appointed to devise a plan, the Congress enacted
appropriate measures that included the following:

> Whereas it has been the wise policy of these states to extend the protec-
> tion of their laws to all those who should settle among them, of whatever
> nation or religion they might be, and to admit them to a participation of
> the benefits of civil and religious freedom; and, the benevolence of this
> practice, as well as its salutary effects, have rendered it worthy of being
> continued in future times.
>
> RESOLVED, That the foregoing resolution be committed to the committee,
> who brought in the report, and that they be directed to have it translated
> into German, and to take proper measures to have it communicated to the
> foreign troops.[39]

Here was a definite assurance of religious freedom within the United
States from the highest governmental authority. Any Hessian deserter
could settle in any of the states and enjoy all civil and religious freedoms
enjoyed by the citizens of that state.[40] Thousands of copies of this resolution were printed in German, to be circulated among the foreign
troops, and the backs of tobacco wrappers were also used to publicize
this information. Congress at one time even toyed with the idea of raising
a corps of German volunteers consisting entirely of Hessian deserters.[41]

It is unknown how many German mercenaries actually deserted the
royal army. Carl Wittke has estimated that anywhere from 5,000 to 12,000

remained in the United States after the war;[42] Frederick Harling and Martin Kaufman put the number closer to 12,000.[43] At the close of the war, pamphlets were printed in German in New Jersey and South Carolina inviting the Hessians to stay and purchase land at bargain prices. Many Hessian prisoners in Virginia and Pennsylvania (where they could easily fraternize with their countrymen and hear their own tongue spoken) were helped by German settlers to escape to the West and become farmers. Of the 1,100 Hessian prisoners brought to Reading, Pennsylvania, only about 300 returned to Germany. A large number settled in Baltimore as farmers and gardeners. Many were absorbed in the Pennsylvania German counties as farmers, and some found employment as schoolteachers.[44]

The Hessians added to the already diverse religious makeup of American society. Increasingly, religious and ethnic pluralism was a reality in the young nation, and it was receiving official sanction by the Continental Congress. The diversity of religions made religious toleration imperative, and the separation of church and state that came to be embodied in the Constitution and Bill of Rights was perhaps in many ways less a matter of democratic theory than a practical and inescapable necessity.

### Conscientious Objectors during the American Revolution

During the Revolutionary War, the Continental Congress was faced with the problem of whether to grant exemptions from military service for conscientious objectors. Actually, the problem was not a new one. In early colonial America, there were several religious sects whose principles forbade them the use of arms in warfare. The Quakers came to America in 1656; the Mennonites (including the Amish and the Hutterites) came in 1683; the Brethren (sometimes called Dunkers, Dunkards, or Tunkers) in 1719. Smaller pacifist sects—the Shakers, Christadelphians, Rogerenes—joined them soon after. These groups stood aside when their neighbors fought off Native American tribes and repaired the breastworks of the forts. They refused to drill or carry arms. They were considered heretics and blasphemers, freethinkers who would be subversive of law and order. However small the burdens of militia duty may have been in the seventeenth and early eighteenth centuries, pacifists were scrupulous in withdrawing from military engagements.[45]

During the Revolution, conscientious objectors suffered many inconveniences and some actual mistreatment at the hands of both individuals and government. Though there was no draft law during the war, public sentiment in favor of the war was so high that pacifists were usually considered traitors. The Catholic patriot Charles Carroll considered that "Quakers, Dunkers, and Mennonists are almost to a man against us, and I believe they will make near $1/4$ of the whole People."[46] In Pennsylvania, where the Quakers and Mennonites were most numerous, Benjamin Franklin, as a member of that state's legislative Committee of Safety, became interested in providing exemption from military service for the conscientious objector. The Pennsylvania legislature responded by allowing exemption, provided an assessment of money approximating the expense and loss of time of those who served in the militia was paid.[47] Other states who retained their militias, even after the Revolutionary War commenced, also frequently required pacifists to pay a tax or to provide substitutes, but they were rarely coerced to do either.[48] The Moravians of North Carolina, however, submitted to a triple tax in lieu of military service.[49] Some volunteered in hospitals, carried the dead from the battlefield, or served as cooks for the soldiers. Some even served as bodyguards to General George Washington.[50]

The Continental Congress in 1775 also took cognizance of the presence of conscientious objectors. It acknowledged the position of the objectors by passing this resolution:

> As there are some people, who, from religious principles, cannot bear arms in any case, this Congress intends no violence to their consciences, but earnestly recommend it to them, to contribute liberally in this time of universal calamity, to the relief of their distressed brethren, in the several colonies, and do all other services to their oppressed Country, which they can consistently with their religious principles.[51]

This resolution was significant because it was Congress's first official recognition of the legal validity of minority religious views. Conscientious objection had achieved a place in the meaning of religious liberty on a national scope.

The Constitution submitted to the states for ratification in 1787 contained no reference to the matter of conscientious objection. Three state ratifying conventions submitted proposals to exempt from military service those persons opposed to bearing arms on religious grounds. Fear was expressed in Pennsylvania's convention that without such an exemption, conscientious objectors might be forced into military service. At the First Congress in 1789, James Madison proposed as part of a constitutional amendment a clause providing that "no person religiously scrupulous of bearing arms shall be compelled to render military service in person."[52] The proposal was not adopted, but several state constitutions did include provisions for conscientious exemption from military service.

In all of the wars in which the United States has been involved since the American Revolution, the issue of conscientious objection has been a subject of considerable controversy. Congress has always sought to provide some measure of protection for conscientious objectors—by designating for exempt status certain pacifist denominations, ordained ministers and theological students, or others who objected on religious grounds. In those cases in which these provisions have been judicially challenged, the legislation has been upheld, although conscientious objection has never been elevated to the status of a constitutional right.[53]

## Treaties with Foreign Nations

After successfully winning its independence from Great Britain, the United States entered into three treaties with foreign countries. These were treaties of friendship in which the nations exchanged guarantees of free trade and commerce, navigation privileges, merchant vessel protections, and related matters of mutual benefit. These treaties were with the Netherlands in 1782, Sweden in 1783, and Prussia in 1785.

Each of these treaties contained provisions for the right of the free exercise of religion of the citizens of the contracting nations located in the jurisdiction of the other. In comparison with commercial treaties entered into by other nations during the same time period, these provisions were innovations in treaties between nations; in the late eighteenth century most nations were still reluctant to grant religious freedom to their own citizens, much less to foreigners. Strictly from the standpoint of the progress of religious liberty in the United States, they are further evidence of the prevailing mood favoring religious freedom for all citizens in the years preceding the adoption and ratification of the U.S. Constitution.

On 8 October 1782 the United States and the Netherlands signed the Treaty of Peace and Commerce. Article Four, in part, reads:

> There shall be an entire and perfect liberty of Conscience allowed to the subjects and inhabitants of each party, and to their families; and no one shall be molested in regard to his worship, provided he submits, as to the public demonstration of it to the laws of the country.[54]

On 3 April 1783 the Treaty of Amity and Commerce was concluded with Sweden, which contains almost verbatim the provision for religious liberty appearing in the treaty with the Netherlands.[55] It is true that these provisions qualify the grant of a generally broad right of religious freedom by permitting "molestation" (presumably arrest) for worshipping in a manner that would violate "the laws of the country." This is a rather open-ended limitation that could be interpreted to mean almost anything, but the spirit of the provision remains admirable, especially in its context as a development in the progress of religious liberty internationally.

The Treaty of Amity and Commerce between the United States and Prussia was subsequently concluded on 10 September 1785. Its Article Eleven contained a guarantee of religious liberty similar to that appearing in the treaties with the Netherlands and Sweden:

> The most perfect freedom of conscience and of worship is granted to the citizens or subjects of either party within the jurisdiction of the other, without being liable to molestation in that respect for any cause other than an insult on the religion of others.[56]

These provisions of course owe as much to the progress of religious liberty in the respective counterpart nations as in the United States. The Netherlands, after breaking free from Spanish rule in the sixteenth century, had become a bastion of religious freedom in the seventeenth century.[57] Amsterdam, in particular, as one writer described it, "was at that time the freest city of the world, in publication, in religion, in the reception of refugees from many a persecution and banishment."[58] The country's leadership in the advancement of religious liberty was interrupted in the early eighteenth century by a renewed persecution of Catholics, but by the latter part of that century the strict temper of Calvinist orthodoxy had subsided considerably.[59]

The treaty with Prussia was signed when Frederick the Great was in power. Under his reign, Prussia's population was made up largely of Catholics and Lutherans, but as one who had been greatly influenced by the French Enlightenment, Frederick advocated the reception and toleration of varying beliefs in the interests of political and economic welfare.[60] Frederick's position is described by historian Preserved Smith:

> Despising Christian dogma as he did, the ruler found in Christian ethics a useful support to the state. He sought, in giving freedom to Catholics, Calvinists, Lutherans, Jews, and all others, not to extirpate the religious sentiments entirely—for that, he feared, would be dangerous to the state—but to encourage all to train men to be good citizens and lovers of their kind. Indeed, far from regarding variety of religion as a danger and weakness to the state, as almost all statesmen had hitherto done, he thought of it as a distinct advantage. Though he esteemed Luther "a mad friar and a barbarous writer," he acknowledged a debt of gratitude to him for dividing the Church so that reason could unfold, philosophy and science enlarge their boundaries, and tolerance increase. The influence of Frederick's example was great and beneficent.[61]

Sweden, a Lutheran state after the early sixteenth century, had by the early eighteenth century relaxed its policy of persecuting dissenting sects. By 1785, when it entered into the treaty just described with the United States, Sweden was ruled by Gustavus III, like Frederick the Great an "Enlightened Despot." Under his reign, the secularism of the Enlightenment, the ethical and devotional emphases of Quietism, and the rise of Swedenborgianism all in varying ways weakened the power of Lutheran dogma. Although a wave of renewed efforts to compel compliance with the state religion was renewed in the nineteenth century, the late eighteenth century was a period of marked emphasis on religious toleration.[62]

The appearance of provisions guaranteeing freedom of faith and practice in the treaties that have been described indicate the advancing status of religious liberty in Western nations in the eighteenth century. This growth was influenced not only by the rationalism of the era but also by the growing belief that coercion of religious belief was harmful to the state as well as to the individual. These factors converged in the new emphases on nationalism, democracy, individual rights, and freedom, all of which found their greatest expression in the United States.

### Religious Liberty under the Northwest Ordinance

The Treaty of Paris recognized the independence of the United States and granted the new nation a vast domain of western territory. In 1787 the Continental Congress developed a comprehensive plan for the development and government of the Northwest Territory—the country between the Mississippi, the Ohio, and the Great Lakes. This plan, called the Northwest Ordinance, laid out three stages for the evolution of each territory into a state. In the first stage, congressionally appointed officials would govern the territory, in the second an elected legislature would share power with them, and in the third, when the people numbered 60,000 or more, they might frame a constitution and apply for statehood.[63]

In its desire to encourage the geographical expansion of the United States, the Congress wanted to assure potential inhabitants that they would enjoy in the territories the same civil and religious liberties they had enjoyed in the states. To this end, the Northwest Ordinance, enacted 13 July 1787, contained a number of significant provisions:

> And for extending the fundamental principles of civil and religious liberty, which form the basis whereon these republics, their laws and constitutions are erected; to fix and establish those principles as the basis of

all laws, constitutions and governments, which forever hereafter shall be formed in the said territory. . . .

It is hereby ordained and declared . . . that the following articles shall be considered as articles of compact between the original States and the people and the States in said territory, and forever remain unalterable, unless by common consent, to wit:

Article 1. No person, demeaning himself in a peaceable and orderly manner, shall ever be molested on account of his mode of worship, or religious sentiments, in the said territory.

Article 3. Religion, morality and knowledge, being necessary to good government and the happiness of mankind, schools and the means of education shall forever be encouraged. . . .[64]

The overall intent of these provisions was to provide a climate of religious freedom in the territories. Given the policy of Congress of recognizing the sovereignty of the various states in regard to religion, and foreseeing that the territories would one day become equally sovereign states, it is implausible that Congress sought a firmer "establishment" policy in the territories.

At the same time, it is undeniable that Article 3 endorses religion in general as something to be encouraged in the educational systems to be formed. But it is important to understand the provision as merely an endorsement of the importance of religion in education—education that in the eighteenth century was almost universally administered by churches—and not as a call for a program of governmentally funded religious instruction. The provision is merely saying that the education that takes place in the new territories should encourage religion, morality, and knowledge, since these are essential to mankind's happiness and to the preparation of citizens' participation in democratic government.

The Northwest Ordinance was reenacted, after the ratification of the Constitution, by the First Congress on 7 August 1789.[65] Because of the Ordinance's implication in Article 3 that religion is an essential component of education, a number of scholars have argued that the First Congress, which adopted the Bill of Rights, could not have intended that the religion clauses require the federal government to be neutral between religion and irreligion.[66] Of course, under a broad interpretation of the Establishment Clause, one that proscribes the advancement, support, or promulgation of religion in general, the Northwest Ordinance would clearly be unconstitutional. And, as Justice William Rehnquist has argued, it is unlikely that the First Congress would have reenacted the Ordinance in 1789 if it thought it was contrary to the meaning of the Establishment Clause.[67]

However, there are a number of factors that work against this view that emerge from a study of the history of the Northwest Ordinance. To begin with, Thomas Jefferson's original 1784 draft of the Ordinance omitted, as would be expected, any reference to or mention of religion. It was April 1785, however, before the congressional committee appointed to produce an ordinance considered in detail Jefferson's proposal. The committee recommended that the central section of every township be reserved for the support of education "and the section immediately adjoining the same to the northward, for the support of religion, the profits arising therefrom in both instances, to be applied forever according to the will of the majority of male residents of full age within the same."[68] Charles Pinckney of South Carolina then proposed that instead of saying "support of religion," the Ordinance should read for the support "of religion and charitable uses."[69] This satisfied some, but not others, who insisted that the word religion be dropped altogether. Pinckney then withdrew his proposed amendment.[70] When the committee's proposal was then put to a vote on 23 April, seventeen members voted in favor, six against. By states, however, there were only five affirmative votes,[71] and the provision therefore was rejected.[72] James Madison was aghast that such a provision so contrary to the spirit of religious liberty should have ever been proposed at all. Commenting on the matter in a letter to James Monroe, Madison remarked: "How a regulation so unjust in itself, so foreign to the authority of Congress, so hurtful to the sale of the public land, and smelling so strongly of an antiquated Bigotry, could have received the countenance of a Committee is truly a matter of astonishment."[73]

All of this parliamentary maneuvering reveals the fundamental uncertainty or ambivalence of the members of the Continental Congress with respect to religion and law. Some were convinced that sharp lines should be drawn between the two; others saw them appropriately linked.

Two years later the whole matter was still one of some controversy. The Northwest Ordinance was approved by the Continental Congress on 13 July 1787. But a draft of the Ordinance considered two days earlier had been rejected on account of similar disagreements over the role that religion should play in the territories. The earlier draft read, in part: "Institutions for the promotion of religion and morality, schools and the means of education shall be forever encouraged."[74] This was an obvious attempt to provide that churches ("institutions for the promotion of religion and morality") and schools would be encouraged. Who could dispute that if religion and morality were necessary to good government, it followed that churches no less than schools must be encouraged? But experience wielded more force than logic. And the experience of many of the delegates was that government should not be in the business of advancing religion, even if religion was essential to good government and human happiness. Others who believed that government ought to have a role in advancing religion, especially in the untamed and un-churched western lands, argued in favor of reserving special sections of land to support the churches. The principle was there, but the votes were not. In the final version, the language calling for the encouragement of religious institutions was dropped in favor of the encouragement of schools and the means of education only. The unmistakable conclusion is that up until the very time of passage of the Northwest Ordinance, there were fundamental differences in both strategy and sentiment re-specting the role that the Continental Congress should play in promoting religion in the West. These differences are no doubt reflected in the somewhat ambiguous language of Article 3: "Religion, morality and knowledge, being necessary to good government and the happiness of mankind, schools and the means of education should be forever encour-aged."[75]

There is a final matter that works against the view that the First Congress would not have reenacted the Ordinance in 1789 if it thought it was contrary to the meaning of the Establishment Clause. The reen-actment of the Ordinance took place on 7 August 1789, eight days before the debates on the proposed religion clauses even began. The argument that Congress, in passing the Northwest Ordinance, did so in contraven-tion of matters that it had not yet even discussed on the floor, is hardly convincing.

These factors tend to make uncertain, in the final analysis, the rela-tionship between the Northwest Ordinance and the intentions of the constitutional framers regarding the separation of church and state. The language in the Ordinance that seemingly advanced religion was, of course, considerably watered down as a result of the objections of some of the members of the Continental Congress that the originally proposed language too obviously advanced religion in the Northwest Territory. The language affecting religion, then, that appeared in the Ordinance in its final form is perhaps best understood as a carryover from the practice of the Continental Congress to legislate rather freely regarding religious matters; after all, even though the legislation was reenacted by the First Congress, the original language was strictly the product of the Conti-nental Congress. The Ordinance, therefore, seems indeed to support an accommodationist interpretation of the Establishment Clause, but it was for this reason the subject of considerable controversy, even at the time of its adoption. Obviously, the implications of the Ordinance's links be-tween religion and government, and ultimately the religion clauses themselves, were not altogether clear even to the framers; there was not then, as there is not today, a uniform comprehension of "original intent."

Many modern commentators have focused on the Northwest Ordinance's apparent advancement of religion in seeking to arrive at the framers' intended meaning of the Establishment Clause. While good arguments can be made on this point by both accommodationists and separationists, a more fundamental contribution of the Northwest Ordinance was to the disestablishment movement. The broad religious freedom granted to settlers under the Ordinance effectively prevented new states from having religious establishments. States admitted to the Union pursuant to the Northwest Ordinance, beginning with Ohio, have all had to conform to the requirements of the Ordinance. Each of the states was therefore settled on the basis of non-establishment, which may in turn have had some influence in the ongoing movement toward disestablishment in the original states.

## Concluding Remarks

The movement for religious liberty in America had three basic components: allowing for freedom of conscience; the removal of civil disabilities on unorthodox sects and non-Christians; and the disestablishment of the churches. More progress toward these reforms was achieved in the revolutionary era than in any other period of American history. Because religion was a matter of either colony or state control, progress toward the disestablishment of churches and the removal of civil disabilities was not generally the result of the efforts of the Continental Congress. The Congress did, however, make a number of notable contributions toward establishing freedom of conscience.

The wartime events afforded Congress the opportunity to grant freedom of conscience and belief to several foreign groups. Because it sought Quebec as an ally in the war, Congress was compelled to act tolerantly and respectfully toward the Catholicism embraced by most Canadians. This attitude led Congress to guarantee to the citizens of Quebec in the Articles of Confederation the right to "maintain any religious worship" without the loss of civil rights if Quebec chose to become a state alongside the existing thirteen. In one respect, this was only an extension of Congress's "states' rights" policy, but in another respect, it was indeed an advancement on religious liberty because none of the thirteen original states had Catholic populations anywhere approaching that of Quebec. These important steps in turn encouraged all Americans to develop tolerant attitudes toward Catholics.

The Continental Congress also granted to deserting foreign mercenaries of the British army of any "religion they might be . . . the benefits of civil and religious freedom" if they chose to settle in the United States. Moreover, in treaties with Sweden, Prussia, and the Netherlands, the United States granted to citizens of those countries "entire and perfect liberty of conscience" while living in or visiting America. The presence of these foreigners added to the growing religious diversity in the United States, and the Continental Congress's actions to assure these foreign citizens that their religious faith would not be an impediment to their enjoyment of civil rights while in America were important events in the progress of religious liberty in America.

The war helped to define the limits of rights of conscience that were to be enjoyed by American citizens as well. Quakers, Mennonites, Brethren, and other pacifist groups objected on religious grounds to bearing arms. Initially looked upon as disloyal traitors to the American cause, gradually these pacifists became better understood and even respected for their conscientious objection. The Continental Congress encouraged the widespread development of these attitudes by formally recognizing the pacifists' objector status and by providing alternative means of wartime service in which the pacifists could participate in the war effort without violating their consciences.

All of these steps taken by the Continental Congress contributed to the meaning of the Free Exercise Clause that later came to be embodied in the First Amendment. The Northwest Ordinance also contributed to the progress of the free exercise of religion in America and ultimately to the meaning of the Free Exercise Clause by prohibiting the arrest of a territorial citizen "on account of his mode of worship, or religious sentiments." Practically speaking, because of the considerable numbers of citizens who came under its provisions, the Northwest Ordinance probably did more to guarantee religious freedom in the United States in the first 100 years of the nation's history than the religion clauses themselves.

*Ten*

## VIRTUE AND THE CONTINENTAL CONGRESS

The occasion was the commencement of Massachusetts's new constitution in October 1780. In attendance at the Brattle Street Congregational Church for the inaugural ceremony were members of the state's senate and house of representatives. At their head sat the governor, John Hancock, a wealthy Bostonian who had served as president of the Continental Congress and who had the distinction of being the first to sign the Declaration of Independence. Dr. Samuel Cooper, pastor of the church, chose Jeremiah 30:20–21 as his text: "Their congregation shall be established before me: and their nobles shall be of themselves, and their governor shall proceed from the midst of them." Dr. Cooper remarked first on the appositness of the verse. "The prophecy seems to have been made for ourselves," he assured Mr. Hancock and the others assembled, "[for] it is so exactly descriptive of that comprehensive, that essential civil blessing, which kindles the lustre, and diffuses the joy of the present day."[1] Then, in a marvel of hermeneutics, the theologian cum patriot declared that the form of government given the Hebrews at Mount Sinai had been a "free republic" in which "sovereignty resided in the people," and which comprised magistracy, council, and an assembly. Dr. Cooper moved forward through the centuries, briefly adverting to the "immortal writings of Sidney and Locke, and other glorious defenders of the liberties of human nature," as well as to the thoughts and accomplishments of Louis XVI and Edmund Burke. But the special focus on that October day was the merit of the state's new constitution. "I need not enlarge before such an audience the particular excellencies of this constitution: How effectually it makes the people the keepers of their own liberties, with whom they are certainly safest: How nicely it poizes the powers of government, in order to render them as far as human foresight can, what God ever designed they should be, powers only to do good."

Yet as Cooper continued, moved by this signal event, warmed in the season of hope after Washington's cold winter on the Delaware three years past, he spoke at once of both the state *and* the larger confederation of which it was a part. So much lay before them. "We seem called by heaven to make a large part of this globe a seat of knowledge and liberty." Theirs, he declared, was the opportunity to "establish the honour and happiness of this new world . . . to invite the injured and oppressed, the worthy and the good to these shores." "Thus," Cooper concluded, "will our country resemble the new city which St. John saw 'coming down from God out of heaven.' "

But the great question before Dr. Cooper and Mr. Hancock was not theirs alone. It challenged, at that moment, the Congress in Philadelphia, just as it had every political theorist since Aristotle, and it was this: How would a new republic, a government whose legitimacy derived explicitly from the people, be maintained? It was a question of the greatest importance, for if they were unable to provide the answer and then effectively implement it across the land, the promising young nation to which they had given birth would surely self-destruct. When Dr. Cooper suggested that the cultivation of a virtuous citizenry was the answer, he stated no novelty. The former president of the Congress who sat before him, the current members of the Congress in Philadelphia, and the authors of the state constitution whose work was that day being implemented would regard the necessity of virtue as axiomatic. If the state and its new constitution were to prosper, if the confederation of which Massachusetts was a part were to fulfill its ambitious destiny, virtue must be the coin of the realm. Again, from Dr. Cooper's sermon:

> Our civil rulers will remember, that as piety and virtue support the honour and happiness of every community, they are particularly requisite in a free government. Virtue is the spirit of a republic; for where all power is derived from the people, all depends on their good disposition. . . . We have now a government free indeed; but after all, it remains with the people, under God, to make it an honorable and happy one: This must ultimately depend on the prudence of their elections, and the virtue of their conduct.[2]

To be sure, not all members of the Continental Congress shared Dr. Cooper's religious zeal. As we have already seen, some opposed overt religious expression by the Congress *qua* an official political body. That upon which they all could agree, however, was that the success of any democratic political society depends on the character of the citizens of which it is comprised; and that virtue is the character to be sought. John Adams, for instance, himself a member of Cooper's Brattle Street Church, in writing his cousin Zabdiel Adams, a Congregational minister, expressed his conviction directly: "Statesmen, my dear sir, may plan and speculate for liberty, but it is religion and morality alone which can establish the principles upon which freedom can securely stand. The only foundation of a free constitution is pure virtue."[3]

But virtue is not self-defining, just as its role is not self-evident. This chapter explores how members of the Continental Congress and their contemporaries understood the term. More especially, it examines the role of virtue in supporting political society, how it is to be fostered, and how virtue and religion in particular are related. Of special interest in the "original intent" context is the question: Did the founders intend to promote virtue among the citizenry by advancing religion? What we find in this period of the Continental Congress is a kind of high water mark for declamations of virtue, both in official and unofficial statements, in remarks of delegates and in anonymous editorials in the colonial press, in sermons (as with Dr. Cooper's) and in political tracts. This would be a republic of virtue, so the consensus seemed to be. Yet when the decade and a half of the life of the Continental Congress closed in 1789, expostulations of virtue and a civic humanism had begun to yield to the ascendance of a Madisonian pragmatism. In an important way, the election of George Washington in 1788 marked both the culmination and end of a classical republican vision and the role of virtue.[4]

Bernard Bailyn, one of a number of preeminent scholars of the colonial period, has written of the historian's task as being that of a "narrator of worlds in motion—worlds as complex, unpredictable, and transient as our own. The historian must re-tell, with a new richness, the story of what some one of the worlds of the past was, how it ceased to be what it was . . . and [how it] developed into what no one could have anticipated."[5] Thus we do here in looking at the world of virtue and the Continental Congress. This was an era when hopes for virtue as foundation and security for an American Republic flourished and then ebbed. We begin with one snapshot of that world in motion, the second day of the First Continental Congress: 6 September 1774.

## Virtue Considered

Patrick Henry, delegate from Virginia, stood to his feet. "Government is dissolved. Fleets and armies and the present state of things show that government is dissolved. Where are your landmarks, your boundaries of colonies? We are in a state of nature. . . . The distinctions between Virginians, Pennsylvanians, New Yorkers, and New Englanders are no more. I am not a Virginian, but an American."[6] As the record of that day's proceedings show, the other members of the newly formed Congress were not so anxious to declare that the colonies had returned to such a pre-societal condition nor to so readily embrace this heady vision of nationalism. They did, however, clearly follow the import of Henry's Lockean reference, and they certainly agreed that theirs was a unique opportunity in the midst of their very real crisis. The Congress had convened in response to the Coercive Acts and the enlarged Quartering Act explicitly to ensure, in the words of their Declaration and Resolves, that "their religion, laws, and liberties may not be subverted." Henry notwithstanding, the Congress, in this initial approach, couched its appeal in terms of English colonists who were loyal subjects of the British sovereign. Yet the tenor of the early deliberations reflected an interest in the nature of government, per se, and not just a simple redress of grievances, showing both sophistication and a distinct American pragmatism. This First Congress drew from a wide number of authorities, classical and modern, interpreted them under the light of their own experiences, and adapted them to their own exigencies. So, for instance, the Declaration and Resolves appealed to Montesquieu ("It is indispensably necessary to good government . . . that the constituent branches be independent of each other"); Locke ("The aforesaid deputies . . . do claim, demand, and insist on . . . their indubitable rights and liberties which cannot be legally taken from them, altered, or abridged by any power whatever, without their own consent"); and the English constitution and common law. Range beyond the formal documents, and one finds the Congress also citing and adapting the work of classical and Renaissance writers, radical Whigs, and New England Puritanism.

Then, as the Congress moved from its tentative steps with the Declaration and Resolves to the truly radical step of the Declaration of Independence two years later, it pointedly shifted focus from *modus vivendi* to establishment of an entirely new government. Even if this were not a state of nature to which the colonies had reverted, the American situation did offer the clearest venue yet to create anew. The delegates understood the enormity of the task and the unparalleled opportunity. "Objects of the most stupendous magnitude," Adams wrote a month before the signing of the Declaration, "and measures in which the lives and liberties of millions yet unborn are intimately interested, are now before us. We are in the very midst of a revolution, the most complete, unexpected, and remarkable, of any in the history of nations."[7]

But of course the challenge of revolution and government building for the millions yet unborn was not straightforward. As the founders scanned history's distant panoramas searching for a guiding political template, they were forced to take another dramatic step. John Diggins's observation nicely captures the crux of the task: the Congress "sought to learn from history in order to defy the past."[8] And why defy the past? Because history did not merely instruct, it warned. History offered its litany of governments that flourished, but it could furnish no such list of those that endured. Describing the attempts to found republics after the fall of Rome, Adams wrote that these efforts had "foamed, raged, and burst, like so many waterspouts upon the ocean."[9] That framed the compelling problem for the Continental Congress as it matured: how to form, not just a separate government or an effective government, but an enduring government. To do that, the Congress would have to devise the best of structures *and* ameliorate the worst tendencies of government's practitioners. The founders and the colonists generally recognized that not only must government restrain injustice and evil, but also it must itself be restrained. That is why Madison wrote in the next decade that government itself is "the greatest of all reflections on human nature." Theory could create the perfect government on paper, but government still comprises imperfect people; and that gave the political deliberations of the Congress and, later, the Constitutional Convention their real seriousness.[10] Defiance of the British would prove the far simpler task.

It is in this war with the past and the vision for a government that could long endure that one must approach the Continental Congress and its revolution of virtue. Talk of virtue was not so much pious cant; it was a serious proposal to arrest the otherwise inevitable mortality of political society. The success of the body politic would, they held, be dependent on the character of the people it comprised. John Witherspoon, president of Princeton and one of the few ministers to serve in the Continental Congress, held exactly that position. Preaching in May 1776, a month before his election as a New Jersey delegate, Witherspoon broadly declared:

> What I have here in view is to point out to you the concern which every good man ought to take in the national character and manners, and the means which he ought to use in bearing down impiety and vice. . . . Nothing is more certain than that a general profligacy and corruption of manners make a people ripe for destruction. A good form of government may hold the rotten materials together for some time, but beyond a certain pitch, even the best constitution will be ineffectual, and slavery must ensue.[11]

Adams, writing as "Novanglus" in February 1775, put it succinctly: "Liberty can no more exist without virtue and independence, than the body can live and move without a soul."[12] But how did the Congress regard virtue? How did the delegates employ the ubiquitous term?[13] They began with the Aristotle of the *Nichomachean Ethics* and secondarily of the *Politics*. To the degree that virtue (Greek *arete*, "excellence") is regarded as "habituated character," the Congress would have concurred.[14] Jefferson certainly emphasized habituation. Writing in 1785 (he was minister to France at the time) to his fifteen-year-old nephew, Jefferson urged, "Encourage all your virtuous dispositions, and exercise them whenever an opportunity arises, being assured that they will gain strength by exercise as a limb of the body does, and that exercise will make them habitual. From the practice of the purest virtue you may be assured you will derive the most sublime comforts in every moment of life and in the moment of death."[15] And much of Franklin's treatment of virtue in the *Autobiography* also had this Aristotelian emphasis on habituation.

Additionally, the Congress adapted Montesquieu, the French theorist who gave them more than just the idea of separation of powers. Montesquieu had adapted the classical trichotomy of three types of governmental structure, making them "despotism," "monarchy," and "republic." Each has, Montesquieu wrote, its animating "principle," a psychological force that informs them. Despotism works by fear, the populace being subservient only as long as the maximum leader can intimidate his people. Monarchies flourish by love of honor; the king must be surrounded by sycophantic courtiers vying for preeminence. But republics can live only so long as there is virtue generally diffused among the citizens. This principle Montesquieu described as "moral virtue directed to the public good," with the emphasis falling on public good.[16]

It is important to note, however, that at no point did the Congress slavishly adhere to earlier views of virtue. They adapted, and sometimes significantly departed from, their predecessors. In part, their reading of Locke was responsible. Aristotle saw political society as essential to realizing man's highest good. Locke saw it not as the route to human perfection, but as a mechanism for securing individual rights. That made a world of difference for virtue. In Aristotle's schema, the polis was a precondition to character. Within this polis men were habituated to a civic virtue, a political excellence. The Continental Congress, because of Locke, laid the stress differently. Human perfectibility was increasingly subordinated to the instrumental idea of government as securing life, liberty, and property; and virtue must antecede good government.[17]

But virtue, as the Congress understood it, had another important intellectual source that modified the classical tradition, one that is obscured if the members of Congress are approached simply as either classical republicans or Lockean liberals. That was the Western Judeo-Christian tradition. The delegates' views about the role of virtue were more than just a sort of political genuflection to Puritan thinking. Where Locke's *Second Treatise* had given the Congress the true individual, a person with unalienable rights prior to his political persona, the Puritans had invested the individual with real psychological depth. Behind much of the founders' writings on values to be inculcated and traits to be eschewed, one finds this Puritan anthropology, often in secularized coloration.[18] In that regard, one can easily describe Benjamin Franklin, who joined the Congress in 1775, as a secularized Puritan.[19] Indeed, Sydney Ahlstrom has suggested that *The Federalist* and the various writings of John Adams "can be read as Puritan contributions to Enlightenment political theory."[20] But this informing Puritan anthropology was unnerving even as it was complicating. This ensured that Congress must be concerned not only with the structure of the republic's government, but also with the character of the republic's citizens, precisely the point Witherspoon sought to make in the sermon cited above.

With this fusion of sources, then, the Congress approached virtue as having a dual aspect, both of which facets find ample illustration in the founders' writings. On the one hand, virtue conveyed a private morality and the ordering of personal affairs. It was at this point that the founders' debt to a Puritan intellectual milieu is most evident. On the other, it had a public dimension that has been well illuminated by those who have stressed the classical republican elements. This public, or civic, virtue inhered in the use of the word "disinterest" and its derivatives. The word, however, did not indicate "no interest"; but, rather, the opposite of self-interest. Samuel Johnson's justly famous dictionary captures the use of disinterest as writers on both sides of the Atlantic employed it in the eighteenth century: "What is contrary to one's wish or prosperity; indifference to profit; superiority to regards of private advantage."[21]

This use of virtue arrayed disinterest and concern for the commonweal on one hand and self-interest, passions, and lack of reason on the other. The popularity of George Washington derives, in no small part, from his embodiment of this virtue of disinterest. Writing his brother in June 1775, after being given command of the army, the general declared:

> I am now to bid adieu to you, and to every kind of domestick ease, for a while. I am imbarked on a wide ocean, boundless in its prospect and from whence, perhaps, no safe harbour is to be found. I have been called upon by the unanimous voice of the colonies to take command of the Continental Army—an honour I neither sought after, nor desired, as I am

thoroughly convinced, that it requires greater abilities and much more
experience than I am master of. . . . That I may discharge the trust to the
satisfaction of my imployers is my first wish.[22]

Adams also commented on just this aspect of virtue. Writing in his
autobiography, Adams reflected on the charge that his proposals of independence for the colonies really stemmed from motives of self-interest.
Adams assiduously denied such charges and then added his conviction
that the one truly fit for public office must renounce the "promising road
to profits, honors, power, [and] pleasure" and instead "devote himself to
labor, danger, and death, and possibly to disgrace and infamy."[23]

Virtue had its Manichaean opposite in the thinking of the members
of Congress, just as it did for writers on the Continent. That dreadful
counterpoise was termed "corruption." Like virtue, corruption embraced
both private and public components. Private corruption was loss of morality, an entropy of the soul. Again, considering Franklin's elaborate
personal scheme to suppress vice and promote the several virtues,[24] one
sees the sort of preoccupation many writers had with this inward dete-
rioration. But corruption certainly could, indeed always did, occur in
the national life. Here the sense was not just that of national sin. A
corrupt and tyrannical government reflected both moral infirmities and
a national departure from first principles. The earlier jeremiads, so much
a part of Puritan preaching, were turned to national aims. These now
secular jeremiads (and joined by explicitly religious ones from the pulpits) traced departure from some earlier purer practice of governance and
a corruptive descent into a debased polity. In a word, the loss of virtue
spelled national doom. And it was a sentiment held by political writers
on both sides of the Atlantic. Indeed, much of the founders' thinking
on virtue reflected that in England only a generation previously. Thomas
Gordon, writing in *Cato's Letters*, warned that the "governors and enemies of Rome destroy[ed] virtue to set up power. . . . The Roman virtue
and the Roman liberty expired together; tyranny and corruption came
upon them almost hand in hand."[25] Edmund Burke recognized that "society cannot exist unless a controlling power upon the will and appetite
be placed somewhere, and the less of it there is within, the more there
must be without."[26]

Consequently, the founders took pains to describe the loss of virtue
in Lycurgus's Sparta and its corruption into a decadent regime; the loss
of virtue in republican Rome as it transmuted into a corrupt empire; and
the English departure from the ancient constitution under the Stuarts or,
later, Walpole and the Hanoverians. Congress, of course, took special note
of the situation in England. Adams, writing as "Novanglus" in January

1775, described England as "one mass of corruption" where "luxury, effeminacy, and venality [had] arrived at . . . a shocking pitch."[27] Again, from Adams: "From being the nursery of heroes, [England] became the residence of musicians, pimps, panders, and catamites." Franklin was equally harsh. Contrasting the "extreme corruption" in the "old rotten state" of England, Philadelphia's printer—one year before the Declaration of Independence—could boast of the "glorious public virtue so predominant in our rising country."[28] Richard Henry Lee, writing to Sam Adams, alluded to the "selfishness and corruption of Europe." He then added, "It would seem as if there were a general jealousy beyond the water, of the powerful effects of to be derived from republican virtue here."[29] Elbridge Gerry, delegate of Massachusetts, wrote in March 1776 that America could "hold her rank in creation, and give law to herself." He little doubted that the time was fast approaching when she must do so because "the people of Great Britain are corrupt, and destitute of publick virtue."[30] And the "long train of abuses and usurpations," which Jefferson recounted in the Declaration, was a litany of sure proofs of corruption in the mother country.

Some saw England's corruption shot through the contemporary world. Sam Adams numbered among them. Writing James Warren in April 1777, Adams declared, "I have always been of the opinion, that we must depend on our own efforts under God for the establishment of our liberties. . . . There seems not to be virtue enough left in the world from generous and disinterested motives to interpose in support of the common rights of mankind."[31] John Adams provided some of the most bleak assessments. The virtue of disinterestedness appeared, he claimed, about once every 500 years, but there were "2,000 instances every year of the semblance of disinterestedness, counterfeited for the most selfish purposes."[32] Unfortunately, there was considerable evidence it had infected the colonies. Franklin was commenting on some of his own countrymen when he said, "Place before the eyes of [some] men a post of honour, that at the same time be a place of profit, and they will move heaven and earth to obtain it."[33] And Adams could apply the same reasoning to his own family. Writing Benjamin Rush, Adams confessed that, without religion, the family would have been "rakes, fops, sots, gamblers, starved with hunger, frozen with cold, scalped by Indians, &c, &c, &c."[34]

Of the various threats to virtue that the Congress noted, two deserve special attention. One was an old fear that had occupied the writings of political theorists for centuries: the great fear of consolidation of power. Members of the Congress were constantly exercised by the dread of accumulated power. In 1777 Thomas Burke, newly elected delegate from North Carolina, wrote the governor, Richard Caswell, of his initial observations. He noted that the other members of the Congress seemed genuinely concerned for the public weal, that they were truly "disinterested." But he perceived something else at work, finding many of the debates pulled toward opposite directions: both toward increasing power and toward restraining it. He concluded, "The more experience I acquire, the stronger is my conviction, that *unlimited power cannot be safely trusted* to any man or set of men on earth." Then, sounding as if he had just laid aside his Newton on gravity and acceleration, Burke wrote, "Power of all kinds has an irresistible propensity to increase a desire for itself. It gives the passion of ambition a velocity which increases in its progress, and this is a passion which grows in proportion as it is gratified."[35] "Power," wrote the Antifederalist "Brutus," "lodged in the hands of rulers to be used at discretion, is almost always exercised to the oppression of the people, and the aggrandizement of themselves."[36]

One of the most dramatic debates about the consolidation of power followed Washington's request, in the darkest days of the war, for increased latitude to make military decisions. Congress communicated to General Washington its approval of his request through the executive committee in Philadelphia (the larger body of Congress had been forced to seek safety in Baltimore because of the British). In its communique, the committee wrote the general, "Happy is this country that the general of their forces can safely be entrusted with the most unlimited power and neither personal security, liberty or property be in the least degree endangered thereby."[37] In light of other deliberations, this marked an extraordinary approbation. Even so, not all were entirely sanguine. In a personal letter to Abigail in April 1777, Adams asserted that this authority did not give Washington "sovereignty" or make him "dictator."[38]

The other great concern was an old fear in new and powerful form. The churches had disparaged the love of money for centuries, but this recrudescent concern could be called the fear of the new economics. Locke wrote of the political individual. But Adam Smith, whose *Wealth of Nations* appeared in 1776, wrote of the economic individual, capping a century of rapidly developing economic thought in Britain and on the Continent. There was little dispute that the new economics could increase a nation's wealth. Debate turned on whether such increase was really desirable. "Not everyone," Forrest McDonald writes, "agreed that increasing the wealth of the nation was entirely desirable, even if it were possible. Many believed that wealth would corrode public virtue by giving the people a taste for luxuries, by spreading a fever for gambling and speculation, and by bringing with it the rise of the 'mobs of great cities.' "[39]

A love of money and the mercantile spirit were much a target of the jeremiads of the day, filled as they were with attacks on land speculators, stockjobbers, and a variety of other opportunists. A greater concern was that this new economics underscored a new, autonomous individual. A burgeoning economy could work, as Smith wrote coolly and Bernard Mandeville ironically, through the synergism of millions of individual economic decisions. Jefferson, while not opposed to expansion of commerce and national capital, certainly numbered among those concerned about where that could lead, if unbridled by virtue. "From the conclusion of this war," he warned during the course of the Revolution, "we shall all be going downhill and these people will forget themselves, but in the sole faculty of making money."[40] Adams, writing to his friend James Warren in 1775, worried whether the colonists would support severe strictures against trade with the British. "Is there temperance, fortitude, and perseverance enough among the people to endure such a mortification of their appetites, passions, and fancies?" In other words, are the private virtues sufficient to withstand the tastes brought by the new commercialism and individual desires? Adams left the question open.[41] Writing to General Horatio Gates only a few months before the Declaration was signed, Adams lamented that "avarice to land" had made "upon this continent so many votaries to mammon."[42] And even Philadelphia, that cradle of American democracy, confronted the delegates with what conventioneers, travelers, and others have faced from time immemorial: price gouging. Writing to his home state's governor, Connecticut delegate William Williams lamented, "The price of everything here are most alarmingly extravagant, much owing to the malicious cunning of our worst enemys, the Torys, and coinciding with the boundless avarice of the merchants, whose gain is the *summum bonum* and all the God they seem to know in these parts."[43]

## The Cultivation of Virtue

In the face of these threats, hoping to "defy the past," the delegates of the Congress deliberated what could be done. What made the American situation seem so auspicious was that the Continental Congress could create a new republic, a republic of virtue, without having first to dissolve an existing government on American lands. They would instead separate from the mother country and pursue their millennial vision on the western side of the Atlantic, an American polis that could, as the Reverend Cooper put it, "invite the injured and oppressed, the worthy and the good to these shores." Of course, to build such a republic of virtue required no little effort. Men both in and out of the Congress debated ideas about how that could be done and the way in which virtue could be employed. Dr. Benjamin Rush, appropriately, approached the connection between national and moral decay and hope for antidote in a scientific way: "We daily see matter of a perishable nature rendered durable by certain chemical operations. In like manner I conceive that it is possible to analyze and combine power in such manner as not only to increase the happiness but to promote the duration of republican forms of government far beyond the terms limited for them by history."[44] As the deliberations continued in the colonies, delegates of Congress and citizens alike proposed and debated a number of ways to promote virtue. Yet four avenues in particular stand out as a means to inculcating virtue: family, exemplary leadership, education, and religion.

## The Role of the Family

The family's role in cultivating virtue was axiomatic, and one finds forceful declarations in the letters of the founders, public addresses, sermons, and the press. The image of the family permeated the writings because it represented in small the order that providence had ordained for all creation. The king was portrayed as father to the nation. England was mother to its constituent colonies. Locke, for instance, in examining the "infancies of commonwealths," described early rulers not as monarchs, but as "nursing fathers tender and carefull of the publick weale."[45]

But the founders did not treat the family as mere metaphor, a literary device to describe something else. Writers on both sides of the Atlantic had understood the family to be essential to the development of both individual virtue and the larger political order. Locke maintained that virtue, not knowledge, is the primary end of education; and virtue is best developed at home. "I think it is the worst sort of good husbandry," Locke declared in *Some Thoughts on Education*, "for a father not to strain himself a little for his son's breeding; which, let his condition [i.e., social circumstances] be what it will, is the best portion he can leave him." And character so acquired had national implications, because "virtue, ability, and learning . . . has hitherto made *England* considerable in the world."[46] Similarly, Joseph Addison wrote in *The Spectator*, "The obedience of children to parents is the basis of all government."

In the colonies those same sentiments flourished. New England clergyman James Lockwood declared in a sermon of 1754, "As the civil state, as well as the churches of Christ, is furnish'd with members of private families: if the governors of these little communities, were faithful to the great trust reposed in them, and family-religion and discipline were thoroughly, prudently & strictly, maintained & . . . , the civil state would prosper and flourish from generation to generation."[47] Benjamin Rush, believing man to be a "naturally ungovernable animal," thought that the family (which he and others termed "domestick" or "family government"), with church and civil government, could produce the "highest degrees of order and virtue."[48] Similarly, an anonymous writer to the *Boston Gazette* stated ideas about virtue, corruption, and the family that the delegates in the Congress shared generally. This jeremiad to the press held:

> There is an inseparable connection between publick virtue and publick happiness. . . . I think it is worth consideration, whether the decay of morality, which is too visible among us, is not very much owing to too much laxness in *family government*. . . . [M]agistrates—ministers of the gospel and heads of families—all who have a regard for the future happiness of their country . . . [ought] to use all possible means to destroy vice and immorality of every kind and to cultivate and promote the fear of God and a love to religion in the minds of our young people—I cannot help thinking that this chiefly depends upon the *good government and institution of families*.[49]

A reflection of Adams during his years in France carries particular force. Writing in his diary in June 1778, the American minister asserted, "The foundations of national morality must be laid in private families. In vain are schools, academies and universities instituted, if loose principles and licentious habits are impressed upon children in their earliest years." He then pointedly asked, "How is it possible that children can have any just sense of the sacred obligations of morality or religion if, from their infancy, they learn that their mothers live in habitual infidelity to their fathers, and their fathers in as constant infidelity to their mothers." Then, Adams asserted the pivotal role of women in the home and their ultimate impact on the whole republican experiment:

> From all that I had read of history and government, of human life and manners, I had drawn this conclusion, that the manners of women were the most infallible barometer, to ascertain the degree of morality and virtue in a nation. . . . The manners of women, are the surest criterion by which to determine whether a republican government is practicable, in a nation or not. The Jews, the Greeks, the Romans, the Swiss, the Dutch, all lost their public spirit, their republican principles and habits, and their republican forms of government, when they lost the modesty and domestic virtues of their women.[50]

Dr. Benjamin Rush numbered among those who stressed the contribution of women to inculcating virtue within the home and inspiring it without. "The first impressions on the minds of children are generally derived from the women," Dr. Rush wrote, thus necessitating their thorough education in "the great subject of liberty and government." This remark followed his declaration that "the only useful education in a republic is to be laid in religion. Without this there can be no virtue, and without virtue there can be no liberty." Thus women, educated in virtue, trained as students of liberty, would transmit the same to their children in the home. Beyond the home, their influence would extend even further, Rush believed, because "the opinions and conduct of men are often regulated by the women in the most arduous enterprises of life."[51]

### The Role of Exemplary Leadership

Exemplary leadership was both an extension of the views on the role of "domestick government" and the belief in a hierarchical social universe. There were those, the Congress and citizenry believed, who had a special ability for leadership and on whose shoulders the responsibility for virtuous living lay especially heavy: they should both lead in virtue and model the same for others. To be sure, one can find here sentiments that are rather aristocratic, sentiments that sometimes had little connection with the leveling democratization of the French Revolution in the next decade. Roger Sherman, delegate of Connecticut and one of only two men to sign the Articles of Confederation, the Declaration, and the Constitution, held that in a republic there would be no higher rank than that of "common citizen." However, there were yet "some men in every society [who] have natural and acquired abilities superior to others, and greater wealth . . . [which] will doubtless give them some degree of influence; and justly, when they are men of integrity." And with considerably more optimism than Adams, who had once called election to the senate a protective "ostracism," Sherman believed that "the senators will doubtless be in general some of the most respectable citizens in the States for wisdom and probity, superior to mean and unworthy conduct."[52] Gouverneur Morris, who served as a delegate from New York, then Pennsylvania, held even stronger views. Shortly before the convening of Congress in 1774, Morris wrote:

> The belwethers [during Grenville's administration] jingled merrily, and roared out liberty, and property, and religion, and a multitude of cant terms, which every one thought he understood, and was egregiously mistaken. The mob begin to think and reason. Poor reptiles! it is with them

a vernal morning; they are struggling to cast off their winter's slough, they bask in the sunshine, and ere noon they will bite, depend upon it. ... And if these instances continue ... farewell aristocracy.[53]

Yet while Adams, Jefferson, Gouverneur Morris, and others might debate what should constitute a "true" aristocracy, they could agree on the criticality of virtuous leaders to model and inspire virtue in others of the body politic. Without such a virtuous elite to lead and inspire, Edmund Burke maintained there could "be no nation." Similarly, Jefferson wrote of an aristocracy of virtue and talent as:

> the most precious gift of nature, for the instruction, the trusts, and government of society. And indeed, it would have been inconsistent in creation to have formed man for the social state, and not to have provided virtue and wisdom enough to manage the concerns of society. May we not even say, that that form of government is best, which provides the most effectually for a pure selection of these natural *aristoi* into the offices of government?[54]

Members of Congress and other writers of the period were particularly exercised with the importance of exemplary leadership in the military. Sam Adams was distressed by "the abominable practice of prophane swearing in our army. It is indeed alarming. Congress has repeatedly injoynd the general officers to discountenance this practice by their authority and influence."[55]

Thus, the Congress supported a military chaplaincy: it was not just a concern for regular worship or comfort for the dying, but a concern for the living (and cursing) soldier that prompted the delegates to act. Writing in his capacity as president of the Congress, John Hancock communicated to General Washington the delegates' view that "regulations respecting chaplains are highly necessary. By increasing their pay, and enlarging the bounds of their duty, the Congress are in hopes of engaging gentlemen of superior learning and virtue to fill these stations."[56] And apparently such men of virtue could not be commissioned too soon. Daniel Roberdeau, in writing Washington about this concern of cursing, lamented, "[O]ur army vies with the most abandoned of the English troops."[57]

This principle worked negatively as well. That is, to promote virtue society not only held forth good examples but also pilloried the bad. Jefferson's characterization of George III in the Declaration followed the pattern, and many of the letters one finds in the journals of the Congress did so as well. For instance, Adams, writing Mercy Otis Warren in March 1775, observed, "If we look into human nature, and run through the various classes of life, we shall find it is really a dread of satyr [i.e., 'satire'] that restrains our species from exorbitances, more than laws, human, moral, or divine. . . . Now the business of satyr is to expose vice and vicious men as such to this scorn and to invoke virtue."[58] Adams and his fellow delegates were clearly ready, pens in hand, to uncover breaches of virtue.

### The Role of Education

An even larger role was accorded education in promoting virtue, and it was a view virtually universal. Writing late in life in the "Report of the Commissioners for the University of Virginia," Jefferson, now a retired gentleman farmer, declared, "Education generates habits of application, of order, and the love of virtue; and controls, by force of habit, any innate obliquities in our moral organization. . . . [It] engrafts a new man on the native stock, and improves what in his nature was vicious and perverse into qualities of virtue and social worth."[59] But that view had long flourished on American soil. Franklin was quite clear on the connection. Writing a friend in 1750, Franklin averred:

> Nothing is of more importance for the public weal, than to form and train up youth in wisdom and virtue. Wise and good men are, in my opinion, the strength of a state: much more so than riches or arms. . . . I think also, that general virtue is more probably to be expected and obtained from the education of youth, than from the exhortation of adult persons; bad habits and vices of the mind being, like diseases of the body, more easily prevented than cured.[60]

Dr. Benjamin Rush numbered among the most ardent and forceful advocates for education in the new nation. Noted professor of chemistry and medicine at the University of Pennsylvania, author of the first treatise in America on mental illness, and proponent for greatly expanded educational opportunities for women, Rush was clear about the connection between learning and virtue on the one hand and a sound and enduring government on the other. Writing in "A Plan for the Establishment of Public Schools," Rush declared, "From the combined and reciprocal influence of religion, liberty, and learning upon the morals, manners, and knowledge of individuals, of these upon government, and of government upon individuals, it is impossible to measure the degrees of happiness and perfection to which mankind may be raised."[61]

The Massachusetts constitution, adopted in 1780, was quite explicit in its view of the importance of education and virtue. "Wisdom and knowledge, as well as virtue, diffused generally among the body of the

people, being necessary for the preservation of their rights and liberties
. . . it shall be the duty of legislators and magistrates, in all future periods
of the Commonwealth, to cherish the interests of literature and the sci-
ences, and all seminaries of them; especially the university at Cambridge,
public schools, and grammar schools." These schools, the constitution
declared, would conduce to all the hallmarks of virtue reminiscent of the
state's Puritan past, as they would "countenance and inculcate the principles of humanity and general benevolence, public and private charity,
industry and frugality, honesty and punctuality in their dealings; sin-
cerity, good humour, and all social affections, and generous sentiments
among the people."[62]

Similarly, the Northwest Ordinance, passed in July 1787, emphasized
the importance of education and its relation to morality. Comprising both
a framework of government for the Northwest Territory and a declaration of rights (styled as "articles of compact"), the Ordinance reflected a
number of critical decisions taken by the Congress, to include those on
American Indian rights, admission of new states, and prohibition of slavery in the territory. Of significance here, after declaring freedom of religion ("No person . . . shall ever be molested on account of his worship"), the Ordinance stated, "Religion, morality, and knowledge being
necessary to good government and the happiness of mankind, schools
and the means of education shall forever be encouraged."[63]

At times, especially in delegates like Rush, who called the public
schools "nurseries of virtue and knowledge," the thoughts on education
seem to have anticipated John Dewey.[64] Writers were unabashed in declaring that education ought to simultaneously inculcate virtue and patriotism. Thus, much of the writing had a clearly utilitarian or instrumental cast. Education in this founding era must clearly lead to
something worthwhile. An anonymous essay in the *Worcester (Mass.)
Magazine* in 1787 urged:

> If America would flourish as a republick, she need only attend to the
> education of her youth. Learning is the *paladium* of her rights—as this
> flourishes, her greatness will increase. . . . [I]n a republican government,
> learning ought to be universally diffused. . . . [E]very one, whether in
> office or not, ought to become acquainted with the principles of civil
> liberty, the constitution of his country, and the rights of mankind in gen-
> eral. Where learning prevails in a community, liberality of sentiment, and
> zeal for the publick good, are the grand characteristic of the people.[65]

Franklin was even more obviously an educational utilitarian, one who
sought to salvage every minute, every activity, from waste. Preaching,
on his view, should serve clear, practical educational aims. After com-

plaining that his own minister was "dry, uninteresting, and unedifying," Philadelphia's leading printer remarked in his *Autobiography* that the sermons' "aim seem[ed] to be rather to make us Presbyterians than good citizens."[66]

Education not only abetted the inculcation of virtue; it provided a defense, as it were, against vice in others. So Madison could write, "Learned institutions ought to be favorite objects with every free people. They throw that light over the public mind which is the best security against crafty and dangerous encroachments on the public liberty."[67] Similarly, Dr. Rush held, "Without learning, men become savages or barbarians, and where learning is confined to a *few* people, we always find monarchy, aristocracy, and slavery."[68]

But education had its limits, and Puritan anthropology (even in secularized form) was there to argue against too optimistic assumptions. Franklin recognized that in his *Autobiography*. For instance, try as he might, he could not eradicate pride by his strenuous efforts at habituation. "I cannot boast of much success in acquiring the *reality* of this virtue; but I had a good deal with regard to the *appearance* of it. . . . In reality there is perhaps no one of our natural passions so hard to subdue as *pride*. Disguise it, struggle with it, beat it down, stifle it, mortify it as much as one pleases, it is still alive."[69] And John Adams, early in Washington's presidency, wrote Sam Adams agreeing that education was important to virtue but also maintaining it was not sufficient to build "dikes against the ocean, its tides and storms. Human appetites, passions, prejudices, and self-love will never be conquered by benevolence and knowledge alone, introduced by human means."[70]

### The Role of Religion

In religion, however, was to be found the most significant resource for developing virtue, in the thinking of the Congress. Americans were not the first to describe the importance, certainly. Locke, for instance, had asserted in *Some Thoughts Concerning Education* that virtue is "the first and most necessary of those endowments, that belong to a man or gentleman." He then continued, "As the foundation of this, there ought very early to be imprinted on his mind a true notion of God, as of the Supreme Being, Author and Maker of all things, from whom we receive all our good, who loves us, and gives us all things."[71] And so also on the western side of the Atlantic. "Among colonial Americans," Vetterli and Bryner write, "it was generally believed that the major source of virtue and morality was religion. . . . The single most important ingredient in virtue as it developed into new world republican philosophy was charity or love, benevolence and its corollary, brotherhood and brotherly love."[72] To be sure, some—even in the ministry—believed virtue could be inculcated and practiced by the exercise of reason and disciplined effort, but the majority view held to the contrary.[73] Adams flatly declared that republican government is supported only by "pure religion or austere morals. Public virtue cannot exist in a nation without private, and public virtue is the only foundation of republics."[74] Again from Adams in 1798: "We have no government armed with power capable of contending with human passions unbridled by morality and religion. . . . Our Constitution was made only for a moral and religious people. It is wholly inadequate to the government of any other."[75] Or Washington in his equally famous comment in his farewell address: "Of all the dispositions and habits, which lead to political prosperity, religion and morality are indispensable supports."[76]

Witherspoon, in his national fast day sermon in May 1776, discussed ways of promoting public virtue, then concluded, "He is the best friend to American liberty, who is most sincere and active in promoting true and undefiled religion. . . . Whoever is an avowed enemy to God, I scruple not to call him an enemy to his country."[77] Rush, whose views on education have already been referenced, made explicit the essential connection between religion and virtue: "The only useful education in a republic is to be laid in religion. Without this there can be no virtue, and without virtue there can be no liberty." And on the relation between religion and virtue, Franklin, responding to a critic with superb irony, wrote:

> You yourself may find it easy to live a virtuous life without the assistance afforded by religion, you having a clear perception of the advantages of virtue, and the disadvantages of vice, and possessing a strength of resolution sufficient to enable you to resist common temptations. But think how great a proportion of mankind consists of weak and ignorant men and women . . . who have need of the motives of religion to restrain them from vice, to support their virtue, and retain them in the practice of it until it becomes *habitual*, which is the great point of security. . . . If men are so wicked as we now see them *with religion*, what would they be if *without it*.[78]

The founders consistently appealed to the role ministers must play. "It is the duty of the clergy," Adams wrote in 1775, "to accommodate their discourses to the times, to preach against such sins as are most prevalent, and recommend such virtues as are most wanted. . . . Justice [for example] is a great christian as well as moral duty and virtue, which the clergy ought to inculcate and explain."[79] Rush concurred: "You are united in inculcating the necessity of morals," he reminded ministers, for "from the success or failure of your exertions in the cause of virtue, we anticipate the freedom or slavery of our country."[80]

The clergy responded with considerable focus and passion to the challenge. Jonas Clark, another of those who spoke before Governor Hancock, declared religion to be "the source of liberty, the soul of government, and the life of a people."[81] Abraham Keteltas, a Dutch Reformed minister educated at Yale and delegate to New York's Provincial Congress, which adopted that state's first constitution, aided the patriots' cause in his 1777 sermon, "God Arising and Pleading His People's Cause." Keteltas's gravaman was to demonstrate that there were not simply opposing sides in the Revolutionary War; there was a categorical separation:

> Our cause, my dear brethren, . . . is the cause of truth against error; the cause of unrighteousness against iniquity; . . . of liberty, against arbitrary power . . . and of virtue against vice. . . . In short, it is the cause of heaven against hell—of the kind Parent of the universe, against the prince of darkness. It is the cause, for which heroes have fought, patriots bled. . . . Nay, it is a cause, for which the son of God came down from his celestial throne, and expired on a cross.

And what should be the response of his audience? "Eminent divines, celebrated poets, have given it as their opinion, that America will be a glorious land of freedom, knowledge, and religion, an asylum for distressed, oppressed, and persecuted virtue. . . . Exert, therefore, your utmost efforts, strain every nerve, do all you can to promote this cause—plead earnestly with God, in its behalf, by continual prayer and supplication, by repentance and reformation, by forsaking every vice, and the practice of universal virtue."[82]

Henry Cumings, the Harvard-trained minister who preached at Lexington on the sixth anniversary of the Revolution's commencement, was more explicit about the connection of true religion to virtue and both to national victory. Providence, he averred, had allowed the wickedness of the British to accomplish His own designs for America. British "tyranny . . . rage and cruelty" had become "the occasion of stirring up a noble spirit of liberty throughout America, and kindling into blaze every spark of virtuous patriotism and true courage." Cumings warned that there had been a "general prevalence of unrighteousness [in] . . . the body politic" and that God had used the wrath of their enemies the British to "teach us righteousness, and make us pious and virtuous." At the same time, God had "remarkably restrained the wrath of our enemies; mercifully defended and protected us; and supported our righteous cause, by many signal interpositions." Then Cumings concluded:

While therefore, you are engaged with a laudable zeal in the cause of civil liberty, you will permit me to remind you, that there is another kind of liberty of an higher and nobler nature, which it is of infinite importance to every one to be possessed of; I mean that glorious internal liberty, which consists in a freedom from the dominion of sin, and in the habit and practice of all the virtues of a good life. This is that noble and exalted liberty of the sons of God, of which our saviour speaks, when he says, If the Son of God shall make you free, then shall ye be free indeed. And this, once gained, will inspire you with the greatest magnanimity and fortitude, in the cause of outward liberty.[83]

Outside the Congress, before disestablishment, one can find more explicit attempts by state government to foster a public virtue through religion. Citing again the Massachusetts constitution of 1780, of which the Reverend Dr. Samuel Cooper was so pleased and in which is found the hand of John Adams, the constitution worked from the *a priori*, "The happiness of a people, and the good order and preservation of civil government essentially depend upon piety, religion, and morality." Article III of its prefatory "Declaration of Rights" then stipulated that:

to promote their happiness and to secure the good order and preservation of their government, the people of this Commonwealth have a right to invest their legislature with power to authorize and require . . . the several towns, parishes, precincts, and other bodies-politic, or religious societies, to make suitable provision, at their own expense, for the institution of the public worship of God, and for the support and maintenance of public protestant teachers of piety, religion, and morality, in all cases where such provision shall not be made voluntarily.[84]

Occasionally, even the Congress itself took steps, although indirect, toward supporting virtue through religious means. In 1777, for instance, as described in chapter 8, the Congress, by a 26 to 12 vote, authorized the Committee of Commerce to import 20,000 Bibles into the colonies, recognizing that "the use of the Bible is so universal and its importance so great."[85] But such acts were done, it seems, in extreme cases and, apart from an institution like the military chaplaincy or the issuance of fast day and thanksgiving proclamations, were never made part of regular government programs to promote virtue.

## Concluding Remarks: Government, Virtue, and Madisonian Pragmatism

All of this brings us to the most critical point about virtue and the Continental Congress, and surely the great paradox of their deliberations on republican government. The Congress could agree on the importance of virtue for the health and longevity of the government they were establishing. They could write freely of the merits of promoting it through various avenues. Yet the Congress, as an official assembly, made no direct attempts to establish it through the promulgation of religion. The communication of the New York delegates back to their state government illustrates. The delegation, which included John Jay and Henry Wisner, remarked on the appropriateness of formal resolutions about religion. "This and the former congress have cautiously avoided the least hint on subjects of this kind, all the members concurring in a desire of burrying [sic] all disputes on ecclesiastical points, which have for ages had no other tendency than that of banishing peace and charity from the world."[86] Similarly, the Congress refused to compel virtue, even as it chose not to establish religion. Perhaps this is one of the most salient points to emerge from a long, sweltering summer of debate in 1787. The delegates to the Constitutional Convention met, conscious of the numerous defects of the Articles of Confederation. But the new structure they proposed strengthened only the government; they made no provision to strengthen, or even to inaugurate, a governmental role in improving people.

In the end, the ideas of Madison prevailed. "If men were angels . . . ," he wrote in the most pungent subjunctive of *The Federalist Papers*. But of course men and women are not. His ideas, however, must not be misunderstood. Madison never denigrated virtue even as he never disparaged religion. At the Virginia ratifying convention, Madison declared:

> I go on this great republican principle, that the people will have virtue and intelligence to select men of virtue and wisdom. Is there no virtue among us? If there be not, we are in a wretched situation. No theoretical checks, no form of government, can render us secure. To suppose that any form of government will secure liberty or happiness without any virtue in the people, is a chimerical idea.[87]

Similarly, Hamilton observed in *Federalist* No. 76, "The supposition of universal venality in human nature is little less an error in political reasoning than the supposition of universal rectitude. The institution of delegated power implies that there is a portion of virtue and honor among mankind which may be a reasonable foundation of confidence."[88]

Thus developed the central paradox of the American approach. On the one hand, the founders realized the criticality of virtue. Still, for all its importance, direct inculcation of virtue lay outside the purview and purpose of government. Madisonian pragmatism, then, was really the best available solution to that dilemma, an attempt to make "such an arrangement," as the Boston *Independent Chronicle* put it in November 1786, "of political power as ensures the existence and security of the government, even in the absence of political virtue."[89] *Federalist* No. 75 is a good illustration that, in matters of great governmental moment, it would be a grave mistake to rest too much confidence on individual virtue. Discussing the provision that the president could make treaties only with the advice and consent of the Senate, Hamilton observed that if the president had authority to act alone, he would be tempted to "sacrifice his duty to his interest." Only the man of "superlative virtue" could withstand such enticement. Hamilton concluded, "The history of human conduct does not warrant that exalted opinion of human virtue which would make it wise in a nation to commit interests of so delicate and momentous a kind, as those which concern its intercourse with the rest of the world, to the sole disposal of a magistrate created and circumstanced as would be a president of the United States."[90]

Such caution was warranted with the people generally, as well. "Has it not," Hamilton asked in *Federalist* No. 6, "invariably been found that momentary passions, and immediate interests, have a more active and imperious control over human conduct than general or remote considerations of policy, utility, or justice?"[91] Even more pointedly, and recognizing the paradox, Madison observed in the crucial *Federalist* No. 10 that "liberty is to faction what air is to fire, an aliment without which it instantly expires. But it could not be a less folly to abolish liberty, which is essential to political life, because it nourishes faction than it would be to wish the annihilation of air, which is essential to animal life, because it imparts to fire its destructive agency." Madison continued, "If the impulse [i.e., self-interest of factions] and the opportunity be suffered to coincide, *we well know that neither moral nor religious motives can be relied on as an adequate control.*" [92] And it is in *Federalist* No. 51 that Madison responded to the dilemma most forcefully. In brief, the way to cut the Gordian knot was not by "exterior provisions" but by "so contriving the interior structure of the government as that its several constituent parts may, by their mutual relations, be the means of keeping each other in their proper places."[93]

It is important to note that at several points the thinking of both Federalist and Antifederalist converged. Both wished for a government effective and enduring. Both understood the importance of virtuous character in citizen and leader alike. Both saw the corrosive effects of power and the corrigibility of men and women. But the Antifederalist, fearing the system of strong federalism as bane and not solution, had a sort of "polis-vision," often as a more loosely confederated republic where virtue might be cultivated and thus save the larger republic. Not so the Federalist. He sought instead an instrumental republic, one that sought to secure Lockean individual rights even as it sought to ameliorate human perversity and its own worst tendencies by structural means. Even the great American Aristotelian himself, Thomas Jefferson, acknowledged the value of this pragmatic view. In the Kentucky Resolutions of 1798, Jefferson declared, "In questions of power, then, let no more be heard of confidence in man, but bind him down from mischief by the chains of the Constitution."[94]

An exchange between two long-retired presidents is instructive. In December 1819 Jefferson wrote from Monticello to Adams. He wondered whether virtue, once lost in a nation, might ever be restored. Reflecting on a corrupt Rome, Jefferson decided that Cicero, Cato, and Brutus, working in concert and with unlimited power, probably could not have halted the entropic tide. But what did Adams, his "Apollo," think? Adams answered promptly. "Have you ever found in history one single example of a nation thoroughly corrupted, that was afterwards restored to virtue, and without virtue there can be no political liberty." But then he added:

> Will you tell me how to prevent riches from becoming the effects of temperance and industry? Will you tell me how to prevent riches from producing luxury? Will you tell me how to prevent luxury from producing effeminacy intoxication extravagance vice and folly? When you answer me these questions, I hope I may venture to answer yours. Yet all these ought not to discourage us from exertion, for . . . I believe no effort in favor of virtue is lost, and all good men ought to struggle both by their council and example.[95]

Adams's answer is interesting on several counts. To begin, he dilated Jefferson's question by moving beyond Rome to the present in America. Further, he had the prescience to recognize that the virtues the Puritans and secular Puritans alike so prized (here, industry and frugality) could, paradoxically, lead to the vices they despised. But most important here, Adams—for all of his concerns for the nation—did not recommend a government course of action to foster virtue. For, as Adams realized, the Constitution was made *for* a moral and religious people, not to *produce* them. The responsibility for virtuous character must rest with the people.

*Eleven*

# THE CONTINENTAL CONGRESS, ORIGINAL INTENT, AND MODERN CONSTITUTIONAL ADJUDICATION

## The Continental Congress and Original Intent

The primary goal of this study has been to examine the record of the Continental Congress on religion for the purpose of discovering what that record might contribute toward a resolution of the modern debate over the original intent of the constitutional framers regarding the interplay of government and religion in the United States. Conclusive statements toward this end do not come easily, due primarily to the fact that the Continental Congress on the one hand, and the Constitutional Convention and First Congress on the other, acted at different times and with different ends. The men of the Continental Congress were called upon first and foremost to prosecute a war, whereas those who framed the Constitution and Bill of Rights were charged with prescribing a comprehensive public philosophy that would ensure the success of a new constitution. The former readily put religion to use, whereas the latter had to think more critically about the long-term role of religion in an untested regime.

But it is possible to draw some conclusions, however tentatively. To begin, our examination has revealed that the notion of the separation of church and state, at the federal level, was virtually nonexistent in the confederation period. Strict notions of separation were occurring in some of the states—most notably Virginia, following Rhode Island, Delaware, and Pennsylvania in this respect—but these developments had little influence on the Continental Congress. It can therefore be said that the Continental Congress rarely sought to excise religion from its governmental function, unless, of course, the matter at issue was considered to be the domain of the states, in which case Congress painstakingly sought to avoid violating the states' reserved jurisdiction.

Much of the Congress's religiosity, of course, consisted of regular and sincere appeals for divine aid in prosecuting a war against a skillful and powerful military force reputed to be the best on the globe. Its thanksgiving and fast day proclamations would probably not have been promulgated had Congress not been prosecuting a war, although both practices were long-time colonial peacetime traditions, and Congress might have continued the traditions even in the absence of the Revolutionary War. The thanksgiving proclamations that became a regular presidential practice beginning in 1789 were a carryover from the wartime tradition of the Continental Congress and were implemented in the new government virtually as a matter of course. Although the wording of the Establishment Clause convinced a number of the First Congress's members that the practice was proscribed to any arm of the federal government, the majority of the congressmen, although they were remarkably casual in their consideration of the constitutional issues, apparently did not see it that way. The wartime fast days promulgated by the Continental Congress were discontinued in the post-1789 regime, almost certainly because of the war's end.

The Continental Congress's practice of having daily prayer offered by its official chaplain was another practice that was continued, again, as virtually a matter of course, by the Congress acting under the Constitution. The modern Supreme Court has upheld the practice of legislative prayers on the basis of a historical argument that looks to an unbroken chain of chaplain-led prayers in Congress that began with the Continental Congress and has continued ever since. Legislative prayers remain a central part of the American civil religion. As such, they acknowledge generally God's sovereignty over the nation, but without the coercive effects that other governmental religious acts entail, such as programmatic prayer in public schools. In a nation that is profoundly religious and does not wish to be hostile toward religion, legislative prayers are an acceptable way of acknowledging the transcendent dimension of nationhood.

The American tradition of appointing military chaplains to serve the nation's armed forces also began with the Continental Congress. Despite objections by some members of the First Congress, James Madison among them, this practice was resumed by the U.S. government operating under the new Constitution and has continued unabated since. If the practice is thought to respect the free exercise rights of servicemen, "establishment" concerns tend to recede so that the military chaplaincy becomes a hallmark of the American tradition of protecting the religious consciences of its citizens.

The absence of religious tests for holding offices in the confederation government might have influenced the framers' decision to proscribe such tests in the Constitution, but Article VI, clause 3 was more likely the product of the framers' realization that a religious test would threaten ratification of the Constitution, since the prevailing religious diversity in the nation would render any test unacceptable to all but a few. Still, as argued in chapter 2, there were many principled arguments advanced against religious tests for civil officeholding that eventually led most of the states, on the model of the Constitution's religious test ban, to abandon their own religious tests.

There are, of course, other practices that were initiated by the Continental Congress that have not continued to be observed as congressional traditions. The Continental Congress frequently attended sermons as a body, although, to avoid favoritism, it made certain to attend the services of a variety of Protestant denominations and, on occasion, Catholic services as well. The Congress also occasionally attended funerals as a body, which, of course, were a form of religious service. As already mentioned, the Continental Congress's practice of declaring fast day observances was not resumed by the post-Constitution congresses. Following the adoption of the Constitution, Congress also discontinued the Continental Congress's practice of invoking the name of God in its official documents. Even the Constitution itself, the official charter of the nation, contains no references to God (see discussion below), whereas the document under which the Continental Congress had functioned, the Articles of Confederation, stated that its provisions were aligned with the pleasure and consent of "the Great Governor of the World."

The Declaration of Independence, drafted by Thomas Jefferson and revised to its final form by the Continental Congress, espoused the view that government and law must be in conformity with higher law—the "Laws of nature and Nature's God." The Continental Congress therefore saw its duty to declare American independence from Britain in religious terms: George III was a tyrant precisely because he had perverted his power by overstepping limits imposed by natural law, and the Englishmen in America were therefore free to revolt and form their own government under the same natural law principles. The natural law foundation of the Declaration was couched in broad, generic terms by Jefferson so that it would appeal to Christian pietists and rationalists alike. The Great Seal, too, the nation's official emblem designed by Jefferson, Franklin, Adams, and the other men of the Continental Congress, also emphasized a providential, higher law theme surrounding the formation of the United States.

These various actions verify that the Continental Congress operated almost totally within an accommodationist paradigm. The present writer will confess that he had expected to find considerably more evidence than he did from the confederation period that would support separationist arguments and help to explain the "non-establishment" restriction in the First Amendment. In fact, only four direct evidences were located. The first is the absence of any kind of religious test for holding office in the confederation government. The Continental Congress was respectful of the diversity of religious views across the states and therefore believed such tests to be repugnant to religious liberty. The gradual disappearance of religious tests for holding public office, both at the federal and state levels, initiated in the founding era, is a sure sign that the meaning of religious liberty in America was progressive and tended increasingly to "separate" church and state, although a complete separation was probably never in view—nor should it be.

The second evidence of the appearance of "separationist" notions is the possibility of an unwillingness by the Continental Congress to publish an American edition of the Bible on grounds that such a project was a religious and not a governmental task. Yet the evidence for this conclusion is flimsy, and Congress's reason for distancing itself from the project may have been no more than that its lack of adequate financial resources to publish the Bibles.

The third evidence supporting separationist arguments is the considerable disagreement that ensued over the question of whether the Continental Congress should play a role in advancing religion in the Northwest Territory. A mild form of advancement (acknowledging that religion, with morality and knowledge, was a goal of the education to take place in the territory) resulted, but it was a far cry from the setting aside of lands for churches that some of the delegates sought.

A fourth development is the apparent acceptance of the view, described in chapter 10, that virtue and morality cannot be effectively cultivated through government efforts. The classical view of government advancing religion for the production of virtue in the people was first questioned, then rejected by various members of the Continental Congress. If we understand the Establishment Clause to have proscribed not only a national religion but, more generally, advancement and promotion of religion, then we can say that this perspective on virtue was written into the Constitution, thus assigning character-building, insofar as it is dependent upon religion, to personal inquiry, families, churches, and other voluntary associations, but not the federal government. And of course after incorporation, the same prohibition on religious advocacy would apply to government at every level.

Finally, there is what we could perhaps identify as a fifth indicia of developing separationist notions in the Continental Congress, that being the clear record of the policy of the Continental Congress to defer to the states, as much as possible, on matters affecting religion. This policy was, strictly speaking, one of "separation" of religion and government, but this assessment is somewhat misleading because the Congress was actually only acknowledging the right of *other* governments to deal with religious matters, which of course is really not "separation" at all.

The record of the Continental Congress on religious liberty is impressive. Its willingness to embrace Canadian Catholics in friendship, even if only to win their support in the American independence movement, accelerated on a broad scale in the colonies the popular acceptance and toleration of Catholics. The lessons the Congress learned from war pacifists about the legitimacy of religious conscientious objection to war helped to broaden the meaning of religious liberty in America. Also, the Congress's willingness to grant religious liberty to foreign mercenaries and foreign citizens helped to further the ideal that peoples of different ethnic and national backgrounds were welcome to come to the United States and enjoy the freedom of religious expression that individual states were willing to grant to them. One could argue that this excellent record is merely representative of the expanding notion of the free exercise of religion that was pervasive throughout the states in the founding era and that was eventually written into the Constitution in the form of the Free Exercise Clause, and thus says very little about "establishment" issues and contributes little to the separationist-accommodationist debate. But if we acknowledge that the religion clauses are interdependent, it is not going too far to suggest that the increased sensitivity to the broad range of religious views deserving of "free exercise" rights that became apparent during the confederation period heightened Americans' sensitivity to the notion that protecting "free exercise" rights also contemplates restrictions on government advancing religious ideas of its own. Thus, an appreciation of "free exercise" naturally and progressively led to an expanded definition of "non-establishment."

## The Constitution and Original Intent

It has been shown that the minimalist attention given to religion in the Constitution was principally the result of the framers' design to neutralize religion as a factor that might threaten the document's ratification. The framers believed that any constitutional provisions that might be

interpreted by the states as a usurpation of the states' long-held jurisdiction over religion would spell certain defeat of the Constitution in the
ratification process. The First Amendment's religion clauses were only a
guarantee of this arrangement: the states would retain full authority to
maintain religious establishments, require religious tests for civil officeholders, or place restrictions on the free exercise of religion; the federal
government, however, was forbidden to pass legislation providing for
an "establishment" of religion or prohibiting the "free exercise" thereof.

### Ratification Controversies

The seeming inattention to religion in the Constitution created real concerns in the ratification process. Whereas the framers assumed that an
overattention to religion in the Constitution would delay ratification, it
happened, coincidentally, that their minimalist approach to religion in
fact threatened ratification. This occurred on two counts: first, the people's demand for an enumeration of basic rights, including religious liberty, and, second, the people's concern that the Constitution was a purely
secular document.

The concern of the people that their religious liberty was in jeopardy
under the Constitution caused the delegates to concede to the people's
demand for a special provision guaranteeing religious liberty. The view
of most of the Convention delegates was that a bill of rights would be
superfluous. They had considered adding a bill of rights (including a
provision guaranteeing religious liberty) during the Convention but had
rejected the inclusion as unnecessary. The new federal government possessed only limited powers delegated to it by the states; no power had
been granted to legislate on any of the subjects that might be included
in a bill of rights. Because no such power existed, none could be exercised or abused, and therefore an enumeration of protected rights was
thought unnecessary. Nevertheless, many of the states were not convinced. Fearful of a national government that would arrogate power unto
itself, they insisted upon specific protections for individual freedoms.
Ratification finally occurred on the assumption of several of the states
that amendments would follow, and in the First Congress James Madison
took the lead in proposing them.

The Convention delegates' answer to the charge that the Constitution
was an overly secular document likewise rested on the framers' commitment to a doctrine of delegated powers. This doctrine holds that all
unenumerated rights and powers are retained by the people. In Lockean
style, the people remain sovereign, relinquishing only those powers that
they choose to assign to a political sovereign. This new Constitution was

a document naming the people, not God, as the creators and overseers of the government formed by it. Although the founders were deeply suspicious of pure democracy and, for some like Alexander Hamilton, even of the participation of the populous within the governmental process, they nevertheless had a strong sense of "the people" as the source of political authority.[1] John Adams explained that "in every government there must exist somewhere, a supreme, sovereign, absolute, and uncontrollable power; but this power resides always in the body of the people."[2] Adams was particularly cautious against ascribing sacred legitimation to political arrangements and wondered whether such justification was the only way to elicit man's obedience to political laws. He referred to the United States as the first government to be erected upon "the simple principles of nature" instead of the more usual attribution to divine origin.[3] Hamilton contended that the fatal flaw of the Continental Congress regime and the Articles of Confederation was that they never had received the mandate or ratification of the people.[4] Thus it would be left up to the federal Constitution to ensure that the ultimate political authority remained with the people while simultaneously ensuring that no one person or body of persons could obtain unassailable decision-making power.

In 1787, within the whole of Western political culture, the secularity of the Constitution of the United States was indeed an isolated anomaly. Religious establishments reigned all over Europe, not just Great Britain. The U.S. Constitution, then, can rightly be viewed as the document that marked the real beginning of political modernity. Government was now to be mostly a human affair; God might lend a helping providential hand, but the formation, maintenance, and dissolution of governments rested with men, not with angels. As the devout Congregationalist from Connecticut, Oliver Ellsworth, saw it, "The business of civil government is to protect the citizen in his rights, to defend the community from hostile powers and to promote the general welfare."[5] Noticeably absent from his description was any attempt to place the new government under divine rule. It is little wonder that as the proposed Constitution was presented to the states for ratification, disconcerted traditionalists made uncomfortable by this break with the past voiced their disapproval.

The specific criticism against the Constitution, voiced repeatedly, was that the document essentially ignored religion. Indeed, the Constitution contained only one reference to religion: Article 6, clause 3 provided that no religious test could be required of any federal officeholder. At the Convention, only Connecticut's Roger Sherman objected to the proposed provision, not because he disagreed with its aim, but because he thought its inclusion "unnecessary, the prevailing liberality being a sufficient security against such tests."[6] Other delegates at the Convention with more principled objections apparently failed to speak up, for Maryland's Luther Martin reported back to his state legislature with a good bit of sarcasm that some of the delegates were "so unfashionable" as to think "that in a Christian country, it would be at least decent to hold out some distinction between the professors of Christianity and downright infidelity or paganism."[7] In Massachusetts the "no religious test" clause generated so much dissent that it nearly resulted in that state's refusal to ratify. One delegate objected to the clause because he "shuddered at the idea that Roman Catholics, Papists and Pagans might be introduced into office; and that Popery and the Inquisition may be established in America."[8] Another thought that "the rulers ought to believe in God or Christ; and that, however a test may be prostituted in England, yet if we thought our public men were to be of those who had a good standing in the Church, it would be happy for the United States; and that a person could not be a good man without being a good Christian."[9] In the North Carolina ratifying convention, concern was expressed that the clause would eventually allow deists, Jews, pagans, Mahometans, even the pope himself to hold federal office.[10]

Similar objections were made to the Constitution's failure to acknowledge God in some specific way. For one Connecticut critic, it was "a sinful omission in the . . . Constitution, in not looking to God for direction, and of omitting the mention of the name of God."[11] Convention delegate William Williams regretted that he had not been farsighted enough to recommend that the Constitution's preamble begin with the words:

> We the people of the United States, in a firm belief of the being and perfections of the one living and true God, the creator and supreme Governor of the world, in his universal providence and the authority of his laws; that he will require of all moral agents an account of their conduct; that all rightful powers among men are ordained of, and mediately derived from God . . . do ordain . . . [etc.][12]

These objections reveal the uneasiness of some Americans who saw the Constitution as an altogether secular text. The ancient requirement of bringing government under divine authority was perspicuously absent. These objections to the omission of religious references in the Constitution do, moreover, raise an important and provocative question: Was the omission due to an overall absence of religious faith on the part of the Convention delegates, or was it explainable on some other basis?

A particular incident that occurred at the Constitutional Convention is somewhat instructive on this question. When in late June 1787 disagreements among the delegates had reached a new high, Benjamin Franklin suggested that perhaps it was time to pray. He reminded his colleagues that "we have been assured . . . in the Sacred Writings, that, 'Except the Lord build this house, they labor in vain that build it!' I firmly believe this."[13] Although the delegates had elected not to invite a chaplain to its sessions, many of the delegates were used to seeing chaplains in the state legislatures and in the Continental Congress. Franklin moved to invite one or more clergymen to lead them in prayer at the beginning of each day. Alexander Hamilton objected on grounds of realpolitik. The majority of the delegates were of the view that to call for a chaplain would be to show the world how badly at odds they were. Edmund Randolph countered with the imaginative suggestion that they invite a clergyman for the Fourth of July celebration and then continue the practice each day thereafter; the public would never realize that a transition had occurred. But neither resolution won much support—only four delegates, Franklin, Randolph, Roger Sherman, and Jonathan Dayton voiced support for either. Hamilton and James Madison solved everyone's discomfort by carrying a motion to adjourn.[14]

The delegates' unwillingness to search out a chaplain is perhaps less an indictment of the vibrancy of their religious commitments as a reflection on their understanding of the task before them. Mark Noll has offered a meaningful insight here. He argues that by the time the Constitution was written, there had developed a noticeable space between religion and politics. For the framers, he says, politics and religion increasingly were perceived to occupy two different "spheres." This, he notes, was not a secular attitude in the modern sense, but it was clearly different from the admixture of religion and politics that characterized the administration of the Continental Congress. He suggests that there was every expectation that Christian principles would continue to play a large role in strengthening the population and even in providing a moral context for legislation. Yet the Constitution, without ever spelling it out precisely, nonetheless was intended to be an acknowledgement that government and religion have distinctively different roles in society.[15] It was a document in no way hostile to Christianity or to religion in general but structured on the belief that government was more a human endeavor than a divine one.

Samuel Spencer of North Carolina said as much when he stated at his state's ratifying convention that religion should stand on its own "without any connection with temporal authority."[16] James Madison also offered this view when, in his final years, he wrote concerning the victory for complete disestablishment of the churches in Virginia in the late 1780s: "We are teaching the world the great truth that Govts. do better

without Kings & Nobles than with them. The merit will be doubled by
the other lesson that Religion flourishes in greater purity, without then
with the aid of Govt."[17] Noll adds this insight:

> The political theory lying behind the Constitution was complex in a way
> that mirrored, to some extent, the complexity of human experience itself.
> The founders had come to see, for example, that reaction against tradi-
> tional abuses of power can lead to new ways of abusing power. To use
> modern jargon, they were aware of the ironic potential in human expe-
> rience. They had come to sense that good solutions to pressing problems
> regularly create new problems of their own. This simple recognition was
> by no means a panacea, but it did protect the founders from the disillu-
> sionment that so often attends crusades. Crusades usually fail, but cru-
> saders stand in even greater risk when they succeed, for the result is
> inevitably disappointment that achievements cannot live up to anticipa-
> tions. The authors of the Constitution, in other words, had learned a lesson
> taught not only by human experience but also by centuries of theological
> reflection on the central teachings of Christianity.[18]

The seemingly secular character of the new Constitution also rested
to some degree on the tendency of many of the leading thinkers of the
day to analogize it to the manner in which God himself was thought to
govern the universe. With the spread of Enlightenment rationalism, the
pervading theological metaphor for God's method of controlling the universe was a constitutional paradigm. This provided the political leaders
with a vocabulary they could use to express the new concepts of a
federal constitutional government. Thus Americans could accept Thomas
Paine's characterization of the republican system of government as "always parallel with the order and immutable laws of nature, and meets
the reason of man in every part."[19] Madison also could defend the idea
of a constitutional government by appealing to its progenitor as God,
"the supreme lawgiver of the universe."[20] And John Adams would note
to Jefferson that the "general principles of Christianity are as eternal and
immutable as the existence and attributes of God; and that those principles of liberty are as unalterable as human nature and our terrestrial,
mundane system."[21] The kind of constitutionalism conceived by the
founders was infused with a divine imprimatur—a necessary advantage
to obtain and sustain the support in the hearts and minds of the people.
Thus the new Constitution was never presented as a completely secular
document; the idea of the providential hand of God was consistently
retained. This image was effectively used by James Madison in *Federalist*
No. 37 when arguing for acceptance of the federal Constitution: "It is
impossible, for the man of pious reflection, not to perceive in it a finger

of that Almighty Hand, which has been so frequently and signally extended to our relief in the critical stages in the revolution."[22]

The concept of a federal Constitution was in turn planted and nurtured within the minds of the people through the sermons of the clergy and their tendency to analogize an earthly constitution to a divine constitution. God was presented as governing the universe according to the laws of a constitution that he himself established, in keeping with his own rational nature.[23] The Constitution was granted a sacred status by such clergy as Abraham Williams, a Congregationalist minister who extolled the virtues of a constitutional government by likening it to the manner in which God governs the universe: "Government is a divine Constitution founded in the nature and relation of things. God is the head . . . and supreme governor."[24] Williams thanked the "great governor of the world" for "placing us under a government so wise and good in its constitution and administration."[25] Similarly, Congregationalist minister Stanley Griswold concluded that the Constitution was "the palladium of all that we hold dear. Let it be venerated as the sanctuary of our liberties and all of our best interests. Let it be kept as the ark of God."[26]

### Religion's Role in the New System

All of this points to a federal system of government that had only begun to think in separationist terms during the constitutional era. There were strong objections to the apparent secularity of the document, but those who understood it knew that it was in no way hostile to religion. As Walter Berns has noted, the Constitution was ordained to secure liberty and its blessings, not to acknowledge God or even move people to faith in God.[27] Had the framers desired to create a Christian commonwealth, calculated to cause Americans to endeavor to keep God's laws, they could easily have done so. But they chose not to because, in their minds, the government derived not from God but from the people. Religion was to be subordinate to liberty; liberty was to free all persons to exercise their faith absent government prescription. As Berns insightfully asserts, "Instead of establishing religion, the Founders established religious freedom."[28] Because the nation was not founded on religious truth, it would act to protect the right of all citizens to believe and act upon divergent views of religious truth. Religious liberty was a natural human right, with which the federal government had no right or authority to interfere.

In the minds of many government leaders, of course, this arrangement still did not contemplate a radical separation of religion from government. In their view, the happiness of the people and the good order and preservation of civil government still depended on religion and piety. If the nation was not theocratic in the primary sense, it remained so in a subordinate sense. This was the position of John Turner at the Massachusetts ratifying convention, who stated that "without the prevalence of Christian piety and morals, the best republican constitution can never save us from slavery and ruin."[29] John Adams, writing to his wife Abigail, declared: "Statesmen may plan and speculate for liberty, but it is religion and morality alone which can establish the principles upon which freedom can securely stand."[30] In his later years, Adams added that the Constitution "was made only for a moral and religious people. It is wholly inadequate to the government of any other."[31] Moreover, President George Washington, in his inaugural address in 1789, gave thanks "to the Great Author of every public and private good" and suggested that Americans must "acknowledge and adore the invisible Hand which conducts the affairs of men."[32] There is no specifically Christian message here, but certainly it is proof that Washington acknowledged a connection between religion and the sustaining of the new nation. A similar perspective appears in Washington's Farewell Address:

> Of all the dispositions and habits which lead to political prosperity, religion and morality are indispensable supports. In vain would that man claim the tribute of patriotism who should labor to subvert these great pillars of human happiness, these firmest props of the duties of men and citizens. The mere politician, equally with the pious man, ought to respect and to cherish them. A volume could not trace all their connections with private and public felicity. Let it simply be asked where is the security for property, for reputation, for life, if the sense of religious obligation *desert* the oaths, which are the instruments of investigation in courts of justice? And lest us with caution indulge the supposition that morality can be maintained without religion. Whatever may be conceded to the influence of refined education on minds of peculiar structure, reason and experience both forbid us to expect that national morality can prevail in exclusion of religious principle.[33]

Accommodationists are understandably pleased by statements like those just quoted, since they are evidence that the framers did not intend to withdraw religion from public life. Yet while all of these statements exalt religion as a necessary support for human government, none expresses the view that it is *government itself* that must promulgate religion. Such statements might, then, be looked upon as arguments for separationism as much as for accommodationism. Separationists usually look to religion to supply the civic virtue so essential to successful democratic government but hold that human government should play a limited role, if any role at all, in promulgating religion as the underlying source of civic virtue. As set forth in chapter 10, there is strong evidence that many of the founders decidedly became proponents of this view. Thus, today most separationists contend that it is the private, non-public sphere that must be respected as the domain of religion and that will supply, in turn, the morality and virtue so essential to the successful functioning of democratic government.

Accommodationists, in arguing that the founders believed that the federal government should have a role in promulgating religion, also point to later presidential proclamations by John Adams and others who have offered presidential prayers and thanksgiving proclamations, usually in general language acceptable to most faiths. But even if it is conceded that such proclamations and prayers do indeed assign to the federal government a role in promulgating religion, there is contrary evidence. There were a number of men of the First Congress who objected to the practices. James Madison, for one, had strong reservations about such practices. He held that "thanksgiving and fasts . . . seem to imply and certainly nourish the erroneous idea of a national religion"[34] and called them "establishments."[35] He remained flexible on the subject, however, proclaiming several days for thanksgiving, reportedly because he found extenuating circumstances in the fact that he was president during the time a war was fought on American soil.[36] Thomas Jefferson, too, opposed official prayer, believing that it was best left in the hands of the people, "where the Constitution has deposited it."[37] Andrew Jackson shared Jefferson's views and steadfastly refused to issue any thanksgiving proclamations.

Accommodationists also frequently cite the congressional practice of appointing paid chaplains as further proof that the framers never intended a posture of complete government neutrality toward religion. This practice too was essentially a carryover from the period of the Continental Congress that has since been judicially upheld as a constitutionally valid historical practice. But Stephen Botein, by analyzing two sermons preached in 1795 by chaplains Ashbel Green and William White on the day recommended by Washington's second thanksgiving proclamation, shows how thoroughly unofficial such occasions were at the federal level of government. Green emphasized that the thanksgiving proclamation left everyone "to his own inclination"; it was not a command but a "signal to a willing people," as he put it. White, with Washington present at Christ Church, plainly said that he preached "within his privilege as a citizen." His sermon gave no indication whatsoever that the federal government should be looked to for support of religion. Instead, as Botein points out, it was to the states that White looked for support of all religious interests.[38]

It is probably best to conclude from these diverse perspectives that the framers were on the whole themselves unclear and in some disagreement about the role that religion should play in national life. There is no dispute that, as a body, they were firmly of the view that the federal government should not interfere with the free exercise of religion so long as it did not disrupt peace and order. They were also of the view that the government should disaffirm any special competence in religious matters. They were of differing opinions, however, about whether the federal government might exercise some subordinate, supportive role that would encourage religion or acknowledge the government's accountability to God as a human institution. Early presidential thanksgiving proclamations, congressional chaplaincies, and legislation reciting the merits of religion (such as the Northwest Ordinance) are evidence that many of the framers believed that the Establishment Clause should be read to countenance at least a very indirect role for religion in national life.

Nevertheless, because most of the framers were respectful of differing religious views, the religious references in presidential proclamations, public prayers, and legislation that in some way interfaced with religion were typically generic, broad, and free of language that was identified with any particular community of faith. This has led some modern historians to argue for an interpretation of the interplay of religion, morality, and politics in the founding era that in many ways transcends both the accommodationist and separationist approaches to interpretation. These historians, Robert Bellah in particular,[39] argue that the framers perceived quite clearly the inherent tensions and conflicts associated with the interplay of religion, morality, and politics and therefore sought to encourage a more generic form of religion discussed today under such categories as democratic faith, societal religion, common faith, or, most often, civil religion.

Was a civil religion indeed advocated by the framers or is this rather abstract form of religion merely a category of faith that developed later in American history that historians like Bellah falsely attribute to the founders? If the founders did in fact promote a civil religion, was it to be outside the strictures of the First Amendment? Even if the founders did not advocate a civil religion (i.e., it was not a part of "original intent"), if such a common American faith has since developed that is broadly acknowledged and practiced, should it be given constitutional protection on the same scale as that enjoyed by traditional forms of religion? Questions such as these must necessarily be dealt with in any discussion of the original intent of the framers with respect to the role of religion in public life. Accordingly, the ensuing section deals specifically with the place of civil religion in the overall framework of original intent as well as the measure of recognition to which it should be entitled in constitutional terms in our own day. Following the section on civil religion, some conclusions are drawn concerning the founders' "original intent" and its place in today's heated venues of legislative and judicial policymaking.

## Civil Religion and the Constitution

The term "civil religion" was coined by Jean-Jacques Rousseau (1712–1778). Rousseau did not invent civil religion—it can be observed in most ancient societies—but all who study civil religion have to deal with Rousseau. Moreover, Rousseau's description of civil religion is important because his most important work, *The Social Contract*, which appeared in 1762, included a lengthy treatment of civil religion and was a work that many of the founders were familiar with and may have been influenced by.[40] Among other matters, Rousseau in his *Social Contract* attempted to resolve the problem of the relationship of religion and society in an enlightened but religiously pluralistic state. He held that Christianity, the most pervasive faith in the West, was defective for his purposes because it weakened the state by creating a dual allegiance (to religion and state) in its followers. Civil religion was the device that he hit upon to solve the dilemma by circumventing the problem of religious diversity, yet cementing man's religious allegiance to civil society. In his conception, citizens were to view their duties to the state as a religious commitment, without allowing their religious differences to subvert their common allegiance. Civil religion, then, was to provide the moral glue for the body politic. Simply put, civil religion was to be the "general will" of the people expressed religiously in the life of the state.[41]

Rousseau's civil religion has no transcendental reference point. The general will of the people is sovereign and stands under no higher law. In this respect Rousseau's civil religion differs from that described by most interpreters of American civil religion in which the state stands under the judgment of a "higher law."

### Civil Religion and the Founding Fathers

None of the founding fathers wrote anything more than isolated statements on the subject of civil religion. Most of these statements, however, contrary to what Bellah would have us believe, had more to do with their deistic religious views than with any systematic attempt to construct a civil religion around which American society could grow and prosper. Thomas Jefferson, for example, is well known for his Unitarian position and his desire that it might become in his own lifetime "the general religion of the United States."[42] He fully expected his own religious views to take hold because, as Americans would inevitably become liberated from their foolish theological controversies and therefore more sensitive to right reason, competing religious views would wither away. For Jefferson, civil government should also be conducted according to right reason, its object being the achievement of "peace and good order."[43] Thus there is no tension between religious belief and civic responsibility because both should accord with common sense and reason; therefore, religious and political disputes are a sign of faulty thinking and should therefore be mostly ignored. "Why," he asked, "should we be dissocialized by mere differences of opinion in politics, in religion, in philosophy, or anything else? [Another's] opinions are as honestly formed as my own. Our different views of the same subject are the result of a difference in our organization and experience."[44]

Jefferson's views, then, on the relationship between religion and civic responsibility can appropriately be called a "civil religion." The reason is obvious: the same rationality that directs the civil order to regulate life in keeping with peace, order, and civic unity also provides for affirming nature's God as the promoter and protector of peace, order, and civic unity. Man's drive for civic order and his perception of God naturally come to the same thing. For this reason, there can be no real tension within Jefferson's civil religion between religious belief and civic responsibility. Properly understood, they mirror one another almost precisely.[45]

In one sense, Jefferson's civil religion was much like Rousseau's in that it collapsed religion into civic duty and therefore made duty to the state the highest responsibility of human beings. In another sense, however, Jefferson's God was still sovereign over all events, maintaining "the universe in its course and order,"[46] so that ultimately duty to God was superior to duty to the state. This enabled him in his inaugural address to refer to God as that "infinite power which rubs the destinies of the universe" and "that Being in whose hands we are."[47] Jefferson, after all, was a realist, and while he held optimistic views about the inevitable upsurge in deistic religion, he also knew that sectarian strife abounded on sincere differences in religious opinion. Thus he thought the religion clauses to be a good idea because they would protect the right of citizens to freely exercise their divergent faiths.[48]

While it would be correct, then, to say that Jefferson had a civil religion, it would not be correct to say that he advocated it as the religion to which everyone should adhere or that it represented the kind of religion envisioned to be protected by the religion clauses. If Unitarianism was to become the dominant faith and if citizens were to increasingly promote order, peace, and civic unity, it would be because time and experience rightly ordered people's thinking, not because such goals were advocated by governments or their leaders. Jefferson's civil religion, from his perspective, would be good for America, but in the meantime society must find creative ways, such as the religion clauses, to limit the effects of political and religious strife.

The present author contends, with Robert Linder,[49] that civil religion had only minimal influence before the Civil War. By that time a considerable civil religion was able to be constructed around certain myths about the founding fathers, God's special concern for America (cast in deistic as well as evangelical Christian terms), and the special character of the founding documents. As Bellah has noted, the American Revolution is seen as the final event of the exodus from Egypt across the Atlantic; the Declaration of Independence and the Constitution are the sacred scriptures of the new civil religion; and George Washington is the Moses who leads his people from tyranny to freedom.[50] But prior to the Civil War, civil religion was still in formation and not a readily recognizable form of American religion.[51] This effectively eliminates, for the purposes of this study, the need to consider civil religion as an element of the framers' "original intent" respecting the desired relationship between religion and the federal government.

### Civil Religion as a Judicial Doctrine

As civil religion, however, has become an American cultural reality in the twentieth century, and since some Americans have begun to insist that civil religion should be given constitutional protection, it is appropriate here to give both a basic description of American civil religion in its present form as well as its current constitutional status. Moreover, such an examination is useful to show that many features of American civil religion indeed had their genesis in the acts and proceedings of the Continental Congress.

The classic definition of civil religion in America is Robert Bellah's. Bellah contends that "certain common elements of religious orientation," shared by the great majority of Americans, "have played a crucial role in the development of American institutions and still provide a religious dimension for the whole fabric of American life, including the political sphere."[52] For Bellah, following Émile Durkheim,[53] the absence of a civil religion within any given society would lead to moral and spiritual decay among its people and, eventually, the decline or disappearance of the society altogether. According to Bellah, the four basic dogmas of this religious dimension are the existence of a transcendent God, the life to come, the reward of virtue and the punishment of vice, and the exclusion of religious intolerance.[54] These dogmas play themselves out in public rituals that, first, involve a public acknowledgment of God's existence and, second, embrace a "theology" that America will only prosper to the extent to which it is just and honorable.

Public acknowledgment of the existence of God has been part of American civil religion from the earliest days of nationhood. As already seen, the Continental Congress opened its sessions each day with the prayers of its chaplain. To ensure that its prayers were nonsectarian, the Congress made special efforts to appoint chaplains of different Protestant faiths. Its official documents, including the Declaration of Independence and the Articles of Confederation, included generic references to God designed not only to reflect the Congress's theistic worldview but to appeal to and capture the approval of a wide variety of religious adherents.

Every president has mentioned God in his inaugural address, although none has used sectarian references.[55] At his first inaugural, as previously mentioned, President Washington noted that "it would be peculiarly improper to omit in this first official act my fervent supplications to that Almighty Being who rules the universe."[56] President Adams addressed the "Being who is supreme above all."[57] The tradition has continued, unbroken, to this day. President John F. Kennedy made three references to God in his inaugural speech,[58] President Ronald Reagan constantly made references to the deity, and evangelist Billy Graham led a prayer at George Bush's oath-taking ceremony in 1988.

Public acknowledgment of God occurs not only at presidential inaugurations but at many other public events as well. Every president, with the exception of Jefferson and Jackson, has promulgated thanksgiving day proclamations; and Congress, beginning in the period of the Continental Congress, has never functioned without the services of a chaplain.

According to Bellah, the God acknowledged in civil religion's rituals is a God unknown to any traditional religion. Civil religion's prayers are not the prayers of any church. No doctrine of traditional religion is promoted or offended by these invocations. The God of the civil religion is *sui generis*.[59] As Bellah puts it:

> Though much is selectively derived from Christianity, this religion is clearly not itself Christianity. . . . The God of the civil religion is not only rather "unitarian," he is also on the austere side, much more related to order, law, and right than to salvation and love. Even though he is somewhat deist in cast, he is by no means simply a watchmaker God.[60]

According to Bellah, the second aspect of civil religion that is perpetually repeated in the rituals of American public life is the belief that God has uniquely blessed America and will assure its prosperity if it is virtuous. As with the invocations of God, this ritual has been present from colonial days and continues to this day. John Winthrop's speech aboard the *Arabella* in which he told the tiny group of travelers, essentially exiled from their own country, that "the eyes of all people are upon us"[61] was perhaps the earliest articulation of this theme. Most Americans have always believed that they are a unique people, that their land is a unique land, chosen by God for special favor. The imagery of the United States as a "New Israel" was vivid, even in the minds of the founders. When John Adams, Benjamin Franklin, and Thomas Jefferson, appointed as a committee by the Continental Congress, met to design a seal for the new nation (see chapter 8), Franklin proposed as the device Moses lifting up his wand and dividing the Red Sea while Pharaoh was overwhelmed by its waters, with the motto "Rebellion to Tyrants is Obedience to God." Jefferson proposed the children of Israel in the wilderness "led by a cloud by day and a pillar of fire by night."

In his second inaugural, Jefferson continued his imagery of a new Israel when he acknowledged that he would "need . . . the favor of that being in whose hands we are, who led our fathers, as Israel of old, from their native land and planted them in a country flowing with all the necessaries and comforts of life."[62] Abraham Lincoln expanded the idea of America as a holy place in the Gettysburg Address when he spoke of "hallowing and consecrating ground" already blessed by the blood of those union martyrs "who here gave their lives, that the nation might live."[63] The chosen people imagery continues today. Ronald Reagan explicitly revived Winthrop's "city on a hill" language. And the seal of the United States, designed and adopted by the Continental Congress, still has the inscription, in Latin, "God has favored our undertaking."

The corollary to the belief that America is a chosen nation is the belief that it must be virtuous if it seeks to continue to prosper. Once again, this theme has been continuously present since the beginning of the country. In his first inaugural address, President Washington remarked that:

> No people can be bound to acknowledge and adore the Invisible Hand which conducts the affairs of man more than those of the United States. Every step by which we have advanced to the character of an independent nation seems to have been distinguished by some token of providential agency. . . .
> The propitious smiles of Heaven can never be expected on a nation that disregards the eternal rules of order and right which Heaven itself has ordained.[64]

Perhaps President Lyndon B. Johnson best articulated the "we will prosper if we are virtuous" element of American civil religion. In his inaugural address he spoke of the first settlers of this country, "the exile and the stranger, brave but frightened" who "made a covenant with this land." Johnson believed that the covenant "binds us still" and added that "if we keep its terms, we shall flourish."[65] What emerges from this focus on the two principal themes in American public life that manifest civil religion is the extent to which civil religion is in many ways independent of both the church and the state. Civil religion is independent of the church because its conception of God is unique and does not follow the doctrine of any particular religious group. Moreover, it is unconcerned with much of what preoccupies traditional religion. Civil religion has no theology of the person, no view of creation, no eschatology, no ecclesiology, no single creed. In a religiously pluralistic society, any sectarian civil religion would be unable to unite the society's diverse groups. Many Americans, with the notable exception of some small groups, such as the Amish, embrace both the civil religion and involvement in more traditional churches, seeing, for the most part, no conflict between the two.

Civil religion in America manifests itself most clearly in public (governmental) acknowledgments to God. While civil religion is mixed with elements of the mythic, patriotic, and secular, it is also religious. Its religious character causes expressions of civil religion such as legislative prayer, graduation prayers in public schools, and Christmas and Hanukkah displays to be challenged as violations of the Establishment Clause. In the case of legislative prayer, the Supreme Court has held that such practices, because they have a long and unbroken tradition in American political life, do not violate the Establishment Clause.[66] Holiday displays have been held not to violate the Establishment Clause if their religious message is muted by surrounding secular symbols.[67] Prayer offered by clergy at a public school graduation ceremony has been held to violate the Establishment Clause as an inappropriate government sponsorship of religion.[68]

The federal courts have struggled in their efforts to assess the constitutional propriety of these kinds of public acknowledgment cases. The difficulty in evaluating such cases is that the religion advanced is typically nonsectarian, symbolic, and without specific theological content—in short, civil religion. The courts, with lawyers sitting as judges, have not been particularly sophisticated in their ability to distinguish civil religion from traditional religion. Occasionally, the Supreme Court has applied a vague concept called "ceremonial deism"[69] to justify some practices of civil religion, but for the most part the Court has seemed to be totally unaware of the large body of scholarly literature that has appeared in recent decades giving analysis to civil religion as a distinctive form of religion. The Court has never defined "ceremonial deism"; the term seems to be mere shorthand for the Court's judgment that a practice ought to be constitutional because it is not really religious, either because it has culturally lost the significance it once had or because it is used only to solemnize a public occasion.

Only recently have the courts begun to consider the possibility of carving out a special test that might constitutionally sanction certain expressions of civil religion. In *Stein v. Plainwell Community Schools*,[70] a federal appeals court considered the constitutionality of including prayers in high school commencement ceremonies. The plaintiffs, parents of students at two Michigan high schools, argued that the prayers "invoke[d] the image of a God or Supreme Being" and thus violated the First Amendment values of "liberty of conscience, state neutrality and noninterference with religion."[71] Attendance at the commencement ceremonies was voluntary, and failure to attend did not affect the receipt of a diploma. In one school a student delivered the prayer; at the other a member of the local clergy offered the prayer.

The court concluded that the religion clauses, taken together, guarantee "equal liberty of conscience," erecting "a neutral state designed to foster the most extensive liberty of conscience compatible with a similar or equal liberty for others."[72] Treating commencement prayers as analogous to legislative prayers, the court concluded that *Marsh v. Chambers* (authorizing legislative prayers) governed the case, permitting some accommodation to the nation's religious traditions. In analyzing the nature of commencement prayers, the court sought to place them within an overall framework of a "civil religion":

So long as the invocation or benediction on these public occasions does not go beyond "the American civil religion," so long as it preserves the substance of the principle of equality of liberty of conscience, no violation of the Establishment Clause occurs under the reasoning of *Marsh*.[73]

In sustaining commencement prayers generally, the court emphasized that, unlike classroom prayer, they presented little danger of religious coercion or indoctrination. The court, however, found the prayers unacceptable because they were so distinctively Christian that they connoted a governmental endorsement of Christianity. Thus the prayers failed to qualify as permissible invocations and benedictions under a special category of "American civil religion."

In 1992, in *Lee v. Weisman*,[74] the U.S. Supreme Court considered a similar case involving commencement prayer. There, a middle school principal had invited a Jewish rabbi to give the invocation and benediction at the school's commencement ceremony. The rabbi recited nonsectarian prayers, following the school's instructions that prayers reflect "inclusiveness in sensitivity." The plaintiff, the father of a fourteen-year-old student of the school, complained that the prayers were an impermissible governmental advancement of religion contrary to the prohibitions of the Establishment Clause.

The Court held that the prayers bore the imprint of the Providence, Rhode Island, school system and were therefore unlawful advancements of religion. The Court stated that even for those students who objected to the religious ceremony, their attendance was in a "fair and real sense" obligatory, even though attendance was not required as a condition for receipt of a diploma. The Court reasoned that this constituted an indirect coercion, which could be as real as any overt compulsion to participate in the state-sponsored religious activity. The atmosphere of the commencement proceeding was distinguished from that of a state legislature, as in *Marsh*. In the latter, the Court said, adults are free to enter and leave with little comment and for any number of reasons, whereas in the former, children are constrained to attend in its entirety the one most important event of their school year.

Of special interest here is the attention that Justice Anthony Kennedy, writing for the majority, gave to the brief discussion of civil religion set forth in the *Stein* case:

We are asked to recognize the existence of a practice of nonsectarian prayer, prayer within the embrace of what is known as the Judeo-Christian tradition, prayer which is more acceptable than one which, for example, makes explicit references to the God of Israel, or to Jesus Christ, or to a patron saint. There may be some support, as an empirical observation, to the statement of the Court of Appeals for the Sixth Circuit, picked up by Judge Campbell's dissent in the Court of Appeals in this case, that there has emerged in this country a civic religion, one which is tolerated when sectarian exercises are not. . . . If common ground can be defined which permits once conflicting faiths to express the shared conviction that there is an ethic and morality which transcend human invention, the sense of community and purpose sought by all decent societies might be advanced. But though the First Amendment does not allow the government to stifle prayers which aspire to these ends, neither does it permit the government to undertake that task for itself.[75]

Kennedy's point here is that "civic religion," whatever its merits and however it might represent consensus, is religion just the same and, if promulgated by government, violates the Establishment Clause. While Kennedy's was not an extended inquiry into the nature of civil religion, his recognition of it as a distinctive form of religion that is different from creedal religions at least gives Court-watchers some glimpse of how the Court might adjudicate future attempts to seek a special status for civil religion under the Establishment Clause.

In addition to Kennedy's assertion that civil religion is only another form of religion and therefore suspect under the Establishment Clause, there are other valid reasons for not enshrining civil religion as a test for measuring the constitutionality of time-honored religious practices. First, an impossible definitional task would ensue. According civil religion a preferred status under the Establishment Clause would require that its contours be closely defined. As a religion without a formal set of theological tenets, clergy, history, mission, or confessional adherents, civil religion would not possess the content it would have to have as the comparative paradigm for assessing the acceptability of religious symbols and practices in public life.[76]

Any definition of civil religion would tend to embrace certain faith traditions and exclude others. Robert Wuthnow distinguishes a conservative civil religion in modern America from a more liberal version, each drawing on a different set of values and portraying the nation in a different light.[77] The conservative version, traditionally advanced by Christian evangelicals and fundamentalists, grants America a special place in the divine order, sees the nation as God's instrument to evangelize the world, gives biblical legitimacy to capitalism, and understands the American form of government to enjoy lasting legitimacy because it was created by founding fathers—Washington, Franklin, Witherspoon, Adams, and others—who were deeply influenced by Judeo-Christian values. On the final tenet just described, Wuthnow offers, as one example of the conservative form of civil religion, the perspective of Francis Schaeffer, who wrote of the founding fathers in his book *A Christian Manifesto:*

These men truly understood what they were doing. They knew they were building on the Supreme Being who was the Creator, the final reality. And they knew that without that foundation everything in the Declaration of Independence and all that followed would be sheer unadulterated nonsense. These were brilliant men who understood exactly what was involved.[78]

On the other side, says Wuthnow, few spokespersons for the liberal version of American civil religion make reference to the religious views of the founding fathers or suggest that America is a chosen nation. References to world evangelization or religious apologetics for capitalism are also rare. Instead of focus on the nation as such, there is an emphasis on humanity in general. Rather than drawing specific attention to the distinctiveness of the Judeo-Christian tradition, liberal civil religion is much more likely to stress basic human rights and common human problems. Issues like world hunger, peace and justice, and nuclear disarmament tend to receive special emphasis. Rather than claiming chosen nation status for America, proponents of a liberal civil religion stress America's interdependence with the rest of the world.[79]

The conservative and liberal wings of American civil religion, therefore, have different understandings of those symbols that are unique to the American experience. For each, civil religion represents a generic set of theological ideals on which the nation is built. Each has the potential to achieve consensus and unity amidst the burgeoning pluralism that characterizes the American situation, yet they are enough at odds to make a mutual collaboration highly unlikely. Under such a state of affairs, it is improbable that the Supreme Court could, even if it wanted to, sufficiently identify and define the American civil religion that would become the constitutional standard for government promulgation of religious symbols.

A second problem with raising the American civil religion to constitutional status is the risk it poses for civil religion's becoming a threat to authentic religious faith.[80] A civil religion tends to enshrine the political order and, as Senator Mark Hatfield has said, for those of traditional faith, borders on idolatry and "fails to speak of repentance, salvation, and God's standard of justice."[81] Finally, constitutionally establishing a civil religion gives the government, through the courts, a tool to justify and reinforce its own policies. As the standard for acceptability, the civil religion would enjoy a preferred status that could be used to exclude traditional religious advocacy from the public arena.[82]

In summary, civil religion has been for much of American history, and remains, a vital cultural force. It is manifested in our own day in prayers at presidential inaugurations, the invocation used each time the Supreme

Court itself hears argument ("God save this honorable court"), Thanks-giving and National Day of Prayer proclamations, the words "under God" in the Pledge of Allegiance, the phrase "In God We Trust" on coins, various Scripture quotations inscribed on government buildings ("Moses the Lawgiver" is the inscription above the Supreme Court's bench), and even the often recited, ritual presidential benediction "God Bless America."

All of these practices are violations of a strict notion of the separation of church and state. Yet they form a rich tradition of practices that are culturally and judicially accommodated. That the judiciary continues to validate these practices without elevating them to constitutionally pro-tected status is an appropriate fusion of the separationist and accom-modationist traditions that form the background of church-state relations in America.[83]

### Concluding Remarks: Accommodationism and Separationism as Competing Paradigms

As stated earlier in this chapter, the record of the Continental Congress on religion, on its face, tends to dramatically favor an accommodationist interpretation of the religion clauses. The overt religiosity of the Conti-nental Congress, as part of the background to the Constitutional Con-vention and the First Congress, does not readily allow for any other conclusion. But this fact is muted by two considerations that surface upon closer examination of the historical evidence.

First, as argued in chapter 5, many of the practices adopted by the First Congress—legislative chaplaincies, military chaplaincies, and pres-idential thanksgiving proclamations in particular—were routine carry-overs from the practices of the Continental Congress and were not, therefore, considered by a majority of the members of the First Congress to violate the First Amendment. These practices were reflexive, even episodic; indeed, the evidence from the proceedings of the First Congress gives little indication that the constitutional legitimacy of these practices were given more than a modicum of serious thought. Second, the religion clauses were drafted in a period when the nation was in an important period of transition—moving away from an accommodationist paradigm to a separationist paradigm—as concerns the desirable relationship be-tween religion and government. An appreciation of this paradigm shift is imperative to an understanding of the American tradition of church and state—a tradition that is appropriately sensitive to accommodationist ideals but is now moored, to the advantage of both church and state, in separationist ideals.

The separation of church and state as a political principle is often misunderstood. For many eighteenth-century thinkers, the separation principle was a means of achieving religious liberty. It did not refer to a cultural separation of religion from society, as many today assume, but rather an institutional separation of governmental and ecclesiastical power. The separation of church and state in late eighteenth-century America had three basic components. The primary component was the disestablishment of churches in the various states; the second was the decriminalization of religious activity, thus making real for Americans the free exercise of religion according to the dictates of conscience; and the third was the removal of religious disabilities for civil officeholding. Substantial progress in all three of these areas was made in local, state, and federal governments during the founding era, but it was the first area—disestablishing churches, that is, making them fiscally independent of government aid—that was at the time only beginning to make noticeable progress.

This progress in making the churches autonomous resulted in citizens being freed from the requirement of paying taxes for the support of churches with whose doctrines they were not in agreement and ended the operational and political advantages that some churches maintained over others. These principles of religious voluntarism and equality among sects were believed by separationists like James Madison, Thomas Jefferson, and Isaac Backus to preserve the integrity of both government and religion.

So compelling were these principles in the founding era that the states, one by one, began to "disestablish" their churches. By the time of the Constitutional Convention, seven of the original thirteen states had altogether abandoned governmental support of religion. Those states that had not by 1787 disestablished their churches eventually did so: South Carolina in 1790, Georgia in 1798, Maryland in 1810, Connecticut in 1818, New Hampshire in 1819, and Massachusetts in 1833.

The Constitution, with its first set of ten amendments, left the issue of church and state firmly located within the framework of limited government. This strategy was part of an amalgam of strategies—including the separation of powers, the system of checks and balances, belief in an informed citizenry, and a theory of reserved powers—that provided the governmental framework for the new nation. For religion, however, the design was that government at the federal level would be conducted without regard to religion. This design, moreover, left the states free to conduct their own governmental affairs with as much attention to religion as they desired. As we have seen, this was essential to the framers' hope of securing ratification of the Constitution, since the states, especially in New England, scrupulously guarded their right to maintain existing religious establishments.

Thus, while all of the states would eventually end their religious establishments, several states had not yet done so when the Constitution was written, and these states were unwilling to consider any arrangement that might jeopardize their jurisdiction over religion. In 1789, when the First Congress was considering amendments to the Constitution, James Madison proposed such an arrangement. His amendment would have imposed on the states the same restrictions against passing laws to create establishments or to prohibit the free exercise of religion that the First Amendment in its final form imposed on Congress.[84] In effect, his proposal would have resulted in the same requirement of the states to abide by the First Amendment that resulted in the twentieth century under the Supreme Court's incorporation doctrine. The House approved of Madison's proposal, but the Senate voted it down, thus preserving the various state establishments.

One way to view the founding era is to place it at a critical juncture in a roughly 200-year movement for religious liberty that began in the 1630s with Roger Williams's call for the disestablishment of the Congregational church in New England and culminated in the 1830s, when the last of the states disestablished its churches. Seen in this light, the disestablishment of the churches becomes the primary dimension of the religious liberty movement. The framing of the Constitution and the Bill of Rights, then, occurred at a stage in the movement when the conviction that disestablishment was a preserver of religious liberty was not as widely held as it later would be. As a result, the Constitution and First Amendment's provisions on religion, as we have seen, were formulated in terms that might best secure the ratification of the documents of which they were a part, without requiring, as under Madison's rejected proposal, prohibitions on state establishments.

The last of the original states to sever all formal ties between civil authority and the churches were Connecticut, New Hampshire, and Massachusetts. The New England Congregational establishments did not die easily; in each state, church and government leaders alike clung to the theocratic ideals of the interdependence of religion and government that had long been the hallmark of the Puritan Way. The winds of change prevailed, however, and eventually many of the Congregationalist leaders began to see the establishments as non-Congregationalists did—as violations of the principle of equality before the law. It is possible, however, that the New England states finally succumbed to disestablishment of the Congregationalist churches as much for practical as for principled reasons. One writer has asserted that the growing presence of the Unitarian church in early nineteenth-century New England caused Congregational legislators to fear that their churches' establishments would eventually be replaced by ones favoring the Unitarian church. To prevent such a development, or so the argument goes, the Congregationalists rallied to support their own disestablishment.[85]

Once disestablishment prevailed across America, it found virtually unanimous support among respected churchmen, statesmen, and historians. Philip Schaff, America's leading church historian in the nineteenth century, wrote in 1857 that "the glory of America is a free Christianity, independent of the secular government, and supported by the voluntary contributions of a free people. This is one of the greatest facts in modern history."[86] Almost never challenged was James Lord Bryce's conclusion after a lengthy visit to America in 1888 that it was "accepted as an axiom by all Americans that the civil power ought to be not only neutral and impartial as between different forms of faith, but ought to leave these matters entirely on one side. . . . There seem to be no two opinions on this subject in the United States."[87]

The importance of separationism for vibrant, authentic religious expression was attested by Alexis de Tocqueville, the French journalist and historian who traveled extensively in the United States in the 1830s. He commented that "the religious atmosphere of the country was the first thing that struck me on my arrival in the United States." He expressed "astonishment" because in his native Europe religion and freedom marched "in opposite directions." After questioning pastors, priests, and laypersons from all of the various churches he visited, he found that "they all agreed with each other except about the details; all thought that the quiet sway of religion over their country was the complete separation of church and state. I have no hesitation in stating that throughout my stay in America I met nobody, lay or cleric, who did not agree about that."[88]

All of these observers had the advantage of witnessing firsthand the growth, spread, and final victory of disestablishment. These developments were a phenomenon that the founding fathers could not totally foresee. The merits of separationism, while appreciated by many of the founding fathers, could only be fully verified by the passage of time and the acceptance of the disestablishment principle in the states.

Separationism declares the state to be neutral in matters of religion. Some would say that America is a secular state, which is essentially true, although it is suggested here that the term "secular state" is so commonly associated with the promotion of secularism, which has never been true of the American state, that the term "neutral state" might be preferable. Adherence to the concept of the neutral state,[89] accompanied by the lack of state patronage and support of religion, has unfortunately been often viewed as an attack upon or threat to religion. Such a view is to misunderstand the very nature of the neutral state, which is to be neither hostile nor subservient to the church or the interests of religion. In matters of religious faith and ultimate belief the neutral state always is uncommitted. The neutral state is neither religious nor irreligious.[90] Philip Schaff expressed it pointedly when he wrote that the Constitution "is neither hostile nor friendly to any religion; it is simply silent on the subject, as lying beyond the jurisdiction of the general government."[91]

The neutral state ought not to be regarded as a barrier but as a benefit to religion. Certainly the phenomenal growth and marked vitality of religion in America—Catholic, Protestant, Jewish, and diverse other minority religions—clearly attest to the fact that religion has not suffered from the American tradition in church and state. This is as one of the founding fathers, Benjamin Franklin, would have wanted it. Franklin, a strong believer in the secular state, wrote of religion: "When a religion is good, I conceive that it will support itself; and, when it cannot support itself, and God does not take care to support it, so that its professors are obliged to call for the help of the civil power, it is a sign, I apprehend, of it being a bad one."[92]

All of the evidence, then, when examined in historical context, supports separationism as that paradigm of church-state thought that best captures the progressively evolving intentions of the founding fathers. Human government functions best when it does not advance, promote, or side with religion, thereby leaving the pursuit of genuine, authentic, and vibrant religious faith to the individual. As government is a human institution, it probably will never escape the attribution to it of the need to conform to religious obligations. Religion, however, is primarily concerned with individuals, not governments, and should therefore be relegated mostly to the individual sphere.

During the period of the Continental Congress, this perspective was in its nascent stage of development and only beginning to make an impression on the nation's best political thinkers. The Continental Congress, therefore, operated almost exclusively within an accommodationist paradigm. This fact recedes in significance, however, when it is recognized that the separationist paradigm was at that time only beginning to be recognized for its advantages to national life. For this reason, the various religious practices of the Continental Congress that were retained by the First Congress—namely, chaplaincies and thanksgiving proclamations—were not widely understood by the framers to violate the religion clauses. Moreover, although such practices do in fact violate a strict notion of the separation of church and state, they are in keeping with a fundamental principle of separationism, namely, that government is not to be hostile to religious faith. Some accommodationism is wise, indeed probably essential, to a people who have been throughout American history, and remain, pervasively religious. An interpretation of the Constitution that allows the federal government to engage in a minimum of religious expression, short of permitting a pattern of governmental support of religion (including civil religion), best serves both the cause of religion and the cause of government[93] and acknowledges the belief of most Americans that the nation remains accountable to the sovereign God.

Government policymakers will do well, however, to accommodate in public life only those practices, such as chaplaincies and thanksgiving observances, that have longstanding traditions in American life. To commit the mistake of naming such practices as proof-positive that the framers embraced a concept of unlimited support and advancement of religion so long as such advocacy is performed nondiscriminatorily is to violate the separationist principles that underlie the religion clauses and that became dominant in nineteenth-century American political thought.

Attempting to distribute nondiscriminatory support among religious institutions pursuant to the accommodationist directive, one of the main goals of the so-called Religious Freedom Amendment, which failed to receive the necessary two-thirds vote for approval as a constitutional amendment when it was voted on in the U.S. House of Representatives on 4 June 1998, would inevitably result in chaos.[94] Under such an arrangement, it would never be possible to allocate government funds fairly and proportionately among the literally thousands of religious groups entitled to assistance. Inevitably, those with the most financial resources and political influence would benefit the most; smaller groups with fewer resources and less influence would suffer, and some would undoubtedly be forced to dissolve due to an inability to compete on equal terms. The principles of equality and fair treatment that underlie the entire Bill of Rights would be seriously undermined.

In addition to violating the purpose and spirit of the First Amendment, government preference accorded to religion in the public sphere is, in many other ways, unfair to minority religions and to unbelievers. Government-sponsored religious displays, for example, although displayed seasonally, nonetheless put forth a clear message—that some religions are officially recognized and preferred above all others. Accommodationists sometimes argue that the solution is for the offended citizen to turn the other way; but that does not alleviate the pain, reduce the isolation, or eliminate the feeling by persons of different religious beliefs or no religious beliefs that they are merely tolerated guests in their own country. The same problems attend prayers and other religious exercises in public schools. As Protestant faiths still command a majority among students (and their parents) in the nation's public schools, the religious exercises to be performed under an accommodationist framework would inevitably support Protestant values. When one considers that the plural character of American religious life now includes communities of faith such as Mormons, Jehovah's Witnesses, Hari Krishnas, Buddhists, Muslims, Hindus, Christian Scientists, and a host of other minority religions, not to mention a large number of unbelievers, it becomes obvious that the only safe course is one of the separation of church and state in which most religious exercises are relegated strictly to forums outside those of governmental sponsorship.

Separationism, provided it remains sensitive to longstanding accommodationist practices, is indeed the best course for the future of America. Government officials charged with the duty of formulating policy in the admittedly complex field of church and state will do well to recall that the essential elements of governmental sponsorship of religion that animate and form the foundation of accommodationist arguments in our own day are those governmental practices in the early life of the nation, including those of the Continental Congress, that were at that point in history undergoing abatement in favor of a new body of political thought that embodied separationist ideals. It is therefore a mistake to consider that early governmental practices such as congressional chaplaincies and presidential prayer proclamations form the basis of the framers' "original intent." Indeed a closer approximation of the framers' original intent is located in the affirmation of that one who was the principal architect of the Constitution, James Madison, who solemnly declared that "any alliance or coalition between Government and Religion . . . cannot be too carefully guarded against."[95]

The Necessity for Taking Up Arms (sometimes called
"A Declaration of Rights") In Congress, July 6, 1775

If it was possible for men who exercise their reason to believe that the
Divine Author of our existence intended a part of the human race to
hold an absolute property in and an unbounded power over others,
marked out by His infinite goodness and wisdom, as the objects of a
legal domination never rightfully resistible, however severe and oppressive, the inhabitants of these colonies might at least require from the
Parliament of Great Britain some evidence that this dreadful authority
over them has been granted to that body. But a reverence for our great
Creator, principles of humanity, and the dictates of common sense must
convince all those who reflect upon the subject that government was
instituted to promote the welfare of mankind and ought to be administered for the attainment of that end.

The legislature of Great Britain, however, stimulated by an inordinate
passion for a power not only unjustifiable but which they know to be
peculiarly reprobated by the very constitution of that kingdom, and
desperate of success in any mode of contest where regard should be had
to truth, law, or right, have at length, deserting those, attempted to effect
their cruel and impolitic purpose of enslaving these colonies by violence,
and have thereby rendered it necessary for us to close with their last
appeal from reason to arms. Yet, however blinded that assembly may be
by their intemperate rage for unlimited domination so to slight justice
and the opinion of mankind, we esteem ourselves bound, by obligations
of respect to the rest of the world, to make known the justice of our
cause. Our forefathers, inhabitants of the island of Great Britain, left their
native land to seek on these shores a residence for civil and religious
freedom. At the expense of their blood, at the hazard of their fortunes,
without the least charge to the country from which they removed, by

unceasing labor and an unconquerable spirit, they effected settlements in the distant and inhospitable wilds of America, then filled with numerous and warlike nations of barbarians. Societies or governments, vested with perfect legislatures, were formed under charters from the Crown, and a harmonious intercourse was established between the colonies and the kingdom from which they derived their origin. The mutual benefits of this union became in a short time so extraordinary as to excite astonishment. It is universally confessed that the amazing increase of the wealth, strength, and navigation of the Realm arose from this source; and the minister, who so wisely and successfully directed the measures of Great Britain in the late war, publicly declared that these colonies enabled her to triumph over her enemies.

Toward the conclusion of that war, it pleased our sovereign to make a change in his counsels. From that fatal moment, the affairs of the British empire began to fall into confusion, and gradually sliding from the summit of glorious prosperity to which they had been advanced by the virtues and abilities of one man, are at length distracted by the convulsions that now shake it to its deepest foundations. The new Ministry finding the brave foes of Britain though frequently defeated yet still contending, took up the unfortunate idea of granting them a hasty peace, and of then subduing her faithful friends.

These devoted colonies were judged to be in such a state as to present victories without bloodshed and all the easy emoluments of statuteable plunder. The uninterrupted tenor of their peaceable and respectful behavior from the beginning of colonization; their dutiful, zealous, and useful services during the war, though so recently and amply acknowledged in the most honorable manner by His Majesty, by the late King, and by Parliament, could not save them from the meditated innovations. Parliament was influenced to adopt the pernicious project, and, assuming a new power over them, have, in the course of eleven years, given such decisive specimens of the spirit and consequences attending this power as to leave no doubt concerning the effects of acquiescence under it. They have undertaken to give and grant our money without our consent, though we have ever exercised an exclusive right to dispose of our own property; statutes have been passed for extending the jurisdiction of Courts of Admiralty and Vice-Admiralty beyond their ancient limits; for depriving us of the accustomed and inestimable privilege of trial by jury, in cases affecting both life and property; for suspending the legislature of one of the colonies; for interdicting all commerce to the capital of another; and for altering fundamentally the form of government established by charter, and secured by acts of its own legislature solemnly confirmed by the Crown; for exempting the "murderers" of colonists from legal trial and, in effect, from punishment; for erecting in a neighboring province, acquired by the joint arms of Great Britain and America, a despotism dangerous to our very existence; and for quartering soldiers upon the colonists in time of profound peace. It has also been resolved in Parliament that colonists charged with committing certain offenses shall be transported to England to be tried.

But why should we enumerate our injuries in detail? By one statute it is declared that Parliament can "of right make laws to bind us in all cases whatsoever." What is to defend us against so enormous, so unlimited a power? Not a single man of those who assume it is chosen by us, or is subject to our control or influence; but, on the contrary, they are all of them exempt from the operation of such laws; and an American revenue, if not diverted from the ostensible purposes for which it is raised, would actually lighten their own burdens in proportion as they increase ours. We saw the misery to which such despotism would reduce us. We for ten years incessantly and ineffectually besieged the throne as supplicants; we reasoned, we remonstrated with Parliament, in the most mild and decent language.

Administration, sensible that we should regard these oppressive measures as freemen ought to do, sent over fleets and armies to enforce them. The indignation of the Americans was roused, it is true; but it was the indignation of a virtuous, loyal, and affectionate people. A congress of delegates from the United Colonies was assembled at Philadelphia, on the 5th day of last September. We resolved again to offer a humble and dutiful petition to the King, and also addressed our fellow subjects of Great Britain. We have pursued every temperate, ever respectful measure; we have even proceeded to break off our commercial intercourse with our fellow subjects, as the last peaceable admonition, that our attachment to no nation upon earth should supplant our attachment to liberty. This, we flattered ourselves, was the ultimate step of the controversy; but subsequent events have shown how vain was this hope of finding moderation in our enemies.

Several threatening expressions against the colonies were inserted in His Majesty's speech; our petition, though we were told it was a decent one, and that His Majesty had been pleased to receive it graciously, and to promise laying it before his Parliament, was huddled into both houses among a bundle of American papers and there neglected. The Lords and Commons in their address, in the month of February, said, that "a rebellion at that time actually existed within the province of Massachusetts Bay; and that those concerned in it had been countenanced and encouraged by unlawful combinations and engagements, entered into by His Majesty's subjects in several of the other colonies; and therefore they besought His Majesty that he would take the most effectual measures to enforce due obedience to the laws and authority of the supreme legislature." Soon after, the commercial intercourse of whole colonies with foreign countries, and with each other, was cut off by an act of Parliament; by another, several of them were entirely prohibited from the fisheries in the seas near their coasts, on which they always depended for their sustenance; and large reinforcements of ships and troops were immediately sent over to General Gage.

Fruitless were all the entreaties, arguments, and eloquence of an illustrious band of the most distinguished peers and commoners, who nobly and strenuously asserted the justice of our cause to stay, or even to mitigate, the heedless fury with which these accumulated and unexampled outrages were hurried on. Equally fruitless was the interference of the City of London, of Bristol, and many other respectable towns in our favor. Parliament adopted an insidious maneuver calculated to divide us, to establish a perpetual auction of taxations where colony should bid against colony, all of them uninformed what ransom would redeem their lives; and thus to extort from us, at the point of the bayonet, the unknown sums that should be sufficient to gratify, if possible to gratify, ministerial rapacity, with the miserable indulgence left to us of raising, in our own mode, the prescribed tribute. What terms more rigid and humiliating could have been dictated by remorseless victors to conquered enemies? In our circumstances to accept them would be to deserve them.

Soon after intelligence of these proceedings arrived on this continent, General Gage, who in the course of the last year had taken possession of the town of Boston in the province of Massachusetts Bay, and still occupied it as a garrison, on the 19th day of April, sent out from that place a large detachment of his army, who made an unprovoked assault on the inhabitants of the said province, at the town of Lexington, as appears by the affidavits of a great number of persons, some of whom were officers and soldiers of that detachment, murdered eight of the inhabitants, and wounded many others. From thence the troops proceeded in warlike array to the town of Concord, where they set upon another party of the inhabitants of the same province, killing several and wounding more, until compelled to retreat by the country people suddenly assembled to repel this cruel aggression. Hostilities, thus commenced by the British troops, have been since prosecuted by them without regard to faith or reputation.

The inhabitants of Boston being confined within that town by the general their governor, and having, in order to procure their dismission, entered into a treaty with him, it was stipulated that the said inhabitants having deposited their arms with their own magistrates, should have liberty to depart, taking with them their other effects. They accordingly delivered up their arms; but in open violation of honor, in defiance of the obligation of treaties, which even savage nations esteemed sacred, the governor ordered the arms deposited as aforesaid, that they might be preserved for their owners, to be seized by a body of soldiers; detained the greatest part of the inhabitants in the town, and compelled the few who were permitted to retire to leave their most valuable effects behind. By this perfidy, wives are separated from their husbands, children from their parents, the aged and the sick from their relations and friends who wish to attend and comfort them; and those who have been used to live in plenty and even elegance are reduced to deplorable distress.

The general, further emulating his ministerial masters by a proclamation bearing date on the 12th day of June, after venting the grossest falsehoods and calumnies against the good people of these colonies, proceeds to "declare them all, either by name or description, to be rebels and traitors, to supersede the course of the common law, and instead thereof to publish and order the use and exercise of the law martial." His troops have butchered our countrymen, have wantonly burned Charlestown, besides a considerable number of houses in other places; our ships and vessels are seized; the necessary supplies of provisions are intercepted; and he is exerting his utmost power to spread destruction and devastation around him.

We have received certain intelligence that General Carleton, the governor of Canada, is instigating the people of that province and the Indians to fall upon us; and we have but too much reason to apprehend that schemes have been formed to excite domestic enemies against us. In brief, a part of these colonies now feel, and all of them are sure of feeling, as far as the vengeance of administration can inflict them, the complicated calamities of fire, sword, and famine. We are reduced to the alternative of choosing an unconditional submission to the tyranny of irritated ministers, or resistance by force.

The latter is our choice. We have counted the cost of this contest and find nothing so dreadful as voluntary slavery. Honor, justice, and humanity forbid us tamely to surrender that freedom which we received from our gallant ancestors, and which our innocent posterity have a right to receive from us. We cannot endure the infamy and guilt of resigning succeeding generations to that wretchedness which inevitably awaits them, if we basely entail hereditary bondage upon them.

Our cause is just. Our union is perfect. Our internal resources are great; and if necessary, foreign assistance is undoubtedly attainable. We gratefully acknowledge, as signal instances of the divine favor toward us, that His providence would not permit us to be called into this severe controversy until we were grown up to our present strength, had been previously exercised in warlike operation, and possessed of the means of defending ourselves. With hearts fortified with these animating reflections, we most solemnly, before God and the world, *declare* that, exerting the utmost energy of those powers which our beneficent Creator has graciously bestowed upon us, the arms we have been compelled by our enemies to assume, we will, in defiance of every hazard, with unabating firmness and perseverance, employ for the preservation of our liberties; being with one mind resolved to die free men rather than live slaves.

Lest this declaration should disquiet the minds of our friends and fellow subjects in any part of the empire, we assure them that we mean not to dissolve that union which has so long and so happily subsisted between us and which we sincerely wish to see restored. Necessity has not yet driven us into that desperate measure, or induced us to excite any other nation to war against them. We have not raised armies with ambitious designs of separating from Great Britain and establishing independent states. We fight not for glory or for conquest. We exhibit to mankind the remarkable spectacle of a people attacked by unprovoked enemies, without any imputation or even suspicion of offense. They boast of their privileges and civilization, and yet proffer no milder conditions than servitude or death.

In our own native land, in defense of the freedom that is our birthright and which we ever enjoyed till the late violation of it, for the protection of our property acquired solely by the honest industry of our forefathers and ourselves, against violence actually offered, we have taken up arms. We shall lay them down when hostilities shall cease on the part of the aggressors and all danger of their being renewed shall be removed, and not before.

With a humble confidence in the mercies of the supreme and impartial Judge and Ruler of the universe, we most devoutly implore his divine goodness to protect us happily through this great conflict, to dispose our adversaries to reconciliation on reasonable terms, and thereby to relieve the empire from the calamities of civil war.

On a motion made, *Resolved*, that a letter be prepared to the lord mayor, aldermen, and livery of the City of London expressing the thanks of this Congress for their virtuous and spirited opposition to the oppressive and ruinous system of colony administration adopted by the British Ministry.

*Ordered,* that the committee appointed to draft an address to the people of Great Britain do prepare this.

Letter to the Inhabitants of Quebec
in Congress, October 26, 1774

Friends and fellow-subjects,

We, the Delegates of the Colonies of New-Hampshire, Massachusetts-Bay, Rhode-Island and Providence Plantations, Connecticut, New-York, New-Jersey, Pennsylvania, the Counties of Newcastle Kent and Sussex on Delaware, Maryland, Virginia, North-Carolina and South-Carolina, deputed by the inhabitants of the said Colonies, to represent them in a General Congress at Philadelphia, in the province of Pennsylvania, to consult together concerning the best methods to obtain redress of our afflicting grievances, having accordingly assembled and taken into our most serious consideration the state of public affairs on this continent, have thought proper to address your province as a member therein deeply interested.

When the fortune of war, after a gallant and glorious resistance, had incorporated you with the body of English subjects, we rejoiced in the truly valuable addition, both on our own and your account; expecting, as courage and generosity are naturally united, our brave enemies would become our hearty friends, and that the Divine Being would bless to you the dispensations of his over-ruling providence, by securing to you and your latest posterity the inestimable advantages of a free English constitution of government, which it is the privilege of all English subjects to enjoy.

These hopes were confirmed by the King's proclamation, issued in the year 1763, plighting the public faith for your full enjoyment of those advantages.

Little did we imagine that any succeeding Ministers would so audaciously and cruelly abuse the royal authority, as to with-hold from you the fruition of the irrevocable rights to which you were thus justly entitled.

But since we have lived to see the unexpected time when Ministers of this flagitious temper have dared to violate the most sacred compacts and obligations, and as you, educated under another form of government, have artfully been kept from discovering the unspeakable worth of *that* form you are now undoubtedly entitled to, we esteem it our duty, for the weighty reasons herein after mentioned, to explain to you some of its most important branches.

"In every human society," says the celebrated Marquis *Beccaaria*, "there is an *effort, continually tending* to confer on one part the heighth of power and happiness, and to reduce the other to the extreme of weakness and misery. The intent of good laws is to *oppose this effort*, and to diffuse their influence *universally* and *equally*."

Rulers stimulated by this pernicious "effort," and subjects animated by the just "intent of opposing good laws against it," have occasioned that vast variety of events that fill the histories of so many nations. All these histories demonstrate the truth of this simple position, that to live by the will of one man, or set of men, is the production of misery to all men.

On the solid foundation of this principle, Englishmen reared up the fabrick of their constitution with such a strength as for ages to defy time, tyranny, treachery, internal and foreign wars: And, as an illustrious author of your nation, hereafter mentioned [Montesquieu] observes,— "They gave the people of their Colonies, the form of their own government, and this government carrying prosperity along with it, they have grown great nations in the forests they were sent to inhabit."

In this form, the first grand right is that of the people having a share in their own government by their representatives chosen by themselves, and, in consequence of being ruled by *laws* which they themselves approve, not by *edicts* of *men* over whom they have no control. This is a bulwark surrounding and defending their property, which by their honest cares and labours they have acquired so that no portions of it can legally be taken from them, but with their own full and free consent, when they in their judgment deem it just and necessary to give them for public service, and precisely direct the easiest, cheapest, and most equal methods, in which they shall be collected.

The influence of this right extends still farther. If money is wanted by Rulers who have in any manner oppressed the people, they may retain it until their grievances are redressed; and thus peaceably procure relief, without trusting to despised petitions or disturbing the public tranquility.

The next great right is that of trial by jury. This provides that neither life, liberty nor property can be taken from the possessor until twelve of his unexceptionable countrymen and peers of his vicinage, who from that neighbourhood may reasonably be supposed to be acquainted with his character and the characters of the witnesses, upon a fair trial, and full enquiry, face to face in open Court before as many people as choose to attend, shall pass their sentence upon oath against him; a sentence that cannot injure him without injuring their own reputation and probably their interest also, as the question may turn on points that in some degree concern the general welfare; and if it does not, their verdict may form a precedent that on a similar trial of their own may militate against themselves.

Another right relates merely to the liberty of the person. If a subject is seized and imprisoned, tho' by order of Government, he may by virtue of this right immediately obtain a writ termed a Habeas Corpus, from a Judge whose sworn duty it is to grant it, and thereupon procure any illegal restraint to be quickly enquired into and redressed.

A fourth right is that of holding lands by the tenure of easy rents and not by rigorous and oppressive services, frequently forcing the possessors from their families and their business to perform what ought to be done in all well regulated states by men hired for the purpose.

The last right we shall mention regards the freedom of the press. The importance of this consists, besides the advancement of truth, science, morality, and arts in general, in its diffusion of liberal sentiments on the administration of Government, its ready communication of thoughts between subjects, and its consequential promotion of union among them, whereby oppressive officers are shamed or intimidated into more honourable and just modes of conducting affairs.

These are the invaluable rights that form a considerable part of our mild system of government; that, sending its equitable energy through all ranks and classes of men, defends the poor from the rich, the weak from the powerful, the industrious from the rapacious, the peaceable from the violent, the tenants from the lords, and all from their superiors.

These are the rights without which a people cannot be free and happy, and under the protecting and encouraging influence of which these colonies have hitherto so amazingly flourished and increased. These are the rights a profligate Ministry are now striving by force of arms to ravish from us, and which we are with one mind resolved never to resign but with our lives.

These are the rights *you* are entitled to and ought at this moment in perfection to exercise. And what is offered to you by the late Act of Parliament in their place? Liberty of conscience in your religion? No.

God gave it to you; and the temporal powers with which you have been and are connected, firmly stipulated for your enjoyment of it. If laws, divine and human, could secure it against the despotic caprices of wicked men, it was secured before. Are the French laws in *civil* cases restored? *It seems so.* But observe the cautious kindness of the Ministers, who pretend to be your benefactors. The words of the statute are—that those "laws shall be the rule, until they shall be *varied* or *altered* by any ordinances of the Governor and Council." Is the "certainty and lenity of the *criminal* law of England, and its benefits and advantages," commended in the said statute, and said to "have been sensibly felt by you," secured to you and your descendants? No. They too are subjected to arbitrary "*alterations*" by the Governor and Council; and a power is expressly reserved of appointing "such courts of *criminal, civil* and *ecclesiastical* jurisdiction, as shall be thought proper." Such is the precarious tenure of mere *will* by which you hold your lives and religion. The Crown and its Ministers are empowered, as far as they could be by Parliament, to establish even the *Inquisition* itself among you. Have you an Assembly composed of worthy men, elected by yourselves and in whom you can confide, to make laws for you, to watch over your welfare, and to direct in what quantity and in what manner your money shall be taken from you? No. The Power of making laws for you is lodged in the governor and council, all of them dependent upon and removable at the *pleasure* of a Minister. Besides, another late statute, made without your consent, has subjected you to the impositions of *Excise*, the horror of all free states, thus wresting your property from you by the most odious of taxes and laying open to insolent tax-gatherers, houses, the scenes of domestic peace and comfort and called the castles of English subjects in the books of their law. And in the very act for altering your government, and intended to flatter you, you are not authorized to "assess levy, or apply any *rates* and *taxes*, but for the inferior purposes of *making roads*, and erecting and repairing *public buildings*, or for other *local* conveniences, within your respective towns and districts." Why this degrading distinction? Ought not the property, honestly acquired by *Canadians*, to be held as sacred as that of *Englishment*? Have not Canadians sense enough to attend to any other public affairs than gathering stones from one place and piling them up in another? Unhappy people! who are not only injured, but insulted. Nay more! With such a superlative contempt of your understanding and spirit has an insolent Ministry presumed to think of you, our respectable fellow-subjects, according to the information we have received, as firmly to persuade themselves that your gratitude for the injuries and insults they have recently offered to you will engage you to take up arms and render yourselves the ridicule and detestation of the world, by becoming tools in their hands, to assist them in taking that freedom from *us* which they have treacherously denied to *you*; the unavoidable consequence of which attempt, if successful, would be the extinction of all hopes of you or your posterity being ever restored to freedom. For idiocy itself cannot believe that, when their drudgery is performed, they will treat you with less cruelty than they have us who are of the same blood with themselves.

What would your countryman, the immortal *Montesquieu*, have said to such a plan of domination as has been framed for you? Hear his words, with an intenseness of thought suited to the importance of the subject.— "In a free state, every man, who is supposed a free agent, *ought to be concerned in his own government:* Therefore the *legislative* should reside in the whole body of the *people*, or their *representatives*."—"The political liberty of the subject is a *tranquility of mind*, arising from the opinion each person has of his *safety*. In order to have this liberty, it is requisite the government be so constituted, as that one man need not be *afraid* of another. When the power of *making* laws, and the power of *executing* them, are *united* in the same person, or in the same body of Magistrates, *there can be no liberty*; because apprehensions may arise, lest the same *Monarcch* or *Senate*, should *enact* tyrannical laws, to *execute* them in a tyrannical manner."

"The power of *judging* should be exercised by persons taken from the *body of the people*, at certain times of the year, and pursuant to a form and manner prescribed by law. *There is no liberty*, if the power of *judging* be not *separated* from the *legislative* and *executive* powers."

"Military men belong to a profession, which *may be* useful, but *is often* dangerous."—"The enjoyment of liberty, and even its support and preservation, consists in every man's being allowed to speak his thoughts, and lay open his sentiments."

Apply these decisive maxims, sanctified by the authority of a name which all Europe reveres, to your own state. You have a Governor, it may be urged, vested with the *executive* powers of the powers of *administration*. In him and in your Council is lodged the power of *making* laws. You have *Judges* who are to *decide* every cause affecting your lives, liberty or property. Here is, indeed, an appearance of the several powers being *separated* and *distributed* into *different* hands for checks one upon another, the only effectual mode ever invented by the wit of men to promote their freedom and prosperity. But scorning to be illuded by a tinsel'd outside, and exerting the natural sagacity of Frenchmen, *examine* the specious device and you will find it, to use an expression of holy writ, "a whited sepulcre" for burying your lives, liberty and property.

Your *Judges* and your *Legislative Council*, as it is called, are *dependent* on your Governor, and he is dependent on the servant of the Crown in Great-Britain. The *legislative, executive* and *judging* powers are *all* moved by the nods of a Minister. Privileges and immunities last no longer than his smiles. When he frowns, their feeble forms dissolve. Such a treacherous ingenuity has been exerted in drawing up the code lately offered you, that every sentence, beginning with a benevolent pretension, concludes with a destructive power; and the substance of the whole, divested of its smooth words, is—that the Crown and its Ministers shall be as absolute throughout your extended province as the despots of Asia or Africa. What can protect your property from taxing edicts and the rapacity of necessitous and cruel masters, your persons from Letters de Cachet, goals, dungeons, and oppressive services, your lives and general liberty from arbitrary and unfeeling rulers? We defy you, casting your view upon every side, to discover a single circumstance promising from any quarter the faintest hope of liberty to you or your posterity, but from an entire adoption into the union of these Colonies.

What advice would the truly great man before-mentioned, that advocate of freedom and humanity, give you, was he now living and knew that we, your numerous and powerful neighbours, animated by a just love of our invaded rights and united by the indissoluble bands of affection and interest, called upon you by every obligation of regard for yourselves and your children, as we now do, to join us in our righteous contest, to make common cause with us therein and take a noble chance for emerging from a humiliating subjection under Governors, Intendants, and Military Tyrants, into the firm rank and condition of English freemen, whose custom it is, derived from their ancestors, to make those tremble who dare to think of making them miserable?

Would not this be the purport of his address? "Seize the opportunity presented to you by Providence itself. You have been conquered into liberty, if you act as you ought. This work is not of man. You are a small people, compared to those who with open arms invite you into a fellowship. A moment's reflection should convince you which will be most for your interest and happiness, to have all the rest of North-America your unalterable friends, or your inveterate enemies. The injuries of Boston have roused and associated every colony, from Nova-Scotia to Georgia. Your province is the only link wanting, to compleate the bright and strong chain of union. Nature has joined your country to theirs. Do you join your political interests? For their own sakes, they never will desert or betray you. Be assured, that the happiness of a people inevitably depends on their liberty, and their spirit to assert it. The value and extent of the advantages tendered to you are immense. Heaven grant you may not discover them to be blessings after they have bid you an eternal adieu."

We are too well acquainted with the liberality of sentiment distinguishing your nation to imagine, that difference of religion will prejudice you against a hearty amity with us. You know that the transcendant nature of freedom elevates those who unite in her cause above all such low-minded infirmities. The Swiss Cantons furnish a memorable proof of this truth. Their union is composed of Roman Catholic and Protestant States, living in the utmost concord and peace with one another and thereby enabled, ever since they bravely vindicated their freedom, to defy and defeat every tyrant that has invaded them.

Should there be any among you, as there generally are in all societies, who prefer the favours of Ministers and their own private interests to the welfare of their country, the temper of such selfish persons will render them incredibly active in opposing all public-spirited measures from an expectation of being well rewarded for their sordid industry, by their superiors; but we doubt not you will be upon your guard against such men, and not sacrifice the liberty and happiness of the whole Canadian people and their posterity to gratify the avarice and ambition of individuals.

We do not ask you, by this address, to commence acts of hostility against the government of our common Sovereign. We only invite you to consult your own glory and welfare, and not to suffer yourselves to be inveigled or intimidated by infamous ministers so far as to become the instruments of their cruelty and despotism, but to unite with us in one social compact, formed on the generous principles of equal liberty and cemented by such an exchange of beneficial and endearing offices as to render it perpetual. In order to complete this highly desirable union, we submit it to your consideration whether it may not be expedient for you to meet together in your several towns and districts and elect Deputies, who afterwards meeting in a provincial Congress, may chuse Delegates to represent your province in the Continental Congress to be held at Philadelphia on the tenth day of May, 1775.

In this present Congress, beginning on the fifth of the last month and continued to this day, it has been with universal pleasure and an unanimous vote resolved: That we should consider the violation of your rights, by the act for altering the government of your province, as a violation of our own, and that you should be invited to accede to our confederation, which has no other objects than the perfect security of the natural and civil rights of all the constituent members according to their respective circumstances, and the preservation of a happy and lasting connection with Great Britain on the salutary and constitutional principals herein before mentioned. For effecting these purposes, we have addressed an humble and loyal petition to his Majesty praying relief of our and your grievances; and have associated to stop all importations from Great-Britain and Ireland, after the first day of December, and all exportations to those Kingdoms and the West-Indies after the tenth day of next September, unless the said grievances are redressed.

The Almighty God may incline your minds to approve our equitable and necessary measures, to add yourselves to us, to put your fate whenever you suffer injuries which you are determined to oppose not on the small influence of your single province but on the consolidated powers of North-America, and may grant to our joint exertions an event as happy as our cause is just, is the fervent prayer of us, your sincere and affectionate friends and fellow-subjects.

> By order of the Congress,
> Henry Middleton, *President.*
> 26 October, 1774

# NOTES

*Preface*

1. Richard B. Morris, *The Forging of the Union, 1781–1789* (San Francisco: Harper & Row, 1987), 269. Seven had served in the First Continental Congress, eight had signed the Declaration of Independence, and two had signed the Articles of Confederation.

2. How the Constitution should be interpreted is, of course, only one area of hermeneutical inquiry. The interpretation of texts generally comes under the field of literary theory, where the sophistication of analysis, according to Stanford Levinson in Levinson and Steven Mailloux, eds., *Interpreting Law and Literature: A Hermeneutic Reader* (Evanston, Ill.: Northwestern University Press, 1988), xx, "has far surpassed anything that [has] occurred in the legal academy." The term "hermeneutics" did not even enter American legal discourse until 1839, when Francis Lieber, a German immigrant, published *Legal and Political Hermeneutics; or, Principles of Interpretation and Construction in Law and Politics with Remarks on Precedents and Authorities*, 3d ed. (St. Louis: F. H. Thomas, 1880). For a good introduction to modern literary theory, see Raman Selden, *A Reader's Guide to Contemporary Literary Theory* (Lexington: University of Kentucky Press, 1989). Some of the best works on constitutional interpretation are Leonard Levy, *Original Intent and the Framers' Constitution* (New York: Macmillan, 1988), and Erwin Chemerinsky, *Interpreting the Constitution* (New York: Praeger, 1987).

3. Among the best works presenting accommodationist interpretations are Chester James Antieu, Arthur L. Downey, and Edward C. Roberts, *Freedom from Federal Establishment: Formation and Early History of the First Amendment Religion Clauses* (Milwaukee: Bruce Publishing, 1964); Walter Berns, *The First Amendment and the Future of American Democracy* (New York: Basic Books, 1976); Michael J. Malbin, *Religion and Politics: The Intentions of the Authors of the First Amendment* (Washington, D.C.: American Enterprise Institute for Public Policy Research, 1978); and Robert L. Cord, *Separation of Church and State: Historical Fact and Current Fiction* (New York: Lambeth Press, 1982). Among the best with separationist stances are Leo Pfeffer, *Church, State and Freedom*, 2nd ed. (Boston: Beacon Press, 1967); Leonard Levy, *The Establishment Clause: Religion and the First Amendment* (New York: Macmillan,

1986); Anson Phelps Stokes, *Church and State in the United States: Historical Development and Contemporary Problems of Religious Freedom under the Constitution*, 3 vols. (New York: Harper & Brothers, 1950); and Isaac Kramnick and R. Laurence Moore, *The Godless Constitution: The Case against Religious Correctness* (New York: Norton, 1996).

4. Undisputably the best work here is Thomas J. Curry, *The First Freedoms: Church and State in America to the Passage of the First Amendment* (New York: Oxford University Press, 1986). A still valuable source is Sanford H. Cobb, *The Rise of Religious Liberty in America: A History* (New York: Macmillan, 1902).

5. See, for example, Edwin S. Gaustad, *Liberty of Conscience: Roger Williams in America* (Grand Rapids, Mich.: Eerdmans, 1991); Mary Maples Dunn, *William Penn: Politics and Conscience* (Princeton: Princeton University Press, 1967); and Robert S. Alley, *James Madison on Religious Liberty* (Buffalo, N.Y.: Prometheus Books, 1985).

6. See, for example, Philip Kurland, *Religion and the Law: Of Church and State and the Supreme Court* (Chicago: Aldine Publishing, 1962); Gerard V. Bradley, *Church-State Relationships in America* (Westport, Conn.: Greenwood Press, 1987); and Leo Pfeffer, *Religion, State, and the Burger Court* (Buffalo, N.Y.: Prometheus Books, 1984).

7. Edward Frank Humphrey, "Continental Congress and Religion," chap. 14 in *Nationalism and Religion in America, 1774–1789* (Boston: Chipman Law Publishing, 1924).

*Chapter One*

1. Leonard Levy, *Original Intent and the Framers' Constitution* (New York: Macmillan, 1988), x, xi. The most comprehensive work on "original intent" is Jack N. Rakove, *Original Meanings: Politics and Ideas in the Making of the Constitution* (New York: Vintage, 1997).

2. Quoted in Alfred H. Kelly and Winfred A. Harbison, *The American Constitution: Its Origins and Development*, 3d ed. (New York: W. W. Norton, 1963), 1.

3. Jonathan K. Van Patten, "The Partisan Battle over the Constitution: Meese's Jurisprudence of Original Intention and Brennan's Theory of Contemporary Ratification," *Marquette Law Review* 70 (Spring 1987): 399.

4. James Madison to Thomas Ritchie, 15 September 1791, *The Founders' Constitution*, 5 vols., ed. Philip B. Kurland and Ralph Lerner (Chicago: University of Chicago Press, 1987) 1: chap. 2, no. 28, 74.

5. H. Jefferson Powell, "The Original Understanding of Original Intent," *Harvard Law Review* 98 (March 1985): 888.

6. Quoted *ibid.*, 915.

7. U.S. Constitution, art. 1, Sec. 8 ("The Congress shall have Power . . . to make all laws which shall be necessary and proper for carrying into Execution the foregoing Powers and all other Powers vested by this Constitution in the Government of the United States, or in any Department or Officer thereof").

8. Alexander Hamilton, "Opinion on the Constitutionality of an Act to Establish a Bank" (1791), reprinted in *Papers of Alexander Hamilton*, ed. Harold C. Syrett (New York: Columbia University Press, 1961), 15:102–3; quoted in Powell, "The Original Understanding," 916.

9. U.S. Constitution, amend. 10.

10. Powell, "The Original Understanding," 916–17.

11. *Ibid.*, 945–46.

12. *Congressional Globe*, 39th Cong., 1st sess., 1866, 677; quoted in Powell, "The Original Understanding," 947.

13. Jefferson H. Powell, "The Compleat Jeffersonian: Justice Rehnquist and Federalism," *Yale Law Journal* 91 (1982): 1321–22.

14. Edwin Meese (speech given to the Federalist Society in Washington, D.C., 30 January 1987 hereafter "Meese Speech"); reprinted in *Marquette Law Review* 70 (Spring 1987): 380–88.

15. Edwin Meese, "The Supreme Court of the United States: Bulwark of a Limited Constitution" (address given to the American Bar Association, Washington, D.C., 9 July 1985); reprinted in *South Texas Law Review* 27 (1986): 455–66.

16. *Ibid.*, 469–70; quoted portions are from Alexander Hamilton's *The Federalist*, No. 78.

17. Meese Speech, 458.

18. Quoted in Howard Ball, "The Convergence of Constitutional Law and Politics in the Reagan Administration: The Exhumation of the 'Jurisprudence of Original Intention' Doctrine," *Cumberland Law Review* 17 (Summer 1987): 880.

19. Irving R. Kaufman, "What Did the Founding Fathers Intend?" *New York Times Magazine*, 23 February 1986, 42.

20. *Ibid.*

21. William J. Brennan, Jr., "The Constitution of the United States: Contemporary Ratification" (address given at Georgetown University, 12 October 1985); reprinted in *South Texas Law Review* 27 (1986): 433–45.

22. *Ibid.*, 436.

23. *Ibid.*

24. *Ibid.*

25. *Ibid.*, 438.

26. Robert H. Bork, "Original Intent and the Constitution," *Humanities* 7 (1986): 26.

27. See generally, Derek Davis, *Original Intent: Chief Justice Rehnquist and the Course of American Church-State Relations* (Buffalo, N.Y.: Prometheus Books, 1991).

28. Jonathan K. Van Patten, "In the End Is the Beginning: An Inquiry into the Meaning of the Religion Clauses," *Saint Louis University Law Journal* 27 (February 1983): 5.

29. See *Engel v. Vitale*, 370 U.S. 421, 429–30 (1962); *Zorach v. Clauson*, 343 U.S. 306, 313–14 (1952); *Everson v. Board of Education*, 330 U.S. 1, 8–11 (1947); Leo Pfeffer, *Church, State and Freedom*, 2d ed. (Boston: Beacon Press, 1967), 122; Jesse H. Choper, "The Religion Clauses of the First Amendment: Reconciling the Conflict," *University of Pittsburgh Law Review* 41 (Spring 1980): 677.

30. *Abington School District v. Schempp*, 374 U.S. 203, 232 (1963) (Brennan, J., concurring).

31. Van Patten, "In the End Is the Beginning," 32.

32. John Locke, "A Letter Concerning Toleration" (1685), reprinted in *Main Currents of Western Thought*, 4th ed., ed. Franklin Le Van Baumer (New Haven: Yale University Press, 1978), 355.

33. 117 Sup. Ct. 2157 (1997).

34. See Carl H. Esbeck, "Five Views of Church-State Relations in Contemporary American Thought," *Brigham Young University Law Review* 86 (1987): 371.

35. 330 U.S. 1 (1947).

36. *Ibid.*, 15–16.

37. Leonard Levy, "The Original Meaning of the Establishment Clause of the First Amendment." In *Religion and the State: Essays in Honor of Leo Pfeffer*, ed. James E. Wood, Jr. (Waco, TX.: Baylor University Press, 1985), 44.

38. Pfeffer, *Church, State and Freedom*, 127.

39. Levy, "The Original Meaning," 44.

40. J. M. O'Neill, *Religion and Education under the Constitution* (New York: Harper & Row, 1949), 56.

41. Levy, "The Original Meaning," 44.

42. 98 U.S. 145 (1878). The *Reynolds* case dealt with a Mormon who was convicted in 1875 in the Utah Territory for violating a federal statute prohibiting polygamy. The defendant claimed that practicing polygamy was his religious duty, but the Court ruled that protection under the Free Exercise Clause extended only to one's opinions, not one's actions. Because the defendant's actions violated "social duties" and "good order," the Court upheld his conviction.

43. See *Employment Division of Oregon v. Smith*, 494 U.S. 872 (1990), in which two men were fired from their jobs as drug counselors after their employer learned the pair had used the drug peyote during ceremonies in the Native American church. The State of Oregon had a criminal statute prohibiting the ingestion of peyote. Believing that an exemption should be carved out for their religious use of the drug, the two men applied for unemployment compensation but were turned down. The U.S. Supreme Court reversed the Oregon Supreme Court's finding that the men were entitled to benefits pursuant to the Free Exercise Clause, holding that state and local governments are free to enact facially neutral, generally applicable laws even though such laws might place minority religions at the mercy of legislatures. Concerned that the *Smith* decision vitiated the free exercise of religion, Congress passed the Religious Freedom Restoration Act in 1993. This legislation reinstated the pre-*Smith* standard for evaluating free exercise claims: government must show a "compelling state interest" to override one's claim that a state's action interferes with religious acts. Subsequently, on separation of power grounds, the Supreme Court found the 1993 act to be unconstitutional, which effectively reinstated the *Smith* rule. See *Boerne v. Flores*, 117 Sup. Ct. 2157 (1997).

44. For the most extensive treatment available of founding era views, see Michael W. McConnell, "The Origins and Historical Understanding of the Free Exercise of Religion," *Harvard Law Review* 103 (1990): 1409.

45. The Free Exercise Clause was made applicable to the states in *Cantwell v. Connecticut*, 310 U.S. 296 (1940), and the Establishment Clause in *Everson v. Board of Education*.

46. 333 U.S. 203, 215 (1948).

47. John Wilson, "Religion, Government, and Power in the New American Nation." In *Religion and American Politics: From the Colonial Period to the 1980s*, ed. Mark Noll (New York: Oxford University Press, 1990), 79–80.

48. *Ibid.*, 80.

49. See generally, Davis, *Original Intent*, especially chap. 8. For the accommodationist views of Justice Clarence Thomas, see Davis, "The Fraternity of Original Intent: Clarence Thomas, the Newest Inductee," *Liberty* 91 (1996): 16.

50. Wilson, "Religion, Government, and Power," 80–81.

51. James Madison, *Notes of Debates in the Federal Convention of 1787*, ed. Adrianne Koch (Athens: Ohio University Press, 1966), 561.

52. James E. Wood, Jr., " 'No Religious Test Shall Ever Be Required': Reflections on the Bicentennial of the U.S. Constitution," *Journal of Church and State* 29 (Spring

1987): 200. For an exhaustive treatment of the "No Religious Test" Clause, see Daniel L. Dreisbach, "The Constitution's Forgotten Religion Clause: Reflections on the Article VI Religious Test Ban," *Journal of Church and State* 38 (Spring 1996): 261.

53. Levy, "The Original Meaning," 45.

54. *The Federalist,* No. 84.

55. Levy, "The Original Meaning," n. 14.

56. *Ibid.,* 46—47.

57. *Ibid.,* 47.

58. Jonathan Elliot, *The Debates in the Several State Conventions on the Adoption of the Federal Constitution,* 5 vols. (Philadelphia: J. B. Lippincott, 1941), 2:236.

59. *Ibid.*

60. Charles C. Tansill, ed., *Documents Illustrative of the Formation of the Union of the American States* (Washington D.C.: Government Printing Office, 1927), 1026.

61. *Ibid.,* 1031; Elliott, *Debates,* 3:659.

62. Tansill, *Documents,* 1035.

63. *Ibid.,* 1047. Levy presents a brief but cogent account of the debates of the New York convention regarding the matter of religious liberty. See Levy, "The Original Meaning," 51—52.

64. *Ibid.,* 1053.

65. James E. Wood, Jr., E. Bruce Thompson, and Robert T. Miller, *Church and State in Scripture, History, and Constitutional Law* (Waco, Tex.: Baylor University Press, 1958), 101—02.

66. Joseph Gales, ed., *Annals of the Congress of the United States: The Debates and Proceedings of the Congress of the United States,* 42 vols. (Washington, D.C.: Gales and Seaton, 1834), 1:441; reprinted in Kurland and Lerner, *The Founders' Constitution,* 5: Bill of Rights, no. 11, pp. 21—32.

67. *Annals of Congress,* 1:451, as appearing in Kurland and Lerner, *The Founders' Constitution,* 5: Bill of Rights, no. 11, p. 25.

68. Robert L. Cord, *Separation of Church and State: Historical Fact and Current Fiction* (New York: Lambeth Press, 1982), 5.

69. Robert A. Rutland, ed., *The Papers of James Madison,* 9 vols. (Charlottesville: University of Virginia Press, 1976), 8:298—306.

70. Elizabeth Fleet, ed., "Madison's Detached Memoranda," *William and Mary Quarterly* 3 (1946): 554—59.

71. *Annals of Congress,* 1:729.

72. *Ibid.*

73. Michael J. Malbin, *Religion and Politics: The Intentions of the Authors of the First Amendment* (Washington, D.C.: American Enterprise Institute for Public Policy Research, 1978), 7.

74. *Ibid.,* 7, 40.

75. Levy, "The Original Meaning," 58.

76. *Annals of Congress,* 1:796.

77. Linda Grant DePauw, ed., *Documentary History of the First Federal Congress of the United States of America,* 3 vols. (Baltimore: Johns Hopkins University Press, 1971), 1:151.

78. *Ibid.*

79. *Ibid.*

80. *Ibid.*

81. *Ibid.*

82. Levy, "The Original Meaning," 60.

83. Douglas Laycock, " 'Nonpreferential' Aid to Religion: A False Claim about Original Intent," *William and Mary Law Review* 27 (Special Issue, 1985–1986), 880.

84. Gerard V. Bradley, *Church-State Relationships in America* (Westport, Conn.: Greenwood Press, Inc., 1987), 93–94.

85. DePauw, *Documentary History*, 1:151.

86. *Ibid.*, 1:166

87. Levy, "The Original Meaning," 59–60.

88. *Annals of Congress*, 1:913; DePauw, *Documentary History*, 1:181.

89. Levy, "The Original Meaning," 61–65.

90. Ball, "The Convergence of Constitutional Law," 886.

91. Philip B. Kurland, "The Origins of the Religion Clauses of the Constitution," *William and Mary Law Review* 27 (Special Issue, 1985–1986), 860.

92. Levy, "The Original Meaning," 58.

93. *Ibid.*, 44.

94. Steven D. Smith, "Wrong Jurisdiction," *Liberty* 93 (March/April 1998): 23. For an enlargement of Smith's thesis, see his *Foreordained Failure: The Quest for a Constitutional Principle of Religious Freedom* (New York: Oxford University Press, 1995).

95. Smith, *Foreordained Failure*, 49.

96. Smith, "Wrong Jurisdiction," 26.

*Chapter Two*

1. Sanford Cobb, *The Rise of Religious Liberty in America: A History* (New York: Macmillan, 1902), 2.

2. Steven D. Smith, *Foreordained Failure: The Quest for a Constitutional Principle of Religious Freedom* (New York: Oxford University Press, 1995). See discussion of Smith's thesis in the final pages of chap. 1.

3. John M. Murrin, "A Roof without Walls: The Dilemma of American National Identity," in *Beyond Confederation: Origins of the Constitution and American National Identity*, ed. Richard Beeman, Stephen Botein, and Edward C. Carter II (Chapel Hill: University of North Carolina Press, 1987), 339.

4. James E. Wood, Jr., E. Bruce Thompson, and Robert T. Miller, *Church and State in Scripture, History, and Constitutional Law* (Waco, Tex.: Baylor University Press, 1958), 76.

5. *Ibid.*

6. John M. Murrin, "Religion and Politics in America from the First Settlements to the Civil War," in *Religion and American Politics: From the Colonial Period to the 1980s*, ed. Mark A. Noll (New York: Oxford University Press, 1990), 21.

7. M. L. Fergeson, *The Church-State Problem and the American Principle of Separation* (Waco, Tex.: Baylor University Press, 1966), 57.

8. Thomas J. Curry, *The First Freedoms: Church and State in America to the Passage of the First Amendment* (New York: Oxford University Press, 1986), 134–48.

9. Leonard Levy, *The Establishment Clause: Religion and the First Amendment* (New York: Macmillan, 1986), 15.

10. William G. McLoughlin, *New England Dissent, 1630–1833: The Baptists and the Separation of Church and State*, 2 vols. (Cambridge: Harvard University Press, 1971), 1:165–99.

11. Levy, *The Establishment Clause*, 2, 16–17.

12. L. H. Butterfield, ed., *Diary and Autobiography of John Adams*, 4 vols. (Cambridge: Belknap Press of Harvard University Press, 1961), 2:152. Also, for a general

discussion of church-state separation in the colonies in the eighteenth century, see Ernest Sutherland Bates, *American Faith: Its Religious, Political and Economic Foundations* (New York: W. W. North, 1940), 217.

13. Murrin, "Religion and Politics," 22.

14. See generally, Randall Balmer, *A Perfect Babel of Confusion: Dutch Religion and English Culture in the Middle Colonies* (New York: Oxford University Press, 1989).

15. Murrin, "Religion and Politics," 22.

16. *Ibid.*

17. Anson Phelps Stokes, *Church and State in the United States: Historical Development and Contemporary Problems of Religious Freedom under the Constitution*, 3 vols. (New York: Harper & Brothers, 1950), 1:436.

18. Wood, Thompson, and Miller, *Church and State*, 85.

19. Murrin, "Religion and Politics," 22.

20. Frederick Lewis Weis, *The Colonial Clergy of Virginia, North Carolina, and South Carolina* (Boston: Society of the Descendants of the Colonial Clergy, 1955), 58–70.

21. Newton B. Jones, ed., "Writings of the Reverend William Tennent, 1740–1777," *South Carolina Historical Magazine* LXI (July-October 1960), 197; quoted in Levy, *The Establishment Clause*, 5.

22. *Ibid.*

23. *Ibid.*, 198–99; quoted in Levy, *The Establishment Clause*, 5–6.

24. Jones, "Writings of the Reverend William Tennent," 203.

25. Francis Newton Thorpe, ed., *The Federal and State Constitutions, Colonial Charters, and Other Organic Laws*, 7 vols. (Washington, D.C.: 1909), 6:3252.

26. Connecticut and Rhode Island waited until 1818 and 1843, respectively, to adopt new state constitutions.

27. Levy, *The Establishment Clause*, 48.

28. Curry, *The First Freedoms*, 136–48.

29. *Ibid.*, 137–38.

30. Lance Banning, "James Madison, the Statute for Religious Freedom, and the Crisis of Republican Convictions," in *The Virginia Statute for Religious Freedom*, ed. Merrill D. Peterson and Robert D. Vaughan (Cambridge: Cambridge University Press, 1988), 113.

31. The other six states were Delaware, Pennsylvania, Rhode Island, New Jersey, New York, and North Carolina.

32. The disestablishments among the remaining six states occurred in the following order: South Carolina (1790), Georgia (1798), Maryland (1810), Connecticut (1818), New Hampshire (1819), and Massachusetts (1833).

33. John F. Wilson, "Religion under the State Constitutions, 1776–1800," *Journal of Church and State* 32 (Autumn 1990): 764. As Wilson explains, Rhode Island's requirement that officeholders be Protestants was not enacted until 1719. This is somewhat of a surprise, he notes, "Because at the time of Roger Williams, in 1665, a law provided that no religious tests for office or voting were allowed, which made it the most tolerant state in the colonies, and possibly in the Western World." But freedom atrophied in Rhode Island after Williams's death in 1683, and the colony often tended thereafter, at least until the revolutionary era, to persecute non-Protestants even more so than its other New England counterparts, Massachusetts, Connecticut, and New Hampshire.

34. *Ibid.*

35. Daniel L. Dreisbach, "The Constitution's Forgotten Religion Clause: Reflections on the Article VI Religious Test Ban," *Journal of Church and State* 38 (Spring 1996): 267.

36. *Ibid.*, 268, 282.

37. *Ibid.*, 286.

38. *Ibid.*, 272–73.

39. See Stokes, *Church and State in the United States*, 1:358–446, and Carl Zollman, "Religious Liberty in the American Law," *Michigan Law Review* 17 (1991): 355.

40. *Torcaso v. Watkins*, 367 U.S. 488 (1961).

41. Oliver Ellsworth, "A Landholder, No. 7," *Connecticut Covenant*, 17 December 1787; quoted in Dreisbach, "The Constitution's Forgotten Religious Clause," 275.

42. *Ibid.*, 275–76.

43. New England Presbyterians to George Washington, in Stokes, *Church and State in the United States*, 1:536.

44. Quoted in Jonathan Elliot, ed., *The Debates in the Several State Conventions, on the Adoption of the Federal Constitution*, 2d ed., 5 vols. (Philadelphia: J. B. Lippincott, 1859), 2:148.

45. Ellsworth, "A Landholder," quoted in Dreisbach, "The Constitution's Forgotten Religion Clause," 276.

46. Samuel Spencer, in Elliot's *Debates*, 4:200.

47. Ellsworth, "A Landholder," quoted in Dreisbach, "The Constitution's Forgotten Religion Clause," 281.

48. Daniel Shute, in Elliot's *Debates*, 2:119.

49. James Iredell, in Elliot's *Debates*, 4:196.

50. See Dreisbach, "The Constitution's Forgotten Religion Clause," 281–84.

51. Steven A. Smith, "Prelude to Article VI: The Ordeal of Religious Test Oaths in Pennsylvania," in *1992 Free Speech Yearbook*, ed. Dale A. Herbeck (Carbondale: Southern Illinois University Press, 1992), 18.

52. See, for example, James E. Wood, Jr., " 'No Religious Test Shall Ever Be Required': Reflections on the Bicentennial of the U.S. Constitution," *Journal of Church and State* 29 (Spring 1987): 206 (ban on religious tests was a "profound acknowledgment of the secular character of the New Republic"); and Isaac Kramnick and Laurence R. Moore, *The Godless Constitution: The Case against Religious Correctness* (New York: Norton, 1996), 168 ("the 'godless politics' dictated by the 'no religious test' clause means that a person's religious faith, or lack thereof, should never be an issue in partisan politics").

53. Smith, *Foreordained Failure*.

54. John Adams to Benjamin Kent, 22 June 1776, *Letters of Delegates to Congress, 1774–1789*, 18 vols., ed. Paul H. Smith (Washington: Library of Congress, 1979–) 4: 290.

*Chapter Three*

1. Charles W. Akers, *Called Unto Liberty: A Life of Jonathan Mayhew, 1720–1766* (Cambridge: Harvard University Press, 1964), 198.

2. Mark A. Noll, *Christians and the American Revolution* (Washington, D.C.: Christian University Press, 1977), 25.

3. Sidney E. Mead, *The Lively Experiment: The Shaping of Religion in America* (New York: Harper & Row, 1963), 38.

4. Nathan O. Hatch, *The Sacred Cause of Liberty: Republican Thought and the Millennium in Revolutionary New England* (New Haven: Yale University Press, 1977), 6.

5. Mead, "American Protestantism During the Revolutionary Epoch," *Church History* 22 (December 1953): 279.

6. Frank L. Mott and Chester E. Jorgenson, *Benjamin Franklin* (New York: American Book, 1936), 70; quoted *ibid.*, 280.

7. John Wesley, *Sermons on Several Occasions*, 4 vols. (Nashville: E. Stephenson and F. A. Owen, 1855), 1:392; quoted *ibid.*

8. Mott and Jorgenson, *Benjamin Franklin*, 280–81.

9. Noll, *Christians in the American Revolution*, 26.

10. Moses Coit Tyler, *Patrick Henry* (Ithaca, N.Y.: Cornell University Press, 1962), 144–45; quoted *ibid.*

11. Samuel Langdon, "Government Corrupted by Vice, and Recovered by Righteousness" (sermon preached to the Congress of the Massachusetts Bay Colony, 31 May 1775), in *Religion and the Coming of the American Revolution*, ed. Peter N. Carroll (Waltham, Mass.: Ginn-Blaisdell, 1970), 141.

12. Charles Frances Adams, ed., *Familiar Letters of John Adams and His Wife, Abigail*, 2 vols. (Boston: Chipman Publishing, 1875), 1:65.

13. Carroll, *Religion and the Coming of the American Revolution*, xv.

14. Gordon S. Wood, *The Creation of the American Republic, 1776–1787* (Chapel Hill: University of North Carolina Press, 1969), especially chap. 3. For a similar emphasis, see J. G. A. Pocock, *The Machiavellian Moment: Florentine Political Thought and the Atlantic Republican Tradition* (Princeton: Princeton University Press, 1974).

15. For example, Hatch, *The Sacred Cause of Liberty*; Ruth H. Bloch, Visionary Republic: Millennial Themes in American Thought, 1756–1800 (New York: Cambridge University Press, 1985); Alan Heimert, *Religion and the American Mind from the Great Awakening to the Revolution* (Cambridge: Harvard University Press, 1966); and Patricia U. Bonomi, *Under the Cope of Heaven: Religion, Society, and Politics in Colonial America* (New York: Oxford University Press, 1986).

16. Heimert, *Religion and the American Mind*, especially chap. 9.

17. *Ibid.*

18. Jonathan Edwards, "Some Thoughts Concerning the Revival of Religion in New England," in *The Works of Jonathan Edwards*, ed. C. C. Goen (New Haven: Yale University Press, 1972), 4:343–70.

19. For an excellent discussion of this theme, see Jerald C. Brauer, "Puritanism, Revivalism, and the Revolution," in *Religion and the American Revolution*, ed. Brauer (Philadelphia: Fortress Press, 1976).

20. William G. McLoughlin, "The Role of Religion in the Revolution," in *Essays on the American Revolution*, ed. Stephen G. Kurtz and James H. Hutson (Chapel Hill: University of North Carolina Press, 1973), 198.

21. *Ibid.*, 198–99.

22. *Ibid.*, 199.

23. Edmund S. Morgan, "The Puritan Ethic and the American Revolution," *William and Mary Quarterly* 24 (January 1967): 3.

24. Bernard Bailyn, *The Ideological Origins of the American Revolution* (Cambridge: Harvard University Press, 1967), 32.

25. Noll, *Christians in the American Revolution*, 30.

26. Lester Douglas Joyce, *Church Clergy in the American Revolution* (New York: Exposition Press, 1966), 38–39.

27. For representative Puritan writings supporting the revolutionary cause, see Benjamin Trumbull, *A Discourse Delivered at the Town of New Haven* (New Haven, 1773), and Dan Foster, *A Short Essay on Civil Government, the Substance of Six Sermons* (Hartford, 1775).

28. Noll, *Christians in the American Revolution*, 30.

29. *Ibid.*, 30–31.

30. Brauer, "Puritanism," 7–8.

31. *Ibid.*, 8.

32. *Ibid.*

33. Kenneth D. Wald, "Religion and Politics: Points of Contact," in his *Religion and Politics in the United States* (New York: St. Martin's Press, 1987), 39.

34. *Ibid.*

35. Perry Miller, *Nature's Nation* (Cambridge: Harvard University Press, 1967), 97–98.

36. Wald, *Religion and Politics*, 40.

37. William G. McLoughlin, *Revivals, Awakening, and Reform: Religion and Social Change in America, 1607–1977* (Chicago: University of Chicago Press, 1978); see especially his discussion on the First Great Awakening in chap. 3.

38. Harry Stout, *The New England Soul* (Oxford: Oxford University Press, 1986), especially 296, 302.

39. Charles Chauncy, "A Discourse on the Good News from a Far Country" (1766), in *The Pulpit of the American Revolution*, ed. John Thornton (New York: DaCapo Press, 1970), 129, 137.

40. Leonard J. Kramer, "Muskets in the Pulpit, 1776–1783: Part I," *Journal of the Presbyterian Historical Society* 31 (December 1953): 48.

41. Cyprian Strong, *God's Care of the New England Colonies . . . A Sermon Preached in the First Society of Chatham* (Hartford, Conn., 1777), 5.

42. *The Parishioner, Having Studied the Point* (Hartford, Conn.: Green and Watson, 1769), 22; quoted in Noll, *Christians in the American Revolution*, 71.

43. Ebenezer Baldwin, *The Duty of Rejoicing under Calamities and Afflictions* (New York: Hugh Gaine, 1776), 38; quoted in Noll, *Christians in the American Revolution*, 58.

44. See, for example, *Blazing Stars: Messengers of God's Wrath* (Boston, 1759); A. F., *A Poem on the Rebuke of God's Hand in the Awful Desolation Made by Fire* (Boston, 1760); and *An Account of a Surprising Phenomenon* (Philadelphia, 1765). This theme is discussed in Bloch, *Visionary Republic*, 33–37.

45. Ruth H. Bloch, "Religion and Ideological Change in the American Revolution," in Mark A. Noll, ed., *Religion and American Politics: From the Colonial Period to the 1980s* (New York: Oxford University Press, 1990), 49–50.

46. Catherine L. Albanese, *Sons of the Fathers: The Civil Religion of the American Revolution* (Philadelphia: Temple University Press, 1976), 14.

47. Edmund S. Morgan, *The Challenge of the American Revolution* (New York: W. W. Norton, 1976), 66.

48. Sydney Ahlstrom, *A Religious History of the American People*, 2 vols. (Garden City, N.Y.: Image Books, 1975), 1:444.

49. Henry F. May, *The Enlightenment in America* (New York: Oxford University Press, 1976), 164.

50. Ceasar Rodney to Thomas Jefferson, September 1790, *Papers of Thomas Jefferson*, 21 vols., ed. Julian P. Boyd (Princeton: Princeton University Press, 1950–1983), 17:547.

51. May, *The Enlightenment in America*, 164.

52. Levi Hart, *Christian Minister Described* (New Haven, Conn., 1772), 10.

53. Samuel Finley, *An Essay on the Gospel Ministry* (Wilmington, Del., n.p., 1763), 34.

54. *Ibid.*, 46.

55. *Ibid.*, 66–67.

56. Bloch, *Visionary Republic*, 188.

57. *Boston Gazette*, 23 January 1775; 1 January 1774.

58. *New York Journal*, 1 September 1774.

59. Thomas Paine, "Common Sense," in Thoms Paine, *Common Sense and the Crisis* (New York: Anchor Books, 1973), 59.

60. "Suffolk Resolves" (September 1774) and "Address to the People of Ireland" (July 1775) in *Journals of the Continental Congress, 1774–1789*, 34 vols., ed. Worthington C. Ford et al. (Washington, D.C., 1904–1937), 1:15, 172 (hereafter cited as *Journals of Congress*).

61. Bonomi, *Under the Cope of Heaven*, 188.


*Chapter Four*

1. Lord Chatham (speech to House of Lords), 20 January 1775; quoted in William J. Bacon, *The Continental Congress: Some of Its Actors and Their Doings, with the Results Thereof* (Utica, N.Y.: Ellis H. Roberts, 1881), 3–4.

2. *Ibid.*

3. Quoted in Ellis Sandoz, "Power and Spirit in the Founding," *This World* 9 (Fall 1984): 67.

4. *Ibid.*

5. Thomas Jefferson, "A Summary View of the Rights of British America," 1 August 1774, in *American Archives*, 6 vols., ed. Peter Force (Washington D.C.: n.p., 1837–1846), 1:690.

6. Jacob Duché, "The Duty of Standing Fast in Our Spiritual and Temporal Liberties," 7 July 1775, in *Patriot Preachers of the American Revolution*, ed. Frank Moore (New York: Charles T. Evans, 1862), 80.

7. *Journals of Congress*, 1:43.

8. James Otis, *The Rights of the British Colonies Asserted and Proved* (Boston, 1764), in *Pamphlets of the American Revolution, 1750–1776*, ed. Bernard Bailyn (Cambridge: Harvard University Press, 1965), 1:423.

9. William Smith, D. D., "The Crisis of American Affairs" (sermon), 23 June 1775, in Moore, *Patriot Preachers*, 105.

10. Oliver Wolcott to Laura Wolcott, 14 April 1778, *Letters of Delegates to Congress, 1774–1789*, 18 vols., ed. Paul H. Smith (Washington D.C.: Library of Congress, 1979–), 9:413.

11. Oliver Wolcott to Laura Wolcott, 2 May 1778, *ibid.*, 9:568.

12. Samuel Chase to Thomas Johnson, 3 May 1778, *ibid.*, 9:572.

13. Samuel Chase to Philip Schuyler, 9 August 1776, *ibid.*, 4:644.

14. John Adams to James Warren, 18 May 1776, *ibid.*, 4:31.

15. Samuel Adams, "Oration on the Steps of the Continental State House," Philadelphia, 1 August 1776; quoted in Benjamin F. Morris, *Christian Life and Character of the Civil Institutions of the United States* (Philadelphia: George W. Childs, 1864), 115.

16. Elbridge Gerry to Samuel Adams, 13 December 1775, quoted *ibid.*, 119.

17. John Witherspoon, "The Dominion of Providence over the Passions of Men," May 1776, in *The Works of the Rev. John Witherspoon*, 4 vols. (Philadelphia: William W. Woodward, 1802), 3:33.

18. William Williams to Oliver Wolcott, 12 August 1776, *ibid.*, 4:666.

19. *Journals of Congress*, 13 September 1779, 5:261. The *Pennsylvania Gazette*, funded partially by the Continental Congress, was its official organ, and in it were published the communications of the Congress to the people.

20. Mark A. Noll, *One Nation under God? Christian Faith and Political Action in America* (New York: Harper & Row, 1988), 36.

21. *Ibid.*, 38. For an analysis of founding-era sermons tying Christian virtue to the success, if not the survival, of the nation, see Nathan O. Hatch, *The Sacred Cause of Liberty: Republican Thought and the Millennium in Revolutionary New England* (New Haven: Yale University Press, 1977), especially chap. 3. This emphasis on the need for virtue among the citizenry, and especially among civic rulers, was indeed one of the most apparent connections between religion and politics in late eighteenth-century literature; religion, of course, was identified as the essential source of virtue. In *Federalist* No. 10, James Madison strongly emphasized the need for virtue in the people if a democracy were to succeed, but he assigned to institutions other than government the responsibility for inculcating virtue. For more on the virtue theme, see chap. 10 herein.

22. Noll, *One Nation under God*, 37.

23. *Ibid.*, 37–38.

24. *Ibid.*, 38–39.

25. Gordon S. Wood, *The Creation of the American Republic: 1776–1787* (Chapel Hill: University of North Carolina Press, 1969), 93.

26. Thomas Paine, "Common Sense," in Thomas Paine, *Common Sense and the Crisis* (New York: Anchor Books, 1973), 21.

27. Thomas Jefferson to Benjamin Franklin, 3 August 1777, *Papers of Thomas Jefferson*, 21 vols., ed. Julian P. Boyd (Princeton: Princeton University Press, 1950–1983), 2:26.

28. John Adams, *"Thoughts on Government,"* in *The Works of John Adams, Second President of the United States*, 10 vols., ed. Charles F. Adams (Boston: Little, Brown, 1850–1856), 4:194.

29. John Adams to J. H. Tiffany, 30 April 1819, in Adams, *The Works of John Adams*, 10:378.

30. Benjamin Rush to Granville Sharp, 7 April 1783, "The Correspondence of Benjamin Rush and Granville Sharp, 1773–1809," ed. John A. Woods, *Journal of American Studies* 1 (April 1967): 17.

31. Benjamin Rush, "On the Defects of the Confederation" (1787), in *The Selected Writings of Benjamin Rush*, ed. Dagobert D. Runes (New York: Philosophical Library, 1947), 31.

32. Edward Frank Humphrey, *Nationalism and Religion in America, 1774–1789* (Boston: Chipman Law Publishing, 1924), 407.

33. *Journals of Congress*, 2:140–57.

34. Catherine Albanese, *Sons of the Fathers: The Civil Religion of the American Revolution* (Philadelphia: Temple University Press, 1976), 193.

35. Humphrey, *Nationalism and Religion*, 408.

36. *Journals of Congress*, 12 June 1778, 11:592–93 (death of Philip Livingston of New York).

37. *Journals of Congress*, 11:364.

38. *Journals of Congress*, 20 October 1774, 1:3. See chap. 10 for the argument that the constitutional framers eventually concluded that the cultivation of virtue must rest with the people, not government.

39. *Gaines' New York Gazette*, 9 January 1775, in *The Diary of the American Revolution: From Newspapers and Original Documents*, 2 vols., ed. Frank Moore (New York: Charles Scribner, 1860), 1:11.

40. John Adams to Abigail Adams, 23 July 1775, *Familiar Letters of John Adams and His Wife, Abigail*, 2 vols., ed. Charles Frances Adams (Boston: Chipman Publishing, 1875), 1:84.

41. Moore, *Diary of the American Revolution*, 1:87–88.

42. William Duane, ed., *Extracts from the Diary of Christopher Marshall, Kept in Philadelphia and Lancaster, during the American Revolution, 1774–1781* (Albany, N.Y.: Joel Munsell, 1877), 71.

43. *Ibid.*, 216.

44. *Journals of Congress*, 2:81, 87, 192. The members of Congress attended mass on four occasions—two were Te Deums and two were Requiems. On each of these occasions the mass took place at St. Mary's Church, Philadelphia. The Te Deums were the independence commemoration on 4 July 1779 and the celebration for victory at Yorktown, 4 November 1781. The Requiems were 18 September 1777, for General Du Coudray, a French officer, and 8 May 1780, for Don Juan de Miralles, a Spanish agent. See "The Continental Congress at Mass," *American Catholic Historical Researches* 6 (1889): 50–76.

45. Albanese, *Sons of the Fathers*, 199.

46. John Jay to Louis XVI, 17 September 1779, *The Diplomatic Correspondence of the American Revolution*, 12 vols., ed. Jared Sparks (Boston: N. Hale and Gray & Bowen, 1829–1830), 5:641.

47. John Hanson to Louis XVI, 20 May 1782, *ibid.*, 6:65.

48. John Adams to John Hanson, 17 April 1780, *ibid.*, 6:5.

49. John Adams to Abigail Adams, 17 September 1775, in Smith, *Letters of Delegates*, 2:23–24.

50. The states were Maryland, Virginia, North Carolina, South Carolina, Georgia, New York, and Delaware. Leo Pfeffer, *Church, State and Freedom*, 2d ed. (Boston: Beacon Press, 1967), 118.

51. *McDaniel v. Paty*, 435 U.S. 618, 622 (1978). The *McDaniel* case, which originated in Tennessee, struck down the last of the state statutes prohibiting ministers from seeking state office.

52. Anson Phelps Stokes, *Church and State in the United States: Historical Development and Contemporary Problems of Religious Freedom under the Constitution*, 3 vols. (New York: Harper & Brothers, 1950), 1: 622. For a contrary argument that disqualification of ministers was a practice inherited from the Church of England, i.e., a product of establishment rather than separation, see William M. Hogue, "The Civil Disability of Ministers of Religion in State Constitutions," *Journal of Church and State* 36 (Spring 1994):329.

53. Thomas Jefferson to Jeremiah Moore, 13 March 1800, in Boyd, *Papers of Thomas Jefferson*, 6:297.

54. Benjamin Rush to Patrick Henry, 16 July 1776, in Smith, *Letters of Delegates*, 4: 473–75. Rush's letter complained of Virginia's practice of disqualifying clergymen from public office, a practice supported by Patrick Henry.

55. Gaillard Hunt, ed., *The Writings of James Madison*, 9 vols. (New York: G. P. Putnam's Sons, 1900–1910), 5:288.

56. *Journals of Congress*, 1: 15–16.

57. Jack N. Rakove, *The Beginnings of National Politics: An Interpretive History of the Continental Congress* (New York: Knopf, 1979), 44–49.

58. Quoted in Henry Steele Commager and Richard B. Morris, eds., *The Spirit of "Seventy-Six"* (Indianapolis: Bobbs–Merrill, 1958), 46.

59. *Journals of Congress*, 1: 33–36.

60. Charles Turner, Massachusetts Election Sermon (1773), in *They Preached Liberty*, ed. Franklin P. Cole (Indianapolis: Liberty Press, 1976), 161.

61. Adams's letter is reprinted *Journals of Congress*, 1:26.

62. Political Discourse No. 9, "For the Fast Day Appointed by Congress, April 1778," *United States Magazine*, May 1779.

63. Thomas Paine, "Common Sense," in *Complete Writings of Thomas Paine*, 2 vols., ed. Philip S. Foner (New York: Harper & Row, 1945), 1:3.

*Chapter Five*

1. Abraham Clark to James Caldwell, 2 August 1776, *Letters of Delegates to Congress, 1774–1789*, 18 vols., ed. Paul H. Smith (Washington, D.C.: Library of Congress, 1979–), 4:605.

2. *Journals of Congress*, 1:26.

3. Charles Frances Adams, ed., *Familiar Letters of John Adams and His Wife, Abigail*, 2 vols. (Boston: Chipman Publishing, 1875), 1:23. Many may consider Samuel Adams's ecumenical spirit admirable, but at least one author has characterized him more generally as puritanical, even caustic toward Catholics and freethinkers. See Norman Cousins, ed., *In God We Trust: The Religious Beliefs and Ideas of the American Founding Fathers* (New York: Harper & Brothers, 1958). Cousins's book also contains chapters describing the religious beliefs of John Adams and John Jay.

4. John M. Swomley, *Religious Liberty and the Secular State* (Buffalo, N.Y.: Prometheus Books, 1985), 54.

5. Silas Deane to Elizabeth Deane, 7 September 1774, in Smith, *Letters of Delegates*, 1:34.

6. Dr. Samuel Cooper (1725–1783) was pastor of Brattle Street Congregational Church in Boston, John Adams's home church.

7. Adams, *Familiar Letters of John Adams*, 1:23–24.

8. *Journals of Congress*, 1:27.

9. *Ibid.*

10. *Ibid.*

11. Quoted in Edward Frank Humphrey, *Nationalism and Religion in America, 1774–1789* (Boston: Chipman Law Publishing, 1924), 412.

12. Quoted *ibid.*, 413.

13. John Witherspoon, "Caspipina's Catechism," in Varnum Lansing Collins, *President Witherspoon: A Biography* (Princeton: Princeton University Press, 1925), 235–37.

14. Humphrey, *Nationalism and Religion*, 414. Regarding the correspondence between Duché and General Washington, see Worthington C. Ford, ed., *The Washington-Duché Letters* (Brooklyn, N.Y.: Cole Printing, 1890).

15. George Reeser Prowell, *Continental Congress at York, Pennsylvania and York County in the Revolution* (York, Penn.: York Printing, 1914), 293.

16. Anson Phelps Stokes, *Church and State in the United States: Historical Development and Contemporary Problems of Religious Freedom under the Constitution*, 3 vols.

(New York: Harper & Brothers, 1950), 451. See chap. 8 on the topic of Congress's involvement in the publication of an American Bible.

17. *Journals of Congress*, 24:331.

18. *Ibid.*, 454.

19. *Ibid.*, 811.

20. Joseph Gales, ed., *Annals of the Congress of the United States: The Debates and Proceedings of the Congress of the United States*, 42 vols. (Washington, D.C.: Gales and Seaton, 1834), 1:19.

21. *Ibid.*, 1:24.

22. *Ibid.*, 1:242.

23. James Madison to Edward Livingston, 10 July 1822, *The Writings of James Madison*, 9 vols., ed. Gaillard Hunt (New York: G. P. Putnam's Sons, 1900–1910), 9: 100.

24. *Marsh v. Chambers*, 463 U.S. 783 (1983).

25. *Ibid.*, 788.

26. *Ibid.*, 803–4.

27. Elizabeth Fleet, ed., "Madison's Detached Memoranda," *William and Mary Quarterly* 3 (October 1946): 554.

28. *Ibid.*, 558.

29. *Ibid.*, 559.

30. Rufus W. Griswold, *The Republican Court; or, American Society in the Days of Washington*, rev. ed. (New York: Appleton, 1856), 433–34.

31. Fleet, "Madison's Detached Memoranda," 559.

32. *Engel v. Vitale*, 370 U.S. 421 (1962); *Wallace v. Jaffree*, 472 U.S. 38 (1985); *Marsh v. Chambers*; and *Lee v. Weisman*, 505 U.S. 577 (1992).

33. *Lee v. Weisman*, 592.

34. Robert L. Cord, *Separation of Church and State: Historical Fact and Current Fiction* (New York: Lambeth Press, 1982), 23.

35. *Reports of Committees of the House of Representatives* (Washington, D.C.: A. O. P. Nicholson, 1854), 2:4.

36. *Journals of Congress*, 2:220.

37. Jared Sparks, ed., *The Writings of George Washington*, 12 vols. (Boston: American Stationers' Company, 1834–1837), 12:401.

38. George Washington to Governor Dinwiddie, 12 June 1757, *The Writings of George Washington*, 39 vols., ed. John C. Fitzpatrick (Washington, D.C.: U.S. Government Printing Office, 1931–1944), 2:56; quoted by George Hunston Williams, "The Chaplaincy in the Armed Forces of the United States of America in Historical and Ecclesiastical Perspective," in *Military Chaplains: From a Religion Military to a Military Religion*, ed. Harvey G. Cox, Jr. (New York: American Report Press, 1972), 18.

39. Fitzpatrick, *Writings of George Washington*, 5:367.

40. George Washington to the President of Congress, 8 June 1777, *ibid.*, 8:203.

41. General Orders from Valley Forge, 2 May 1778, *ibid.*, 8:203.

42. Richard Peters, ed., *The Public Statutes at Large of the United States of America* (Boston: Charles C. Little and James Brown, 1845), 1:222.

43. *Ibid.*, 223.

44. Fleet, "Madison's Detached Memoranda," 560–61.

45. *Abington School District v. Schempp*, 374 U.S. 203, 222 (1963).

46. *Ibid.*, 296.

47. *Ibid.*, 299.

48. Lorenzo D. Johnson, *Chaplains of the General Government* (New York: Buford Press, 1856), 24.

49. Samuel A. Bates, ed., *Records of the Town of Braintree, 1640–1793* (Randolph, Mass.: Matson Press, 1886), 421.

50. P. L. Ford, ed., *The Writings of Thomas Jefferson*, 10 vols. (New York: G. P. Putnam's Sons, 1892–1899), 1:9.

51. *Ibid.*, 11.

52. Philip Davidson, *Propaganda and the American Revolution, 1763–1783* (Chapel Hill: University of North Carolina Press, 1941), 96.

53. *Henry Laurens Papers*; quoted in Davidson, *Propaganda and the American Revolution*, 355.

54. Kate M. Rowland, *Life and Correspondence of George Mason, 1725–1792*, 2 vols. (New York: G. P. Putnam's Sons, 1892), 1:320.

55. *Journals of Congress*, 2:87–88.

56. John Adams to Abigail Adams, 12 June 1775, in John Adams, *Familiar Letters of John Adams and His Wife Abigail Adams during the Revolution* (Freeport, N.Y.: Books for Libraries Press, 1970), 66.

57. William De Loss Love, *The Fast and Thanksgiving Days of New England* (Boston: Houghton, Mifflin, 1895), 343–44.

58. John Adams to James Warren, 23 July 1775, in Smith, *Letters to Delegates*, 1:650.

59. *Journals of Congress*, 9:854–55.

60. *Ibid.*

61. Quoted in Stokes, *Church and State*, 453.

62. *Ibid.*, 453.

63. Quoted *ibid.*

64. *Constitutional Gazette*, December 1775, *The Diary of the American Revolution: From Newspapers and Original Documents*, 2 vols., ed. Frank Moore (New York: Charles Scribner, 1860), 1:185.

65. Jonathan Trumbull to George Washington, 13 July 1775, *Correspondence of the American Revolution*, ed. Jared Sparks (Freeport, N.Y.: Books for Library Press, 1970), 2:2.

66. Elbridge Gerry to Samuel Adams, 13 December 1775; quoted in Catherine Albanese, *Sons of the Fathers: The Civil Religion of the American Revolution* (Philadelphia: Temple University Press, 1925), 83.

67. Samuel Adams, oration on the steps of the Continental State House, 1 August 1776; quoted *ibid.*

68. Benjamin Rush to Granville Sharp, 20 September 1774, "The Correspondence of Benjamin Rush and Granville Sharp 1773–1809," ed. John A. Woods, *Journal of American Studies* 1 (April 1967): 12.

69. *Journals of Congress*, 8 May 1778, 10:214.

70. *Ibid.*, 26 May 1779, 12:543.

71. Thomas McKean to Caesar Rodney, 28 April 1778, *Letters to and from Caesar Rodney, 1756–1784*, ed. George Herbert Ryden (New York: DeCapo Press, 1970), 264.

72. *Journals of Congress*, 23:647.

73. *Ibid.*, 25:989–90. The proclamation was approved on 18 October 1783; see *ibid.*, 25:699–701.

74. Albanese, *Sons of the Fathers*, 199.

75. Leo Pfeffer, *Church, State and Freedom*, 2d ed. (Boston: Beacon Press, 1967), 223.

76. *Annals of Congress*, 25 September 1789, 1:949.

77. *Ibid.*

78. *Ibid.*, 1:950.

79. *Ibid.*

80. *Ibid.*

81. Quoted in Pfeffer, *Church, State and Freedom*, 224.

82. Hunt, *The Writings of James Madison*, 9:100.

83. William T. Hutchinson et al., eds., *The Papers of James Madison*, 8 vols. (Chicago: Caperton Press, 1962), 3:560.

84. *Ibid.*

85. *Ibid.*

86. Quoted *ibid.*

87. Stephen Botein, "Religious Dimensions of the Early American State," in *Beyond Confederation: Origins of the American Constitution and American National Identity*, ed. Richard Beeman, Stephen Botein, and Edward C. Carter II, (Chapel Hill: University of North Carolina Press, 1987), 320.

*Chapter Six*

1. *Journals of Congress*, 5: 424–26.

2. Quoted in Mark A. Noll, Nathan O. Hatch, and George M. Marsden, *The Search for Christian America* (Westchester, Ill.: Crossway Books, 1983), 73.

3. Thomas Jefferson to James Smith, 8 December 1822; quoted in Gary North, *Political Polytheism: The Myth of Pluralism* (Tyler, Tex.: Institute for Christian Economics, 1989), 406–7.

4. Thomas Jefferson to Benjamin Waterhouse, 26 June 1822, in *The Writings of Thomas Jefferson*, 10 vols., ed. Paul Leicester Ford (New York: G. P. Putnam's Sons, 1892–1899), 10:219.

5. Thomas Jefferson to Peter Carr, 10 August 1787, *ibid.*, 4:427.

6. David Hawke, *A Transaction of Free Men: The Birth and Course of the Declaration of Independence* (New York: Scribner's, 1964), 81–82.

7. Cushing Strout, *The New Heavens and the New Earth: Political Religion in America* (New York: Harper & Row, 1974), 81.

8. Franklin B. Dexter, ed., *The Literary Diary of Ezra Stiles*, 3 vols. (New York: G. P. Putnam's Sons, 1901), 3:387.

9. Carl Van Doren, *Benjamin Franklin* (New York: Viking, 1938), 655.

10. Bernard Fay, *Revolution and Freemasonry, 1680–1800* (Boston: Little, Brown, 1935), viii.

11. Ronald E. Henton, *Masonic Membership of the Founding Fathers* (Silver Spring, Md.: Masonic Service Association, 1965), 100–1, says that there is no proof that Sherman was a Mason, but that he might have been. But see Philip Roth, *Masonry in the Formation of Our Government* (Milwaukee, Wisc.: privately printed, 1927), 53, for the claim that Sherman was in fact a Mason, although he offers no convincing proof.

12. David Hawke, *Honorable Treason: The Declaration of Independence and the Men Who Signed It* (New York: Viking, 1976), 57–59, 61.

13. Frank Donovan, *Mr. Jefferson's Declaration: The Story behind the Declaration of Independence* (New York: Dodd, Mead, 1968), 55.

14. Hawke, *Honorable Treason*, 125.

15. Quoted *ibid.*, 98.

16. Roth, *Masonry in the Formation of Our Government*, 114. One source has described the Masonic God in the following way: "The Nature of the Masonic God is best seen in their favorite title for him: the Supreme Architect. The Masonic God is first of all a deistic God who is found at the top of the ladder of Masonic wisdom. From God emanates a rational order for the universe, which includes a moral order for the affairs of humanity. Nature is order ruled by immutable and absolute laws laid down at the beginning of the universe as it is so ordained by the Supreme Architect. Civilizations, so long as they are in complete accord with nature and its laws, can survive." Pamela M. Jolicoeur and Louis L. Knowles, "Fraternal Associations and Civil Religion: Scottish Rite Freemasonry," *Review of Religious Research* 20 (Fall 1978): 14–15.

17. Thomas Jefferson to James Madison, 30 August 1823, reprinted from the Jefferson Papers of the Library of Congress in *A Casebook on the Declaration of Independence*, ed. Robert Ginsberg (New York: Thomas Y. Crowell, 1967), 31. John Adams's account, written probably in 1805, was slightly different. He claimed that he and Jefferson were appointed as a two-man subcommittee and that Adams himself insisted that Jefferson prepare the draft. See L. H. Butterfield, ed., *Diary and Autobiography of John Adams*, 4 vols. (Cambridge, Mass.: Belknap Press of Harvard University Press, 1961), 3:335–37.

18. *Journals of Congress*, 5: 427–31. Excellent, detailed accounts of the events that transpired between 11 June (appointment of the five-man committee) and 4 July are available. Among them are Edward Dumbald, *The Declaration of Independence and What It Means Today* (Norman: University of Oklahoma Press, 1950); Donovan, *Mr. Jefferson's Declaration*; and Garry Wills, *Inventing America: Jefferson's Declaration of Independence* (Garden City, N.Y.: Doubleday, 1978). An excellent five-page summary account is offered as an editorial note in Julian Boyd, ed., *The Papers of Thomas Jefferson*, 8 vols. (Princeton: Princeton University Press, 1950), 1:413–17.

19. Ford, *Writings of Thomas Jefferson*, 7:407.

20. *Journals of Congress*, 2:127–40.

21. Ibid., 2:140–57.

22. Charles Frances Adams, ed., *The Works of John Adams*, 10 vols. (Boston: Chipman Publishing, 1850–1856), 2:513–14n.

23. Ford, *Writings of Thomas Jefferson*, 10:266.

24. Carl Becker, *The Declaration of Independence: A Study in the History of Political Ideas* (1922; reprint, New York: Vintage Books, 1958), 26.

25. James Madison, during the proceedings of the First Congress in 1789, asserted this view by stating that the colonies in 1776 remained "as a political society, detached from their former connection with another society, without dissolving into a state of nature; but capable of substituting a new form of government in the place of the old one, which they had, for special considerations, abolished." Joseph Gales, ed., *Annals of the Congress of the United States: The Debates and Proceedings of the Congress of the United States*, 42 vols. (Washington, D.C.: Gales and Seaton, 1834), 1:421–22.

26. Becker, *The Declaration of Independence*, 30–36.

27. Brian Tierney, *Religion, Law, and the Growth of Constitutional Thought, 1150–1650* (Cambridge: Cambridge University Press, 1982), chap. 3. Marsilius's *Defender of Peace*, authored in 1324, set forth his pathbreaking position. An excellent translation is Alan Gewirth, trans., *The Defender of Peace* (Toronto: Toronto University Press, 1980).

28. Ginsberg, "The Declaration as Rhetoric," in *Casebook on the Declaration of Independence*, 219, takes the view that Franklin's recommended language was to make the phrase more understandable to the public than Jefferson's more "scientistic" phrase. Ginsberg proposes that the committee, to avoid another area of conflict in the public mind, opted to avoid use of the term "social contract" in favor of a phrase more familiar in Calvinistic rhetoric, "governments are instituted among men." Ginsberg adds: "These persuasive turns of phrase reflect more than the guile of the Declaration's authors; they reveal how much public considerations affected the Declaration as it finally appeared, decisively affected it as a document for the education of future generations."

29. The close reader will notice the shift from "inalienable" in Jefferson's draft to "unalienable" in the final copy. This may have been a typographical error, or it may have been a change that either Franklin or Adams suggested as a preferred spelling. For a more comprehensive discussion, see Donovan, *Mr. Jefferson's Declaration*, 47–48, 92.

30. *Ibid.*, 36–37.

31. Lloyd Weinrib, *Natural Law and Justice* (Cambridge: Harvard University Press, 1987), 20–30.

32. *Ibid.*, 32–35.

33. *Ibid.*, 35–39.

34. *Ibid.*, 45–49.

35. *Ibid.*, 37–39.

36. *Ibid.*, 39–40.

37. Morton White, *The Philosophy of the American Revolution* (New York: Oxford University Press, 1978).

38. *Ibid.*, chap. 2.

39. *Ibid.*, 39.

40. Actually the number of U.S. citizens with college degrees on the eve of the American Revolution was quite small. One estimate is that there were no more than 3,000 with degrees from American institutions; those with degrees from British institutions numbered no more than 2,000. That 5,000 citizens out of a population of 2.5 million had college degrees means that in 1776 roughly only one-fifth of 1 percent of the American population owned college degrees. The colleges did not issue annual catalogs, but the total enrollment in the nine American colleges in 1776 was about 750 students and had probably never exceeded that figure. See Harry Gehman Good and James D. Teller, *A History of American Education* (New York: Macmillan, 1973), 213–14.

41. Sir David Brewster, *Memoirs of the Life, Writings, and Discoveries of Sir Isaac Newton*, 2 vols. (Edinburgh: T. Constable, 1855), 1:340.

42. Samuel Quincy, *Twenty Sermons*; quoted in Becker, *The Declaration of Independence*, 77.

43. Quoted in Becker, *The Declaration of Independence*, 78.

44. *Ibid.*

45. John Wise, *A Vindication of the Government of New England Churches* (Boston: John Boyles [1719], 1772); excerpts reprinted in Page Smith, ed., *Religious Origins of the American Revolution* (Missoula, Mont.: Scholars Press, 1976), 144–53.

46. C. Gregg Singer, "Theological Aspects of the Revolution," *Christianity Today* 3 (22 June 1959): 6.

47. Samuel West, *A Sermon Preached before the Honorable Council of the State of Massachusetts, Being the Anniversary for the Election*, 29 May 1776, in John Wingate Thornton, *The Pulpit of the American Revolution* (1860; reprint, New York: DeCapo Press, 1970), 272.

48. Thomas Jefferson, *Notes on the State of Virginia* (New York: Harper & Row, 1964), 152.

49. Samuel Adams to Elbridge Gerry, *The Writings of Samuel Adams*, 4 vols., ed. H. A. Cushing (New York: J. P. Lippincott, 1904–1908), 2:349 (emphasis added).

50. Annapolis *Maryland Gazette*, 16 June 1787.

51. North, *Political Polytheism*, 406.

52. *Ibid.*, 407–8.

53. *Ibid.*, 403.

54. C. Gregg Singer, *A Theological Interpretation of American History* (Nutley, N.J.: Craig Press, 1964), 43–45.

55. Patricia U. Bonomi, *Under the Cope of Heaven: Religion, Society and Politics in Colonial America* (New York: Oxford University Press, 1986), 199.

56. Quoted *ibid.*, 200.

57. William G. McLoughlin, "The Role of Religion in the Revolution," in *Essays on the American Revolution*, ed. Stephen G. Kurtz and James H. Hutson (Chapel Hill: University of North Carolina Press, 1973), 204.

58. Anson Phelps Stokes, *Church and State in the United States: Historical Development and Contemporary Problems of Religious Freedom under the Constitution*, 3 vols. (New York: Harper & Brothers, 1950), 1:247.

59. Kate Mason Rowland, *The Life of Charles Carroll, of Carrollton, 1737–1832, with His Correspondence and Public Papers*, 2 vols. (New York: G. P. Putnam, 1900), 2: 357–58. For a discussion of Carroll's contributions as a member of the Continental Congress, see Thomas O'Brien Hanley, *Revolutionary Statesman: Charles Carroll and the War* (Chicago: Loyola University Press, 1983), 41–54.

60. Douglas Laycock, "The Declaration Is Not Law," *Christian Legal Society Quarterly* 12 (Fall 1991): 8.

61. Roger Sherman, 28 June 1787, *Journal of the Federal Convention*, repr., 2 vols., ed. E. H. Scott (Chicago: Scott, Foresman, 1898), 1:258.

62. Laycock, "The Declaration Is Not Law," 8.

63. *Ibid.*, 12.

64. Alfred H. Kelly and Winfred A. Harbison, *The American Constitution: Its Origins and Development*, 3d ed. (New York: W. W. Norton, 1963), 89.

*Chapter Seven*

1. Claude Van Tyne, "Sovereignty in the American Revolution: A Historical Study," *American Historical Review* 12 (1907): 529.

2. Richard Morris, " 'We the People of the United States': The Bicentennial of a People's Revolution," *American Historical Review* 82 (1977): 1; Edward S. Corwin, "The Passing of Dual Federalism," *Virginia Law Review* 36 (1950): 1; Max Beloff, *The American Federal Government* (New York: Oxford University Press, 1959), 15–16; and Raoul Berger, *Federalism: The Founders' Design* (Norman, Okla.: University of Oklahoma Press, 1987).

3. Berger, *Federalism*, 28.

4. Van Tyne, "Sovereignty in the American Revolution," 542.

5. Merrill Jensen, *The Articles of Confederation: An Interpretation of the Social-Constitutional History of the American Revolution* (Madison: University of Wisconsin Press, 1940), 56, n. 5.

6. Berger, *Federalism*, 23.

7. John B. McMaster and Frederick D. Stone, *Pennsylvania and the Federal Constitution, 1787–1788* (Lancaster, Penn.: Inquirer Printing, 1888), 291.

8. Quoted in Berger, *Federalism*, 23.

9. Max Farrand, ed., *The Records of the Federal Convention of 1787*, 3 vols. (New Haven: Yale University Press, 1911), 1:173.

10. *Ware v. Hylton*, 3 U.S. 199, 224 (1796).

11. *Journals of Congress*, 5:424.

12. Jensen, *Articles of Confederation*, 119, n. 5, notes that "most of the states, in the instructions permitting their delegates in Congress to vote for independence and for a confederation, reserved to themselves the complete control of their internal affairs and particularly of their 'internal police.' "

13. Quoted in Berger, *Federalism*, 40.

14. This is apparent even to Jefferson Powell, who, as a strong proponent of the Hamiltonian nationalist school that developed following ratification of the Constitution, admits that "with the exception of a few ultranational Federalists, all the participants in the dispute over the Constitution's ratification . . . had regarded the Articles as a compact among the States as independent sovereigns, and the Confederation Congress as the agent, not the superior of the states." Jefferson Powell, "The Original Understanding of Original Intent," *Harvard Law Review* 98 (1985): 885, 928–29.

15. William Staples Read, *Rhode Island in the Continental Congress, 1765–1790* (New York: De Capo Press, 1971), 690.

16. The nuncio's note is reprinted in Jules A. Baisnee, *France and the Establishment of the American Catholic Hierarchy: The Myth of French Interference, 1783–1784* (Baltimore: Johns Hopkins Press, 1934), 49–50.

17. Reprinted *ibid.*, 50–51.

18. Quoted *ibid.*, 51.

19. Quoted *ibid.*, 33.

20. Reprinted *ibid.*, 79.

21. *Secret Journals of the Acts and Proceedings of Congress*, 3:493.

22. Catholic leaders in America supported the idea of a papal representative in the United States because of the growing number of Catholics in its regions. In 1784 there were in New England about 600; in New York and New Jersey, 1,700; in Pennsylvania and Delaware, 7,700; in Maryland, about 20,000; in the southern states, about 2,500; and living within French establishments on the Mississippi, about 12,000. This data is recited in letter from Barbç-Marbois to the Comte de Vergennes; reprinted *ibid.*, 91–92.

23. Harvey Skilton, "John Carroll," in *The New International Dictionary of the Christian Church*, rev. ed., ed. J. D. Douglas (Grand Rapids, Mich.: Zondervan, 1978), 195–96.

24. Quoted in W. R. Estep, *Religious Liberty: Heritage and Responsibility* (North Newton, Kans.: Bethel College, 1988), 68.

25. William G. McLoughlin, *New England Dissent, 1630–1833: The Baptists and the Separation of Church and State* (Cambridge: Harvard University Press, 1971), 547–56; Estep, *Religious Liberty*, 68–69.

26. Estep, *Religious Liberty*, 68–69.

27. Quoted in McLoughlin, *New England Dissent*, 557.

28. *Ibid.*

29. Peter S. Onuf, *The Origins of the Federal Republic: Jurisdictional Controversies in the United States, 1775–1787* (Philadelphia: University of Pennsylvania Press, 1983), 16.

30. McLoughlin, *New England Dissent*, 557.

31. William G. McLoughlin, ed., *The Diary of Isaac Backus*, 3 vols. (Providence: Brown University Press, 1979), 2:915.

32. The memorial is printed in Alvah Hovey, *A Memoir of the Life and Times of the Rev. Isaac Backus* (Boston: Printers Press, 1858), 280ff.

33. McLoughlin, *The Diary of Isaac Backus*, 2:916.

34. *Ibid.*, 917.

35. L. H. Butterfield, ed., *Diary and Autobiography of John Adams*, 4 vols. (Cambridge: Harvard University Press, 1961), 2:152–54.

36. McLoughlin, *New England Dissent*, 561, 564.

37. *Ibid.*, 563.

38. Thomas Gilpin, one of the affected Quakers, authored a firsthand account of the episode that was later published as *Exiles in Virginia: With Observations on the Society of Friends during the Revolutionary War* (Philadelphia: C. Sherman, 1848), 2.

39. *Ibid.*, 35.

40. *Pennsylvania Packet*, 6 September 1777.

41. *Journals of Congress*, 8:642.

42. *Journals of Congress*, 8:707–8.

43. *Ibid.*, 714, 718.

44. *Ibid.*, 723.

45. *Ibid.*, 714, 718–19.

46. Quoted in Edward Frank Humphrey, *Nationalism and Religion in America, 1774–1789* (Boston: Chipman Law Publishing, 1924), 149–50.

47. *Journals of Congress*, 10:98.

48. *Ibid.*, 10:258.

49. Quoted in Gilpin, *Exiles in Virginia*, 42.

50. *Ibid.*, 234–38.

51. See, James Madison, *The Federalist*, No. 10.

52. *Connecticut Courant*, 17 December 1787.

53. See chap. 1, infra.

54. John F. Wilson, "Religion, Government, and Power in the New American Nation," in Mark A. Noll, ed., *Religion and American Politics: From the Colonial Period to the 1980s* ed. Mark A. Noll (New York: Oxford University Press, 1990), 84.

55. On the passage of the Fourteenth Amendment, however, specifically on the view that it was an attempt to "complete" the Constitution that James Madison had envisioned, see Michael P. Zuckert, "Completing the Constitution: The Fourteenth Amendment and Constitutional Rights," *Publius: The Journal of Federalism* 22 (Spring 1992): 76.

*Chapter Eight*

1. *Journals of Congress*, 5:517–18.

2. *The Great Seal of the United States* (Washington, D.C.: U.S. Government Printing Office, 1986), 1.

3. Richard S. Patterson and Richardson Dougall, *The Eagle and the Shield: A History of the Great Seal of the United States* (Washington, D.C.: U.S. Government Printing Office, 1976), 6–10.

4. Franklin note, undated (August 1776). Thomas Jefferson Papers, Manuscript Division, Library of Congress; quoted in *The Great Seal*, 14.

5. Julian P. Boyd, ed., *Papers of Thomas Jefferson*, 21 vols. (Princeton: Princeton University Press, 1950–1983), 1:677–79.

6. Patterson and Dougall, *The Eagle and the Shield*, 16.

7. L. H. Butterfield, *Diary and Autobiography of John Adams*, 4 vols. (Cambridge: Harvard University Press, 1961), 2: ix–x.

8. Patterson and Dougall, *The Eagle and the Shield*, 10–13.

9. *Ibid.*, 19.

10. *Ibid.*, 25–27.

11. *Journals of Congress*, 5:691.

12. Harry Stout, *The New England Soul* (Oxford: Oxford University Press, 1986), 54.

13. Patterson and Dougall, *The Eagle and the Shield*, 32–35.

14. *Ibid.*, 35, 38–39.

15. *Journals of Congress*, 17:423.

16. *Ibid.*, 434.

17. The appointment of this committee is not noted in the *Journals of the Continental Congress* but is recorded in the "Committee Book" of Congress's official secretary, Charles Thomson. Patterson and Dougall, *The Eagle and the Shield*, 44; also, see Papers of the Continental Congress, item 186, folio 25, RG 360, N.A.

18. *Ibid.*, 57.

19. *Ibid.*, 69, *The Great Seal*, 4.

20. Patterson and Dougall, *The Eagle and the Shield*.

21. *The Great Seal*, 4–5.

22. *Ibid.*, 5.

23. *Ibid.*, 5–6.

24. Papers of the Continental Congress, item 23, folios 131–32; reproduced *ibid.*

25. *The Great Seal*, 6, 12.

26. *Ibid.*, 7–14.

27. Patterson and Dougall, *The Eagle and the Shield*, 22–25.

28. *Journals of Congress*, 8:536.

29. *Journals of Congress*, 8:734–35.

30. D. W. Belisle, *History of Independence Hall: From the Earliest Period to the Present Time* (Philadelphia: James Challen & Son, 1859), 371–72; Anson Phelps Stokes, *Church and State in the United States: Historical Development and Contemporary Problems of Religious Freedom under the Constitution*, 3 vols. (New York: Harper & Brothers, 1950), 1:471.

31. Margaret T. Hills, "The First American Bible, as Published by Robert Aitken," *Bible Society Record* 113 (January 1968): 2; William H. Gaines, "The Continental Congress Considers the Publication of a Bible, 1777," *Studies in Bibliography* 3 (1950–1951): 274.

32. Gaines, "The Continental Congress Considers the Publication of a Bible," 280.

33. *Journals of Congress*, 18:979.

34. *Journals of Congress*, 20:549. Also see Hills, "The First American Bible," 3.

35. *Ibid.*, 4.

36. Edwin A. R. Rumball-Petre recorded that by 1940 seventy-one extant copies of the Aitken Bible had been traced; however, he surmised that several were untraced and estimated that probably more than a hundred copies were extant. Edwin A. R. Rumball-Petre, *America's First Bibles, with a Census of 555 Extant Bibles* (Portland, Maine: Southworth-Anthoensen Press, 1940), 96.

37. *Journals of Congress*, 23:572–74.

38. Rumball-Petre, *America's First Bibles*, 86.

39. See Charles Thomson to Robert Morris, 14 and 16 November, 1781, and Morris's diary entry for 16 November, *The Papers of Robert Morris, 1781–1784*, ed. E. James Ferguson (Pittsburgh: University of Pittsburgh Press, 1977), 3:186–87, 188, 191.

40. Rumball-Petre, *America's First Bibles*, 86–88.


*Chapter Nine*

1. *Journals of Congress*, 1:33.

2. William Addison Blakely, *American State Papers on Freedom in Religion*, 3d rev. ed. (Tacoma Park, Wash.: Review and Herald, 1943), 62.

3. Elihu Hall, *The Present Way* (New London, 1749), 45; quoted in Richard Bushman, *From Puritan to Yankee: Character and the Social Order in Connecticut, 1690–1765* (Cambridge: Harvard University Press, 1967), 226.

4. Edwin S. Gaustad, "Religion," in *The Encyclopedia of Colonial and Revolutionary America*, ed. John Mack Faragher (New York: Sachem Publishing, 1990), 357–59.

5. Robert T. Handy, *A History of the Churches in the United States and Canada* (New York: Oxford University Press, 1977), 122–23.

6. *Ibid.*, 137.

7. Harold C. Syrett and Jacob E. Cooke, eds., *The Papers of Alexander Hamilton*, 27 vols. (New York: Columbia University Press, 1961–1987), 1:169–70.

8. Richard Smith's diary, 5 February 1776, *Letters of Delegates to Congress, 1774–1789*, 18 vols., ed. Paul H. Smith (Washington, D.C.: Library of Congress, 1979–), 3:203.

9. M. Searle Bates, *Religious Liberty: An Inquiry* (New York: International Missionary Council, 1945), 216; Francis Newton Thorpe, *The Federal and State Constitutions*, 7 vols. (Washington, D.C.: n.p., 1909), 5:2636–38; Oscar Handlin and Mary Handlin, ed., *The Popular Sources of Political Authority: Documents on the Massachusetts Constitution of 1780* (Cambridge: Harvard University Press, 1966), 467–68.

10. Carl Bridenbaugh, *Mitre and Sceptre: Transatlantic Faiths, Ideas, Personalities and Politics, 1689–1775* (New York: Oxford University Press, 1962). Indeed, the chief aim of Bridenbaugh's book was to prove a conspiracy by the English church and state to impose Anglicanism on the colonies. But see William M. Hogue, "The Religious Conspiracy Theory of the American Revolution: Anglican Motive," *Church History* 45 (1976): 277, for the view that the movement to anglicize America was active only within the English ecclesiastical establishment, not within Parliament.

11. Letter from a gentleman, 20 February 1775, to his brother in London, *Letters on the American Revolution, 1774–1776*, ed. Margaret Willard (Boston: Houghton Mifflin, 1925), 67.

12. *Journals of Congress*, 1:105–13. This letter is also discussed and reproduced in Charles S. Hyneman and Donald S. Lutz, eds., *American Political Writings during the Founding Era, 1760–1805* (Indianapolis: Liberty Press, 1983), 231–39.

13. Handy, *A History of the Churches*, 123.

14. *Journals of Congress*, 1:117.

15. *Ibid.*, 2:68–70.

16. John C. Fitzpatrick, ed., *The Writings of George Washington*, 39 vols. (Washington, D.C.: U.S. Government Printing Office, 1931), 3:495–96.

17. *Ibid.*, 3:492.

18. *Journals of Congress*, 15 February 1776, 4:152.

19. *Ibid.*, 4:217.

20. James Dana, *A Century Discourse Delivered at the Anniversary Meeting of the Freemen of Wallingford*, 9 April 1770 (New Haven, Conn., 1770), 20–21. Also, see generally, Ruth H. Bloch, *Visionary Republic: Millennial Themes in American Thought, 1756–1800* (New York: Cambridge University Press, 1985), especially chaps. 3–4.

21. John T. Ellis, *Catholics in Colonial America* (Baltimore: Helicon, 1965), 232, estimates that there were only 20,000 Catholics in the colonies in 1776, less than 1 percent of the population. The number of Jews nearly equaled the number of Catholics. Most of the remaining religious population (97–98 percent) was Protestant.

22. On this point, see Lynn Montross, *The Reluctant Rebels: The Story of the Continental Congress, 1774–1789* (New York: Harper & Brothers, 1950), 251–52, who credits Charles Carroll of Carrollton with much of the progress made during the Revolution in colonial attitudes toward Catholics. Without ever becoming a religious propagandist, he says, Carroll "set an example which melted the prejudices of rebel leaders, many of whom had never known anyone of his faith." Carroll's tolerant spirit could be observed from the earliest days of the convening of the Continental Congress. He wrote to William Graves in 1774: "I am a warm friend to toleration. I execrate the intolerating spirit of the Church of Rome and of other churches." See Charles Carroll to William Groves, 14 August 1774, "Extracts from the Carroll Papers," *Maryland Historical Magazine* 32 (1920): 222.

23. Carl Brent Swisher, *American Constitutional Development*, 2d ed. (Westport, Conn.: Greenwood Press, 1978), 18.

24. *Journals of Congress*, 5:424–26. On earlier forms of cooperation among the colonies in the seventeenth and eighteenth centuries, see Harry M. Ward, *"Unite or Die": Intercolony Relations, 1690–1763* (Port Washington, N.Y.: Lefert's Press, 1971).

25. *Ibid.*, 5:433.

26. *Ibid.*, 2:195–98.

27. Jack Rakove, *The Beginnings of National Politics: An Interpretive History of the Continental Congress* (New York: Knopf, 1979), 136–38. For an interpretation of the Franklin draft, see Gerald Stourzh, *Benjamin Franklin and American Foreign Policy*, 2d ed. (Chicago: University of Chicago Press, 1969), chaps. 3 and 4.

28. The proposed Articles are printed in the *Papers of the Continental Congress*, No. 47; see also *Journals of Congress*, 5:546.

29. Rakove, *Beginnings of National Politics*, 138–39; Merrill Jensen, *The Articles of Confederation: An Interpretation of the Social-Constitutional History of the American Revolution* (Madison: University of Wisconsin Press, 1940), 128.

30. Swisher, *American Constitutional Development*, 18–19; Valerie A. Earle, "The Federal Structure," *Founding Principles of American Government: Two Hundred Years of Democracy on Trial*, ed. George G. Graham, Jr., and Scarlett G. Graham (Bloomington: Indiana University Press, 1977), 135.

31. Rakove, *Beginnings of National Politics*, 151–52.

32. Art. III of Dickinson draft; see *Journals of Congress*, 5:547.

33. Rakove, *Beginnings of National Politics*, 152.

34. *Journals of Congress*, 5:547.

35. Rakove, *Beginnings of National Politics*, 153.

36. *Journals of Congress*, 9:907.

37. The Tenth Amendment reads: "The powers not delegated to the United States by the Constitution, nor prohibited by it to the States, are reserved to the States respectively, or to the people."

38. Anson Phelps Stokes, *Church and State in the United States: Historical Development and Contemporary Problems of Religious Freedom under the Constitution*, 3 vols. (New York: Harper & Brothers, 1950), 1:466; Johann Conrad Dohla, *A Hessian Diary of the American Revolution* (Norman: University of Oklahoma Press, 1990), x–xi.

39. *Journals of Congress*, 5:640, 653, 708.

40. Not only had Congress apparently forgiven these soldiers' participation in the war, but also they had been forced to collect depositions against a great many of the Hessians who were accused of multiple rapes of young girls in New Jersey and Connecticut in 1779. See Mary Beth North, *Liberty's Daughters: The Revolutionary Experience of American Women, 1750–1800* (Boston: Little, Brown, 1980), 203–4.

41. Frederick Harling and Martin Kaufman, *The Ethnic Contribution to the American Revolution* (Westfield, Mass.: Westfield Bicentennial Committee, 1976), 27–30.

42. Carl Wittke, *We Who Built America: The Saga of the Immigrant* (Cleveland: Press of Case Western Reserve University, 1967), 92.

43. Harling and Kaufman, *Ethnic Contribution to the American Revolution*, 32.

44. Wittke, *We Who Built America*, 92.

45. Lillian Schlissel, *Conscience in America: A Documentary History of Conscientious Objection in America, 1757–1967* (New York: E. P. Dutton, 1968), 17–18.

46. Charles Carroll to Charles Carroll, Sr., 5 October 1777, in Smith, *Letters of Delegates*, 8:168–69.

47. Robert T. Miller and Ronald B. Flowers, *Toward Benevolent Neutrality: Church, State, and the Supreme Court*, 3d ed. (Waco, Tex.: Baylor University Press, 1987), 104.

48. Schlissel, *Conscience in America*, 18.

49. Harling and Kaufman, *Ethnic Contribution to the American Revolution*, 32.

50. *Ibid.*, 32–33.

51. *Journals of Congress*, 2:18.

52. Joseph Gales, ed., *The Debates and Proceedings in the Congress of the United States: With an Appendix Containing Important State Papers and Public Documents, and All the Laws of a Public Nature; With a Copious Index*, 42 vols. (Washington D.C.: Gales & Seaton, 1834–1856), 1:451.

53. See, for example, *Arver v. United States*, 245 U.S. 366 (1918), in which the Court upheld the Selective Draft Act of 1917, which exempted regularly ordained ministers and theological students, as well as "any well-recognized religious sect or organization at present organized and existing and whose existing creed or principles forbid its members to participate in war in any form"; and *United States v. Seeger*, 380 U.S. 163 (1965), which upheld the Selective Training and Service Act of 1940, as amended in 1948, which exempted one "who, by religious training and belief, is conscientiously opposed to participation in war in any form." It is interesting to note that in the *Seeger* case, the U.S. Supreme Court broadened the meaning of the term "religious training and belief" to also exempt those who hold "a given belief that is sincere and . . . occupies a place in the life of its possessor parallel to that filled by the orthodox belief in God."

54. *Journals of Congress* (as ratified by the Congress, 22 January 1783), 24:67–80. The treaty is also reproduced in William M. Malloy, *Treaties, Conventions, International Acts, Protocols and Agreements between the United States of America and Other Powers*, 3 vols. (New York: Greenwood Press, 1910), 2:1233–44.

55. *Journals of Congress* (as ratified by the Congress, 29 July 1783, and proclaimed by Congress, 25 September 1783), 24:457–73; also reproduced in Malloy, *Treaties*, 2: 1725–35.

56. *Journals of Congress* (as ratified by the Congress, 17 May 1786), 30:269–85; also reproduced in Malloy, *Treaties*, 2:1477–86.

57. Frederick A. Norwood, *Strangers and Exiles: A History of Religious Refugees*, 2 vols. (Nashville: Abingdon Press, 1969), 2:57–60.

58. Bates, *Religious Liberty*, 167.

59. Henry Kamen, *The Rise of Toleration* (London: World University Library, 1967), 145–48.

60. Gerald R. Cragg, *The Church and the Age of Reason, 1648–1789* (1960; reprint, New York: Penguin Books, 1985), 215–18.

61. Preserved Smith, *A History of Modern Culture*, 2 vols. (New York: Holt, 1930–1934), 2:561.

62. Bates, *Religious Liberty*, 204–5; Cragg, *The Church in the Age of Reason*, 216.

63. See generally, Peter S. Onuf, *Statehood and Union: A History of the Northwest Ordinance* (Bloomington: Indiana University Press, 1987).

64. United States Code (1976 Edition), 1:xlii–xliii.

65. Public Statutes at Large, "First Congress, of the Territory Northwest of the River Ohio," 1:50.

66. John S. Baker, for example, in "James Madison and Religious Freedom," *Benchmark* 3 (January–April 1987): 71–78, argues that the Northwest Ordinance has been almost entirely overlooked in modern discussions of the religion clauses. He says, for instance, that the U.S. Supreme Court, in cases involving the interpretation of the religion clauses, has only three times made reference to the Northwest Ordinance. Two of the references, one by Justice Frank Murphy in a dissenting opinion in *Jones v. City of Opelika*, 316 U.S. 584, 622 (1942), and the other by Justice William O. Douglas in a concurring opinion in *Engel v. Vitale*, 370 U.S. 421, 443 n. 9 (1962), were only passing references that gave the Northwest Ordinance no meaningful attention. The other reference, by Justice William H. Rehnquist in a dissenting opinion in *Wallace v. Jaffree*, 105 Sup. Ct. 2479, 2513 (1985), finally, according to Baker, gave the Northwest Ordinance its justly deserved attention as a piece of legislation that can help to illuminate the founders' intent with respect to the religion clauses.

Rehnquist, at p. 2513 in his opinion in *Wallace*, a 1985 case dealing with moments of silence for prayer and meditation in public schools, argued that the Northwest Ordinance confirms "the view that Congress did not mean that the government should be neutral between religion and irreligion." In considering the relationship between the religion clauses and the Ordinance, he added that "it seems highly unlikely that the House of Representatives would simultaneously consider proposed amendments to the Constitution and enact an important piece of legislation which conflicted with the intent of the proposals."

67. *Wallace*, 2513.

68. *Journals of Congress*, 28:293.

69. *Ibid.*

70. *Ibid.*, 28:294.

71. The affirmative votes were cast by New Hampshire, Massachusetts, Delaware, Pennsylvania, and Virginia.

72. William Ellery of Rhode Island and Melancton Smith of New York led the successful assault against the appropriation of public lands for the use of religion. The question was oddly put so that the vote was taken on whether the religion clauses should stand. In that way only a few noes were required to defeat the question and consequently strike the offensive phrases. Harry Ammon, in *James Monroe: The Quest for National Identity* (New York: McGraw-Hill, 1971), 52, takes the view that by this manner, although few of the delegates favored the support of the religion clause, few had to go on record against it.

73. James Madison to James Monroe, 29 May 1785, *The Papers of James Madison*, 9 vols., ed. Robert A. Rutland (Charlottesville: University of Virginia Press, 1976), 8:286. Monroe seems never to have responded to Madison's condemnation of the clause, nor to explain why he and his fellow Virginia delegates voted for retention of the provision.

74. *Journals of Congress*, 32:318.

75. These points are also discussed in Bernard Schwartz, *The Bill of Rights: A Documentary History*, 2 vols. (New York: Chelsea House, 1971), 1:395; Edwin S. Gaustad, *Faith of Our Fathers: Religion and the New Nation* (San Francisco: Harper & Row, 1987), 115–17; and Edmund Cody Burnett, *The Continental Congress: A Definitive History of the Continental Congress from Its Inception in 1774 to March, 1789* (New York: Macmillan, 1941), 624.

*Chapter Ten*

1. Dr. Cooper's sermon appears in Ellis Sandoz, *Political Sermons of the American Founding Era, 1730–1805* (Indianapolis: Liberty Press, 1991), 627–56. This and the following citations are found at 631, 634, 639, 644, 655, 656.

2. *Ibid.*, 647, 53.

3. Cited in Edwin Gaustad, *Neither King nor Prelate* (Grand Rapids, Mich.: William B. Eerdman's Publishing Co., 1993), 92.

4. Clearly Washington, regarded as the American Cincinnatus, enjoyed immense popularity because of what he embodied, not because of his astute abilities as a political philosopher. Like the Roman general before him, Washington readily surrendered his sword to the Congress, hoping to return to private life. As the Duché affair makes clear (see chap. 5), Washington established his bona fides beyond question as the virtuous leader who sought public good, not private advantage. He made, then, the ideal candidate for the inaugural presidency. A good presentation of this public persona of Washington is found in Richard Pierard and Robert Linder, *Civil Religion and the Presidency* (Grand Rapids, Mich.: Zondervan Publishing House, 1988), 65–86.

5. Bernard Bailyn, "The Challenge of Modern Historiography," *American Historical Review* 87 (February 1982): 24.

6. Edmund C. Burnett, ed., *Letters of Members of the Continental Congress*, 8 vols. (Washington, D.C.: Carnegie Institution, 1921–1936), 1:14.

7. Letter to William Cushing, 9 June 1776, Burnett, *Letters*, 1:478.

8. John Diggins, *The Lost Soul of American Politics* (New York: Basic Books, 1984), 6.

9. *Ibid.*, 6.

10. For example, it was no aesthetic appeal of symmetry or desire for efficiency but a deliberation on unpleasant features of human nature that led the Constitutional Convention to adopt bicameralism. An unsigned editorial in the *Essex Result* (Mass.) in 1778 illustrates this by arguing: "The legislative power must not be trusted with one assembly. A single assembly is frequently influenced by the vices, follies, passions, and prejudices of an individual. It is liable to be avaricious, and to exempt itself from the burdens it lays upon its constituents." And with typical acerbity, Adams commented on the special role of a senate. Concerned that the "rich, well-born, and the able" would overpower those possessed only of "simple honesty and plain sense," Adams recommended the former be put in a body that would be "to all honest and useful intents, an ostracism." Cited in Philip Kurland and Ralph Lerner, eds., *The Founders' Constitution*, 5 vols. (Chicago: Chicago University Press, 1987), 1:365, 366–67. *The Federalist*, of course, would later argue this precise point at some length.

11. From "The Dominion of Providence over the Passions of Men," in Sandoz, *Political Sermons*, 553. Witherspoon's influence was enormous. The only clergyman to sign the Declaration, Witherspoon counted among his pupils one future president (Madison), one vice president, twenty-one senators, twenty-nine representatives, and thirty-three judges. Nine of the fifty-five delegates to the 1787 Constitutional Convention had been his pupils.

12. In Robert Taylor, ed., *Papers of John Adams*, 10 vols. (Cambridge: Harvard University Press, 1977), 2:245.

13. Several sources provide a good survey of the historical development and employment of the term "virtue." Some of the more recent include Richard Sinopoli, *The Foundations of American Citizenship: Liberalism, the Constitution, and Civic Virtue* (New York: Oxford University Press, 1992); Gordon Wood, *The Radicalism of the American Revolution* (New York: Random House, 1991); and Richard Vetterli and Gary Bryner, *In Search of the Republic* (Totowa, N.J.: Rowman and Littlefield, 1987). Ellis Sandoz, while not focusing primarily on virtue, does a nice job in locating the basis for moral action in the tradition of law and religion in his *A Government of Laws* (Baton Rouge: Louisiana State University Press, 1991).

14. The central passage of the *Ethics*, at least regarding virtue, is that in Book II where Aristotle differentiated between "moral" and "intellectual" virtue. In the ensuing discussion, Aristotle held that virtue is not innate but is a matter of choice based on rational principles and that it is inculcated through habituation. In the matter of education and character, Locke may be seen as Aristotelian. As his *Thoughts Concerning Education* made clear, moral formation had primacy, not particular subject matter. For instance, Locke wrote, " 'Tis virtue then, direct virtue, which is the hard and valuable part to be aimed at in education. . . . All other considerations and accomplishments should give way and be postponed to this." Aristotle's "habituation" became "good breeding" in Locke. See, for instance, the discussion in Section 70, *The Educational Writings of John Locke*, ed. James Axtell (New York: Cambridge University Press, 1968), 169ff.

15. Letter to Peter Carr, 19 August 1785, *The Portable Jefferson*, ed. Merrill Peterson (New York: Penguin Books, 1975), 381.

16. His definition appears in III.5.6 of *The Spirit of Laws*, and he returns to it in V.2. In an appendix to the 1757 edition, Montesquieu stressed again that he had in view political virtue, not a moral or Christian virtue, and he defined it there quite succinctly as "love of one's country," the "spring which sets republican government

in motion." Citations are from the Carrither's edition (Berkeley: University of California Press, 1977).

17. The ideas here derive in part from suggestive comments made in Vetterli and Bryner's "Public Virtue and the Roots of Republican Government," the introductory chapter to *In Search of the Republic*.

18. Clinton Rossiter, who has described American democracy as a "highly moral adventure," writes in *The First American Revolution* that "Puritanism was the goad to the American conscience that insisted on communal responsibility before individual freedom, constitutionalism before democracy, order before liberty" ([New York: Harcourt, Brace, and World, 1956], 94). To the degree that early American historiography presents the founding era as simply a debate between classical republicanism and Lockean liberalism, it also truncates other critical intellectual components that informed the founders' worldview. Although this chapter does not attempt to trace the historiographic debate, it is written from the perspective that other elements, particularly Puritanism, had major impact. Perry Miller, of course, should be accorded credit for raising the visibility of Puritanism's influence and for critiquing writings that have ignored it. Some recent works that have contributed to our understanding of Puritanism's (and religion generally) contribution include John Diggins, *The Lost Soul of American Politics*; Barry Shain, *The Myth of American Individualism* (Princeton: Princeton University Press, 1994); Donald Lutz, *A Preface to American Political Theory* (Lawrence: University Press of Kansas, 1992); Ellis Sandoz, *Government of Laws*; and Mark Noll, ed., *Religion and American Politics* (New York: Oxford University Press, 1990), especially Ruth Bloch's essay, "Religion and Ideological Change in the American Revolution," 44–61. Noll's collection of essays provides an accessible bibliography for those who wish to do more reading in the area.

19. Perry Miller, in an engaging interpretative essay comparing Jonathan Edwards and Franklin, describes the two as "heirs of a once unitary tradition, which they split asunder, but of which they are alike legitimate descendants. . . . Although Franklin blithely put aside the theology out of which this particular code arose [that of work and calling], he as much as Edwards exemplified it every day of his life." Perry Miller, ed., *Major Writers of America* (New York: Harcourt, Brace, and World, 1962), 1:84–85.

20. Sydney Ahlstrom, *A Religious History of the American People* (New Haven: Yale University Press, 1972), 363. See his discussion of "Religion and the American Revolution," *ibid.*, 361ff. Bernard Bailyn has described the transduction of Puritan thought into a broader milieu as having "been consolidated and amplified by a succession of writers in the course of the seventeenth century, [then] channeled into the mainstream of eighteenth-century political and social thinking by a generation of enlightened preachers, and softened in its denominational rigor by many hands." *The Ideological Origins of the American Revolution*, enlarged ed. (Cambridge: Harvard University Press, 1992), 32.

21. S.v. "disinterest." Citations are from Samuel Johnson's *Dictionary of the English Language* (New York, Arno Press, 1979). Reprint of the 1775 edition published in London by W. Strahan. For more on the classical republican strain of founding era thought generally and "disinterest" specifically, see Gordon S. Wood, "Interests and Disinterestedness in the Making of the Constitution," in *Beyond Confederation: Origins of the American Constitution and American National Identity* ed. Richard Beeman, Stephen Botein, and Edward C. Carter III (Chapel Hill: University of North Carolina Press, 1987), 69.

22. Burnett, *Letters*, 1:138–39.

23. Cited in Burnett, *Letters*, 2:435–36, n. 3.

24. See Franklin's *Autobiography*, ed. Kenneth Silverman (New York: Viking-Penguin, 1986), 90ff.

25. Ronald Hamowy, ed., *Cato's Letters* (Indianapolis: Liberty Fund, 1995), 195.

26. Cited in Vetterli and Bryner, *In Search of the Republic*, 1.

27. Taylor, *Papers of John Adams*, 2:242.

28. This and the immediately preceding Adams quote are cited in Bailyn, *Ideological Origins*, 236.

29. Letter of 14 March 1785, Kurland and Lerner, *The Founders' Constitution*, 1:160.

30. Burnett, *Letters*, 1:409–10.

31. Letter of 17 April 1777, *ibid.*, 2:330.

32. Cited in Wood, *Radicalism*, 289.

33. Cited in Wood, *Radicalism*, 108.

34. Cited in Gaustad, *Neither King nor Prelate*, 93.

35. Burnett, *Letters*, 2:294–95 (italics in original).

36. "Brutus," writing 29 November 1787, to "The People of the State of New York," *The Anti-Federalist*, ed. Herbert Storing (Chicago: University of Chicago Press, 1985), 132.

37. Burnett, *Letters*, 1:198. The Congress's action was to give Washington full power within the nascent war department, which included the authority to raise additional battalions, appoint officers, and provision his men. As the records of the Congress make clear, it had sought to direct the war effort in all its particulars, to include the most mundane details of logistics. Military necessity dictated that Congress give Washington more latitude. For instances of the Congress trying to manage the war effort, see the numerous letters of congressional delegates in Burnett, *passim*, especially 1775–1777. See also the relevant correspondence in Worthington Ford, ed., *Journals of Congress* (Washington: Government Printing Office, 1906), during the same period, esp. 6:1027, 1053.

38. Burnett, *Letters*, 2:317.

39. Forrest McDonald, *Novus Ordo Seclorum* (Lawrence: University Press of Kansas, 1985), 98.

40. Cited in Vetterli and Bryner, *In Search of the Republic*, 225.

41. Burnett, *Letters*, 1:239–40.

42. Burnett, *Letters*, 1:406.

43. Letter of 5 July 1777, in *ibid.*, 2:401.

44. From Rush's "Plan for the Establishment of Public Schools," in *American Political Writings during the Founding Era, 1760–1805*, 2 vols., ed. Charles S. Hyneman and Donald Lutz (Indianapolis: Liberty Press, 1983), 1:685.

45. Peter Laslett, ed., *Two Treatises of Government* (New York: Cambridge University Press, 1988), 342. Locke's discussion of commonwealths is, of course, part of a polemic, one intended to refute the views of Filmer and others with respect to monarchy and divine right.

46. In Axtell, *Educational Writings of John Locke*, 170–71 (italics in original).

47. The Addison and Lockwood quotes are cited in Wood, *Radicalism*, 43–44.

48. Hyneman and Lutz, *American Political Writings*, 1:682–83.

49. The letter is found in *ibid.*, 1:38–39 (italics in original).

50. L. H. Butterfield, ed., *Diary and Autobiography of John Adams* (Cambridge: Harvard University Press, 1961), 4:123. Adams's own relationship with Abigail, as regards "domestick government," is itself a rich study. Abigail did not scruple to

remind John of the delegates' responsibilities to their wives in the whole revolutionary affair. In a letter dated 31 March 1776, Abigail wrote, "I long to hear that you have declared an independency—and by the way in the new code of laws which I suppose it will be necessary for you to make I desire you would remember the ladies, and be more generous and favorable to them than your ancestors. Do not put such unlimited power into the hands of the husbands. Remember all men would be tyrants if they could." The letter is available in Kurland and Lerner, *The Founders' Constitution*, 1:518–20.

51. Hyneman and Lutz, *American Political Writings*, 691.

52. Both citations are letters to John Adams written in July 1789 and are in Kurland and Lerner, *The Founders' Constitution*, 2:232, 403.

53. Letter to John Penn, 20 May 1774, in *ibid.*, 1:517–18. A disdain or fear of "the people" was not an isolated sentiment. Sherman wrote that he hoped the "people . . . have as little to do as may be about the government." William Livingston, who served both as governor of New Jersey and as a delegate to the Continental Congress, stated: "The people have ever been and ever will be unfit to retain the exercise of power in their own hands." And Federalist writer John Jay declared: "The people who own the country ought to govern it." Citations in Richard Hofstadter, "The Founding Fathers: An Age of Realism," in *The Moral Foundations of the American Republic*, ed. Robert Horwitz (Charlottesville: University of Virginia Press, 1986), 63, 73.

54. The Burke and Jefferson citations are both from Vetterli and Bryner, *In Search of the Republic*, 171, 172–73.

55. Letter to Samuel Cooper, 23 April 1777, in Burnett, *Letters*, 2:339.

56. *Ibid.*, 2:376.

57. *Ibid.*

58. Taylor, *Papers of John Adams*, 2:407–8.

59. In Peterson, *The Portable Jefferson*, 335, 336. This remarkable document of 1818, with its reflections on reason, habit, and virtue, in many ways shows Jefferson the unreconstructed classical republican yet in others clearly reflects the passage of twenty-two centuries since Aristotle. The Aristotelian systematization of the domain of knowledge appears again, but with an early nineteenth-century adaptation.

60. Cited in Ralph Ketcham, *The Political Thought of Benjamin Franklin* (Indianapolis: Bobbs-Merrill, 1965), 57.

61. Hyneman and Lutz, *American Political Writings*, 1:682.

62. The complete text of the Massachusetts constitution may be found in Kurland and Lerner, *The Founders' Constitution*, 1:11–23. These passages are found on p. 21. The 1780 Constitution is clearly Lockean: government is instituted to secure "natural rights and the blessings of life" and is a "voluntary association of individuals" who retain the unalienable right to "reform, alter, or totally change the same." But the constitution also reflects the Puritan heritage of Massachusetts Bay, as indicated below in the section on religion.

63. See chap. 9 for a more extensive discussion of the Northwest Ordinance.

64. For instance, Rush observed in his "Plan" that "our schools of learning, by producing one general, and uniform system of education, will render the mass of the people more homogeneous, and thereby fit them more easily for uniform and peaceable government." See Hyneman and Lutz, *American Political Writings*, 1:681. Also see Peter S. Onuf, "State Politics and Republican Virtue: Religion, Education, and Morality in Early American Federalism," in *Toward a Usable Past: Liberty under*

*State Constitutions*, ed. Paul Finkelman and Stephen E. Gottlieb (Athens: University of Georgia Press, 1991).

65. The essay appears in *ibid.*, 1:699–701. The cited passages here are 700–1 (italics in original).

66. *Autobiography*, 90.

67. Cited in Vetterli and Bryner, *In Search of the Republic*, 140.

68. In Hyneman and Lutz, *American Political Writings*, 1:676 (italics in original).

69. *Autobiography*, 102–3 (italics in original).

70. Letter of 18 October 1790, in Kurland and Lerner, *The Founders' Constitution*, 1:352.

71. In Axtell, *Educational Writings of John Locke*, 241.

72. Vetterli and Bryner, *In Search of the Republic*, 52–53. An extended treatment of civil religion in particular and the republican vision is also in Vetterli and Bryner, especially 89–120. The treatment also will give an idea of the vast bibliography that has developed in this area.

73. One of those who believed it possible to inculcate virtue apart from religion was Samuel McClintock. Graduate of Princeton and chaplain to the army during the Revolution, McClintock declared, "Altho' true religion, the religion of the heart, consisting in faith and love unfeigned, and a real conformity to the divine character, is necessary in all who on good grounds would hope for eternal life; yet those who are wholly destitute of this religion, have it in their power to practice, on natural principles, that virtue, which according to the constitution of the divine government over nations, will ensure their temporal prosperity and glory." In Sandoz, *Political Sermons*, 810. McClintock later became, not unnaturally, a staunch supporter of Jefferson, who sought to propound a universal moral sense that operated even apart from religion, much as the Scottish common sense philosophers. Although McClintock's view was, at the time, a minority view, he anticipated a modern temper. See his sermon, cited here, in *ibid.*, 789–813. A more "orthodox" view for the time was that of the Reverend Asa Burton. Preaching an election sermon in 1786 in Vermont, Burton declared, "Political virtue may serve as a support for a while, but it is not a lasting principle." Ruth Bloch, who provides this citation, summarizes Burton's solution: "The true basis of free states [is] a popular spirit of religious benevolence that [arises] from the fear of God." From "Religion and Ideological Change in the American Revolution," in Noll, *Religion and American Politics*, 55.

74. Letter to Mercy Otis Warren, 16 April 1776, in Kurland and Lerner, *The Founders' Constitution*, 1:670.

75. Cited in Vetterli and Bryner, *In Search of the Republic*, 70.

76. Kurland and Lerner, *The Founders' Constitution*, 1:684. The text of the full address is in *ibid.*, 681–85. Some modern writers, typically "Christian Nation" advocates, cite these quotes from Adams (n. 75) and Washington as proof-positive that the founders believed that the federal government should advance religion. See, for example, David Barton, *Original Intent: The Courts, the Constitution, and Religion* (Aledo, Tex.: Wallbuilder Press, 1996), 156–57, 116–17. But neither statement should be so interpreted. They reflect only the view, widely held among the founders, that no government can long survive without the virtue that religion produces in the citizenry; they say nothing about government advancement of religion.

77. "The Dominion of Providence," in Sandoz, *Political Sermons*, 554.

78. Cited in Vetterli and Bryner, *In Search of the Republic*, 69 (italics in original). In his *Autobiography* (p. 89), Franklin confessed, "Tho I seldom attended any public

worship, I had still an opinion of its propriety, and of its utility when rightly conducted, and I regularly paid my annual subscription for the support of the only
presbyterian minister or meeting we had in Philadelphia."

79. Taylor, *Papers of John Adams*, 2:266–67.

80. Cited in Wood, *Radicalism*, 334.

81. Cited in Gordon Wood, *The Creation of the American Republic, 1776–1787*
(Chapel Hill: University of North Carolina Press, 1969), 427.

82. Sandoz, *Political Sermons*, 603–4.

83. Sermon of 19 April 1781, in Sandoz, *Political Sermons*, 673, 677–78, 680–81.

84. Kurland and Lerner, *The Founders' Constitution*, 1:12.

85. *Journals of Congress*, 11:364.

86. Burnett, *Letters*, 1:156.

87. Cited in Bailyn, *Ideological Origins*, 369.

88. *The Federalist*, 431. Citations are from the edition edited by Isaac Kramnick
(New York: Penguin Books, 1987).

89. Cited in Wood, *Creation*, 429.

90. *The Federalist*, 425–26.

91. *Ibid.*, 106.

92. *Ibid.*, 123, 126 (italics added).

93. *Ibid.*, 318, 319. And those in the ministry could agree. Samuel McClintock,
preaching before the state officials on the occasion of the adoption of the New Hampshire constitution, observed, "Government is necessary, and must be supported; and
it ought to be a humiliating consideration that the necessity and expences of this
divine institution, is founded on the corruption and vices of human nature; for if
mankind were in a state of rectitude there would be no need of the sanctions of
human law to restrain them from vice or to oblige them to do what is right." Sandoz,
*Political Sermons*, 812.

94. Quoted in Peterson, *Portable Jefferson*, 288.

95. Lester J. Cappon, ed., *The Adams-Jefferson Letters* (Chapel Hill: University of
North Carolina Press, 1959), 549–51.

*Chapter Eleven*

1. David Nicholls, *God and Government in an Age of Reason* (London: Routledge,
1995), 111.

2. Ibid., quoting John Adams in "Proclamation of the Great and General Court,"
in *The Works of John Adams*, ed. C. F. Adams, 10 vols. (Boston: Chipman Publishing,
1850–1856), 1:193.

3. *Ibid.*, 109, citing John Adams, preface to "A Defense of the Constitution"
(1787), in *Works of John Adams*, 1:291–92.

4. *Ibid.*, 111, quoting Alexander Hamilton, *The Federalist*, No. 22.

5. *The Connecticut Courant*, 17 December 1787, "To the Landholders and Farmers"
by "A Landholder" (Oliver Ellsworth).

6. James Madison, *Notes of Debates in the Federal Convention of 1787*, ed. Adrianne Koch (Athens: Ohio University Press, 1966), 561.

7. Max Farrand, ed., *The Records of the Federal Convention of 1787*, 3 vols. (New
Haven: Yale University Press, 1911), 3:227.

8. Jonathan Elliott, *The Debates in the Several State Conventions on the Adoption
of the Federal Constitution*, 5 vols., 2d ed. (Philadelphia: J. P. Lippincott, 1988), 2:
148.

9. *Ibid.*, 2:119.

10. Louise Irby Trenholme, *The Ratification of the Federal Constitution in North Carolina* (New York: Columbia University Press, 1932), 178–80.

11. Quoted in Edward Frank Humphrey, *Nationalism and Religion in America, 1774–1789* (Boston: Chipman Law Publishing, 1924), 462.

12. William Williams, letter to the *American Mercury*, 11 February 1788, *The Documentary History of the Ratification of the Constitution*, 16 vols., ed. Merrill Jensen (Madison: State Historical Society of Wisconsin, 1978), 3:588.

13. Farrand, *Records of the Federal Convention of 1787*, 3:467.

14. *Ibid.*, 1:450–52; 3:467–73.

15. Mark A. Noll, *One Nation under God? Christian Faith and Political Action in America* (New York: Harper & Row, 1988), 69.

16. Elliott, *Debates*, 4:200.

17. Philip B. Kurland and Ralph Lerner, eds., *The Founders' Constitution*, 5 vols. (Chicago: University of Chicago Press, 1987), 5:106.

18. Noll, *One Nation under God*, 73.

19. Nicholls, *God and Government*, 106, quoting Thomas Paine, *The Rights of Man (Representative Selections)*, ed. H. H. Clark (New York: Heritage Press, 1961), 195.

20. *Ibid.*, 108, quoting Madison, "Memorial and Remonstrance against Religious Assessments (1785)" in *American Political Writings during the Founding Era, 1760–1805*, ed. Charles Hyneman and Donald S. Lutz (Indianapolis: Liberty Press, 1983), 637.

21. *Ibid.*, 108, quoting a letter from Adams to Jefferson, 28 June 1813.

22. *Ibid.*, 108, quoting Madison, *The Federalist*, No. 37.

23. *Ibid.*, 105, 114.

24. *Ibid.*, 118.

25. *Ibid.*, 119, quoting "An Election Sermon (1762)," in Hyneman and Lutz, *American Political Writings*, 6ff.

26. Ibid., 121, quoting "Overcoming Evil with Good (1801)," in Ellis Sandoz, *Political Sermons of the American Founding Era, 1730–1805* (Indianapolis: Liberty Press, 1991), 1549.

27. Walter Berns, "Religion and the Founding Principle," *The Moral Foundations of the American Republic*, 3d ed., ed. Robert H. Horwitz (Charlottesville: University Press of Virginia, 1986), 214.

28. *Ibid.*, 215.

29. Bernard Schwartz, *The Bill of Rights: A Documentary History*, 2 vols. (New York: Chelsea House, 1971), 2:709.

30. Quoted in Lynn R. Buzzard and Samuel Ericsson, *The Battle for Religious Liberty* (Elgin, Ill.: David C. Cook Publishing, 1982), 180.

31. Adams, *The Works of John Adams*, 9:229.

32. John C. Fitzpatrick, ed., *The Writings of George Washington*, 39 vols. (Washington, D.C.: U.S. Government Printing Office, 1931), 30:291–96.

33. *Ibid.*, 35:229.

34. Elizabeth Fleet, ed., "Madison's Detached Memoranda," *William and Mary Quarterly* 3 (October 1946): 560.

35. *Ibid.*, 554–59.

36. *Ibid.*, 560.

37. Quoted in *Wallace v. Jaffree*, 105 Sup. Ct. 2479, 2514 (1985) (Rehnquist, J., dissenting).

38. Stephen Botein, "Religious Dimensions of the Early American State," in *Beyond Confederation: Origins of the American Constitution and American National Identity,* ed. Richard Beeman, Stephen Botein, and Edward C. Carter, II (Chapel Hill: University of North Carolina Press, 1987), 324.

39. Robert Bellah, "Civil Religion in America," in *Beyond Belief: Essays on Religion in a Post-Traditional World* (New York: Harper & Row, 1970), 141.

40. Donald Lutz, "The Relative Influence of European Writers on Late Eighteenth-Century American Political Thought," *American Political Science Review* 189 (1984): 189–97, surveyed more than 15,000 items of political literature printed in the period 1760–1805 and found that Rousseau was the fifteenth most frequently cited political thinker.

41. Jean-Jacques Rousseau, *The Social Contract and Discourses,* trans. and ed. G. D. H. Cole (New York: E. P. Dutton, 1950). Regarding the "general will" of the people, see especially pp. 368–75.

42. Adrienne Koch and William Peden, eds., *The Life and Selected Writings of Thomas Jefferson* (New York: Random House, 1944), 704. While Jefferson used the term "Unitarianism," he employed it in a very broad sense as more or less synonymous with "deism." It did not imply a specific denominational view of religion.

43. *Ibid.,* 313.

44. Quoted in Daniel Boorstin, *The Lost World of Thomas Jefferson* (Boston: Beacon Press, 1960), 120.

45. David Little, "The Origins of Perplexity: Civil Religion and Moral Belief in the Thought of Thomas Jefferson," in *American Civil Religion,* ed. Russell E. Richey and Donald G. Jones (New York: Harper & Row, 1974), 194–95. Little holds that the views of Adams, Franklin, and Madison were similar to Jefferson's. *Ibid.,* 204, n. 3.

46. Koch and Peden, *Life and Selected Writings of Thomas Jefferson,* 707.

47. Thomas Jefferson, First Inaugural Address, 4 March 1801, in *Thomas Jefferson: Writings,* ed. Merrill D. Peterson (New York: Viking Press, 1984), 492.

48. Jefferson was in Paris during the Constitutional Convention, but upon receiving a copy of the proposed Constitution, he wrote James Madison expressing his concern over the lack of a bill of rights, which would include a provision "for freedom of religion." See Jefferson to Madison, 20 December 1787, in Koch and Peden, *Life and Selected Writings of Thomas Jefferson,* 436.

49. Robert Linder, "Civil Religion in Historical Perspective: The Reality That Underlies the Concept," *Journal of Church and State* 17 (Autumn 1975): 416.

50. Bellah, "Civil Religion in America," 173, 177.

51. Linder, "Civil Religion in Historical Perspective," 416.

52. Bellah, "Civil Religion in America," 171.

53. Émile Durkheim, *The Elementary Forms of the Religious Life,* rev. ed. (New York: Free Press, 1965).

54. Bellah, "Civil Religion in America," 171.

55. *Ibid.,* 187, n. 3.

56. *Ibid.*

57. *Ibid.*

58. *Ibid.,* 168–72.

59. *Ibid.,* 175.

60. *Ibid.*

61. Robert C. Winthrop, ed., *Life and Letters of John Winthrop* (Boston: Ticknor and Fields, 1867), 19.

62. Philip S. Foner, ed., *Basic Writings of Thomas Jefferson* (New York: Willey Book Company, 1944), 359.

63. Quoted in Bellah, "Civil Religion in America," 176, 179.

64. Fitzpatrick, *Writings of George Washington*, 30:291.

65. Quoted in Bellah, "Civil Religion in America," 175.

66. *Marsh v. Chambers*, 463 U.S. 783 (1983).

67. *Lynch v. Donnelly*, 465 U.S. 668 (1984) (Christmas creche paid for with public monies constitutional when surrounded by Santa Claus, reindeer, elves, and related secular Christmas decorations); *County of Allegheny v. A.C.L.U.*, 492 U.S. 573 (1989) (Jewish menorah displayed on public property constitutional when located next to a Christmas tree and a sign saluting liberty).

68. *Lee v. Weisman*, 505 U.S. 577 (1992).

69. For example, see *Lynch v. Donnelly*, 465 U.S. 668 (1984) at 716 (Brennan, J., dissenting), and *County of Allegheny v. A.C.L.U.*

70. 822 F.2d 1406 (6th Cir. 1987).

71. *Ibid.*, 1408.

72. *Ibid.*

73. *Ibid.*, 1409.

74. *Lee v. Weisman*, 505 U.S. 577 (1992).

75. *Ibid.*, 580–81.

76. Arlin M. Adams and Charles J. Emmerich, *A Nation Dedicated to Religious Liberty: The Constitutional Heritage of the Religion Changes* (Philadelphia: University of Pennsylvania Press, 1990), 87.

77. Robert Wuthnow, *The Restructuring of American Religion: Society and Faith Since World War II* (Princeton: Princeton University Press, 1988), 244–57.

78. Quoted *ibid.*, 245.

79. *Ibid.*, 250–51.

80. Adams and Emmerich, *A Nation Dedicated to Religious Liberty*, 87.

81. Mark Hatfield, *Between a Rock and a Hard Place* (Waco, Tex.: Word Books, 1976), 92.

82. Adams and Emmerich, *A Nation Dedicated to Religious Liberty*, 87.

83. For the view that civil religion should be legitimated under Establishment Clause adjudication, see Yehudah Mirsky, "Civil Religion and the Establishment Clause," *Yale Law Journal* 95 (1986): 1237; and Michael M. Maddigan, "The Establishment Clause, Civil Religion, and the Public Church," *California Law Review* 81 (1993): 293.

84. Joseph Gales, ed., *Annals of the Congress of the United States: The Debates and Proceedings of the Congress of the United States*, 42 vols. (Washington, D.C.: Gales and Seaton, 1834), 1:783–84.

85. Charles H. Lippy, "The 1780 Massachusetts Constitution: Religious Establishment or Civil Religion?" *Journal of Church and State* 20 (Autumn 1978): 533.

86. Quoted in Martin E. Marty, "Living with Establishment and Disestablishment in Nineteenth-Century Anglo-America," *Journal of Church and State* 18 (Winter 1976): 72.

87. Quoted *ibid.*

88. Alexis de Tocqueville, *Democracy in America*, ed. J. P. Mayers and Max Lerner, trans. George Lawrence (New York: Harper & Row, 1969), 271–72.

89. What constitutes a "neutral" state is, of course, no small problem. For treatments on the meaning of neutrality, see Douglas Laycock, "Formal, Substantive, and

Disaggregated Neutrality Toward Religion," *DePaul Law Review* 39 (1990): 993; Michael W. McConnell, "Neutrality under the Religion Clauses," *Northwestern Law Review* 81 (1986): 146; Steven D. Smith, *Foreordained Failure: The Quest for a Constitutional Principle of Religious Freedom* (New York: Oxford University Press, 1995), chap. 7; and Stephen V. Monsma, *Positive Neutrality: Letting Religious Freedom Ring* (Westport, Conn.: Greenwood Press, 1993).

90. James E. Wood, Jr., "The Secular State," *Journal of Church and State* 7 (Spring 1965): 169.

91. Quoted *ibid.*, 175.

92. Kurland and Lerner, *The Founders' Constitution*, 5:48.

93. This position is consistent with the Supreme Court's doctrine of "benevolent neutrality," first expressed in *Walz v. Tax Commission*, 397 U.S. 664 (1970). "Benevolent neutrality" is appropriately sensitive to the institutional difference between religion and government that was intended by the framers while simultaneously allowing for some governmental expressions of religion in public life.

94. For a summary of the Religious Freedom Amendment in its various stages, see Derek H. Davis, "Equal Treatment: A Christian Separationist Approach," *Equal Treatment of Religion in a Pluralistic Society*, ed. Stephen V. Monsma and T. Christopher Soper (Grand Rapids, Mich.: Eerdmans, 1998), 142–50.

95. Gaillard Hunt, ed., *The Writings of James Madison*, 9 vols. (New York: G. P. Putnam's Sons, 1900–1910), 9:100.

*Appendix A*

Reprinted from *Journals of Congress*, 2:140–57.

*Appendix B*

Reprinted from *Journals of Congress*, 1:105–13.

# BIBLIOGRAPHY

*Primary Sources*

A. F., *A Poem on the Rebuke of God's Hand in the Awful Desolation Made by Fire.* Boston, 1760.

Adams, Charles Frances, ed. *Familiar Letters of John Adams and His Wife, Abigail.* 2 vols. Boston: Chipman Publishing, 1875.

————, ed. *The Works of John Adams, Second President of the United States.* 10 vols. Boston: Little, Brown, 1850–1856.

Adams, John. *Diary and Autobiography of John Adams.* 4 vols. Edited by L. H. Butterfield. Cambridge: Harvard University Press, 1961.

*An Account of a Surprising Phenomenon.* Philadelphia, 1765.

Bailyn, Bernard, ed. *Pamphlets of the American Revolution, 1750–1776.* Cambridge: Harvard University Press, 1965.

Baldwin, Ebenezer. *The Duty of Rejoicing under Calamities and Afflictions.* New York: Hugh Gaine, 1776.

Bates, Samuel A., ed. *Records of the Town of Braintree, 1640–1793.* Randolph, Mass.: Matson Press, 1886.

Blakely, William Addison. *American State Papers on Freedom in Religion.* 3d rev. ed. Tacoma Park, Wash.: Review and Herald, 1943.

*Blazing Stars: Messengers of God's Wrath.* Boston, 1759.

*Boston Gazette.*

Boyd, Julian P., ed. *Papers of Thomas Jefferson.* 21 vols. Princeton: Princeton University Press, 1950–1983.

Burnett, Edmund C., ed. *Letters of Members of the Continental Congress.* 8 vols. Washington, D.C.: Carnegie Institution, 1921–1936.

Butterfield, L. H., ed. *Diary and Autobiography of John Adams.* 4 vols. Cambridge: Belknap Press of Harvard University Press, 1961.

Cappon, Lester J., ed. *The Adams-Jefferson Letters.* 2 vols. Chapel Hill: University of North Carolina Press, 1959.

Chauncy, Charles. "A Discourse on the Good News from a Far Country." 1766. In *The Pulpit of the American Revolution.* Edited by John Thornton. New York: DaCapo Press, 1970.

Cole, Franklin P., ed. *They Preached Liberty.* Indianapolis: Liberty Press, 1976.

*Connecticut Courant.*

*Constitutional Gazette.*

Cushing, H. A., ed. *The Writings of Samuel Adams.* 4 vols. New York: J. P. Lippincott, 1904–1908.

Dana, James. *A Century Discourse Delivered at the Anniversary Meeting of the Freemen of Wallingford.* 9 April 1770. New Haven, Conn., 1770.

DePauw, Linda Grant, ed. *Documentary History of the First Federal Congress of the United States of America.* 3 vols. Baltimore: Johns Hopkins University Press, 1971.

Dexter, Franklin B., ed. *The Literary Diary of Ezra Stiles.* 3 vols. New York: G. P. Putnam's Sons, 1901.

Duane, William, ed. *Extracts from the Diary of Christopher Marshall, Kept in Philadelphia and Lancaster, during the American Revolution, 1774–1781.* Albany, N.Y.: Joel Munsell, 1877.

Edwards, Jonathan. "Some Thoughts Concerning the Revival of Religion in New England." In *The Works of Jonathan Edwards.* Edited by C. C. Goen. New Haven: Yale University Press, 1972.

Elliot, Jonathan, ed. *The Debates in the Several State Conventions on the Adoption of the Federal Constitution.* 5 vols. 2d ed. Philadelphia: J. B. Lippincott, 1941.

Farrand, Max, ed. *The Records of the Federal Convention of 1787.* 3 vols. New Haven: Yale University Press, 1911.

Ferguson, E. James, ed. *The Papers of Robert Morris, 1781–1784.* Pittsburgh: University of Pittsburgh Press, 1977.

Finley, Samuel. *An Essay on the Gospel Ministry.* Wilmington, Del., 1763.

Fitzpatrick, John C., ed. *The Writings of George Washington.* 39 vols. Washington, D.C.: U.S. Government Printing Office, 1931–1944.

Fleet, Elizabeth, ed. "Madison's Detached Memoranda." *William and Mary Quarterly* 3 (October 1946): 554–59.

Foner, Philip S. *Complete Writings of Thomas Paine.* 2 vols. New York: Harper & Row, 1945.

———, ed. *Basic Writings of Thomas Jefferson.* New York: Willey Book Company, 1944.

"For the Fast Day Appointed by Congress, April 1778." *United States Magazine,* May 1779.

Force, Peter, ed. *American Archives: Fourth Series, Containing a Documentary History of the English Colonies in North America, from the King's Message to Parliament, of March 7, 1774, to the Declaration of Independence by the United States.* 6 vols. Washington, D.C., 1837–1846.

Ford, Paul Leicester, ed. *The Writings of Thomas Jefferson.* 10 vols. New York: G. P. Putnam's Sons, 1892–1899.

Ford, Worthington C., ed. *The Washington-Duché Letters.* Brooklyn, N.Y.: Cole Printing, 1890.

———, et al., eds. *Journals of the Continental Congress, 1774–1789.* 34 vols. Washington, D.C., 1904–1937.

Foster, Dan. *A Short Essay on Civil Government, the Substance of Six Sermons.* Hartford, Conn., 1775.

Franklin, Benjamin. *Autobiography.* Edited by Kenneth Silverman. New York: Viking-Penguin, 1986.

———. *The Political Thought of Benjamin Franklin*. Edited by Ralph Ketcham. Indianapolis: Bobbs-Merrill, 1965.

Gales, Joseph, ed. *Annals of the Congress of the United States: The Debates and Proceedings of the Congress of the United States*. 42 vols. Washington, D.C.: Gales and Seaton, 1834.

Gilpin, Thomas. *Exiles in Virginia: With Observations on the Society of Friends during the Revolutionary War*. Philadelphia: C. Sherman, 1848.

Goen, C. C., ed. *The Works of Jonathan Edwards*. New Haven, Conn.: Yale University Press, 1972.

Hall, Elihu. *The Present Way*. New London, Conn., 1749.

Hamilton, Alexander. "Opinion on the Constitutionality of an Act to Establish a Bank." 1791. Reprint in *Papers of Alexander Hamilton*. Ed. Harold C. Syrett. New York: Columbia University Press, 1961.

Hamilton, J. G. de Rhoulac, ed. *The Best Letters of Thomas Jefferson*. New York: Houghton Mifflin, 1926.

Hamowy, Ronald, ed. *Cato's Letters*. Indianapolis: Liberty Fund, 1995.

Hart, Levi. *Christian Minister Described*. New Haven, Conn., 1772.

Hiltzheimer, Jacob. *Extracts from the Diary of Jacob Hiltzheimer*. Philadelphia: W. F. Fell, 1893.

Hunt, Gaillard, ed. *The Writings of James Madison*. 9 vols. New York: G. P. Putnam's Sons, 1900–1910.

Hutchinson, William T., et al., eds. *The Papers of James Madison*. 8 vols. Chicago: Caperton Press, 1962–.

Hyneman, Charles S., and Donald S. Lutz, eds. *American Political Writings during the Founding Era, 1760–1805*. Indianapolis: Liberty Press, 1983.

Jefferson, Thomas. *Notes on the State of Virginia*. New York: Harper & Row, 1964.

Johnson, Samuel. *Dictionary of the English Language*. New York: Arno Press, 1979. Reprint of the 1775 edition published in London by W. Strahan.

Koch, Adrienne, and William Peden, eds. *The Life and Selected Writings of Thomas Jefferson*. New York: Random House, 1944.

Kurland, Philip B., and Ralph Lerner, eds. *The Founders' Constitution*. 5 vols. Chicago: University of Chicago Press, 1987.

Langdon, Samuel. "Government Corrupted by Vice, and Recovered by Righteousness." Sermon preached to the Congress of the Massachusetts Bay Colony. 31 May 1775. In *Religion and the Coming of the American Revolution*. Edited by Peter N. Carroll. Waltham, Mass.: Ginn-Blaisdell, 1970.

Law, Nathaniel. *An Astronomical Diary; or, Almanac for the Year of Christian Era, 1775*. Boston: John Kneeland, 1774.

Locke, John. *The Educational Writings of John Locke*. Edited by James Axtell. New York: Cambridge University Press, 1968.

———. *Two Treatises of Government*. Edited by Peter Laslett. New York: Cambridge University Press, 1988.

Madison, James. *Notes of Debates in the Federal Convention of 1787*. Edited by Adrienne Koch. Athens: Ohio University Press, 1966.

Malloy, William M. *Treaties, Conventions, International Acts, Protocols and Agreements between the United States of America and Other Powers*. 3 vols. New York: Greenwood Press, 1910.

McLoughlin, William G., ed. *The Diary of Isaac Backus*. 3 vols. Providence: Brown University Press, 1979.

Miller, Perry, ed. *Major Writers of America*. 2 vols. New York: Harcourt, Brace, and World, 1962.

Montesquieu, Charles de Secondat, baron de. *The Spirit of Laws*. Edited by David W. Carrithers. Berkeley: University of California Press, 1977.

Moore, Frank, ed. *The Diary of the American Revolution: From Newspapers and Original Documents*. 2 vols. New York: Charles Scribner, 1860.

———, ed. *Patriot Preachers of the American Revolution*. New York: Charles T. Evans, 1862.

*New york Gazette*.

*New York Journal*.

Otis, James. *The Rights of the British Colonies Asserted and Proved*. Boston, 1764. In *Pamphlets of the American Revolution, 1750–1776*. Edited by Bernard Bailyn. Cambridge: Harvard University Press, 1965.

Paine, Thomas. *Common Sense*. In *Complete Writings of Thomas Paine*. 2 vols. Edited by Philip S. Foner. New York: Harper & Row, 1945.

———. *Common Sense and the Crisis*. New York: Anchor Books, 1973.

———. *The Rights of Man (Representative Sections)*. Edited by H. H. Clark. New York: Heritage Press, 1961.

*The Parishioner, Having Studied the Point*. Hartford, Conn.: Green and Watson, 1769.

Penn, William. *The Great Case of Liberty of Conscience*. London, 1670.

*Pennsylvania Gazette*.

Peters, Richard, ed. *The Public Statutes at Large of the United States of America*. Boston: Charles C. Little and James Brown, 1845.

Peterson, Merrill, ed. *The Portable Jefferson*. New York: Penguin Books, 1975.

Peterson, Merrill D., ed. *Thomas Jefferson: Writings*. New York: Viking Press, 1984.

Post, Lydia. *Personal Recollections of the American Revolution*. Edited by Sidney Barclay. Port Washington, N.Y.: Kennicut Press, 1970.

Public Statutes at Large, "First Congress, of the Territory Northwest of the River Ohio." Washington, D.C.

*Reports of Committees of the House of Representatives*. Washington, D.C.: A.O.P. Nicholson, 1854.

Rousseau, Jean-Jacques. *The Social Contract and Discourses*. Translated and edited by G. D. H. Cole. New York: E. P. Dutton, 1950.

Rowland, Kate Mason. *Life and Correspondence of George Mason, 1725–1792*. 2 vols. New York: G. P. Putnam's Sons, 1892.

———. *The Life of Charles Carroll, of Carrollton, 1737–1832, with His Correspondence and Public Papers*. 2 vols. New York: G. P. Putnam, 1900.

Runes, Dagobert D., ed. *The Selected Writings of Benjamin Rush*. New York: Philosophical Library, 1947.

Rutland, Robert A., ed. *The Papers of James Madison*. 9 vols. Charlottesville: University of Virginia Press, 1976.

Ryden, George Herbert. *Letters to and from Caesar Rodney, 1756–1784*. New York: DeCapo Press, 1970.

Sandoz, Ellis, ed. *Political Sermons of the American Founding Era, 1730–1805*. Indianapolis: Liberty Press, 1991.

Schlissel, Lillian. *Conscience in America: A Documentary History of Conscientious Objection in America, 1757–1967*. New York: E. P. Dutton, 1968.

Schwartz, Bernard. *The Bill of Rights: A Documentary History*. 2 vols. New York: Chelsea House, 1971.

Smith, Paul H., ed. *Letters of Delegates to Congress, 1774–1789*. 18 vols. Washington, D.C.: Library of Congress, 1979–.

Smith, William, D.D. "The Crisis of American Affairs." Sermon, 23 June 1775. In *Patriot Preachers of the American Revolution*. Edited by Frank Moore. New York: Charles T. Evans, 1862.

Sparks, Jared. *Correspondence of the American Revolution*. 4 vols. Freeport, N.Y.: Books for Library Press, 1970.

———, ed. *The Diplomatic Correspondence of the American Revolution*. 12 vols. Boston: N. Hale and Gray & Bowen, 1829–1830.

———, ed. *The Writings of George Washington*. 12 vols. Boston: American Stationers' Company, 1834–1837.

Storing, Herbert, ed. *The Anti-Federalist*. Abridged by Murray Dry. Chicago: University of Chicago Press, 1985.

Strong, Cyprian. *God's Care of the New England Colonies . . . A Sermon Preached in the First Society of Chatham*. Hartford, Conn., 1777.

Syrett, Harold C., and Jacob E. Cooke, eds. *The Papers of Alexander Hamilton*. 27 vols. New York: Columbia University Press, 1961–1987.

Tansill, Charles C., ed. *Documents Illustrative of the Formation of the Union of the American States*. Washington D.C.: Government Printing Office, 1927.

Taylor, Robert, ed. *Papers of John Adams*. 10 vols. Cambridge: Harvard University Press, 1977.

Thornton, John Wingate. *The Pulpit of the American Revolution*. 1860. Reprint, New York: DeCapo Press, 1970.

Thorpe, Francis Newton, ed. *The Federal and State Constitutions, Colonial Charters, and Other Organic Laws*. 7 vols. Washington, D.C.: n.p., 1909.

"The Times." In *Songs and Ballads of the American Revolution*. Edited by Frank Moore. New York: Charles Scribner, 1856.

Trenholm, Louise Irby. *The Ratification of the Federal Constitution in North Carolina*. New York: Columbia University Press, 1932.

Trumbull, Benjamin. *A Discourse Delivered at the Town of New Haven*. New Haven, 1773.

Turner, Charles. *Massachusetts Election Sermon, 1773*. In *They Preached Liberty*. Edited by Franklin Cole. Indianapolis: Liberty Press, 1976.

Watson, John Fanning. *Historic Tales of Olden Time, Concerning the Early Settlement and Progress of Philadelphia and Pennsylvania*. Philadelphia: E. Littell and T. Holden, 1833.

Webster, Daniel. "A Discourse in Commemoration of the Lives and Services of John Adams and Thomas Jefferson." In *The Works of Daniel Webster*. 6 vols. Boston: Charles C. Little and James Brown, 1851.

Wesley, John. *Sermons on Several Occasions*. 4 vols. Nashville: E. Stephenson and F. A. Owen, 1855.

West, Samuel. *A Sermon Preached before the Honorable Council of the State of Massachusetts, Being the Anniversary for the Election*. 29 May 1776. In *The Pulpit of the American Revolution*. Edited by John W. Thornton. New York: DeCapo Press, 1970.

Willard, Margaret, ed. *Letters on the American Revolution, 1774–1776*. Boston: Houghton Mifflin, 1925.

Williams, Roger. *The Bloudy Tenet, of Persecution, for Cause of Conscience*. London, 1644. In *The Complete Writings of Roger Williams*. 7 vols. Boston: Russell & Russell, 1963.

Williams, William. Letter to the *American Mercury*. 11 February 1788. In *The Doc-umentary History of the Ratification of the Constitution*. Edited by Merrill Jensen. 16 vols. Madison, Wisc.: State Historical Society of Wisconsin, 1978.

Winthrop, Robert C., ed. *Life and Letters of John Winthrop*. Boston: Ticknor and Fields, 1867.

Witherspoon, John. "The Dominion of Providence over the Passions of Men." May 1776. In *The Works of the Rev. John Witherspoon*. 4 vols. Philadelphia: William W. Woodward, 1802.


*Secondary Sources*

Abraham, Henry J. "Religion, the Constitution, the Court, and Society: Some Con-temporary Reflections on Mandates, Words, Human Beings, and the Art of the Possible." In *How Does the Constitution Protect Religious Freedom?* Edited by Robert A. Goldwin and Art Kaufman. Washington, D.C.: American Enterprise Institute, 1987.

Ahlstrom, Sydney E. *A Religious History of the American People*. 2 vols. Garden City, N.Y.: Image Books, 1975.

Akers, Charles W. *Called Unto Liberty: A Life of Jonathan Mayhew, 1720–1766*. Cam-bridge: Harvard University Press, 1964.

Albanese, Catherine L. *Sons of the Fathers: The Civil Religion of the American Revo-lution*. Philadelphia: Temple University Press, 1976.

Alley, Robert S. *James Madison on Religious Liberty*. Buffalo, New York: Prometheus Books, 1985.

Antieu, Chester James, Arthur L. Downey, and Edward C. Roberts. *Freedom from Federal Establishment: Formation and Early History of the First Amendment Re-ligion Clauses*. Milwaukee: Bruce Publishing, 1964.

Bacon, William J. *The Continental Congress: Some of Its Actors and Their Doings, with the Results Thereof*. Utica, N.Y.: Ellis H. Roberts, 1881.

Bailyn, Bernard. "The Challenge of Modern Historiography." *American Historical Review* 87 (February 1982): 1–24.

———. *The Ideological Origins of the American Revolution*. Cambridge: Harvard Uni-versity Press, 1967.

Baisnee, Jules A. *France and the Establishment of the American Catholic Hierarchy: The Myth of French Interference, 1783–1784*. Baltimore: Johns Hopkins Press, 1934.

Baker, John S. "James Madison and Religious Freedom." *Benchmark* 3 (January–April 1987): 71–78.

Ball, Howard. "The Convergence of Constitutional Law and Politics in the Reagan Administration: The Exhumation of the 'Jurisprudence of Original Intention' Doctrine." *Cumberland Law Review* 17 (Summer 1987): 877–90.

Balmer, Randall. *A Perfect Babel of Confusion: Dutch Religion and English Culture in the Middle Colonies*. New York: Oxford University Press, 1989.

Bancroft, George. *History of the United States of America, from the Discovery of the Continent*. 6 vols. New York: Appleton, 1891.

Banning, Lance. "James Madison, the Statute for Religious Freedom, and the Crisis of Republican Convictions." In *The Virginia Statute for Religious Freedom*. Edited by Merrill D. Peterson and Robert D. Vaughan. Cambridge: Cambridge Univer-sity Press, 1988.

Bates, Ernest Sutherland. *American Faith: Its Religious, Political and Economic Foundations*. New York: W. W. North, 1940.

Bates, M. Searle. *Religious Liberty: An Inquiry*. New York: International Missionary Council, 1945.

Becker, Carl. *The Declaration of Independence: A Study in the History of Political Ideas*. New York: Vintage Books, 1958.

Beeman, Richard, Stephen Botein, and Edward C. Carter II, eds. *Beyond Confederation: Origins of the American Constitution and American National Identity*. Chapel Hill: University of North Carolina Press, 1987.

Belisle, D. W. *History of Independence Hall: From the Earliest Period to the Present Time*. Philadelphia: James Challen & Son, 1859.

Bellah, Robert H. "Civil Religion in America." In *Beyond Belief: Essays on Religion in a Post-Traditional World*. Edited by Bellah. New York: Harper & Row, 1970.

———. "Religion and the Legitimization of the American Republic." In *America, Christian or Secular: Readings in American Christian History and Civil Religion*. Edited by Jerry S. Herbert. Portland, Ore.: Multnomah Press, 1984.

Beloff, Max. *The American Federal Government*. New York: Oxford University Press, 1959.

Berger, Raoul. *Federalism: The Founders' Design*. Norman: University of Oklahoma Press, 1987.

Berns, Walter. *The First Amendment and the Future of American Democracy*. New York: Basic Books, 1976.

———. "Religion and the Founding Principle." In *The Moral Foundations of the American Republic*. 3d ed. Edited by Robert H. Horwitz. Charlottesville: University Press of Virginia, 1986.

Bloch, Ruth H. "Religion and Ideological Change in the American Revolution." In *Religion and American Politics: From the Colonial Period to the 1980s*. Edited by Mark A. Noll. New York: Oxford University Press, 1990.

———. *Visionary Republic: Millennial Themes in American Thought, 1756–1800*. New York: Cambridge University Press, 1985.

Boles, Donald E. *The Bible, Religion, and the Public Schools*. 2d ed. Ames: Iowa State University Press, 1963.

Bonomi, Patricia U. *Under the Cope of Heaven: Religion, Society and Politics in Colonial America*. New York: Oxford University Press, 1986.

Boorstin, Daniel. *The Lost World of Thomas Jefferson*. Boston: Beacon Press, 1960.

Bork, Robert H. "Original Intent and the Constitution." *Humanities* 7 (1986): 26–38.

Botein, Stephen. "Religious Dimensions of the Early American State." In *Beyond Confederation: Origins of the American Constitution and American National Identity*. Edited by Richard Beeman, Stephen Botein, and Edward C. Carter II. Chapel Hill: University of North Carolina Press, 1987.

Bradley, Gerard V. *Church-State Relationships in America*. Westport, Conn.: Greenwood Press, 1987.

Brauer, Jerald C. "Puritanism, Revivalism, and the Revolution." In *Religion and the American Revolution*. Edited by Brauer. Philadelphia: Fortress Press, 1976.

Brennan, William J., Jr. "The Constitution of the United States: Contemporary Ratification." *South Texas Law Review* 27 (1986): 433–45.

Brewster, David. *Memoirs of the Life, Writings, and Discoveries of Sir Isaac Newton*. 2 vols. Edinburgh: T. Constable, 1855.

Bridenbaugh, Carl. *Mitre and Sceptre: Transatlantic Faiths, Ideas, Personalities and Politics, 1689–1775*. New York: Oxford University Press, 1962.

Burnett, Edmund Cody. *The Continental Congress: A Definitive History of the Continental Congress from Its Inception in 1774 to March, 1789.* New York: Macmillan, 1941.

Bushman, Richard. *From Puritan to Yankee: Character and the Social Order in Connecticut, 1690–1765.* Cambridge: Harvard University Press, 1967.

Buzzard, Lynn R., and Samuel Ericsson. *The Battle for Religious Liberty.* Elgin, Ill.: David C. Cook Publishing, 1982.

Carroll, Peter N., ed. *Religion and the Coming of the American Revolution.* Waltham, Mass.: Ginn-Blaisdell, 1970.

Chemerinsky, Erwin. *Interpreting the Constitution.* New York: Praeger, 1987.

Choper, Jesse H. "The Religion Clauses of the First Amendment: Reconciling the Conflict." *University of Pittsburgh Law Review* 41 (Spring 1980): 673–701.

Cobb, Sanford H. *The Rise of Religious Liberty in America: A History.* New York: Macmillan, 1902.

Coleman, John A. "Civil Religion." *Sociological Analysis* 31 (1970): 67–77.

Collins, Herman LeRoy, and Wilfred Jordan. *Philadelphia: A Story of Progress.* 3 vols. New York: Lewis Historical Publishing, 1941.

Collins, Varnum Lansing. *President Witherspoon: A Biography.* Princeton: Princeton University Press, 1925.

Commager, Henry Steele, and Richard B. Morris, eds. *The Spirit of "Seventy-Six."* Indianapolis: Bobbs-Merrill, 1958.

Cord, Robert L. *Separation of Church and State: Historical Fact and Current Fiction.* New York: Lambeth Press, 1982.

Corwin, Edward S. "The Passing of Dual Federalism." *Virginia Law Review* 36 (1950): 1–24.

Cousins, Norman, ed. *In God We Trust: The Religious Beliefs and Ideas of the American Founding Fathers.* New York: Harper & Brothers, 1958.

———. *The Republic of Reason: The Personal Philosophies of the Founding Fathers.* San Francisco: Harper & Row, 1988.

Cox, Harvey G., Jr., ed. *Military Chaplains: From a Religion Military to a Military Religion.* New York: American Report Press, 1972.

Cragg, Gerald R. *The Church and the Age of Reason, 1648–1789.* 1960. Reprint, New York: Penguin Books, 1985.

Cremin, Lawrence A. *American Education: The Colonial Experience, 1607–1783.* New York: Harper & Row, 1970.

Cunliffe, Marcus. *George Washington: Man and Monument.* Boston: Little and Brown, 1958.

Current, Richard N., T. Harry Williams, and Frank Feidel. *American History: A Survey.* 2d ed. New York: Knopf, 1961.

Curry, Thomas J. *The First Freedoms: Church and State in America to the Passage of the First Amendment.* New York: Oxford University Press, 1986.

Davidson, Philip. *Propaganda and the American Revolution, 1763–1783.* Chapel Hill: University of North Carolina Press, 1941.

Davis, Derek H. "Equal Treatment: A Christian Separationist Approach." In *Equal Treatment of Religion in a Pluralistic Society.* Edited by Stephen V. Monsma and T. Christopher Soper. Grand Rapids, Mich: Eerdmans, 1998.

———. "The Fraternity of Original Intent: Clarence Thomas, the Newest Inductee." *Liberty* 91 (March–April 1996): 16–20.

———. *Original Intent: Chief Justice Rehnquist and the Course of American Church-State Relations.* Buffalo, N.Y.: Prometheus Books, 1991.

DeSchweinitz, Edmund Alexander. *The Life and Times of David Zeisberger: The Western Pioneer and Apostle of the Indians*. Philadelphia: J. B. Lippincott, 1871.

Diggins, John Patrick. *The Lost Soul of American Politics*. New York: Basic Books, 1984.

Dohla, Johann Conrad. *A Hessian Diary of the American Revolution*. Norman: University of Oklahoma Press, 1990.

Donovan, Frank. *Mr. Jefferson's Declaration: The Story behind the Declaration of Independence*. New York: Dodd, Mead, 1968.

Dreisbach, Daniel L. "The Constitution's Forgotten Religion Clause: Reflections on the Article VI Religious Test Ban." *Journal of Church and State* 38 (Spring 1996): 261–95.

Dumbald, Edward. *The Declaration of Independence and What It Means Today*. Norman: University of Oklahoma Press, 1950.

Dunn, Mary Maples. *William Penn: Politics and Conscience*. Princeton: Princeton University Press, 1967.

Durkheim, Émile. *The Elementary Forms of the Religious Life*. Rev. ed. New York: Free Press, 1965.

Earle, Valerie A. "The Federal Structure." In *Founding Principles of American Government: Two Hundred Years of Democracy on Trial*. Edited by George G. Graham, Jr., and Scarlett G. Graham. Bloomington: Indiana University Press, 1977.

Ellis, John T. *Catholics in Colonial America*. Baltimore: Helicon, 1965.

Esbeck, Carl H. "Five Views of Church-State Relations in Contemporary American Thought." *Brigham Young University Law Review* 86 (1986): 371–404.

Estep, W. R. *Religious Liberty: Heritage and Responsibility*. North Newton, Kans.: Bethel College, 1988.

Fay, Bernard. *Revolution and Freemasonry, 1680–1800*. Boston: Little, Brown, 1935.

Fergeson, M. L. *The Church-State Problem and the American Principle of Separation*. Waco, Tex.: Baylor University Press, 1966.

Gaines, William H. "The Continental Congress Considers the Publication of a Bible, 1777." *Studies in Bibliography* 3 (1950–1951): 274–81.

Gaustad, Edwin S. *Faith of Our Fathers: Religion and the New Nation*. San Francisco: Harper & Row, 1987.

———. *Liberty of Conscience: Roger Williams in America*. Grand Rapids, Mich.: Eerdmans, 1991.

———. *Neither King nor Prelate*. Grand Rapids, Mich.: Eerdman, 1993.

———. "Religion." In *The Encyclopedia of Colonial and Revolutionary America*. Edited by John Mack Faragher. New York: Sachem Publishing, 1990.

Gewirth, Alan, trans. *The Defender of Peace*. Toronto: Toronto University Press, 1980.

Ginsberg, Robert, ed. *A Casebook on the Declaration on Independence*. New York: Thomas Y. Crowell, 1967.

Good, Harry Gehman, and James D. Teller. *A History of American Education*. New York: Macmillan, 1973.

Gordon, William. *The History of the Rise, Progress and Establishment of the Independence of the United States of America*. 4 vols. London, 1788.

Graham, George G., Jr., and Scarlett G. Graham, eds. *Founding Principles of American Government: Two Hundred Years of Democracy on Trial*. Bloomington: Indiana University Press, 1977.

Griswold, Rufus W. *The Republican Court; or, American Society in the Days of Washington*. Rev. ed. New York: Appleton, 1856.

Handy, Robert T. *A History of the Churches in the United States and Canada.* New York: Oxford University Press, 1977.

Hanley, Thomas O'Brien. *Revolutionary Statesmen: Charles Carroll and the War.* Chicago: Loyola University Press, 1983.

Harling, Frederick F., and Martin Kaufman. *The Ethnic Contribution to the American Revolution.* Westfield, Mass.: Westfield Bicentennial Committee, 1976.

Hatch, Nathan O. *The Sacred Cause of Liberty: Republican Thought and the Millennium in Revolutionary New England.* New Haven: Yale University Press, 1977.

Hatfield, Mark. *Between a Rock and a Hard Place.* Waco, Tex.: Word Books, 1976.

Hawke, David. *Honorable Treason: The Declaration of Independence and the Men Who Signed It.* New York: Viking, 1976.

———. *A Transaction of Free Men: The Birth and Course of the Declaration of Independence.* New York: Scribner's, 1964.

Heimert, Alan. *Religion and the American Mind from the Great Awakening to the Revolution.* Cambridge: Harvard University Press, 1966.

Henderson, H. James. "The Structure of Politics in the Continental Congress." In *Essays on the American Revolution.* Edited by Stephen G. Kurtz and James H. Hutson. Chapel Hill: University of North Carolina Press, 1973.

Henton, Ronald E. *Masonic Membership of the Founding Fathers.* Silver Spring, Md.: Masonic Service Association, 1965.

Herbert, Jerry S., ed. *America, Christian or Secular: Readings in American Christian History and Civil Religion.* Portland, Ore.: Multnomah Press, 1984.

Hills, Margaret T. "The First American Bible, as Published by Robert Aitken." *Bible Society Record* 113 (January 1968): 1–4.

Hofstadter, Richard. "The Founding Fathers: An Age of Realism." In *The Moral Foundations of the American Republic.* Edited by Robert Horwitz. Charlottesville: University of Virginia Press, 1986.

Hogue, William M. "The Civil Disability of Ministers of Religion in State Constitutions." *Journal of Church and State* 36 (Spring 1994): 329–55.

———. "The Religious Conspiracy Theory of the American Revolution: Anglican Motive." *Church History* 45 (1976): 277–92.

Horwitz, Robert H., ed. *The Moral Foundations of the American Republic.* 3d ed. Charlottesville: University Press of Virginia, 1986.

Hovey, Alvah. *A Memoir of the Life and Times of the Rev. Isaac Backus.* Boston: Printers Press, 1858.

Howe, Mark DeWolfe. *The Garden and the Wilderness: Religion and Government in American Constitutional History.* Chicago: University of Chicago Press, 1965.

Humphrey, Edward Frank. *Nationalism and Religion in America, 1774–1789.* Boston: Chipman Law Publishing, 1924.

Jensen, Merrill. *The Articles of Confederation: An Interpretation of the Social-Constitutional History of the American Revolution.* Madison: University of Wisconsin Press, 1940.

Johnson, Lorenzo D. *Chaplains of the General Government.* New York: Buford Press, 1856.

Johnson, W. F. *America's Foreign Relations.* 2 vols. New York: Century, 1916.

Jolicoeur, Pamela M., and Louis L. Knowles. "Fraternal Associations and Civil Religion: Scottish Rite Freemasonry." *Review of Religious Research* 20 (Fall 1978): 3–22.

Jones, Newton B., ed. "Writings of the Reverend William Tennent, 1740–1777." *South Carolina Historical Magazine* LXI (July–October 1960): 197–204.

Joyce, Lester Douglas. *Church Clergy in the American Revolution*. New York: Exposition Press, 1966.

Kamen, Henry. *The Rise of Toleration*. London: World University Library, 1967.

Katz, Wilbur. "Radiations from Church Tax Exemption." *Supreme Court Review*. Chicago: University of Chicago Press, 1970.

Kaufman, Irving R. "What Did the Founding Fathers Intend?" *New York Times Magazine*, 23 February 1986.

Kelly, Alfred H., and Winfred A. Harbison. *The American Constitution: Its Origins and Development*. 3d ed. New York: Norton, 1963.

Kramer, Leonard J. "Muskets in the Pulpit, 1776–1783: Part I." *Journal of the Presbyterian Historical Society* 31 (December 1953): 48–62.

Kramnick, Isaac, and R. Laurence Moore. *The Godless Constitution: The Case against Religious Correctness*. New York: Norton, 1996.

Kurland, Philip B. "The Origins of the Religion Clauses of the Constitution." *William and Mary Law Review* 27 (Special Issue, 1985–1986): 839–61.

———. *Religion and the Law: Of Church and State and the Supreme Court*. Chicago: Aldine Publishing, 1962.

Kurtz, Stephen G., and James H. Hutson, eds. *Essays on the American Revolution*. Chapel Hill: University of North Carolina Press, 1973.

Laycock, Douglas. "The Declaration Is Not Law." *Christian Legal Society Quarterly* 12 (Fall 1991): 8–11.

———. "Formal, Substantive, and Disaggregated Neutrality Toward Religion." *DePaul Law Review* 39 (1990): 993–1018.

———. " 'Nonpreferential' Aid to Religion: A False Claim about Original Intent." *William and Mary Law Review* 27 (Special Issue, 1985–1986): 875–923.

Levinson, Stanford, and Steven Mailloux, eds. *Interpreting Law and Literature: A Hermeneutic Reader*. Evanston, Ill.: Northwestern University Press, 1988.

Levy, Leonard W. *The Establishment Clause: Religion and the First Amendment*. New York: Macmillan, 1986.

———. *Original Intent and the Framers' Constitution*. New York: Macmillan, 1988.

———. "The Original Meaning of the Establishment Clause of the First Amendment." In *Religion and the State: Essays in Honor of Leo Pfeffer*. Edited by James E. Wood, Jr. Waco, Tex.: Baylor University Press, 1985.

Lieber, Francis. *Legal and Political Hermeneutics; or, Principles of Interpretation and Construction in Law and Politics with Remarks on Precedents and Authorities*. 3d ed. St. Louis: F. H. Thomas, 1880.

Linder, Robert. "Civil Religion in Historical Perspective: The Reality That Underlies the Concept." *Journal of Church and State* 17 (Autumn 1975): 399–421.

Lippy, Charles H. "The 1780 Massachusetts Constitution: Religious Establishment or Civil Religion?" *Journal of Church and State* 20 (Autumn 1978): 533–49.

Little, David. "The Origins of Perplexity: Civil Religion and Moral Belief in the Thought of Thomas Jefferson." In *American Civil Religion*. Edited by Russell E. Richey and Donald D. Jones. New York: Harper & Row, 1974.

Locke, John. "A Letter Concerning Toleration." Reprint in *Main Currents of Western Thought*. Edited by Franklin Le Van Baumer. 4th ed. New Haven: Yale University Press, 1978.

Love, William DeLoss, Jr. *The Fast and Thanksgiving Days of New England*. Boston: Houghton Mifflin, 1895.

Lutz, Donald. *A Preface to American Political Theory*. Lawrence: University Press of Kansas, 1992.

————. "The Relative Influence of European Writers on Late Eighteenth-Century American Political Thought." *American Political Science Review* 189 (1984): 189–97.

Maas, David E. "The Watchwords of 1774." *Fides et Historia,* 18 October 1986.

Maddigan, Michael M. "The Establishment Clause, Civil Religion, and the Public Church." *California Law Review* 81 (1993): 245–99.

Malbin, Michael J. *Religion and Politics: The Intentions of the Authors of the First Amendment.* Washington, D.C.: American Enterprise Institute for Public Policy Research, 1978.

Marnell, William H. *The First Amendment: The History of Religious Freedom in America.* Garden City, N.Y.: Doubleday, 1964.

Marty, Martin E. "Living with Establishment and Disestablishment in Nineteenth-Century Anglo-America." *Journal of Church and State* 18 (Winter 1976): 61–78.

May, Henry F. *The Enlightenment in America.* New York: Oxford University Press, 1976.

McConnell, Michael. "Accommodation of Religion." *Supreme Court Review.* Chicago: University of Chicago Press, 1985.

————. "Neutrality under the Religion Clauses." *Northwestern Law Review* 81 (1986): 146–167.

————. "The Origins and Historical Understanding of the Free Exercise of Religion." *Harvard Law Review* 103 (1990): 1409–1517.

McDonald, Forrest. *Novus Ordo Seclorum.* Lawrence: University Press of Kansas, 1985.

McLoughlin, William G. *New England Dissent, 1630–1833: The Baptists and the Separation of Church and State.* 2 vols. Cambridge: Harvard University Press, 1971.

————. *Revivals, Awakening, and Reform: Religion and Social Change in America, 1607–1977.* Chicago: University of Chicago Press, 1978.

————. "The Role of Religion in the Revolution." In *Essays on the American Revolution.* Edited by Stephen G. Kurtz and James H. Hutson. Chapel Hill: University of North Carolina Press, 1973.

McMaster, John B., and Frederick D. Stone. *Pennsylvania and the Federal Constitution, 1787–1788.* Lancaster, Pa.: Inquirer Printing, 1888.

Mead, Sidney E. "American Protestantism During the Revolutionary Epoch." *Church History* 22 (December 1953): 279–97.

————. "Christendom, Enlightenment, and the Revolution." In *Religion and the American Revolution.* Edited by Jerald C. Brauer. Philadelphia: Fortress Press, 1976.

————. *The Lively Experiment: The Shaping of Religion in America.* New York: Harper & Row, 1963.

Meese, Edwin. "The Supreme Court of the United States: Bulwark of a Limited Constitution." Washington, D.C., 9 July 1985. Reprint, *South Texas Law Review* 27 (1986): 455–66.

————. Speech. Federalist Society, Washington, D.C., 30 January 1987. Reprint, *Marquette Law Review* 70 (Spring 1987): 381–88.

Meigs, Cornelia Lynde. *The Violent Men: A Study of Human Relations in the First American Congress.* New York: Macmillan, 1949.

Miller, Perry. *Nature's Nation.* Cambridge: Harvard University Press, 1967.

Miller, Robert T., and Ronald B. Flowers. *Toward Benevolent Neutrality: Church, State, and the Supreme Court.* 3d ed. Waco, Tex.: Baylor University Press, 1987.

Mirsky, Yehudah. "Civil Religion and the Establishment Clause." *Yale Law Journal* 95 (1986): 1237–62.

Monsma, Stephen V. *Positive Neutrality: Letting Religious Freedom Ring*. Westport, Conn.: Greenwood Press, 1993.

Montross, Lynn. *The Reluctant Rebels: The Story of the Continental Congress, 1774–1789*. New York: Harper & Brothers, 1950.

Moore, John Norton. "The Supreme Court and the Relationship between the 'Establishment' and 'Free Exercise' Clauses." *Texas Law Review* 42 (1963): 149–98.

Morgan, Edmund S. *The Challenge of the American Revolution*. New York: Norton, 1976.

———. "The Puritan Ethic and the American Revolution." *William and Mary Quarterly* 24 (January 1967): 3–43.

Morris, Benjamin F. *Christian Life and Character of the Civil Institutions of the United States*. Philadelphia: George W. Childs, 1864.

Morris, Richard. *The Forging of the Union, 1781–1789*. San Francisco: Harper & Row, 1987.

———. " 'We the People of the United States': The Bicentennial of a People's Revolution." *American Historical Review* 82 (1977): 1–19.

Mott, Frank L., and Chester E. Jorgenson. *Benjamin Franklin*. New York: American Book, 1936.

Murrin, John M. "Religion and Politics in America from the First Settlements to the Civil War." In *Religion and American Politics: From the Colonial Period to the 1980s*. Edited by Mark A. Noll. New York: Oxford University Press, 1990.

——— "A Roof without Walls: The Dilemma of American National Identity." In *Beyond Confederation: Origins of the Constitution and American National Identity*. Edited by Richard Beeman, Stephen Botein, and Edward C. Carter II. Chapel Hill: University of North Carolina Press, 1987.

Nicholls, David. *God and Government in an Age of Reason*. London: Routledge, 1995.

Noll, Mark A. *Christians and the American Revolution*. Washington, D.C.: Christian University Press, 1977.

———. *One Nation under God? Christian Faith and Political Action in America*. New York: Harper & Row, 1988.

———. ed. *Religion and American Politics: From the Colonial Period to the 1980s*. New York: Oxford University Press, 1990.

Noll, Mark A., Nathan O. Hatch, and George M. Marsden. *The Search for Christian America*. Westchester, Ill.: Crossway Books, 1983.

North, Gary. *Political Polytheism: The Myth of Pluralism*. Tyler, Tex.: Institute for Christian Economics, 1989.

North, Mary Beth. *Liberty's Daughters: The Revolutionary Experience of American Women, 1750–1800*. Boston: Little, Brown, 1980.

Norwood, Frederick A. *Strangers and Exiles: A History of Religious Refugees*. 2 vols. Nashville: Abingdon Press, 1969.

O'Neill, J. M. *Religion and Education under the Constitution*. New York: Harper & Row, 1949.

Onuf, Peter S. *The Origins of the Federal Republic: Jurisdictional Controversies in the United States, 1775–1787*. Philadelphia: University of Pennsylvania Press, 1983.

———. *Statehood and Union: A History of the Northwest Ordinance*. Bloomington: Indiana University Press, 1987.

Patterson, Richard S., and Richardson Dougall. *The Eagle and the Shield: A History of the Great Seal of the United States*. Washington, D.C.: U.S. Government Printing Office, 1976.

Pearson, Samuel C., Jr. "Nature's God: A Reassessment of the Religion of the Founding Fathers." *Religion in Life* 46 (Summer 1977): 152–65.

Pepper, Stephen. "Reynolds, Yoder, and Beyond: Alternatives for the Free Exercise
Clause." *Utah Law Review* (1981): 309–78.

Pfeffer, Leo. *Church, State and Freedom.* 2d ed. Boston: Beacon Press, 1967.

———. *Religion, State, and the Burger Court.* Buffalo, N.Y.: Prometheus Books, 1984.

Pierard, Richard, and Robert Linder. *Civil Religion and the Presidency.* Grand Rapids,
Mich.: Zondervan, 1988.

Pocock, J. G. A. *The Machiavellian Moment: Florentine Political Thought and the
Atlantic Republican Tradition.* Princeton: Princeton University Press, 1974.

Powell, H. Jefferson. "The Compleat Jeffersonian: Justice Rehnquist and Federalism."
*Yale Law Journal* 91 (1982): 1317–70.

———. "The Original Understanding of Original Intent." *Harvard Law Review* 98
(March 1985): 885–948.

Prowell, George Reeser. *Continental Congress at York, Pennsylvania and York County
in the Revolution.* York, Pa.: York Printing, 1914.

Quafe, Milo Milton. *The Flag of the United States.* New York: Grossett & Dunlap,
1942.

Rakove, Jack N. *The Beginnings of National Politics: An Interpretive History of the
Continental Congress.* New York: Knopf, 1979.

———. *Original Meanings: Politics and Ideas in the Making of the Constitution.* New
York: Vintage, 1997.

Read, William Staples. *Rhode Island in the Continental Congress, 1765–1790.* New
York: DeCapo Press, 1971.

Richey, Russell E., and Donald G. Jones, eds. *American Civil Religion.* New York:
Harper & Row, 1974.

Robinson, Stewart M. "God and the Continental Congress." *Christianity Today* 3 (4
February 1957): 1–3.

Rossiter, Clinton. *The First American Revolution.* New York: Harcourt, Brace, and
World, 1956.

Roth, Philip. *Masonry in the Formation of Our Government.* Milwaukee, Wisc.: privately printed, 1927.

Rumball-Petre, Edwin A. R. *America's First Bibles, with a Census of 555 Extant Bibles.*
Portland, Maine: Southworth-Anthoensen Press, 1940.

Sandoz, Ellis. *A Government of Laws.* Baton Rouge: Louisiana State University Press,
1991.

———. "Power and Spirit in the Founding." *This World* 9 (Fall 1984): 66–77.

Schaff, Philip. *Church and State in the United States.* New York: Arno Press, 1972.

Scott, E. H., ed. *Journal of the Federal Convention.* 2 vols. Reprint, Chicago: Scott,
Foresman, 1898.

Selden, Raman. *A Reader's Guide to Contemporary Literary Theory.* Lexington: University of Kentucky Press, 1989.

Shain, Barry. *The Myth of American Individualism.* Princeton: Princeton University
Press, 1994.

Singer, C. Gregg. "Theological Aspects of the Revolution." *Christianity Today* 3 (22
June 1959): 5–7.

———. *A Theological Interpretation of American History.* Nutley, N.J.: Craig Press,
1964.

Sinopoli, Richard. *The Foundations of American Citizenship: Liberalism, the Constitution, and Civic Virtue.* New York: Oxford University Press, 1992.

Skilton, Harvey. "John Carroll." In *The New International Dictionary of the Christian Church*. Rev. ed. Edited by J. D. Douglas. Grand Rapids, Mich.: Zondervan, 1978.

Smith, Page, ed. *Religious Origins of the American Revolution*. Missoula, Montana: Scholars Press, 1976.

Smith, Preserved. *A History of Modern Culture*. 2 vols. New York: Holt, 1930–1934.

Smith, Steven A. "Prelude to Article VI: The Ordeal of Religious Test Oaths in Pennsylvania." In *1992 Free Speech Yearbook*. Edited by Dale A. Herbeck. Carbondale: Southern Illinois University Press, 1992.

Smith, Steven D. *Foreordained Failure: The Quest for a Constitutional Principle of Religious Freedom*. New York: Oxford University Press, 1995.

Stevens, William Perry. *The Faith of the Signers of the Declaration of Independence*. New Haven: Yale University Press, 1926.

Stokes, Anson Phelps. *Church and State in the United States: Historical Development and Contemporary Problems of Religious Freedom under the Constitution*. 3 vols. New York: Harper & Brothers, 1950.

Stourzh, Gerald. *Benjamin Franklin and American Foreign Policy*. 2d. ed. Chicago: University of Chicago Press, 1969.

Stout, Harry. *The New England Soul*. Oxford: Oxford University Press, 1986.

Strout, Cushing. *The New Heavens and the New Earth: Political Religion in America*. New York: Harper & Row, 1974.

Swisher, Carl Brent. *American Constitutional Development*. 2d ed. Westport, Conn.: Greenwood Press, 1978.

Swomley, John M. *Religious Liberty and the Secular State*. Buffalo, N.Y.: Prometheus Books, 1985.

Tierney, Brian. *Religion, Law, and the Growth of Constitutional Thought, 1150–1650*. Cambridge: Cambridge University Press, 1982.

Tocqueville, Alexis De. *Democracy in America*. Edited by J. P. Mayers and Max Lerner. Translated by George Lawrence. New York: Harper & Row, 1969.

Trenholme, Louise Irby. *The Ratification of the Federal Constitution in North Carolina*. New York: Columbia University Press, 1932.

Tyler, Moses Coit. *Patrick Henry*. Ithaca, N.Y.: Cornell University Press, 1962.

Van Doren, Carl. *Benjamin Franklin*. New York: Viking, 1938.

Van Patten, Jonathan K. "In the End Is the Beginning: An Inquiry into the Meaning of the Religion Clauses." *Saint Louis University Law Journal* 27 (February 1983): 1–95.

————. "The Partisan Battle over the Constitution: Meese's Jurisprudence of Original Intention and Brennan's Theory of Contemporary Ratification." *Marquette Law Review* 70 (Spring 1987): 389–422.

Van Tyne, Claude. "Sovereignty in the American Revolution: A Historical Study." *American Historical Review* 12 (1907): 529–45.

Vetterli, Richard, and Gary Bryner. *In Search of the Republic*. Totowa, N.J.: Rowman and Littlefield, 1987.

Wald, Kenneth D. "Religion and Politics: Points of Contact." In *Religion and Politics in the United States*. Edited by Wald. New York: St. Martin's Press, 1987.

Ward, Harry M. *"Unite or Die": Intercolony Relations, 1690–1763*. Port Washington, N.Y.: Lefert's Press, 1971.

Weinrib, Lloyd. *Natural Law and Justice*. Cambridge: Harvard University Press, 1987.

Weis, Frederick Lewis. *The Colonial Clergy of Virginia, North Carolina, and South Carolina*. Boston: Society of the Descendants of the Colonial Clergy, 1955.

Weslager, Clinton A. *The Delaware Indians: A History*. New Brunswick, N.J.: Rutgers University Press, 1973.

White, Morton. *The Philosophy of the American Revolution*. New York: Oxford University Press, 1978.

Wilcox, Clyde. "Public Attitudes Toward Church-State Issues: Elite-Mass Differences." *Journal of Church and State* 34 (Spring 1992): 259–78.

Williams, George Hunston. "The Chaplaincy in the Armed Forces of the United States of America in Historical and Ecclesiastical Perspective." In *Military Chaplains: From a Religion Military to a Military Religion*. Edited by Harvey G. Cox, Jr. New York: American Report Press, 1972.

Wills, Garry. *Inventing America: Jefferson's Declaration of Independence*. Garden City, New York: Doubleday, 1978.

Wilson, John. "Religion, Government, and Power in the New American Nation." In *Religion and American Politics: From the Colonial Period to the 1980s*. Edited by Mark Noll. New York: Oxford University Press, 1990.

———. "Religion under the State Constitutions, 1776–1800." *Journal of Church and State* 32 (Autumn 1990): 764–73.

Wise, John. *A Vindication of the Government of New England Churches*. Boston: John Boyles, 1719, 1772.

Witle, John Jr. " 'A Most Mild and Equitable Establishment of Religion': John Adams and the Massachusetts Experiment." *Journal of Church and State* 41 (Spring 1999): 213–52.

Wittke, Carl. *We Who Built America: The Saga of the Immigrant*. Cleveland: Press of Case Western Reserve University, 1967.

Wood, Gordon S. *The Creation of the American Republic, 1776–1787*. Chapel Hill: University of North Carolina Press, 1969.

———. *The Radicalism of the American Revolution*. New York: Random House, 1991.

Wood, James E., Jr. " 'No Religious Test Shall Ever Be Required': Reflections on the Bicentennial of the U.S. Constitution." *Journal of Church and State* 29 (Spring 1987): 199–208.

———. "Religion and Public Education in Historical Perspective." *Journal of Church and State* 14 (Autumn 1972): 397–414.

———. "The Secular State." *Journal of Church and State* 7 (Spring 1965): 169–78.

Wood, James E., Jr., E. Bruce Thompson, and Robert T. Miller. *Church and State in Scripture, History, and Constitutional Law*. Waco, Tex.: Baylor University Press, 1958.

Woods, John A., ed. "The Correspondence of Benjamin Rush and Granville Sharp 1773–1809." *Journal of American Studies* 1 (April 1967): 1–38.

Wright, Esmond, ed. *Causes and Consequences of the American Revolution*. Chicago: Quadrangle Books, 1966.

Wuthnow, Robert. *The Restructuring of American Religion: Society and Faith since World War II*. Princeton: Princeton University Press, 1988.

Zollman, Carl. "Religious Liberty in the American Law." *Michigan Law Review* 17 (1991): 355–375.

*Table of Cases*

*Abington School District v. Schempp*, 374 U.S. 203 (1963).

*Aguilar v. Felton*, 105 S. Ct. 3232 (1985).

*Allegheny County v. Greater Pittsburgh ACLU*, 492 U.S. 573 (1989).

*Arver v. United States,* 245 U.S. 366 (1918).

*Boerne v. Flores,* 117 S. Ct. 2157 (1997).

*Cantwell v. Connecticut,* 310 U.S. 296 (1940).

*Employment Division of Oregon v. Smith,* 494 U.S. 872 (1990).

*Engel v. Vitale,* 370 U.S. 421 (1962).

*Everson v. Board of Education,* 330 U.S. 1 (1947).

*Grand Rapids School District v. Ball,* 473 U.S. 373 (1985).

*Jones v. Opelika,* 316 U.S. 584 (1942).

*Lee v. Weisman,* 505 U.S. 577 (1992).

*Lynch v. Donnelly,* 465 U.S. 668 (1984).

*Marsh v. Chambers,* 463 U.S. 783 (1983).

*McCollum v. Board of Education,* 333 U.S. 203 (1948).

*McDaniel v. Paty,* 435 U.S. 618 (1978).

*Reynolds v. United States,* 98 U.S. 145 (1878).

*Stein v. Plainwell Community Schools,* 822 F.2d 1406 (6th Cir. 1987).

*Thornton v. Caldor,* 472 U.S. 703 (1985).

*Torcaso v. Watkins,* 367 U.S. 488 (1961).

*United States v. Seeger,* 380 U.S. 163 (1965).

*Wallace v. Jaffree,* 472 U.S. 38 (1985).

*Walz v. Tax Commission,* 397 U.S. 664 (1970).

*Ware v. Hylton,* 3 U.S. 199 (1796).

*Watson v. Jones,* 13 Wallace 679 (1872).

*Wisconsin v. Yoder,* 406 U.S. 205 (1972).

*Zorach v. Clauson,* 343 U.S. 306 (1952).

# INDEX

Printed in the United States
67215LVS00002BA/256-270

9 780195 133554